Wordsmith

A Guide to College Writing

Fifth Edition

Pamela Arlov
Macon State College

PEARSON

Boston   Columbus   Indianapolis   New York   San Francisco   Upper Saddle River
Amsterdam   Cape Town   Dubai   London   Madrid   Milan   Munich   Paris   Montreal   Toronto
Delhi   Mexico City   Sao Paulo   Sydney   Hong Kong   Seoul   Singapore   Taipei   Tokyo

Senior Acquisitions Editor:
    Matthew Wright
Development Editor: Erin Reilly
Marketing Manager: Kurt Massey
Supplements Editor:
    Donna Campion
Media Project Manager: Lisa Dotson
Associate Managing Editor: Bayani
    Mendoza de Leon
Production/Project Manager: Raegan
    Keida Heerema

**Project Coordination, Text Design,
    and Electronic Page Makeup:**
    Laserwords
Cover Designer/Manager: Nancy
    Danahy
Manufacturing Manager: Mary Ann
    Gloriande
Printer/Binder: Edwards Brothers
Cover Printer: Lehigh-Phoenix
    Color/Hagerstown

To my husband, Nick: "Love is not love/ Which alters when it alteration finds."

This book was set in 10.5/12.5 Palatino.

Credits and acknowledgments borrowed from other sources and reproduced, with permission, in this textbook appear on page 605.

Copyright © 2012, 2010, 2007, 2004 Pearson Education, Inc.

Library of Congress Cataloging-in-Publication Data

Arlov, Pamela.
    Wordsmith : a guide to college writing / Pamela Arlov.—5th ed.
        p. cm.
Previous ed.: 2010.
    Includes index.
    ISBN-13: 978-0-205-25127-8
    ISBN-10: 0-205-25127-7
    1. English language—Rhetoric.   2. English language—Grammar.
3. College readers.   4. Report writing.   I. Title.
    PE1408.A69 2012
    808'.042—dc23

                                            2011028759

10 9 8 7 6 5 4 3 2 1—EB—14 13 12 11

www.pearsonhighered.com

Student ISBN-13: 978-0-205-25127-8
ISBN-10: 0-205-25127-7
Annotated Instructor's Edition ISBN-13: 978-0-205-21110-4
ISBN-10: 0-205-21110-0

Why Do You Need This New Edition?

If you're wondering why you should buy this new edition of *Wordsmith: A Guide to College Writing,* **Fifth Edition, here are six good reasons!**

1. **Build Confidence and Creativity with Informal Writing Assignments.** Each of the writing modes chapters (Chapters 8, 9, and 10) contains new impromptu writing assignments called *Small Scrawls.* Designed to be completed in one sitting, *Small Scrawls* will help you become quicker and more fluid in your writing.

2. **Recognize Formal and Informal Situations and Write Appropriately for Both.** When you speak, you naturally shift between formal and informal language, depending on the situation. Chapter 26, Word Choice, has been updated to help you fine-tune that skill and to recognize categories of word choice that are generally not appropriate for college writing, such as slang, textspeak, and more.

3. **Write Persuasively.** Arguing effectively and writing persuasively are essential skills not only for college writing but also for the writing you will do in your career and throughout your life. This edition of *Wordsmith* includes an updated section on argument in Chapter 10, Examining Logical Connections.

4. **Explore New Topics in Four New Readings.** The readings section has been updated with four new essays on hot topics in today's culture: Richard Woods' "Has the Internet Killed Privacy?"; Amy Chua's "Why Chinese Parents Are Different"; Tony Kelso's "After 20 Years, I Want to See My Abusive Dad for His Money"; and Larry Fennelly's "Is National Service the Cure for America's Woes?"

5. **Enjoy Reading Your Textbook.** A conversational tone and real-world examples make reading and completing your assignments less tedious. Concise instruction tells you what you need to know in a straightforward manner, making it easier for you to absorb even the most challenging lessons. New exercises, visuals, and chapter openers throughout the text bring the material to life and add humor to the text.

6. **Master Chapter Content with Chapter Goals and Integrated MyWritingLab Prompts.** Each chapter in *Wordsmith* now opens with a chapter goal and ties in to the most powerful online writing tool on the planet, Pearson's *MyWritingLab* (**www.mywritinglab.com**). Now you can truly grasp chapter content and test your understanding of that content with *MyWritingLab* in a more meaningful way!

Contents

Thematic List of Readings

Education and Language

Ourselves and Others

Social Issues

List of Readings by Rhetorical Mode

Example

Description

Narration

Preface

Thank you for choosing *Wordsmith: A Guide to College Writing* as your textbook. Whether you are teaching from this text or learning from it, it is my hope that you will enjoy its simplicity. Writing itself is remarkably complex, incorporating the personality and experience of each writer and each reader. It also requires adherence to agreed-upon rules of grammar, punctuation, and form. Therefore, I have tried to make this book simple in its structure, straightforward in its language and presentation, and easy to use for both instructors and students.

Updates to the Fifth Edition

Several changes have been made in the fifth edition of *Wordsmith: A Guide to College Writing*:

- Each chapter is now preceded by new learning goals to help students and instructors alike see what the chapter is intended to accomplish before they begin work in it.

- In response to requests for more informal writing assignments, each of the writing modes chapters (Chapters 8, 9, and 10) now contains several impromptu writing assignments called *Small Scrawls*. These assignments, intended to be completed in one sitting, inspire students' confidence and creativity as well as help them become quicker and more fluid in their writing.

- The section on argument in Chapter 10, Examining Logical Connections, has been strengthened with new coverage of ethos, pathos, and logos and identifying flawed arguments.

- Because so many instructors and students find *MyWritingLab* to be an invaluable supplement, *MyWritingLab* prompts have been added throughout the text to help instructors and students easily access additional course materials.

- Chapter 26, Word Choice, has been updated with a new section on eliminating the more informal constructions spawned by texting and the Internet.

- The Readings section has been updated with four new essays. Richard Woods' "Has the Internet Killed Privacy?" sheds new light on a topic that has been much discussed in recent years. Amy Chua's "Why Chinese Parents Are Different," an excerpt from her controversial book, *Battle Hymn of the Tiger Mother*, explores differences in parenting styles. Larry Fennelly's "Is National Service the Cure of America's Woes?" looks at proposals to mandate national service—a hot topic in today's political culture. Tony Kelso's "After 20 Years, I Want to See My Abusive Dad for His Money" is an impassioned exploration of a strained parent-child relationship.

- An annotated instructor's edition is available with answers for most exercises in the text.

- There is little throughout the fifth edition that has not been re-examined and revised. For example, the coverage of APA style has been updated to meet the 2009 guidelines, new content on keeping thesis points parallel has been included in Chapter 3, and many new images and new exercises have been added in most chapters.

Features of *Wordsmith: A Guide to College Writing*

- A three-part layout allows the freedom to mix and match writing chapters, grammar chapters, and readings.

- A structured yet flexible approach to writing encourages clarity and creativity.

- A direct, conversational approach is used throughout.

- Lighthearted chapter openings promote a positive and playful approach to learning.

Part 1 Composition

Part 1, Composition, begins with an overview of the basics. Chapter 1 introduces the writing process and a review of the paragraph; a student essay is presented in all drafts and stages, along with a transcript of a student writing group's discussion of the work in progress. From there (in Chapters 2 through 7), the five steps in the writing process are presented in the order in which most writers address them: prewriting, planning, drafting, revising, and proofreading. This includes a complete chapter devoted to writing a thesis statement and planning the essay (Chapter 3). Throughout Part 1, topics for essays, paragraphs, and journal writing provide the bases for assignments and encourage further practice.

Chapters 8 through 10 move into methods of development. I believe it is more realistic to group the modes since they are seldom used in isolation in "real-world" writing. These groupings highlight their relationship to one another and allow students to read about all the methods even if they use only a few. Modes with a similar purpose are grouped together, and the optional "Mixed Methods" assignments at the end of the chapter show how the modes can be used together in a single piece of writing. Two full-length essays and one paragraph provide models for each method of development.

Chapter 11, Writing a Summary, provides a step-by-step guide to summarizing an article, and Chapter 12, Writing a Research Paper, takes students a step further into writing papers based on outside sources. Chapters on summarizing and on writing a research paper help students make the transition from personal writing to academic writing.

Part 2 Grammar

Part 2, Grammar, can be used in a variety of ways: with direct, in-class instruction; in a lab setting, as a supplement to lab assignments; or for independent study. It also works well for instructors who want to combine methods by addressing more difficult topics in class while assigning easier material or review material for independent study.

In the grammar chapters, explanations are clear, logical, and user-friendly. Each topic is dealt with, one skill at a time, with numerous practice exercises for each skill. The step-by-step, easy-to-understand presentation is suitable for classroom discussion or independent study. At the end of each chapter are review exercises in increasing order of difficulty, ending in most chapters with a paragraph-length editing exercise.

✎ Part 3 Readings

Part 3, Readings, offers high-interest essays by professional writers to reinforce reading skills and serve as springboards for discussions and assignments. In any craft, the works of accomplished artisans can inspire the apprentice. These essays model writing at its best: entertaining, challenging, and thought-provoking. Each reading is followed by a comprehension exercise that includes questions about content, questions about the writer's techniques, and related topics for discussion and writing. Diversity in authorship, subject matter, and rhetorical method is emphasized.

✎ Acknowledgments

I could not have written this book without the help, support, and collaboration of a great many people. I owe thanks to all the staff at Pearson, particularly Matthew Wright, Senior Acquisitions Editor, who is a joy to work with and who has given me some great opportunities; and Erin E. Reilly, Development Editor, who has done so much for this edition of the book that I cannot imagine how I ever did the previous editions without her. I owe a debt of gratitude to Raegan Heerema, Project Manager; Bayani Mendoza de Leon, Managing Editor; Tom DeMarco, Marketing Manager; and Eric Stano, Editor in Chief. I also thank the always cheerful, never ruffled Bruce Hobart, Production Coordinator at Laserwords Maine; Rohini Herbert, copyeditor par excellence; and Maxine Barber, proofreader.

I thank my division/department chair, Linda Green, for making sure I had time and space to work on this project. I thank Susan Phillips, Paul Wilson, and Sam and Wendy Johnston for letting me photograph their dog, hands, and daughter, respectively, and I thank Mary Frances Johnston for being my model.

Also, I thank the reviewers, whose comments helped to shape the most recent edition of the *Wordsmith* series: Elizabeth Andrews, South Florida Community College; Sylvia Boyd, Philips Community College; Heather Mobley, Central Georgia Technical College; Sharon Rinkiewicz, Broward College; and Jean Sherrod, Pitt Community College.

I also thank Nick Arlov, my dear husband, for his love and support, and for the sacrifices he made so many years ago so that I could attend college. I will always be grateful.

Pamela Arlov
Macon State College

Instructor Resources

Annotated Instructor's Edition. The *AIE* is a replica of the student text that includes the answers to all exercises. **ISBN: 0-205-21110-0.**

Instructor's Resource Manual. The Instructor's Resource Manual contains sample syllabi, a student answer key, and two chapter tests for each of the 30 chapters in the text. For each chapter, there is one short answer and one multiple-choice test for instructors to choose from. There are also a grammar pre-test and post-test. Additional chapter specific assignments and teaching tips provided by Pamela Arlov are included as well. The Instructor's Resource Manual is available by download at Pearson's Instructor Resource Center, which can be accessed by going to **www.pearsonhighered.com.** **ISBN: 0-205-21283-2.**

PowerPoint Presentation. A presentation for each chapter, which is structured around the chapter learning goals, can be downloaded at Pearson's Instructor Resource Center. You can use these presentations as is or edit them to suit your lecturing style.

Student Resources

My Writing Lab: Where Better Practice Makes Better Writers! **www.mywritinglab.com**

MyWritingLab, a complete online learning program, provides better practice exercises to developing writers.

What makes the practice in MyWritingLab better?

- Diagnostic Testing
- Progressive Learning
- Online Gradebook
- eTextbook

For a complete list of additional supplements to package with the text, including dictionaries, a thesaurus, a grammar or editing workbook, and readers, contact your Pearson sales representative, or visit us at **www.pearsonhighered.com.**

CHAPTER 1

The Writing Process

Chapter Goal: Develop an understanding of the writing process and write a clear, organized paragraph.

The write-o-matic takes pure thought
And funnels it into
A cylinder where it's transformed
To something bright and new.

From deep within, this strange machine
Puffs out an orange vapor,
Then spits out from the other end
A smooth, well-written paper.

Unfortunately, the verse above describes something that does not exist. There is no write-o-matic; there is only the writing process—easy to talk about, but not always easy to do. However, the more familiar you become with the writing process, the more you experiment with your own strategies for writing and practice the ones in this book, the easier and more automatic writing will become for you.

Writing is not a single act, but a process composed of several steps. One writer, Nick, describes the process this way:

> I think first. It's not like it pops out of me; it brews in me for a while. The next thing I do is to begin writing ideas down, good or bad. Once I get the ideas down in rough form—I wouldn't call it an outline necessarily—I write it out from beginning to end. Then the revision process begins, because I'm always unhappy with the first thing I write. It's a thorough examination: cutting, connecting thoughts, shifting ideas around, adding new ideas. I really go back to the beginning, because every time I revise, I have to think more. Then I write out the second draft from beginning to end. I don't worry about punctuation or spelling. I keep revising until I think I've got it; then I start worrying about periods and commas. Then it's ready for another reader.

Focus on the Writing Process: Completing the Steps

Think of the steps that went into making and putting up this sign. Someone planned it right down to the style of the letters and the black border. A company manufactured it and passed it through quality control. A city, state, or county purchased the signs and put them up. Yet clearly, something went wrong during the process.

Taking shortcuts in any process, including the writing process, can result in embarrassing mistakes. So even if "Dash it off and hand it in" has been your motto until now, give the writing process a chance, and allow yourself time to complete all the steps. That way, whatever you are writing—a paper for school, a memo for work, a purchasing request, a legal document—will reflect your best effort.

Reflect on It

1. Write down something you do that requires several steps.
2. List the steps in the order in which you do them.
3. Is it a flexible process, like the writing process, in that you can go back to a previous step if you need to? Or is it a process more like cooking, in that once the cake is in the oven, it's too late to add another egg?
4. Finally, think about the importance of each step in your process. What would happen if you left out a step?

The Writing Process

mywritinglab

Visit MyWriting Lab for additional practice with the writing process.

Although everyone approaches writing a little differently, most of us follow a process similar to the one just described. The writer in the example above is, in fact, following all of the steps in the **writing process:** prewriting, planning, drafting, revising, and proofreading.

Prewriting

mywritinglab

Visit MyWriting Lab for additional practice prewriting.

"I think first."

Prewriting covers a range of activity from casually thinking about your topic to doing a prewriting exercise to get your thoughts on paper. You will find that you prewrite throughout the writing process. When you are waiting at a traffic light and an example to illustrate one of your points pops into your head, you are prewriting. When you realize that a paragraph isn't working the way you planned and you stop to figure out another approach, you are prewriting. Prewriting *is* thinking, and the more thought you put into your paper, the stronger it will be.

Planning

"I get the ideas down in rough form—I wouldn't call it an outline."

Careful and thoughtful **planning** makes an essay easier for you to write and easier for your readers to read. Your plan may include a thesis statement—a statement of the main idea. Because it states the main idea, the thesis statement is the cornerstone of your essay. It may change more than once as your essay takes shape; still, it is important to have a main idea and to keep it in sight. After all, if you are not certain of your main point, you can be sure that your readers won't be, either. Besides a thesis, your plan will probably include an informal outline. Don't be afraid that planning will waste your time. Careful planning—or lack of it—always shows in the final draft.

Drafting

mywritinglab

Visit MyWriting Lab for additional practice drafting.

"I write it out from beginning to end."

Drafting your essay can be easy or difficult. Sometimes your ideas flow freely. At other times, your thoughts grind to a standstill, and you become frustrated and think you have nothing to say. Both situations are a normal part of the creative process. If you get stuck during the drafting process, don't quit in frustration. What is happening to you happens to all writers. Write *through* the problem, or, if necessary, return to the planning or prewriting stage.

The best advice on drafting is "don't procrastinate." Do your planning and prewriting early. If you have a project that involves research or outside reading, do those things early to give the information time to sink in before you write. Writing is easier if you plan ahead, and getting an early start prevents last-minute panic. Then if you get stuck during the drafting process, you will have time to work out the problem rather than going into emergency mode because your paper is due the next day.

As you draft your essay or paragraph, don't worry about grammar, spelling, or punctuation. Stopping to look up a comma rule will only distract you. Concentrate on ideas and save proofreading for later.

If your word processing software highlights or underlines mistakes as you write, then turn the spelling and grammar checker off until you are ready to proofread. You will appreciate your word processing software much more if it does not interrupt you as you write.

Revising

mywritinglab

Visit MyWriting Lab for additional practice revising.

"I'm always unhappy with the first thing I write."

In its Latin roots, the word *revising* means "seeing again." **Revising** is difficult because it is hard to see your work with the eyes of a reader. Writers often see what they *meant* to say rather than what they really said. Sometimes they take for granted background knowledge that the reader may not have. To overcome these difficulties, put your draft aside for a day or so before trying to revise it. With twenty-four hours between writing and revising, you will see your writing more clearly. It is also helpful to let someone else look at your work—a friend, classmate, or relative. Ask the person to focus on the *content* of your paper rather than on grammar, spelling, or punctuation. Ask which ideas are clear and which ones need more explanation. Ask how well your examples illustrate the points you have made. A reader's comments can help you see your work in a new light.

Don't be afraid of making big changes during revision. Throwing a whole paragraph out and starting over may keep an essay on track. Changing the paragraph order sometimes gives your message just the emphasis you want. Or you may find that a first draft contains just a seed of what you really want to say. Don't be afraid to start over. The first words you write are not written in stone.

One word of advice—if you don't know how to use a computer, learn. Taking an essay through multiple drafts and major changes is much easier on a computer. Once you learn to write on a computer, the essays, term papers, and reports that you write in college will look less intimidating.

Proofreading

mywritinglab

Visit MyWriting Lab for additional practice editing the essay.

"Then I start worrying about periods and commas."

Proofreading is the final polish that you put on your paragraph. When you proofread, consider such matters as grammar, spelling, and word choice. Replace vague words with specific words, and mercilessly cut words that are not carrying their weight. Look at connections, making sure ideas flow smoothly from one sentence to the next. Because the stages of the writing process overlap, you have probably done some minor proofreading along the way. Before the final proofreading, set the piece of writing aside for a time. Then proofread it once more to give it the polish of a finished piece.

An Important Point

If you go through the writing process expecting a series of sequential steps like those involved in changing your car's oil, you may think the process is not working for you. However, writing a five-hundred-word essay is not a sequential process but a repetitive one, more like driving a car than changing its oil.

If you take a five-hundred-mile trip, the steps you follow might be described as "Turn on the ignition. Put the car in drive. Accelerate. Brake. Put the car in park. Turn off the ignition." Yet it is not that simple. During a five-hundred-mile journey, you repeat each step not once but several times, and sometimes you stop for rest or fuel.

Writing an essay works the same way. You may list the steps as "Prewrite. Plan. Draft. Revise. Proofread." But again, it is not that simple. You may change the order of paragraphs as you write the first draft or correct a spelling mistake as you revise. Sometimes you repeat a step several times. You probably even stop for rest or fuel. Eventually, both processes—driving and writing—take you where you want to go.

EXERCISE 1	THE WRITING PROCESS

Answer the following questions to review your knowledge of the writing process.

1. The five steps in the writing process are _____, _____, _____, _____, and _____.

2. The "thinking step" in the writing process is called _____.

3. The part of the writing process that involves correcting grammar and punctuation is called _____.

4. Major changes would most likely be made during the _____ step in the writing process.

5. True or false? The steps in the writing process often overlap. T   F

The Writing Process: Carla's Essay

This section follows the development of one writer's essay from start to finish. In writing her essay, Carla went through several forms of prewriting and made two different outlines. She talked with members of her writing group and her instructor, and she wrote two rough drafts. (Only the first rough draft is shown here because the final draft reflects all of the changes made.) Before turning in her final draft, Carla also proofread the essay once from top to bottom and twice from bottom to top. Then she asked a member of her writing group to look over the final draft for any mistakes she might have overlooked.

The steps that Carla goes through are the same steps that you will take as you learn the writing process. You will also share some of her frustrations. But like Carla, you will probably find that what seems difficult at first is attainable, one step at a time.

Carla's Assignment

Carla's instructor handed out a list of three essay topics. Carla chose to write on this one:

> Write an essay about one of your roles in life and the emotions it makes you feel. Discuss positive aspects, negative aspects, or both, but be sure to tie your discussion to specific emotional reactions.

Carla's instructor suggested that the students try one or more forms of prewriting and then make an outline. Earlier, the class had been divided into writing groups of four or five people who would critique and support one another during the term. The instructor suggested that the writing groups meet to discuss each student's outline. Then, each student would write a rough draft to bring to an individual writing conference with the instructor.

Carla's Prewriting

Working on a computer, Carla tried a form of prewriting called invisible writing. (For more information on invisible writing and other forms of prewriting, see Chapter 2.) In this prewriting, Carla did not worry about grammar or spelling. Instead, she focused on gathering ideas. Her prewriting is reproduced here without correction.

Roles, roles. I have many roles in life. I am a student, a worker, a mother, a daughter, a friend. And I have roles within those roles. With my daughter I am a teacher, a doctor, a disciplinarian, a play-mate. With my mother I am sometimes child, sometimes adult. At work I feel competent and at school I often feel lost. As a modern woman I have to do it all, work, school, motherhood, the whole bit and still stay sane. It's juggling roles that gives me such headaches. I get so stressed sometimes when I have to study for a test and I am beat from working all day and Alisa needs her bath and a story. There is so much to say I don't know where to start. And what about the emotions connected with all that. Sometimes I am happy, sometimes I am too tired to feel anything, sometimes I am proud of all I do and sometimes I could just cry from exhaustion and frustration. I don't know what else to say and I don't feel any closer to getting an essay written. I am afraid this is not working for me.

Later, Carla followed up her invisible writing by brainstorming, focusing on her role as a mother.

Role—Mother

Everything I do is for Alisa	spending time with her
school	making sure she knows her grandparents, has a family connection
work	
reading to her	working hard so her future can be secure
tucking her in at night	want to be someone she can look up to
asking about her day	give up a lot but get a lot in return

Carla's Outline

As she looked over her brainstorming, Carla saw that many aspects of her role as a mother were focused on her child's present needs, while still others centered on Alisa's future. She also saw a possible connection to the past through Alisa's grandparents. She decided to structure her outline around her child's past, present, and future.

Outline

Thesis: As a mother, it is my job to see that my daughter is connected to the past, has her present needs met, and is ready for the future.

Paragraph 1—Connect her to the past:
1. Teach her what I have learned
2. Make sure she is connected to a previous generation through grandparents

Paragraph 2—Take care of her present needs:
1. Work to see that she is provided for
2. Spend time with her

Paragraph 3—The future:
1. Go to school to take care of her future
2. Make sure her future needs are met and that she can go to college

Carla's Writing Group Meets

Next, Carla met with her writing group. A transcript of the portion of the session dealing with Carla's outline appears here.

Transcript: Writing Group Session, Wednesday, October 3, 2:10 p.m.

Brenda: Okay, who wants to go first? Antonio?

Antonio: Not me. Carla?

Carla: Well, I just brought an outline. I'll go first. (Carla passes out copies of her outline, and the group reads the outline.)

Antonio: I like it. I like the way you include past, present, and future. It gives the outline a good flow.

Carla: You're just saying that because I got you off the hook. You didn't have to go first. (Laughter.)

Thanh: I like the chronological order, too. But there's one thing I don't see. Where's the emotion?

Carla: What?

Thanh: Remember the assignment said to connect the role to the emotions it made us feel?

Carla: Oh, no! That's right. Now, after all the work I've done, I'll have to change it. Maybe I can just go back and put in how I feel about teaching, working, and going to school.

Kelly: How do you feel about it?

Carla: I feel good. It makes me happy to know that I'm doing all I can for her.

Antonio: No tough times? No bad emotions?

Carla: (laughs) Plenty. I am always tired—no energy, no money. Sometimes it gets me down.

Brenda: Tell me about it. My kids are grown, but I remember. But I wouldn't raise a kid today for anything. The world is too scary.

Carla: I know. Sometimes I lie awake at night and worry about all the things that could happen.

Thanh:	Well, why don't you put some of that in? You know, reality. Tell us what it's really like.
Brenda:	I agree. That will make it more interesting.
Carla:	Okay. I'll try it. What about my three points? Should I keep them?
Brenda:	Maybe. Or you could make the emotions your three points.
Antonio:	But don't get rid of that past, present, and future part. I like that.
Carla:	Thanks, everybody. You've really helped. Okay, Antonio, now it's your turn.

Carla's Journal Entry and New Outline

After talking to her writing group, Carla wrote a journal entry, then made a new outline.

I can't believe I forgot that the assignment said the essay should be about my emotions. Well, let's see. What are the emotions I feel about being a mother? First of all, I feel an overwhelming and protective love for my daughter. I never knew I could feel that way about any living thing. But I also feel discouraged and down-hearted many times. I work hard and just barely get by. I can't remember the last time I bought a new outfit for Alisa or for myself. Financial troubles are the worst. And like Brenda said, it is scary raising a child these days. Some nights I lie awake terrified about what could happen to her or what could happen to me that would keep me from taking care of her. I also feel angry when I hear people talk about single parents not being able to raise their children with the right values. This is not a perfect world. I did not create it, but I have to live in it and I do the best I can. If they haven't walked in my shoes, they can't judge me.

So far, the emotions I can pick out are happiness, love, discouragement, terror, and anger. Maybe I can write about some of those.

Carla's new outline:

Thesis: Since my daughter Alisa was born, I have lived with the joy, the pain, and often, the sheer terror of raising a child alone.

Joy:
1. Seeing her at birth
2. Watching her grow and form a personality

Pain:
1. Being a single parent
2. Not having enough money
3. Working long hours along with going to school

Terror:

1. Something could happen to me—illness or whatever—and keep me from taking care of her
2. Things that could happen to her

Carla's Rough Draft with Notes

From her new outline, Carla wrote a rough draft. Then she met with her instructor for a conference on her draft. Carla's rough draft, with notes she made at the conference with her instructor, follows.

Since my daughter Alisa was born, I have lived with the joy, the pain, and also the sheer terror of raising a child alone. Being a single parent can happen to anyone but I never thought it would happen to me. I had dreams of a marriage that would last forever and of strong, healthy children who would always feel secure in the love of two full-time parents.

Move the thesis to the end of the introduction.

Raising my daughter Alisa is a joy that I would not trade for any-thing. The first time I saw her, I thought she was beautiful even though to anyone else, she probably was not much to look at. Watching her grow into a real little human being with a personality that is not mine or her grandparents' or her father's but uniquely her own has been a delight. Seeing her develop as a person has been and will always continue to be my chief joy in life.

Add description. What did she look like? How did the sight of her affect me? What is her personality like? Make the last sentence less wordy.

At first, I was unhappy not having her father to share the joy of Alisa's first word or to sit up with me through the night when she had a fever. But that kind of pain goes away. What remains is the constant weight of struggling to keep up financially. I wait for child support checks that may or may not come, and if they do not come, I do without. Between school and work, my day often lasts twelve hours. But I know the rewards of building a life for myself and my daughter will one day outweigh the pain I have endured.

Add a topic sentence to this paragraph. Add more support about the ways I cope.

Parenthood has brought with it feelings of terror. No matter how loving and watchful I am, there are so many things that are beyond my control. Sometimes, I wake in the lonely hours before dawn and think, What if something happens to me? What if I die or am in an accident and can't take care of Alisa? Worse yet is the thought that something could happen to her. Every time I hear of a child who is seriously ill or who has been badly hurt, my heart freezes. When I see television news stories about trusted scout leaders, teachers, or pastors being arrested for child molestation or child pornography, I am reminded that I can take nothing for granted. Fortunately, the business of daily living usually keeps those thoughts away, otherwise, I don't know how I would stay sane.

No major changes.

Raising a child is a joy even though it is a full-time job, and it is even harder when money is scarce and the world seems uncertain. Still, I would not trade the joys of raising my daughter for all the wealth and security in the world.

Conclusion is okay.

Carla's Final Draft

Sandoval 1

Carla Sandoval

English 1101

Professor De Luca

7 May 2011

My Feelings about Motherhood

Being a single parent can happen to anyone, but I never thought it would happen to me. I had dreams of a marriage that would last forever and of strong, healthy children who would always feel secure in the love of two full-time parents. But life is not a fairy tale, and dreams don't always come true. Since my daughter Alisa was born, I have lived with the joy, the pain, and the sheer terror of raising a child alone.

Raising my daughter Alisa is a joy that I would not trade for anything. The first time I saw her red, wrinkled face, swollen eyes, and the thin fuzz of hair plastered to her tiny head, I was certain that I would do anything to protect her and keep her safe. Watching her personality develop has been a delight. From the start, she has had incredible focus. At two months, she peered at people intently, as if she were memorizing their faces. At two years, that intentness turned into a stubborn insistence on exploring every cabinet and emptying every drawer and shelf she could reach. Now, at five, she still has that same focus. I see it when she stacks her blocks or looks at her books, shutting out the world in her concentration on the task. She is my joy.

Along with joy, single parenthood holds special pain. Alisa's father was not there to share the joy of Alisa's first word or to sit up with me through the night when she had a fever. But that kind of pain goes away. What remains is the constant weight of financial struggle. I wait for child support checks, and if they do not come, I do without. I scour yard sales for good used clothing for the two of us and stretch my paycheck so that I can still buy groceries at the end of the month. I leave Alisa at my mother's and head out for a day that, between school and work, often lasts twelve hours. If it weren't for Alisa, I don't know how I could endure those long grinding days. But I know the rewards of building a life for myself and my daughter will one day outweigh the pain I have endured.

Parenthood has brought with it feelings of terror that are even more intense because I am raising my child alone. I know that no matter how loving and watchful I am, many things are beyond my control. Sometimes, I wake in the lonely hours before dawn and think, "What if I die or am in an accident and can't take care of Alisa?" Worse yet is the thought that something could happen to her. Every time I hear of a child who is seriously ill or who has been badly hurt, my heart freezes. When I see

Sandoval 3

television news stories about trusted scout leaders or pastors being

arrested for child molestation or child pornography, I am reminded that

I can take nothing for granted. Fortunately, the daily rush usually keeps

those thoughts away; otherwise, I don't know how I would stay sane.

Raising a child is a full-time job, and it is even harder when money

is scarce and the world seems uncertain. Still, I would not trade the joys

of raising my daughter for all the wealth and security in the world.

Carla's Approach to Writing—and Yours

Carla's final draft is the product of many hours' thought and work, and is at least partly a result of her willingness to listen to the advice and comments of others. It is also a result of her willingness to discard ideas that did not work.

Writing is a process of trial and error—sometimes it feels like mostly error. Even experienced writers often find writing difficult, often wonder each time they write if they have anything worthwhile to say or the ability to say it. In addition, the very act of writing makes the writer vulnerable. Your words and experiences are a part of you, and putting them on paper for others' examination can make you feel exposed. So why should you bother to write? You should bother because, at its best, writing can give you power and joy and the ability to move others. Fortunately, writing is a skill that improves with practice, and if you give it serious effort, you will amaze yourself. The following list, "Five Quick Takes on Writing," may help you put the task of writing in perspective.

Five Quick Takes on Writing

1. Take it a step at a time. Writing is often a slow process, and it always requires thought.
2. Take it seriously. The ability to write clearly and well will benefit you academically, professionally, and personally throughout your life.
3. Take it easy. Don't expect yourself to be perfect.
4. Take it to the limit. Stretch the limits of your imagination. Refuse to limit yourself by labeling yourself a poor writer.
5. Take it with you. Writing is a vital part of the real world. Make it a part of your life.

Group Exercise 1 The Ideal Conditions for Writing

In a group of three or four, discuss the ideal conditions for writing. Think about questions such as these: What tools do you enjoy working with? Do you write best with music or in absolute silence? Do you like having others around, or do you prefer to be alone? Do you need coffee or snacks when you write? Do you need room to pace, or do you think best seated in front of a desk or a computer? After each group member has contributed, see what differences and similarities exist among members of your group. Have a spokesperson report your group's findings to the rest of the class.

If You Hate the Thought of a Step-by-Step Approach . . .

This section is for those who rebel at the idea of a step-by-step approach like the one described in this chapter. Although prewriting, planning, drafting, revising, and proofreading are identifiable steps in the writing process, there's no law that says everyone has to approach them in exactly the same way.

For some people, a step-by-step approach does not come naturally. These people have a thinking style that is most often called "right-brained" or "holistic." The human brain is divided into two halves, or hemispheres, and most people are wired to rely heavily on the left hemisphere—the half responsible for logical, sequential, step-by-step thinking. Some people, however, rely more heavily on the right half of the brain, the part responsible for seeing the whole, for thinking in images, and for flashes of insight.

The following questions may help you decide if you are a right-brained thinker.

1. If you were asked to analyze how you write, would your answer be, "I don't know. I just do it"?

2. When you are required to turn in an outline, do you do it last, after you have written the paper?

3. If you were asked to describe your usual prewriting technique, would you say, "I never prewrite"?

4. Do you often arrive at the right answer to math problems without following the steps?

5. Do you have a hard time getting detail into your writing?

6. Are you a "big-picture person" rather than a "detail person"?

If you answered yes to three or more of these questions, you may have sometimes been seen as a rebel because you don't always follow a step-by-step, conventional approach to your work. But chances are that, whatever other characteristics you possess, you are also a right-brained writer.

Right-brained people are often intuitive, seeing the big picture before others do. They have a strong creative streak. They sometimes grasp ideas easily without knowing why or understanding how. But unlike their methodical, list-making, left-brained brothers and sisters, right-brained people often have trouble with the details. Planning isn't in their natures, and they tend not to have systems or specific steps to rely on. Whatever the task is, they "just do it."

If you are right-brained, does that mean that the methods in this text won't work for you? No. They *will* work. But you may have to work at them a bit harder. Give them a chance. Don't count them out until you have had enough experience with them to determine whether they work for you or not.

There are additional strategies you can use. Unlike more conventional methods, the following tips for right-brained writers were crafted with you in mind. These ideas may give you the extra boost you need to harness your creativity and let your right-brained way of thinking work for you, not against you. If your thinking style is left-brained, read on anyway. There may be something here that you can use along with the logical, step-by-step approach that works so well for you.

Tips for Right-Brained Writers

Find your most creative time and use it for writing. Some people find that they are at their best in the mornings. Others find that their creative juices begin to flow around 9:00 or 10:00 P.M. Writing will be easier if you schedule it during your natural period of creativity.

Use your rough draft as your prewriting. Because you think in terms of the whole, you may find it easier to do a rough draft than to prewrite. Consider your rough draft a form of prewriting, to be extensively revised before you turn it in.

Give your brain an assignment. When you have writing to do, let your right brain work on it while you are doing other things. At the beginning of the day, for instance, look over the assignment for a few minutes. Then come back to it in the evening and reap the benefits of having worked on the topic subconsciously. Or think about your topic before you go to sleep at night and write in the morning. This technique can work not only in prewriting but also in revising.

Realize that doing the grunt work is a necessary evil. Right-brained people are less likely to put in the time it takes to master the basics because doing so may be tedious and boring to them. They are also less likely to plan. But even the most creative people need self-discipline. It's a hard lesson to learn, but mastering the basics is essential to creative work. Singers spend endless time on breath control and scales. Artists learn anatomy and basic drawing. It is those efforts that set them free to do their best work. The payoff in mastering the basics is that once you learn them, you can forget about them. They will be second nature. The same goes for planning. Once you have made a plan, you are free to do the creative work. Doing the grunt work now always pays off in more freedom later.

Make a commitment to writing. Many professional writers are right-brained and face the same resistance that you do. Invariably, they say that the only way they can maintain the extended effort it takes to write books, plays, or novels is to have a routine and to write every day.

Review of the Paragraph

mywritinglab

Visit MyWriting Lab for additional practice recognizing a paragraph.

This text will guide you step by step through the process of writing an essay. Before you begin essay writing, take the time to briefly review the single-paragraph composition.

A paragraph has a topic sentence that gives it direction and lets the reader know where the paragraph is headed. It has strong support for the topic sentence in the form of details and examples, all of which contribute to paragraph unity by supporting the topic sentence. Each sentence flows smoothly into the next, providing coherence. Often, the paragraph ends with a summary sentence that restates the topic sentence and brings the paragraph to a strong close.

The Topic Sentence

mywritinglab

Visit MyWriting Lab for additional practice with the topic sentence.

A topic sentence does two things. First, it presents the **general topic** of the paragraph. Then it makes a **specific point** about that topic.

Example Topic Sentences

topic sentences   specific point about the topic
Balancing school and family life can be difficult.

topic   specific point about the topic
My sense of humor often gets me in trouble.

The Supporting Sentences

A topic sentence provides direction—the road map for a paragraph—but supporting sentences supply the scenery. While topic sentences are broad and general, large enough to encompass the entire paragraph, supporting sentences are specific, giving details and examples.

The Summary Sentence

A summary sentence ends the paragraph. Sometimes it sums up the points made in the paragraph, sometimes it restates the topic sentence, but it always brings the paragraph to a graceful and definite close.

A Model Paragraph

People-Watching at the Convenience Store

Topic Sentence —————— My part-time job as a convenience store clerk allows me to observe a fascinating variety of people. If I work the morning shift,

First supporting point ————— my customers are mostly neatly dressed office workers rushing to work. They stop to buy gas for their morning commute or to grab a cup of coffee on the way to the office. They dash up to the register in a cloud of aftershave or perfume, pay for their purchases, and quickly

Second supporting point ————— leave. In the early afternoon, the store fills with children who attend a nearby elementary school. They flock into the store in giggling groups and head straight for the candy aisle. The children take their time choosing fruit-flavored bubble gum, sour candies, and chocolate bars. They bring their purchases and their money to the register, then nois-ily flock out again, happy to be out of school for the day. If I work

Third supporting point ————— the late afternoon shift, I see laborers, grimy and exhausted, buying a single can of beer or a lottery ticket. They are young men with old, tired eyes, yet most of them offer a smile or make a joke as they count out crumpled dollar bills with callused hands. With such a wide variety

Summary sentence ————— of customers, my job at the convenience store is never dull.

Writing Assignments

WRITING ASSIGNMENT 1   Writing and You

Write a paragraph describing your attitudes toward writing. Use the following steps.

Prewrite: Jot down a few of the words that come to mind when you think of writing. Think of any significant experiences you have had that have shaped your attitude toward writing. Consider your writing habits. Are you organized? Do you procrastinate?

Plan: Look over your prewriting. Try to sum up your attitude toward writing in a single word or phrase, and then construct an opening sentence for your paragraph using that word or phrase. Use one of the following sentences, filling in the blank with your word or phrase, or construct your own sentence.

- My attitude toward writing is _____.
- When I think about writing, I feel _____.
- My feelings about writing have always been _____ ones.

Once you have constructed an opening sentence, decide how to organize your paragraph. A couple of possibilities are listed here.

1. Take a historical approach, describing the influences that have shaped your writing. Use chronological (time) order.
2. Take a step-by-step approach, describing what you do and how you feel as you go through a writing assignment.

Finally, complete the planning stage by making an outline that briefly lists the points you plan to make in support of your opening sentence.

Draft: Write out a rough draft of your paragraph. Focus on expressing your ideas rather than on grammar and punctuation.

Revise: Read over your rough draft. Have you left out anything important? Is each idea clearly expressed? Does the paragraph flow smoothly? Is the sequence of ideas logical and effective? If possible, ask a classmate to look over your rough draft with the same questions in mind. Then revise your paragraph, incorporating any necessary changes.

Proofread: Check your paragraph for mistakes in spelling, grammar, and punctuation. Look at each sentence individually. Then proofread once more. You have now completed all the steps in the writing process.

WRITING ASSIGNMENT 2   Reasons For Attending College

People go to college for many reasons. Some attend college to fulfill lifelong goals, others to escape a dead-end job, still others to fulfill their families' expectations. What has brought you to college?

Write a paragraph discussing your reasons for attending college, using the following steps.

Prewrite: Take a sheet of paper and begin with the words, "When I . . . . " Write for five or ten minutes without stopping, then look to see what you have. Does your prewriting focus more on the past (When I was a child, I used to line up my dolls and pretend they were students . . .) or on the future (When I receive my nursing degree, I will be able to fulfill many of my dreams . . .)? Seeing whether your focus is on the past or on the future will help you to decide on the direction your paragraph should take.

Plan: Look over your prewriting and underline the most important words and ideas. Then construct an opening sentence that states the central idea you want to express in your paragraph. Some typical opening sentences follow.

- All of my reasons for attending college are rooted in the past.
- Attending college is one way I can ensure a brighter future for my children.
- Attending college will help me realize my dream of becoming a nurse.
- For me, attending college is a way out of a dead-end job.

Once you have constructed an opening sentence, decide how to organize your paragraph. A couple of possibilities are listed here.

1. Take a historical approach, describing the influences that shaped your decision to attend college. Use chronological (time) order.
2. Take a point-by-point approach, listing your reasons one by one.

Finally, complete the planning stage by making an outline that briefly lists the points you plan to make in support of your opening sentence.

Draft: Write out a rough draft of your paragraph. Focus on expressing your ideas rather than on grammar and punctuation.

Revise: Read over your rough draft. Have you left out anything important? Is each idea clearly expressed? Does the paragraph flow smoothly? Is the sequence of ideas logical and effective? If possible, ask a classmate to look over your rough draft with the same questions in mind. Then revise your paragraph, incorporating any necessary changes.

Proofread: Check your paragraph for mistakes in spelling, grammar, and punctuation. Look at each sentence individually. Then proofread once more. You have now completed all the steps in the writing process.

mywritinglab   For support and practice meeting this chapter's goal, log in to www.mywritinglab.com and select **The Writing Process**.

CHAPTER 2

Preparing to Write

🖋 **Chapter Goal:** Use prewriting strategies to become a more efficient writer.

Dream
         Invent
Play
         Discover
Imagine
         Reflect
Consider

🖋 Prewriting

mywritinglab

Visit MyWriting Lab for additional practice with prewriting.

Prewriting is the first step in the writing process. It is the act of gathering your thoughts on a topic. Depending on the assignment you are given, it may also include narrowing your topic to a manageable size. Prewriting begins the moment you receive an assignment. Immediately, a part of your mind begins to gather information. However, it usually takes a bit of effort to bring that information to the surface. The prewriting methods in this chapter are designed to jump-start the writing process by helping you collect your thoughts on a topic and get them on paper.

Focus on Preparing to Write: Finding Inspiration

When Emilio Estevez was in the process of writing Bobby, *a screenplay about the day Robert F. Kennedy was shot in the kitchen of the Ambassador Hotel, he allowed writer's block to stop him from writing the script for a year. Finally, Estevez checked into a hotel in Pismo Beach, California, to finish the job. He casually mentioned the project to a check-in clerk, who told him that she had been in the kitchen of the Ambassador Hotel on that day. Her story gave him the inspiration he needed to create a new character and finish the script.*

When you write, do you sometimes have difficulty coming up with ideas, or, like Emilio Estevez, get stuck after you come up with the idea? Unlike Estevez, you don't have years to do your writing projects. You need a reliable way of generating ideas. This chapter will help you find various ways to tap into your imagination so that you can get your ideas on paper.

Reflect on It

Whether you are taking a class or pursuing a career, you need ideas. Think about how you best generate ideas. Is your mind most open to new ideas when you are talking with others or when you are alone? Do you need to "sleep on it" to get good ideas, or do they come to you quickly? Think about a time when you solved a problem with a creative idea. How did you come up with it?

Source: http://www.urbancinefile.com.au/home/view.asp?a=12867&s=Interviews

---

Why Prewrite?

It's tempting to skip prewriting. After all, why take the time to prewrite when you can just sit down and start writing? The answer is that taking a few extra minutes to prewrite is more efficient than not prewriting. Prewriting is worth your time for several reasons.

- *Prewriting opens a doorway to your thoughts.* Your mind does not offer instant access to its content. Bits of memory and stored knowledge reveal themselves gradually, one by one. Prewriting allows your mind time to reveal its knowledge on the subject.

- *Prewriting helps prevent writer's block.* Prewriting can never be wrong, so the process of prewriting gives you a certain immunity to writer's block, the paralysis that comes from feeling that every word must be perfect and every sentence correct.

- *Prewriting builds confidence.* By the time you finish prewriting, you will probably find that you have more to say about your subject than you imagined. Therefore, you will write more strongly and confidently.

- *Prewriting sparks creativity.* When you are not worried about whether your ideas are right or wrong, you are more likely to think creatively and let your thoughts flow freely.

- *Prewriting tells you when to quit.* If you just can't get a topic going, maybe it's not worth pursuing. Try something else.

Prewriting Methods

The aim of all **prewriting methods** is the same: to get ideas on paper. At this point in the writing process, it is not the quality of ideas that counts, but the quantity.

When you are ready to prewrite, sit at the computer or in a comfortable spot with pen and paper. Relax your mind and body, and remind yourself that prewriting is a playful exercise of imagination and that it is okay to write down anything that comes to mind. As for the part of your mind that automatically jumps in to criticize what you think and say, give it some time off. Your purpose in prewriting is to put down every thought on your topic, no matter how ridiculous it seems. Later, you can discard what is not usable. But while you are prewriting, there is no good or bad, no right or wrong.

Some of the methods may feel awkward at first, but try them all. One will be right for you.

Brainstorming

mywritinglab
Visit MyWriting Lab for additional practice with brainstorming.

Brainstorming, a listing technique, is one of the easiest prewriting techniques. To brainstorm, take a few minutes to list whatever comes to mind on your topic, no matter how strange it seems. Your purpose is not to censor or come up with the "right" items for your list, but to generate ideas.

Example of Brainstorming

Here's how one writer, Tamiko, approached a brainstorming exercise on clothing:

stores	secondhand stores
fashion models	department stores
slick magazines	occasions
anorexia	job interviews
expensive	professional dress
name brands	uniforms
my red dress	proms
designer labels	my favorites—old jeans and T-shirts
even children are fashion-conscious	"Clothes make the man" (or woman!)

When Tamiko looked over her prewriting, she decided that the part of it that most interested her was the quotation "Clothes make the man." She wasn't quite sure which side she was on, so she did a two-sided brainstorming. Though Tamiko used brainstorming, she could have chosen any form of prewriting to explore both sides of the issue. The result of her brainstorming follows.

Example of Two-Sided Brainstorming

Clothes make the man (or woman).

Agree	Disagree
People judge us by the outside	It's what's inside that counts
Clothing tells people about us	Clothing can hide the truth
Tells our economic status	People who can't look beyond clothing are shallow
Sometimes reveals professional status	
Shows our sense of style	
Different dress for different ages	
Helps us express our personality	
Tells how much we care about appearance	
It's all people have to go on until they know us	

When she looked at her brainstorming, Tamiko was surprised to find that her evidence favored the "agree" side of the issue. "I thought I looked beyond superficial things like clothes," she said, "but I really have more evidence to support the statement than to disagree with it."

Like Tamiko, you may find that willingness to explore both sides of an issue leads you in an unexpected direction.

EXERCISE 1	BRAINSTORMING

Brainstorm on one of the following topics; then see if you have a focus for a possible essay. Feel free to explore more than one side of your idea.

1. Do credit cards do more harm than good?

2. Is it better to be a leader or a follower?

3. Are good manners necessary in the modern world?

4. Do video surveillance systems protect people or violate their privacy?

5. If two people are in love, should large differences in their ages matter?

Freewriting

mywritinglab
Visit MyWriting Lab for additional practice with freewriting.

Freewriting is nonstop writing on a topic for a set period of time. The point of freewriting is that your flow of words never ceases; your pen never stops moving. If you have nothing to say, repeat your last thought again and again until a new thought replaces it. Do not worry about spelling, about clarity, or about whether your thoughts are logically connected. Just write.

Example of Freewriting

Burt's freewriting on "goals" draws on his own experience.

I am supposed to do a freewriting on goals and I can't think of anything to say. I should talk about my goals, I guess, but I haven't even decided on a major yet. My goal has mostly been to get through each day. My sociology professor said that one characteristic of poverty is a focus on today. A poor person wonders, "What will I eat today?" not "How will I provide for my future?" People who are poor can't afford to think of tomorrow because today is such a struggle. I am goal-poor. I have accomplished so little in my life that I feel afraid to set goals.

I guess I fear failure. I am even afraid to commit to a major for fear I won't be able to do it. I can set little goals, like making an A on a test or studying for two hours in the evening, but I just don't set big goals. I can still hear my father saying, "You will never accomplish anything." Maybe it's not too late. I am going in the right direction by starting school.

| EXERCISE 2 | FREEWRITING |

Freewrite on one of the following topics; then see if you have a focus for a possible essay.

1. children
2. friendship
3. morality

4. television
5. physical appearance

Focused Freewriting

Focused freewriting helps you zoom in on a topic and bring ideas into closer focus. Rather than ranging outward in all directions, focused freewriting examines a narrow topic. Use focused freewriting when the assigned topic is a specific question or when you have narrowed your topic through previous prewriting. Focused freewriting is just like any other freewriting, but with a narrower range.

Example of Focused Freewriting

Here is how one writer, Eric, handled a focused freewriting on the question "What rules of etiquette are important today?" His finished essay appears in Chapter 9.

> Some people today totally ignore manners, as if they are not important. Some of the old rules are gone but new ones replace them. Just like that old guy in the health club who said he never opened doors for women. He seemed to think that he didn't have to be polite anymore. That's wrong. Manners is just basic consideration for other people. Maybe there was a time when it was which fork to use, that kind of thing, but now that the world is so crowded, that stuff matters less and respecting people's space matters more. New rules come up for new situations, too. There are rules for computers and email and rules for talking on the phone and texting. All the old stereotypes are out and manners are just practical ways of getting along in the world.

| EXERCISE 3 | FOCUSED FREEWRITING |

Do a focused freewriting on one of the following topics.

1. What kinds of risks are good to take?
2. Why are people superstitious?

3. What kinds of music do you enjoy?

4. What one characteristic is most important in a friend?

5. Is family more or less important than it was in your grandparents' day?

Invisible Writing: A Computer Technique

Invisible writing is a freewriting technique especially for writing on a computer. Turn on your computer and, once you have a blank screen in front of you, type the words "Invisible Writing" at the top of the page. Then turn your monitor off or adjust the contrast until the words are no longer visible and your screen is completely dark.

Freewrite for five or ten minutes. It is especially important not to worry about spelling errors. With this method, you can hardly avoid them. At first, you may feel strange, even anxious, pouring your words into the dark computer screen. Soon, though, your fingers and your thoughts will fly.

EXERCISE 4	INVISIBLE WRITING

If you have access to a computer, do an invisible writing on one of the following topics. Then see if you have a focus for an essay.

1. transportation
2. competition
3. grades
4. newspapers
5. littering

Clustering

mywritinglab

Visit MyWriting Lab for additional practice with clustering.

Clustering is a technique designed to boost your creativity by stimulating both hemispheres, or halves, of your brain. On the one hand, the left brain is the part used in logical tasks that move in 1-2-3 order. When you count to ten, write a sentence, or make an outline, you are using your left hemisphere. Your right hemisphere, on the other hand, specializes in tasks involving imagery or intuition. Since clustering involves both listing (a left-brain task) and drawing (a right-brain task), it allows you to tap both your logical side and your creative side.

To cluster, begin with a circled word—your topic. From there, "map out" associations. Some people branch out ideas from the central word, like quills on a porcupine. Others group ideas when they cluster, with smaller clusters branching out from larger ones. When this latter type of cluster is finished, it resembles the diagram of a molecule in a biology textbook.

What your diagram looks like does not matter. In clustering, what matters is that you get your thoughts on paper using both images and words.

Look at the examples of clustering that follow

Example of a Porcupine Cluster

Here is Kelly's "porcupine" cluster on the topic "If you could change one aspect of your personality, what would it be?"

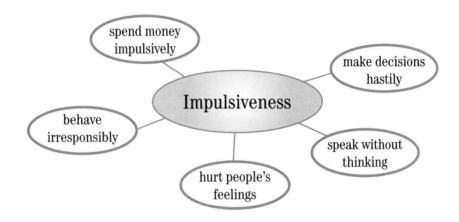

Example of a Molecule Cluster

Jemal's "molecule" cluster is on the topic "computers."

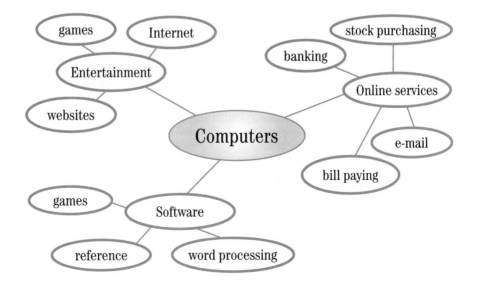

| EXERCISE 5 | CLUSTERING |

Do a cluster diagram on one of the following topics.

1.   managing anger

2.   fitness

3.   making sacrifices to reach a specific goal

4.   automobiles

5.   bad habits

Outlining

Outlining is often the last step in the prewriting process. Once you have used one or more of the other prewriting methods, organizing your thoughts into outline form takes you one step further in the writing process. Forget about the formal outline with its array of Roman numerals, ABCs, and 1-2-3s. A short essay calls for a short outline. Your outline may be just a few words jotted on a page, or it may include a thesis statement, topic sentences, and a brief listing of support for each topic sentence. Following are two sample outlines on the same topic.

Outline 1

Benefits of Karate

1. Confidence
   physical confidence
      walk taller and straighter
      not as klutzy
      feel more comfortable with my physical self
   mental confidence
      believe more in my ability to do things
2. Self-discipline
   plan study time and make better grades
   do my homework on weekdays to leave most of the
      weekend free
   keep my work area neater
3. New view of life
   helps me see life as something I control, not something
      that controls me
   helps me see that hard work turns desire to succeed into
      success
   new hopes for future

Outline 2

Thesis:
　　Karate has given me confidence, self-discipline, and a new view of life.
Topic Sentence 1:
　　Karate has helped me become mentally and physically confident.
Topic Sentence 2:
　　The self-discipline I bring to karate has helped me become more disciplined in other areas.
Topic Sentence 3:
　　Seeing my hard work pay off has given me a new view of life and of my future.

EXERCISE 6   OUTLINING

Choose one of your practice prewritings and make an outline for a paragraph or essay.

Journal Writing

The word *journal* comes from *jour,* the French word for *day.* **Journal writings,** then, are "daily writings." Journals are usually composed of informal writings on a variety of subjects. A journal allows you to experiment with the techniques you are learning in your writing class. In a journal, the only form of writing you should avoid is "diary mode." An "I-got-up-I-fed-the-dog-I-went-to-school" format makes for dull writing and even duller reading. Write about issues that matter to you. Interpret your dreams. Describe your grandfather's tool shed. Work toward detailed writing that follows a logical pattern.

Whether you receive credit for it in class or not, make journal writing a habit. Practice is the only thing that is guaranteed to make you a better writer. Courses and texts are of limited value without time spent alone with a computer or pen and paper. If you think, "It won't matter because I'll never be a good writer," ask yourself this: How good a driver would you be if the only driving you had done was in a driver education course? You *can* be a better writer. Daily writing in your journal will start you on your way.

Journal Topics

1. What are some reasons for keeping a journal or diary?
2. What are the characteristics of a good student?
3. Discuss a person who has been a mentor or a role model to you.

4. A poem by Paul Laurence Dunbar begins, "We wear the mask/That grins and lies . . . " Discuss some of the masks that you wear.

5. Should every able citizen of the United States be required to do some sort of paid public service (not necessarily military service) for a set period?

6. Why are some people unsuccessful in school or at work?

7. Is it necessary for you to own an automobile?

8. Do Americans spend too much time watching television?

9. Is year-round school a good idea?

10. If you could know any one thing about your future, what would you want to know?

11. Have you ever had a dream that was so vivid that it seemed real? Describe it.

12. If you could live anywhere in the world, where would you choose to live?

13. If you could visit any historical period, which one would you choose to visit?

14. Although responsibilities are sometimes burdens, they also tell us who we are. Which of your responsibilities is most important to you?

15. Is it better to have a determined, forceful "Type A" personality or a relaxed, easygoing "Type B" personality?

PROGRESSIVE WRITING ASSIGNMENT

How the Progressive Writing Assignment Works

One of the following topics will serve as the basis for your first essay. In this chapter, you will complete prewriting for the essay. Throughout the next five chapters, each progressive assignment will take you a step further toward a completed essay. By the time you have finished the assignment at the end of Chapter 7, you will have completed all the steps in the writing process and will have a finished essay.

Progressive Writing Assignment: Prewriting

In this chapter, your progressive assignment is a prewriting assignment. Choose one of the topics below and follow the instructions.

Topic 1: Discuss three obstacles to your education.

TIPS FOR PREWRITING

Use any of the methods outlined in this chapter to prewrite on the topic "Discuss three obstacles to your education." As you prewrite, consider all the factors that surround those obstacles. What is the nature of the obstacles? Are they physical, emotional, financial, academic? Does family or work play a role? Are there obstacles you have already overcome? How did you manage to overcome them? Are there obstacles that remain to be conquered? How will you do it?

WHAT NOW?
After you have completed your prewriting, you should have more material than you will be able to use. To prepare for the next step in the Progressive Writing Assignment, choose the three obstacles that you want to focus on in your essay.

Topic 2: Discuss your short-term goals, long-term goals, or both.

TIPS FOR PREWRITING
Use any of the methods outlined in this chapter to prewrite on the topic "Discuss your short-term goals, long-term goals, or both." As you prewrite, consider all the factors that surround those goals. What are the goals? Are they new goals or lifelong ambitions? Is goal-setting easy for you because you have practiced it all your life, or is it difficult because you have not been a goal-oriented person? What is the nature of your goals? Are they academic goals, career goals, physical goals, spiritual goals, or family goals? How do you plan to reach them? How are they related to one another? How will they change your life?

WHAT NOW?
After you have completed your prewriting, you should have more material than you will be able to use. Decide which ideas you want to focus on. Recall that you can discuss long-term goals, short-term goals, or both. To prepare for the next step in the Progressive Writing Assignment, choose three goals to focus on in your essay.

Topic 3: Discuss the values you have learned by observing members of your family.

TIPS FOR PREWRITING
Use any of the methods outlined in this chapter to prewrite on the values reflected in the behavior of your family. Most people learn *values*—ideas about what is important and how we should conduct ourselves—from family members. Often, these values are learned from parents who stress the importance of honesty, hard work, and other positive traits. In this essay, however, you are to consider the values you learned through *observation* of your family members, not through what they have said to you. For example, your grandfather may never have said a word to you about the value of hard work, but if he got up before dawn, worked twelve hours a day, and spent his weekends repairing the plumbing in his house or tending to his yard, he didn't need to tell you about hard work. He showed you. Think about the members of your family, and write down the things they do to show you what is important in life. Be as specific as possible.

ANOTHER POSSIBLE APPROACH
Another approach to this topic is possible. Perhaps you look at certain members of your family and see negative values that you want to avoid. You can present

these negative influences as examples you do not want to follow, changing the names if you wish to protect your relatives' privacy.

What Now?

After you have completed your prewriting, you should have more material than you will be able to use. To prepare for the next step in the Progressive Writing Assignment, decide which ideas you want to focus on in your essay.

Topic 4: Discuss your methods of coping with stress.

Tips for Prewriting

Everyone experiences stress from many sources, such as overwork, family problems, pressure to excel in school, or even boredom. In this essay, you will write about your ways of coping with stress. Begin by brainstorming or freewriting about some of the sources of your stress. Then explore the coping strategies that you use for each source of stress. Think in detail about those methods and about how well they work.

What Now?

After you have completed your prewriting, you should have more material than you will be able to use. To prepare for the next step in the Progressive Writing Assignment, decide which three coping strategies you want to focus on in your essay.

mywritinglab   For support and practice meeting this chapter's goal, log in to **www.mywritinglab.com** and select **Getting Started** and **Prewriting**.

CHAPTER 3

Building a Framework: Thesis and Organization

> 🖋 **Chapter Goal:** Construct an effective thesis and structure an essay to support it.

Built into the framework—
A splash of sunlight across the floor,
The velvety embrace of an old recliner,
The stench of wet dog,
A shout of children's laughter—
Things that make a house a home.

When you are ready to begin writing an essay, you are ready to think about its framework. Just as a builder lays a foundation and builds a framework before building a house, you will set up the framework of your essay through its thesis and organization. You know the subject of your essay, and you have decided, through prewriting, what points your essay will cover. Perhaps you have even made an outline. Now you are ready to write a thesis statement. Several ways of writing a thesis are presented in this chapter, but at heart, a thesis is very simple: It is the main idea of your essay. Once you have stated the main idea clearly and effectively, you are ready to organize your essay to best advantage.

Focus on Building a Framework: Finding Direction in Your Writing

The picture shows a sextant, a navigational instrument invented by Isaac Newton around the turn of the eighteenth century. This tool allowed sailors to measure a star against

the horizon to gauge where their ship was on a nautical chart. Without a sextant, sailors had to use what they knew of the ocean, land, and stars and hope for the best. With sextants, sailors had a much better idea where they were and how to get where they were going.

A thesis statement functions much like a sextant: It provides direction to your readers so that they will know where your essay is going. Without a thesis, both you and your readers may feel lost in a vast ocean of words. An effective thesis statement will ensure smooth sailing for your readers as you guide them through your essay.

Reflect on It

A thesis statement is your statement of the main idea. It sums up your essay in a sentence and lets the reader know where the essay is going.

But a thesis statement is more than just a sentence in a college essay. When you have learned to write a good thesis statement, you have learned to capture a large idea in very few words.

How will you find capturing the heart of an idea useful in your future career? What kinds of documents will you write that will benefit from the inclusion of a single statement of the main idea before you go into details? These may be emails, reports, or proposals. Whatever your career may be, you'll have to write something to someone. Write down at least one detailed example of a document you will write that will benefit from a statement of the main idea.

The Structure of an Essay

mywritinglab

Visit MyWriting Lab for additional practice with recognizing an essay.

Before constructing a thesis, study the diagram of a typical essay below. Then read the essay that follows, noticing how it corresponds to the diagram. A well-planned thesis statement is an important step in writing a well-structured essay.

Structure of an Essay

Title
- Concisely conveys the topic of the essay

Introduction
- Begins with an interesting opening sentence
- Introduces the topic
- Ends with a thesis that presents the main idea and that may list the points that will be covered

---

First Body Paragraph
- Begins with a topic sentence that introduces the first point of discussion
- Presents examples and details that develop the first point
- May close with a summary sentence that restates the first point

---

Second Body Paragraph
- Begins with a topic sentence that introduces the second point of discussion
- Presents examples and details that develop the second point
- May close with a summary sentence that restates the second point

---

Third Body Paragraph
- Begins with a topic sentence that introduces the third point of discussion
- Presents examples and details that develop the third point
- May close with a summary sentence that restates the third point

---

Conclusion
- Provides a two- to four-sentence ending for the essay
- May sum up the points made in the essay
- Ends on a note of finality

A Model Essay

The Advantages of Internet Shopping

Standing in a line at a huge discount store on the Saturday before Christmas, I felt grumpy and impatient. The line had been at a standstill for five minutes, and the toddler behind me in his mother's shopping cart had started to wail loudly. Hunger was beginning to gnaw at the edges of my stomach. When had shopping become such a pain? Recently, however, I have discovered Internet shopping. Convenience, choice, and savings are the reasons I now prefer to do my shopping online.

Convenience is the main advantage of shopping over the Internet. If I want to, I can shop at the same large discount store where I shopped on that miserable Saturday afternoon, but with no long lines and no squalling babies. On the Internet, I do not have to circle a huge parking lot searching for a space. I can shop in the quiet and convenience of my own home, with jazz playing softly and a cup of hot chocolate in my hand. "No shirt, no shoes, no service" does not apply on the Internet. Flannel pajamas and fuzzy bunny slippers are well within the dress code. And if it's midnight, I can still shop. The Internet is open all night.

A second advantage to Internet shopping is choice. Living in a medium-sized city, I don't have access to the full range of shops that a large metropolitan area would offer. However, the Internet connects me in minutes with a full range of retailers. Since the online environment offers a wide range of stores from Walmart to Tiffany, I am sure to find something within my price range. In addition, a wide variety of merchandise is available. I can listen to samples of music at online music stores and buy the tunes I enjoy. I can buy gifts, flowers, candy, and personalized T-shirts for Christmas, birthdays, or Mother's Day. I can even buy textbooks for my classes online. With the variety of merchandise offered on the Internet, I can almost always find what I need.

Finally, shopping on the Internet saves both money and time. I don't have to buy gas for my car before I shop online, nor do I buy lunch as I might if I were at a shopping center. In addition, since online retailers don't need brick-and-mortar stores, they have lower overhead and often, lower prices. I recently saved $200 on a laser printer by purchasing it online. Shopping online also takes less time than shopping in a store. Driving around and shopping at malls or discount stores can easily take the better part of a Saturday. Shopping online usually takes less than an hour, even if I visit multiple sites to compare prices. Saving money and time is a big advantage of online shopping.

Internet shopping has many advantages, including convenience, choice, and savings. Next Christmas, I will not drive to a crowded discount store and wear out my feet and my patience looking for a gift; I will turn on my computer instead. I hear that even Santa surfs the Net these days.

Constructing the Thesis Statement

mywritinglab

Visit MyWriting Lab for additional practice constructing the thesis statement.

A **thesis statement**, usually placed at the end of your introductory paragraph, states the main idea of your essay, often states or implies your attitude or opinion about the subject, and gives your essay **direction**. Direction means that the thesis sets the course that the essay will follow. In an essay, the thesis statement is the controlling force behind every sentence and every word. It is a promise to your reader that you will discuss the idea mentioned in the thesis statement and no other.

Types of Thesis Statements

A thesis statement presents the main idea of an essay. Sometimes, it also presents the points that will be covered in the essay. When you construct your thesis statement, you will decide whether to write a thesis that lists points of developments or one that does not.

As you write, you will find that some topics lend themselves to the listing of points while others do not. Your writing habits can also help you decide which type of thesis to use. Careful, organized writers can usually work with either type. Writers who tend to skip steps, however, often find that listing points forces them to be more thorough and organized.

The Thesis with Points Listed

A thesis with points listed presents the main idea along with the points of development. These points are listed in the order in which they will be discussed in the essay. The thesis that lists points of development has a long tradition in college writing. Listing thesis points provides a road map that lets the reader see where the essay is headed.

Examples of a Thesis with Points Listed

✔ My formula for a successful lawn care business includes *clever advertising, competitive prices,* and *reliable service.*

✔ *Price, performance,* and *fit* are factors to consider when shopping for athletic shoes.

Advantages of a Thesis with Points Listed

1. Listing thesis points forces you to plan your essay carefully. If you habitually skim over the prewriting and planning stages, then listing points forces you to think through your topic before you write the essay.

2. Listing thesis points conveys an impression of careful organization. Your reader sees concrete evidence that you planned before you wrote.

3. Listing thesis points aids clarity by giving the reader a road map to the development of your essay.

4. Listing thesis points keeps you on track. Your thesis serves as a mini-outline for you to follow as you write.

Making Your Thesis Points Parallel

When you list thesis points, the points should be written in **parallel structure;** that is, each point needs to be written in the same grammatical structure. This is easier than it sounds, and parallel structure makes your thesis points sound like exactly what they are: different points that form a single unit.

Look at the difference in the two example thesis statements that follow.

Examples of Nonparallel and Parallel Thesis Statements

Nonparallel thesis points:

✗ New York is an exciting city to visit because of museums such as the Metropolitan Museum of Art or the American Museum of Natural History, many Broadway plays have tickets available, and going to Ellis Island or seeing the Statue of Liberty.

Differing grammatical structures and too much information make the previous example seem awkward and lacking in unity. Now look at the same thesis statement with parallel points.

Parallel thesis points

✔ New York is an exciting city to visit because of its fascinating museums, Broadway plays, and historic sites.

The parallel thesis flows more smoothly, and the points sound as though they belong together. Notice that no specific details, such as the names of plays or historic sites, are given. Details are best reserved for the body paragraphs.

EXERCISE 1 | **PARALLEL STRUCTURE IN THESIS STATEMENTS**

In each pair of thesis statements, circle the letter of the thesis with the strongest parallel structure.

1. **a.** A dog is an ideal animal companion for me because dogs are protective, suit my active lifestyle, and a dog can be trained.

   b. A dog is an ideal animal companion for me because a dog will protect me, join me in outdoor activities, and respond to training.

     c. A dog is an ideal animal companion for me because a dog will protect me, join me in outdoor activities, and trained easily.

2. a. Looking at a Google Maps photo of my childhood home, I see that it is smaller, neater, and prettier than I remember.

     b. Looking at a Google Maps photo of my childhood home, I see that it is much smaller than I remember, the porch and yard are neater, and the paint and roof have been changed and the screen has been taken off the porch, and really, what were my grandparents thinking with the green roof, anyway?

     c. Looking at a Google Maps photo of my childhood home, I see that it is really small, has been taken care of, and pretty.

3. a. Text messaging is perfect for short messages because it is quiet, unlike calling on a cell phone, and it is quick and does not interrupt the person being called.

     b. Text messaging is perfect for short messages because in some places, like movie theaters, it's rude to talk aloud; it is fast, and less distracting than a phone call.

     c. Text messaging is perfect for short messages because it is quieter, faster, and less distracting than a phone call.

For more information on using parallel structure, see Chapter 21, "Parallel Structure."

Three Ways to Write a Thesis Listing Points

When you write a thesis listing points, you may list the points at the end of the thesis statement, at the beginning of the thesis statement, or in a separate sentence.

Points listed at the end of the thesis statement. One way of writing a thesis statement is to present the main idea first and then list the points of development.

Example of a Thesis Listing Points

       thesis   point 1   point 2

✔ I enjoy fishing because it relaxes me, it challenges me, and

             point 3

it occasionally feeds me.

The writer's thesis, or main idea, is that fishing relaxes him, challenges him, and occasionally feeds him. Notice that the thesis also conveys the writer's attitude toward his subject: He enjoys fishing. Even without the word *enjoy,* the positive nature of the points conveys the writer's attitude. Also, note the parallel structure of the thesis points. Each point follows the same pattern.

> it relaxes me
>
> it challenges me
>
> it (occasionally) feeds me

Although perfect parallel structure will not be possible in every thesis, try to make thesis points as parallel as possible.

Points listed at the beginning of the thesis statement. Listing points first is a bit out of the ordinary. With this technique, you can create a thesis that will not look like everyone else's.

Example of Points at the Beginning of a Thesis Statement

       point 1   point 2   point 3

✔ Too little time, money, and self-confidence

              thesis

made me postpone my college education.

Points listed in a separate sentence. Listing points separately works well for longer thesis statements. If you find your thesis statement becoming long and cumbersome, try listing the points separately.

Example of Points Listed in a Separate Sentence

                      thesis

✔ AIDS is changing the dating habits of American men and women.

                  point 1   point 2

People are becoming reluctant to engage in casual sex, choosy about

                        point 3

the men or women they date, and more likely to remain monogamous.

EXERCISE 2	ANALYZING THESIS STATEMENTS

Analyze the three thesis statements below by answering the questions that follow.

1. Good students are likely to attend class regularly, participate enthusiastically, and study often.

    a. What is the topic of the essay? _____

    b. Are the points of development listed first, last, or separately? _____

    _____

    c. List the points in the order of presentation. Note the parallel structure.

    _____

    _____

    _____

2. Accomplishing something important, helping others, and supporting my family will be the rewards of earning my nursing degree.

    a. What is the topic of the essay? _____

    b. Are the points of development listed first, last, or separately? _____

    _____

    c. List the points in the order of presentation. Note the parallel structure.

    _____

    _____

    _____

3. Singing with a jazz band gives me an outlet for my creativity, a source of extra income, and a more active social life.

    a. What is the topic of the essay? _____

    b. Are the points of development listed first, last, or separately? _____

    _____

    c. List the points in the order of presentation. Note the parallel structure.

    _____

    _____

    _____

| EXERCISE 3 | COMPLETING THESIS STATEMENTS |

Complete the following thesis statements, making sure to list the points in parallel structure.

1. The convenient parking, the _____, and the _____ are advantages of shopping in a mall.

2. Classmates who talk in class, _____, and _____ are disruptive influences.

3. _____, _____, and _____ are the main ingredients for a party.

4. Any employer would be fortunate to hire me. I would bring enthusiasm, _____, and _____ to my job.

5. I would like living in a small town. Small towns are _____, _____, and _____.

| EXERCISE 4 | WRITING A THESIS STATEMENT LISTING POINTS |

Write a thesis listing points on three of the following topics. Include one thesis with points listed first, at least one with points listed last, and at least one with points listed separately. Remember to use parallel structure.

1. What are the keys to maintaining good health?

    _____

    _____

2. If you could possess any one talent or ability, what would you choose? Why?

    _____

    _____

3. What are some differences between high school and college classes?

    _____

    _____

4. Do you prefer working alone or in a group?

    _____

    _____

5. Do you enjoy being outdoors? Why or why not?

_____

_____

The Thesis without Points Listed

The thesis without points listed presents the central idea of the essay without listing the points of development. A thesis that does not list points requires you to plan carefully to keep yourself and your reader on track. Without the road map that listing your points provides, it is even more important that your essay flow logically and smoothly. Thus, topic sentences require careful planning so that they are clearly connected to the thesis. When you plan a thesis without points listed, it is a good idea to plan each topic sentence, too, to ensure that you stay on track. Remember, not listing points does not mean that you do not plan them; it simply means you do not list them in the thesis.

Examples of Thesis Statements without Points Listed

✔ Working in a chicken processing plant was a sickening experience.
✔ When I look back ten years from now, I will see that my choice to attend college was the best decision I ever made.

Advantages of a Thesis without Points Listed

1. A thesis without points listed allows you to state your main idea simply and concisely.
2. A thesis without points listed works well when the points are long and cumbersome or difficult to write in parallel structure.
3. A thesis without points listed eliminates the worry that your topic sentences will echo the wording of your thesis too closely.
4. The thesis without points listed is considered a more advanced technique and is more often the choice of professional essayists.

Examples of Development of Thesis Statements without Points Listed

Following are examples of thesis statements that do not list points, along with possible topic sentences for each body paragraph.

Example 1

✔ *Thesis:* At the college level, the proper punishment for those caught cheating is expulsion.

Topic sentences:

> *Body paragraph 1:* Expulsion is a severe penalty that will make potential cheaters think twice before being dishonest.

> *Body paragraph 2:* Expelling cheaters will reassure responsible students that honesty really is the best policy.

> *Body paragraph 3:* Most important, a college's refusal to tolerate cheating ensures that a college degree will retain its value.

Example 2

✔ *Thesis:* Year-round attendance at public schools is a good idea.

Topic sentences:

> *Body paragraph 1:* For working parents, a longer school year would ease summer child-care problems.

> *Body paragraph 2:* Year-round school attendance would prevent "brain drain" during summer vacation.

> *Body paragraph 3:* A longer school year would lead to higher student achievement.

EXERCISE 5	WRITING A THESIS STATEMENT WITHOUT POINTS LISTED

Write a thesis that does not list points on three of the following topics.

1. Do you prefer to write on a computer or with pen and paper?

   _____

   _____

2. Some are promoting the day after Thanksgiving, traditionally a big day for retailers, as "Buy Nothing Day," a day of awareness about holiday over-spending. Would you participate in "Buy Nothing Day"?

   _____

   _____

3. If you could have an all-expenses-paid trip to anywhere for two weeks, where would you go? Why?

   _____

   _____

4. If you were building a house and had enough in your budget for just one porch, would you choose to build a front porch or a back porch? Why?

    _____

    _____

5. Is it better to grow up in a small family or in a large family? Why?

    _____

    _____

Evaluating Your Thesis Points

After you construct your thesis, the next step is to evaluate your thesis points. Specifically, your thesis points should not overlap, should not be too broad, and should not be too narrow.

Avoiding Overlap

When two or more of your points overlap, you risk making the same point more than once. Evaluating the thesis for overlap means making sure that your points of development are distinct, separate points that do not cover the same territory. The following examples show thesis statements with overlapping points.

Example of Thesis with Overlap

           thesis   point 1

✗ <u>Taking out a car loan has helped me</u> <u>to be responsible in making</u>

          point 2   point 3

<u>payments, to handle money wisely,</u> and <u>to obtain reliable transportation.</u>

Analysis:

Points 1 and 2 overlap because making payments is a part of handling money wisely. The writer needs to evaluate the support she plans to use for each point and modify the thesis accordingly.

Revision

✔ Taking out a car loan has helped me to handle my finances responsibly, to establish a good credit rating, and to obtain reliable transportation.

Analysis:

The writer has eliminated the overlap by combining the overlapping points and adding a new point: establishing a credit rating.

EXERCISE 6	ELIMINATING OVERLAP

Each of the following thesis statements contains one point that overlaps with another point. Cross out that point, and write in one that does not overlap with any other point.

1. Although I enjoy my job, I sometimes tire of the long hours, the stress, and pressure.

    _____

2. Our college's snack bar is a place to meet friends, a place to study, and a place to gather.

    _____

3. Trustworthiness, honesty, and a sense of humor are qualities I look for in a friend.

    _____

4. I broke off my engagement because I needed to finish college before marrying, I wanted my freedom, and I was not ready for a long-term commitment.

    _____

5. People on public assistance should work for the money they receive. Such work would prepare them for the job market, give them confidence in their abilities, and give them experience that would help them obtain future employment.

    _____

Avoiding Ideas That Are Too Broad

Ideas that are too broad are too large to develop in a single paragraph. Often, they are also vague because the writer has not taken the time to consider exactly what the paragraph will be about.

Example of a Thesis Point That Is Too Broad

                                    Thesis
✗ A degree in elementary education will give me a chance to work at a

         point 1   point 2   point 3
    challenging career, to support my family well, and to make the world a
    better place.

Analysis:

The third point, "to make the world a better place," is too broad. Narrowing the idea to cover only the writer's community and relating the idea to the writer's field of study makes the point narrower, more realistic, and easier to support.

Revision

✔ A degree in elementary education will give me a chance to work at a challenging career, to support my family well, and to influence the future through my students.

EXERCISE 7 **ELIMINATING POINTS THAT ARE TOO BROAD**

Each of the following thesis statements contains one point that is too broad. Cross out that point, and write in a point that can be developed within one paragraph.

1. Spending a year or two on a job before going to college can provide a student with the opportunity to earn money for a college education, to see what the real world is like, and to learn responsible work habits.

   _____

2. I like Ms. Brennan, my supervisor, because of her fairness, her sense of humor, and her good qualities.

   _____

3. For me, the ideal job provides on-site child care, up-to-date equipment, and great working conditions.

   _____

4. Losing weight, controlling my temper, and improving myself are some New Year's resolutions I am trying to keep this year.

   _____

5. I dislike driving at night because of my poor night vision, fear of something happening to me, and the possibility of a breakdown.

   _____

Avoiding Ideas That Are Too Narrow

Ideas that are too narrow may not produce a paragraph's worth of support. Often, these ideas are better used as supporting details. When an idea is too narrow, see if it is related to a larger idea that could be used as a topic sentence. If the idea cannot be broadened, discard it and look for another.

Example of a Thesis Point That Is Too Narrow

Thesis

✗ My grandmother, the owner of Sally's Bakery, has all the characteris-

point 1   point 2
tics of a good businesswoman. She works hard, says "hello" to cus-

point 3
tomers, and provides quality service.

Analysis:

The second point, "says 'hello' to customers," is too narrow to be developed as a paragraph. However, saying "hello" is part of a larger issue: treating customers with courtesy.

Revision

✔ My grandmother, the owner of Sally's Bakery, has all the characteristics of a good businesswoman. She works hard, treats customers courteously, and provides quality service.

EXERCISE 8 ELIMINATING POINTS THAT ARE TOO NARROW

Each of the following thesis statements contains one point that is too narrow. Cross out that point, and write in a point that is large enough to develop within a paragraph.

1. Growing up with three sisters has taught me to stand up for myself, to share my hair dryer, and to cherish my family ties.

    _____

2. I enjoy my job at First National Bank because the working conditions are pleasant, I make $12.80 per hour, and my coworkers are helpful.

    _____

3. The latest safety devices, a medium blue color, and reliability are the features I look for in a car.

_____

4. My dog is playful, protective, and named Butch.

_____

5. We enjoyed the lake because of its eighty-degree water temperature, its long, sandy beach, and its abundant plant and animal life.

_____

Organizing Your Essay

mywritinglab

Visit MyWriting Lab for additional practice with essay organization.

As you construct your thesis statement, think about the order of the supporting paragraphs within your essay. Four possible ways of organizing your essay are emphatic order, reverse emphatic order, sandwich order, and chronological order. Above all, choose a method of organization that is logical to you and to your readers.

Emphatic Order

One logical way to present your ideas is in **emphatic order**, or **order of importance**. Leading up to a strong idea with emphatic order gives your essay a "snowball effect": The essay becomes more convincing as it goes along.

You may also wish to experiment with **reverse emphatic order**, beginning with your most important idea and leading to the less important ideas. This type of organization suggests that your strongest idea carries such weight that it demands to be heard first. Your lesser points shore up that idea and lend your thesis further support.

Whether you choose emphatic order or reverse emphatic order, your technique will be sound. The first and last body paragraphs are always strong points of emphasis because readers are more likely to remember points that come first or last.

Example of Emphatic Order

✔ *Thesis*: Internet radio is preferable to traditional broadcast radio.

Topic sentence 1: Internet radio has a broader range of content than can be found on a typical FM band.

Topic sentence 2: For those willing to pay, Internet radio is also available without commercials.

Topic sentence 3: Most important, Internet radio stations can be customized according to the user's taste.

Example of Reverse Emphatic Order

✔ *Thesis:* When I bought a new car recently, I looked for cars with the features that were most important to me.

Topic sentence 1: When I began my search for a new car, the most important factor was cost.

Topic sentence 2: After finding cars in my price range, I looked at crash test data to find the cars that were the safest.

Topic sentence 3: Finally, I checked *Consumer Reports* to see which cars were the most reliable.

EXERCISE 9 | **USING EMPHATIC ORDER**

Develop a thesis statement and topic sentences on two of the following four topics. Use emphatic order for one of your chosen topics and reverse emphatic order for the other.

1. Why are people afraid of aging?

2. What do you hope to accomplish within the next five years?

3. What skills—academic or nonacademic—should everyone have?

4. People usually regard anger as destructive and unproductive. Is anger ever useful?

Your Answers

Emphatic Order

Thesis _____

_____

Topic sentence 1 (least important idea) _____

_____

Topic sentence 2 (second most important idea) _____

_____

Topic sentence 3 (most important idea) _____

_____

Reverse Emphatic Order

Thesis _____

_____

Topic sentence 1 (most important idea) _____

Topic sentence 2 (second most important idea) _____

_____

Topic sentence 3 (least important idea) _____

_____

Sandwich Order

The points you develop within an essay are not always equally strong. When one of your points is weaker than the others, try **sandwich order**, placing your weaker point between the two stronger ones. This method employs the same psychology that is at work when you use emphatic order. If ideas are presented in a sequence, people remember the first and last ideas more strongly than those presented in the middle. Thus, the first and last body paragraphs become the "showcase positions" in the essay, the positions where you place the material that you want your readers to remember.

Example of Sandwich Order

✔ *Thesis*: Children benefit from attending day-care centers.

Topic sentence 1: At day-care centers, children benefit from interaction with peers.

Topic sentence 2: Children who attend day-care centers learn rules of behavior and basic skills.

Topic sentence 3: Perhaps most important, day care helps a child become self-reliant.

Analysis:

Point 2 is the weakest point because skills and knowledge children will need in school could also be acquired at home. Point 1 is strong because exposure to many other children is more likely to occur at a day-care center than at home. Point 3 is strong because at a day-care center, without parents to cling to, children are more likely to become independent.

EXERCISE 10   USING SANDWICH ORDER

Develop a thesis and topic sentences for two of the following topics. Determine which point is the weakest, and sandwich it in the middle of your thesis. Be prepared to explain the logic you used to your instructor and classmates.

1. What can parents do to prepare their children for school?

2. What do people reveal about themselves by the way they speak?

3. Is there any college course you would refuse to take? Why?

4. If you controlled pay scales, for which job would you pay the highest salary? Why?

Your Answers

Thesis _____

_____

Topic sentence 1 (strong point) _____

_____

Topic sentence 2 (weak point) _____

_____

Topic sentence 3 (strong point) _____

_____

Chronological Order

Chronological order, also called *time order* or *order of occurrence,* is most often used in narratives and storytelling. But chronological order is also useful in essays. In writing about the hassles of being a first-year student, you would probably discuss problems with registration before discussing the first day of class because registration occurred first. If you were discussing your lifelong love of music, you would probably begin with your childhood piano lessons and end with your participation in your college's community chorus. Chronological order fulfills your reader's expectation to have events described in the order in which they occurred.

Example of Chronological Order

✔ *Thesis:* My first day of classes was difficult.

Topic sentence 1: Finding a parking space on the first day of class was more difficult than I expected.

Topic sentence 2: Finding my way around an unfamiliar campus was frustrating.

Topic sentence 3: After dashing into class late, I was embarrassed to realize that I was in the wrong room.

EXERCISE 11   **USING CHRONOLOGICAL ORDER**

Using chronological order, develop a thesis and three topic sentences for two of the following topics.

1. What should a job candidate do to make a good impression in an interview?

2. Which three people have had the greatest influence on your life?

3. Discuss how you became involved in a hobby that you enjoy.

4. If you had an entire day to spend any way you wanted, what would you do?

Your Answers

Thesis _____

_____

Topic sentence 1 _____

_____

Topic sentence 2 _____

_____

Topic sentence 3 _____

_____

PROGRESSIVE WRITING ASSIGNMENT

Progressive Writing Assignment: Thesis and Outline

If your instructor has assigned the Progressive Writing Assignment, you have already completed your prewriting for one of the following topics. In this chapter, you will complete your thesis and outline. Recall that each assignment takes you a step further in writing an essay, and by the end of Chapter 7, you will have a complete essay.

Topics and Tips for Writing a Thesis and an Outline

The Topics

Topic 1: Discuss three obstacles to your education.

Topic 2: Discuss your short-term goals, long-term goals, or both.

Topic 3: Discuss the values you have learned by observing the members of your family.

Topic 4: Discuss your methods of coping with stress.

Tips for Writing a Thesis and an Outline

- Develop a thesis and an outline from your prewriting, but don't be afraid to add new material if you have new ideas.
- Decide on the points you will cover in your essay and the order in which you will present them. Then write a tentative thesis.
- If you have listed your thesis points, check to make sure that they are parallel and do not overlap.
- Finally, make an outline by writing a topic sentence for each body paragraph and, if you wish, briefly jotting down a couple of the major points you will discuss in the essay.

mywritinglab   For support and practice meeting this chapter's goal, log in to www.mywritinglab.com and select **Thesis Statement**.

CHAPTER 4

Introducing the Essay

✎ **Chapter Goal:** Write effective and engaging introductions.

Temptation

You have just opened a chocolate shop on a busy street. You have only one small display window to catch your customers' attention. What do you do with that bare window, which right now holds only a dead fly? Do you throw in a few boxes of chocolate, unopened, along with a big red SALE sign? Of course not. You clean the window, dispose of the fly, and put down a luxurious velvet cloth. You cover silver trays with lace doilies and artfully arrange the chocolates. You make the display so irresistible that those passing by are drawn into your shop.

Temptation. It works on readers, too. No one *has* to buy your chocolates or read your essay. Your job is to make them want to do those things. An artfully placed image, an exciting story, or a carefully chosen quotation can be irresistible, pulling a reader into your essay. However, an introduction is more than just a way to draw a reader in. It does several jobs that no other part of the essay could do quite so effectively.

Focus on Introducing the Essay: A Look at the Hook

Famous First Lines from Novels

"As Gregor Samsa awoke one morning from uneasy dreams, he found himself transformed in his bed into a gigantic insect."

—Franz Kafka, *The Metamorphosis* (1915)

Once upon a time, there was a woman who discovered she had turned into the wrong person.

—Anne Tyler, *Back When We Were Grownups* (2001)

"Mr. and Mrs. Dursley, of number four, Privet Drive, were proud to say that they were perfectly normal, thank you very much."

—J. K. Rowling, *Harry Potter and the Sorcerer's Stone* (1998)

As any novelist knows, the first line of any book is crucial. Joseph Heller's "It was love at first sight" in Catch-22 *or Herman Melville's "Call me Ishmael" in* Moby-Dick *are among some of the most famous. They demonstrate how first lines can hook a reader into reading the next sentence, and the next, and the next.*

An introduction to an essay does the same thing. A strong and compelling introduction will capture your readers' attention and prepare them for the essay to come.

Reflect on It

If you are doing this exercise in class, look through the Readings section of this book to find an essay with a first line that interests you. If you are at home, choose a book from your bookshelf or an article from a magazine. Then fill in the information below.

Essay, book, or article you chose: _____

First line: _____

Did the first line hook you? _____

Purposes of an Introduction

mywritinglab

Visit MyWriting Lab for additional practice with essay introductions.

1. An introduction draws your reader into the essay.

The first sentence of your introduction should be as irresistible as a box of French chocolates. True, it won't always turn out that way. Aim high anyway. A reader who is drawn in by the first sentence is more likely to read the second and the third.

2. An introduction advances the general topic of your essay.

Have you ever noticed how people approach a topic of conversation? They don't just walk up and say, "The colonization of space may become an increasingly important goal as the world's population increases," or "May I borrow twenty dollars?" Instead, they ease into the conversation, giving their listeners time to make a mental shift to the topic before bringing up the main point.

Your reader needs to make a similar mental shift. When you ease into the thesis by bringing up your general topic first, your reader has time to turn her thoughts away from whatever is on her mind—the price of gas or what to eat for lunch—and to get in the mood to listen to what you have to say.

3. An introduction provides the necessary background.

Background information is not always necessary. But if it is, the introduction is a good place for it. Background information tucked into the introduction gives the necessary details without intruding on the rest of the essay. In an essay about your job, for instance, the introduction should include where you work and what you do. Then you won't have to include the information as an afterthought. In an essay about a short story or a novel, your introduction should include the title of the work and the author's name. If you are writing about an event in your life, use the introduction to establish background details such as your age at the time, where it happened, and who else was involved.

4. An introduction presents your essay's thesis.

The most important job of an introductory paragraph is to present your essay's thesis. Every sentence in the introduction should follow a path of logic that leads directly to your thesis, which will be the last sentence of your introduction. Once you have stated the thesis, stop. Your body paragraphs will flow naturally from a thesis that comes at the end of the introduction.

Types of Introduction

Introductions that draw a reader in don't just happen; they are carefully crafted. Following are several types of introduction. Try them all, using the examples as models.

Broad to Narrow

The **broad-to-narrow introduction** is a classic style of introduction. Sometimes called the *inverted triangle introduction*, it funnels your reader from a broad statement of your topic to the narrowest point in the introduction: your thesis.

Example of Broad-to-Narrow Introduction

Cell phones are almost everyone's number one accessory. They are handy for emergencies or just to keep in touch with family and friends, so people take them everywhere. They tag along to the grocery store, to a shopping center, and even to places where they are not welcome, such as movie theaters and classrooms. They are not welcome everywhere they go, but there is one place where cell phones never belong. Used behind the wheel of a car, cell phones cause driver inattention, close calls in traffic, and even loss of life.

EXERCISE 1 **A BROAD-TO-NARROW INTRODUCTION**

Arrange the following numbered sentences into a broad-to-narrow introduction, ending with the thesis.

1. Among the skillet meals, frozen dishes, boxed dinners, and canned cuisine, one convenience food stands out.
2. Manufacturers have developed a variety of convenience foods for people who do not have the time or the desire to prepare food from scratch.
3. Microwaveable frozen meals offer superior variety, nutrition, and ease of preparation.
4. Most people enjoy eating, but not everyone enjoys cooking.

The sentences should be arranged in the following order: _____,

_____, _____, _____.

Narrow to Broad

The **narrow-to-broad introduction** is just the opposite of the broad-to-narrow introduction. Instead of beginning with a statement of your general topic, the narrow-to-broad introduction begins at a point that is smaller than your thesis and expands toward that thesis. With this method, you can create an unusual and intriguing opening.

Example of Narrow-to-Broad Introduction

Thousands of feet above the earth, a small crystal traces a zigzag path to the bleak landscape below. It is the first snowflake of the season, soon to be followed by many more that will blanket the earth in a layer of white. Winter is my favorite of all the seasons. I love its beauty, I enjoy the opportunity to ski, and, like a kid, I can never wait for Christmas to arrive.

EXERCISE 2 **A NARROW-TO-BROAD INTRODUCTION**

Arrange the following numbered sentences so that they form a narrow-to-broad introduction, ending with the thesis.

1. Seeing my father dying without dignity only reinforces my belief that physicians should be allowed to assist the suicides of terminally ill patients.

2. His eyes show no sign of recognition as I enter the room and say, "Hello, Dad."

3. As I stand in the doorway, I see my father, his hand curled like a fallen leaf and tied to the bed's metal safety bar with a Velcro wrist cuff.

4. When he became terminally ill, my father begged for enough pills to kill himself, but Dr. Abercrombie refused to prescribe them.

The sentences should be arranged in the following order: _____, _____, _____, _____.

Quotation

A **quotation** adds sparkle to your introduction and spares you the work of crafting just the right words for your opening—someone else has already done it for you. You do not necessarily have to quote a book, a play, or a famous person. You may quote your best friend, your mother, or your great-aunt Sally. You may quote a commercial, a bumper sticker, or a popular song. You may quote an expert on your subject to lend authority to your words. For a ready-made source of quotations, consult the reference section of your college library for collections of quotations, such as *Bartlett's Familiar Quotations.*

When opening with a quotation, you need to know how to use quotation marks and how to paraphrase a quotation. (See Chapter 30 for more information on quotations.) It is also important to give credit to the author or, if you do not know who originally said it, to acknowledge that the quotation is not your own. In addition, a quotation cannot just hang in space, unconnected to your essay. You need a transition that shows your reader the connection between the quotation and your thesis.

Examples of Quotation Openings

Quotation Opening—Known Author:

Mark Twain wrote, "Few things are harder to put up with than the annoyance of a good example." He must have had a
transition to thesis
brother just like mine. All my life I have tried to live up to the example of a brother who is more athletic, more studious, and more at ease socially than I am.

Quotation Opening—Unknown Author:

acknowledgment of outside source
A habit has been defined as "a shackle for the free." This
transition to thesis
statement seems particularly relevant to the habit of smoking. A person who smokes is no longer free but is chained to a habit that is expensive, socially unacceptable, and dangerous.

Paraphrased Quotation—Author and Exact Words Unknown:

acknowledgment of outside source   paraphrased quotation
I once heard someone say that we get old too soon and
transition to thesis
smart too late. That statement is certainly true in my case. I have just begun to understand that my parents were right when they told me I should go to college. At seventeen, I disregarded their advice. Now, at thirty-two, I realize that I need a college education to make a comfortable living, to reach my career goals, and to set the right example for my children.

EXERCISE 3   **OPENING WITH A QUOTATION**

Choosing from the list of quotations below, follow the directions for each numbered part of the exercise.

Quotations

The only way to have a friend is to be one.
—Ralph Waldo Emerson, *Essays, First Series: Friendship*

The real problem is not whether machines think but whether men do.
—B. F. Skinner, *Contingencies of Reinforcement*

In spite of everything, I still believe that people are really good at heart.
—Anne Frank, *Anne Frank: The Diary of a Young Girl*

Everyone is a moon and has a dark side which he never shows to anybody.
—Mark Twain, *Following the Equator*, Vol. 1

Wisdom is not bought.
—African proverb

Show me someone not full of herself, and I'll show you a hungry person.
—Nikki Giovanni, *Poem for a Lady Whose Voice I Like*

Beware of all enterprises that require new clothes.
—Henry David Thoreau, *Walden*

1. Write an opening sentence using an exact quotation and the author's name.

    _____

    _____

2. Write an opening sentence using an exact quotation but pretending you do not know the author's name.

    _____

    _____

3. Write an opening sentence paraphrasing one of the quotations and again pretending you do not know the author's name.

    _____

    _____

4. Write a transitional sentence connecting the quotation to the thesis in the following introduction.

    "The brain is like a muscle," Carl Sagan said. "When we use it, we feel good." (Transitional sentence) _____

    _____

    My experiences in a college classroom have made me more self-reliant, more certain of my abilities, and less fearful of being wrong.

5. Write an introduction that opens with a quotation and leads with a transitional sentence into one of the following thesis statements (or one of your own).

a. People reveal a lot about themselves by the way they dress.

b. Every first-year student needs to know how to form new relationships during the first term at a new college.

c. The aspects of my personality that I like least are my impatience, my stubbornness, and my tendency to procrastinate.

_____

_____

_____

_____

Anecdote

An **anecdote** is a brief story that illustrates a point. *Brief* is the key word. Introductions should be short, so keep your story to a few sentences and be sure to include a transition that connects the anecdote to the thesis.

Example of an Anecdotal Introduction

When she saw her front door standing open, the woman knew there had been another break-in. She took her five-year-old daughter next door and returned with a neighbor and a borrowed baseball bat. Hesitantly, she entered. Vulgar graffiti covered the walls, and white stuffing protruded from deep slashes in the sofa. In neighbor-
transition to thesis
hoods like this one where crime is out of hand, residents often feel powerless. Community involvement such as neighborhood watches, neighborhood patrols, and insistence on police presence can help residents reclaim their streets.

EXERCISE 4 | AN ANECDOTAL INTRODUCTION

Read the following anecdotal introduction; then answer the questions that follow.

[1]Last night, my sister Karen picked at her dinner, eating only her salad and her green beans. [2]Before bed, she did fifty

stomach crunches, then stood at the mirror critically eyeing her waist, which is approximately the same size as her hips. [3]When I asked her what she was doing, she said she was too fat and had to lose weight. [4]Karen is only nine years old, but she is already in pursuit of a goal that is impossible and unhealthy. [5]The modern obsession with having a reed-thin body is encouraged by the fashion industry, the media, and even the manufacturers of food.

1. How many sentences does the anecdote contain? _____

2. Which sentence contains the transition to the thesis? _____

Contrasting Idea

Gold placed on black velvet in a jeweler's window takes on extra luster against the contrasting background. Through the drama of contrast, your ideas, too, can shine. Starting with a **contrasting idea** is an easy and effective technique to use, but there are two elements that must not be left out. The first is a change-of-direction signal. When switching from one idea to its opposite, you need a word such as *but* or *however* to signal the change. The second required element is a clear, strong contrast.

Example of a Contrast Introduction

When I hit a home run in the bottom of the ninth to win the game for the McDuffie's Auto Parts Tigers, my dad was not there. He missed many family activities because he believed his first duty was to his job. After I graduate from college, I will have a career, but it will not be my only priority. I hope to have a well-rounded life with time for career, time for family, and time for activities that interest me.

EXERCISE 5	OPENING WITH CONTRASTING IDEAS

In the blank below each introduction, write the word that serves as a change-of-direction signal.

1. One of my professors says that students who see college simply as preparation for a career are in the wrong place. College, she says, is for those who want to become well-rounded and educated. I hate to tell her, but if all this place had to offer were wisdom, there would be an abundance of empty seats in the lecture halls. Colleges should replace classes in art appreciation and French

with career skills courses, additional courses in the student's major field, and internships in various career fields.

___

2. I used to believe in accepting coworkers as they were. I did my job and minded my own business. If my coworkers goofed off, that was their business. Lately, however, I am becoming increasingly intolerant of people who arrive late, gossip, or don't carry their share of the load.

___

Historical

The term "historical introduction" has nothing to do with the Gettysburg Address or the Cuban Missile Crisis. A **historical introduction** provides the reader with background information—the "history" behind your essay. Historical introductions have two functions—to *establish expertise* or authority on a subject or to *set the stage* for your discussion.

Historical Introduction to Establish Expertise

Background material can help you establish your authority or expertise on a particular subject. If you are giving advice on car maintenance, for instance, it might help your reader to know that you've worked summers and weekends at Ace's Auto Repair for the last four years, or that your own car is nearing the 200,000-mile mark on the odometer. Readers are more likely to accept advice from those who have some experience or expertise in a particular area.

Example of a Historical Introduction to Establish Expertise

Through my parents' divorces and subsequent remarriages, I have acquired one stepfather, two stepmothers, three sets of step-grandparents, three stepsisters, two stepbrothers, and assorted step-aunts, step-uncles, and step-cousins. I speak with the voice of experience when I say that getting along with step-families requires compromise, respect of others' privacy, and willingness to share.

Historical Introduction to Set the Stage

Another reason to use a historical introduction is to give the background that sets the stage for your essay. Information the reader needs in order to understand the rest of the essay should be placed in the introduction. If you write about neighbors who donated food, clothing, and money to your family, don't wait until the last paragraph to tell about the house fire that prompted their generosity. Establish background information in the introduction.

Example of a Historical Introduction to Set the Stage

> My dad was a car enthusiast and, almost from the time I could walk, I followed him around on Saturdays, carrying things and being "helpful." He encouraged my love of cars, and when I was fourteen, he bought me an old junker to rebuild. Restoring cars and working on engines has brought enjoyment, won the respect of other car enthusiasts, and helped me to earn extra income.

EXERCISE 6	HISTORICAL INTRODUCTIONS

Look at each of the following thesis statements and decide whether the writer needs to use a historical introduction (1) to establish authority or (2) to set the stage. Write your choice in the blank beneath each question and be prepared to give reasons for your answer.

1. If you are not satisfied with a product or service, complain immediately, speak to the right person, and suggest a solution to the problem.

   _____

2. Moving away from home has made me more independent, more confident in my abilities, and more appreciative of my parents.

   _____

3. Helpful coworkers, a pleasant workplace, and an understanding boss make my job enjoyable.

   _____

4. Setting up your computer and printer is easier than you think.

   _____

5. To get a good bargain in a used car, you must do the proper research, have the car checked by a professional, and know how to negotiate with the dealer.

   _____

PROGRESSIVE WRITING ASSIGNMENT

Progressive Writing Assignment: Introducing the Essay

If your instructor has assigned the Progressive Writing Assignment, you have already completed your prewriting and have written a thesis and an outline. In this chapter, you will write your introduction. Recall that each assignment takes you a step further in writing an essay and that you are now one chapter closer to a complete essay.

Topics and Tips for Introducing the Essay

The Topics

Topic 1: Discuss three obstacles to your education.

Topic 2: Discuss your short-term goals, long-term goals, or both.

Topic 3: Discuss the values you have learned by observing members of your family.

Topic 4: Discuss your methods of coping with stress.

Tips for Introducing Your Essay

- Carefully consider which type of introduction would be most effective for your topic. Ask yourself if there is a quotation or an anecdote that might be particularly effective with your topic. See if there is a contrasting idea that you could use or a way to lead into your thesis with a broad-to-narrow introduction. Once you have thought through each method of introduction, ask yourself which one would work best with your topic and be most appealing to a reader.
- Place your thesis at the end of your introduction. Then make sure that the sentence that leads into the thesis does its job smoothly, providing a logical transition from your lead-in to your main idea.

mywritinglab   For support and practice meeting this chapter's goal, log in to **www.mywritinglab.com** and select **Essay Introductions, Conclusions, and Titles.**

CHAPTER 5

Developing Body Paragraphs

✍ **Chapter Goal:** Recognize the characteristics of effective body paragraphs (direction, unity, coherence, and support) and write paragraphs that embody these qualities.

Sparkle

A jeweler judges the quality of a diamond by "The Four C's"—color, cut, clarity, and carat weight. Evaluating by these four standards, the jeweler can determine the value of the gem.

Wouldn't it be nice if there were similar standards we could apply to writing? **Direction, unity, coherence,** and **support** are the standards that measure paragraph and essay writing. Check your essays against these standards to see if you have created a real gem—or at least a diamond in the rough.

A paragraph is the smallest multiple-sentence unit of communication in the English language. But simply lumping sentences together does not make a paragraph. A **body paragraph** is a paragraph that supports a larger idea: the thesis statement of an essay. An effective body paragraph has four characteristics: direction, unity, coherence, and support.

Focus on Developing Body Paragraphs: Considering the Details

Cartoons take an incredible amount of time to create. Joe Rhodes, columnist for Entertainment Weekly *online, says, "It takes six months to complete a half-hour episode of*

The Simpsons" because "there are 24 frames for every second, 24 minutes in every show. The mechanics of a simple eye blink can take half a page of instructions" ("The Making of The Simpsons," www.ew.com). *Imagine the detail work each of those frames must take so that the audience experiences seamless programming.*

You may not plan to create cartoons for a living, but undoubtedly your career will require attention to detail. If you design clothing, every element of the design must work together in a unified manner. If you are a trial lawyer, you will need to review every piece of evidence to present a coherent case to the jury. As in an essay, the details work together to form a unified and coherent whole.

Reflect on It

Think about the career you plan to pursue. What details will you have to weave into a coherent and unified whole?

Characteristics of an Effective Body Paragraph

mywritinglab
Visit MyWriting Lab for additional practice developing and organizing paragraphs.

1. **Direction** means that the body paragraph has a strong topic sentence that states the main idea and sets the course that the paragraph will follow.

2. **Unity** means that the paragraph makes one main point and sticks to that point.

3. **Coherence** means that the ideas in the paragraph are logically connected and easy to follow.

4. **Support** means that the paragraph contains a specific and detailed discussion of the idea stated in the topic sentence.

Direction: Shaping the Topic Sentences of Body Paragraphs

mywritinglab

Visit MyWriting Lab for additional practice with the topic sentence.

A **thesis statement** gives an essay its overall direction and sometimes provides a road map for the reader by listing points. The **topic sentences** extend that function by charting each leg of the journey as the essay moves through each body paragraph. Each topic sentence outlines one thesis point, thus providing direction for each body paragraph.

The following list outlines the functions of the topic sentences of body paragraphs.

Functions of the Topic Sentence of a Body Paragraph

1. The topic sentence of a body paragraph provides a **thesis link** by mentioning the *general subject* of the essay.

2. The topic sentence of a body paragraph mentions the *specific thesis point* that will be developed within the paragraph.

3. The topic sentence may also provide *transitions* from one paragraph to the next.

Look at the following thesis statements and their topic sentences. Notice that the topic sentences link to the thesis by mentioning the general subject of the essay. A thesis link is simple to write: All you do is mention the general subject of the essay in each topic sentence, and you have forged a relationship between the thesis and your topic sentences. The topic sentences also present each specific thesis point. Notice that if supporting points are listed in the thesis, topic sentences follow the same order.

Example 1: Thesis Statement and Topic Sentences

general subject (thesis link)   point 1
Thesis: A community college is a good choice for students with children,

point 2   point 3
students on a budget, and students with full-time jobs.

point 1
Topic sentence 1: Students who have children find that

general subject (thesis link)
a community college allows them to be students and parents, too.

general subject
(thesis link)   (transition)   point 2
Topic sentence 2: A community college also helps students fit the costs
of college into a tight budget.

point 3
Topic sentence 3: <u>Students who work during the day</u> often prefer to

general subject (thesis link)
attend night school at <u>a community college</u>.

Example 2: Thesis Statement and Topic Sentences

general subject   no points listed
Thesis: <u>Making a daily schedule</u> helps me use my time efficiently.

general subject (thesis link)   point 1
Topic sentence 1: <u>A daily schedule</u> helps me <u>set priorities</u>.

general subject (thesis link)   point 2
Topic sentence 2: <u>By using a daily schedule</u>, I can <u>avoid committing</u>

<u>myself to too many activities</u>.

(transition) general subject (thesis link)   point 3
Topic sentence 3: Finally, <u>my daily schedule</u> helps me <u>keep my day</u>

<u>organized</u>.

EXERCISE 1 | **COMPLETING TOPIC SENTENCES**

A list of incomplete topic sentences follows each of the following thesis statements. Fill in the blanks in each topic sentence. Topic sentences should follow the same order suggested in the thesis.

1. For me, an ideal vacation spot will offer me the opportunity to lie in the sun, to exercise, and to eat a variety of foods.

   a. When I am on vacation, I enjoy _____.

   b. Vacation also gives me the opportunity to _____.

   c. One of the activities I enjoy most on vacation is_____

   _____.

2. My favorite piece of furniture is my grandfather's desk. I love it for its beauty, usefulness, and sense of family history.

   a. I admire the desk for its _____.

   b. Not only is the desk attractive, it is also _____.

   c. The link to my _____, however, is the main reason the desk is important to me.

3. I am attending college so that I can become an accountant, support my children, and make my family proud.

    a. With a college education, I can _____ .

    b. A degree will also help ensure _____ .

    c. As a first-generation college student, I _____ .

4. At my favorite hangout, the Sand Crab, I enjoy the casual atmosphere, the unique blend of music, and the company of friends.

    a. The Sand Crab has a/an _____ that I enjoy.

    b. The combination of old and new _____ makes the Sand Crab unique.

    c. Best of all, _____ also enjoy gathering at the Sand Crab.

5. When parents go through a divorce, children may be plagued by guilt, divided loyalty, and insecurity.

    a. When parents divorce, children may _____ .

    b. Especially if the parents' divorce is a bitter one, children may

    _____ .

    c. Children of divorce may also experience _____ .

The Thesis Link

A **thesis link** is a word or phrase that links the topic sentence directly to the central idea of the essay. It is not always enough for the topic sentence to state a thesis point. Linking the topic sentence to the general subject of the essay or to your attitude about that subject reminds your reader that the paragraph is part of a larger whole. At the same time, a thesis link aids coherence by relating the specific point to the thesis. Notice in the following examples that each topic sentence contains a word or phrase that links the paragraph to the thesis.

Example 1: Thesis Links in Topic Sentences

                                    thesis

Thesis statement: I have achieved higher grades this term by

         point 1   point 2   point 3

improving my study habits, organizing my time, and cutting back my

work hours.

Topic sentence 1: <u>Better study habits</u> have been <u>a key to my improved</u>

<u>grades.</u>

point 1   thesis link

Topic sentence 2: <u>Planning</u> has also <u>helped me improve my grades.</u>

point 2   thesis link

Topic sentence 3: <u>The step that has most affected my GPA</u> was

thesis link

reducing <u>my work hours.</u>

point 3

Example 2: Thesis Links in Topic Sentences

Thesis: An Internet connection is essential for any college student.

thesis

Although the points are not listed in the thesis, the writer presents them in the topic sentences. The thesis link in each topic sentence will be a reference to the idea that the Internet is essential for any college student. Points 1, 2, and 3 will be the specific ways that the Internet is necessary.

Topic sentence 1: <u>College students will find the Internet essential</u>

thesis link

<u>for accessing class material, even if they are not taking an online class.</u>

point 1

Topic sentence 2: <u>For most college students, an Internet connection</u>

thesis link

<u>is a vital link to their professors.</u>

point 2

Topic sentence 3: <u>The Internet is also necessary</u> for everything from

thesis link

<u>planning a class schedule to checking grades.</u>

point 3

EXERCISE 2   **PROVIDING THESIS LINKS**

Following are five thesis statements and topic sentences that relate to them. Circle the letter of the topic sentence that does not have a thesis link, that is, the sentence that does not mention the general subject of the essay. Then rewrite the sentence, linking it to the thesis.

1. *Thesis:* The size, the location, and the design of my house make it an ideal place to live.

    a. My house is easy to enjoy because it's small enough to take care of easily.

    b. Out in the country, my nearest neighbor is five miles away.

    c. The convenient layout and the many windows in my home suit my casual lifestyle.

    _____

    _____

2. *Thesis:* Some students are a pain to have as classmates. These include students who never come prepared, those who are noisy, and those who monopolize the class discussion.

    a. Coming to class unprepared is a common occurrence.

    b. Even worse than the unprepared student is the student who distracts the class with unnecessary noise.

    c. Most tiresome of all is the student who monopolizes the class discussion.

    _____

    _____

3. *Thesis:* In recent years, the public has become increasingly unwilling to report crimes.

    a. Many people fear that reporting a crime will provoke retaliation from the criminal.

    b. Some citizens don't want to get involved.

    c. Other crimes go unreported because crime victims believe the police can do nothing to help.

    _____

    _____

Unity: Sticking to the Point of the Essay

An essay with **unity** is like a completed jigsaw puzzle. Every piece is necessary, and each does its part to contribute to the big picture. Each paragraph and each sentence fit perfectly to support the thesis. When one piece does not fit, the essay lacks unity. Lack of unity occurs within a paragraph when one or more sentences do not support the paragraph's topic sentence. Likewise, when an entire paragraph does not support the thesis of the essay, the essay lacks unity.

Read the paragraph in the example below and see if you can spot the three sentences that interfere with the unity of the paragraph.

Example: Paragraph with Poor Unity

[1]I have heard that inside every fat person, there is a thin person waiting to get out, but I believe that just the opposite is true. [2]Inside every thin person, a fat person is waiting to take control. [3]For most people, maintaining thinness requires self-control at mealtime. [4]A thin person may avoid second helpings of fried chicken and load up on salad instead. [5]But somewhere inside, an inner, fat self is craving ice cream with chocolate sauce for dessert. [6]Staying thin also requires exercise. [7]The thin person may have plans to attend a Pilates class after work, but the fat person inside would rather curl up in front of a fire with a book and a cup of hot cocoa. [8]The thin person who gets up at 5:30 A.M. to jog has to silence the fat self's unhappy voice, which is whining for just an extra half-hour's sleep. [9]Of course, thin people are better off staying thin. [10]Studies have shown that in general, people who eat less live longer. [11]In addition, people who exercise are healthier and more likely to maintain flexibility and mobility well into old age. [12]All it would take is a moment of weakness for the fat person inside to burst forth, no longer held in by the tight cocoon of thinness.

Were you able to spot the sentences that did not fit? The paragraph lacks unity because sentences 9, 10, and 11 do not support the topic sentence of the paragraph.

EXERCISE 3 **SPOTTING PROBLEMS WITH UNITY**

Read the following essay. Find and identify

   a. the body paragraph that does not support the thesis statement, and

   b. the body paragraph that contains two sentences that do not support its topic sentence.

Choosing a Veterinarian

That squirming, tail-wagging furball that you bring home from the pound or pet store needs more than just love and kibble. Good veterinary care is also essential. If you know what to look for, finding the right veterinarian for your pet can be a simple process.

[1]The first step is to evaluate the veterinarian's office. First, consider its location. It should be close enough to your home to be convenient. In an emergency, you should be able to get there in a few minutes. Next, look at the physical facility itself. Cleanliness is a must. The waiting room should be clean and pleasant, and it should be standard practice for the staff to disinfect the tables in the exam rooms before each use. Finally, make sure that the facility's services meet your needs. Some veterinary clinics provide boarding, grooming, and bathing. Some clinics require appointments, while others provide service on a first-come, first-served basis. The clinic you choose should be convenient, clean, and provide the services that you need.

[2]Once you have found a clinic you like, the next step is to evaluate the veterinarian and the staff. They should be kind to you and to your pet. Watch the way your pet is handled. Is he handled gently yet confidently, called by name, and spoken to in a kind tone? The vet's approach to your pet should make you smile. If your pet is treated roughly, find another vet. Your vet's treatment of you should pass muster, too. Good veterinarians do not simply treat animals; they also educate owners. They tell you why and how an illness can occur, signs to look for as the pet gets better, and signs that indicate you should bring the pet back. Caring for a sick pet can be difficult because a pet cannot talk to you like a human can. The pet cannot tell you where it hurts or what is wrong.

[3]Even with good veterinary facilities and a competent, caring vet, chances are that the veterinary clinic will not be your pet's favorite place to visit. Many pet owners report that their pets have an uncanny sixth sense about visits to the vet. When it's time to go to the vet, these apparently psychic pets disappear under beds, into closets, or behind refrigerators. Repeated calling does not bring them out, and they must finally be hunted down and dragged out of hiding. In the car, cats yowl and dogs whine, and some fearful pets even have "accidents" on the way, losing control of their bowel or bladder functions. At the vet's office, most become quiet and docile as the veterinarian handles them. Rarely, animals become aggressive, growling or snapping. But although the visits may be traumatic, they are necessary to a pet's good health.

Ensuring good veterinary care is easier if you know how to pick the right vet for your dog or cat. Good veterinary care is one way you can repay the love, loyalty, and companionship your pet provides.

The paragraph that is entirely off the topic is body paragraph _____.

The paragraph that contains two sentences that do not support the topic sentence is body paragraph _____.

Coherence: Holding the Essay Together

An essay with **coherence** is an essay with solid and strong connections between paragraphs and ideas. To achieve coherence, you must first make sure that the ideas you set down are logically related and well thought out. Coherence between ideas can also be aided by transitional words and expressions.

Following is a list of transitional words and expressions, organized by their function within the sentence.

Some Common Transitional Words and Expressions

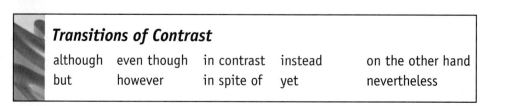

Transitions of Time

after	during	later	now	suddenly	when
as	first	meanwhile	often	temporarily	while
before	immediately	next	previously	then	yet

Transitions of Space

above	beside	down	next to	toward
around	between	in	on	under
behind	by	near	over	

Transitions of Addition

also	finally	furthermore	in addition	next
another	first			

Transitions of Importance

as important	essential	major	primary
equally important	just as important	most important	significant

Transitions of Contrast

although	even though	in contrast	instead	on the other hand
but	however	in spite of	yet	nevertheless

> ### *Transitions of Cause and Effect*
>
> | a consequence of | because | since | therefore |
> |---|---|---|---|
> | as a result | consequently | so | thus |

> ### *Transitions of Illustration or Example*
>
> | for example | for instance | including | such as |
> |---|---|---|---|

Making Transitions between Body Paragraphs

When you move from one body paragraph to the next, **transitional words** act as signposts. In the first body paragraph, often no transition is needed. If you use a transitional word or expression, a simple "first of all," or "one reason . . ." usually works well. But avoid a mechanical "first, second, third" approach. Instead, vary your transitional techniques. In the second and third body paragraphs, transitional words create a bridge between paragraphs that suggests that you have discussed a related idea in the preceding paragraph. Because you are adding an idea to the ones you have already discussed, the transitional words you use will be transitions of addition: *also, another, next, an additional (reason, factor, way)*.

Examples of Transitional Words in Topic Sentences

- ✔ Doing something for someone else is *another* way to shake a bad mood.
- ✔ Some teenagers' unwillingness to use birth control *also* contributes to the high rate of teen pregnancy.
- ✔ The *first* step in resolving a conflict is to define the issues involved.

EXERCISE 4	USING TRANSITIONAL EXPRESSIONS IN TOPIC SENTENCES

Rewrite the following topic sentences using a transitional word or phrase. The word or phrase you choose will depend on whether the sentence is a topic sentence for the first body paragraph, the second body paragraph, or the last body paragraph, but it should be a *transition of addition*.

1. Newspapers are a better source of news than television because newspaper stories go into more detail. (*Make this sentence an appropriate topic sentence for a second body paragraph.*)

_____

_____

2. It is important to find a family doctor after moving to a new town. (*Make this sentence an appropriate topic sentence for a third body paragraph.*)

    _____

    _____

3. The tailgater is a type of bad driver. (*Make this sentence an appropriate topic sentence for a first body paragraph.*)

    _____

    _____

4. Using public transportation is cheaper than owning a vehicle. (*Make this sentence an appropriate topic sentence for a third body paragraph.*)

    _____

    _____

5. Good communication skills are essential in a job interview. (*Make this sentence an appropriate topic sentence for a first body paragraph.*)

    _____

    _____

Making Transitions within Paragraphs

Within paragraphs, transitional words keep your reader oriented in time and space and aware of the relationships between ideas. Within a single paragraph, you may need several types of transitional words to move your reader smoothly from one idea to the next.

| EXERCISE 5 | USING TRANSITIONAL EXPRESSIONS WITHIN PARAGRAPHS |

In the following paragraph, provide the indicated type of transition in the blank.

       [1] _____ (time) the Fresh-Food Supermart was robbed, Shawna had the bad luck to be the only cashier on duty. The

robber came in about 7:00 A.M., [2] _____ (time) the store opened. She noticed him right away [3] _____ (cause-effect) his baseball cap was pulled low over his eyes and he wore a jacket [4] _____ (contrast) the morning was warm. He loitered for a while [5] _____ (space) the door, [6] _____ (time) he walked up to her register. She must have suspected him [7] _____ (cause-effect) she suddenly remembered Mr. Monroe, the store manager, saying: "If you are ever robbed, remember that your life is worth more than whatever is in that cash drawer. Stay cool and hand over the money." [8] _____ (time) the robber leaned [9] _____ (space) her and mumbled, "I have a gun. Put the money in a bag." Remembering Mr. Monroe's words, Shawna quickly withdrew the money from the cash register. [10] _____ (time) she reached for a bag, she was surprised at the words that automatically fell from her lips: "Paper or plastic?" Much [11] _____, (time) Mr. Monroe teased that not only had she remembered his instructions, she had [12] _____ (addition) remembered to offer her "customer" a choice.

The Transitional Topic Sentence

The **transitional topic sentence** takes a backward glance at the topic of the preceding paragraph before moving on to the topic of the paragraph it leads into. Since the first body paragraph presents the first point of discussion, transitional topic sentences are not used there. Transitional topic sentences can be used only in the second and third body paragraphs of a five-paragraph essay. They are an effective way of moving between paragraphs, but like any other technique, they should not be overdone. One per essay is probably enough. Some examples of transitional topic sentences follow.

Example 1: Transitional Topic Sentence

✔ Not only do illegal drugs pose a health risk, they can also land the user in jail.

Discussion: The writer has discussed the health risks posed by illegal drugs in the preceding paragraph and is now going to discuss the possibility that the user may spend time in jail.

Example 2: Transitional Topic Sentence

✔ A lifetime sentence to the prison of addiction is often the worst consequence of drug use.

Discussion: This variation of the first example merely hints at the topic of the preceding paragraph (the possibility of serving time in jail). The hint provides a connection between paragraphs.

Example 3: Transitional Topic Sentence

✔ Although rock music suits my happy, energetic moods, I turn to the sound of blues when I am depressed.

Discussion: This transition outlines a movement from a paragraph about rock music to a paragraph about blues.

EXERCISE 6   **WRITING TRANSITIONAL TOPIC SENTENCES**

The following outlines show a thesis and three topic sentences. For each outline, rewrite topic sentences 2 and 3 as transitional topic sentences. The first one is done for you.

1. *Thesis:* I prefer renting movies to going to a movie theater. When I rent a movie, I watch it when I want to, avoid crowds, and spend less money.

   Topic sentence 1: One advantage of renting a movie is that I can watch it whenever I want to, not when the theater schedules it.

   Topic sentence 2: I also like being able to avoid crowds at the theater.

   Rewritten transitional topic sentence 2: In addition to setting my own schedule, I like being able to avoid the crowded theater.

   Topic sentence 3: Saving money is another important advantage of renting a movie.

   Rewritten transitional topic sentence 3: _____

   _____

2. *Thesis:* Traffic jams, dangerous drivers, and high gas prices all contribute to my dislike of driving.

   Topic sentence 1: My morning commute is often a disaster because of heavy traffic.

   Topic sentence 2: Dangerous drivers also contribute to my dread of driving.

   Rewritten transitional topic sentence 2: _____

   _____

> *Topic sentence 3:* High gas prices make driving expensive,
>
> *Rewritten transitional topic sentence 3:* _____
>
> _____
>
> 3.   *Thesis:* In my spare time, I enjoy tennis, woodworking, and reading.
>
> *Topic sentence 1:* Tennis is one of my favorite spare-time activities.
>
> *Topic sentence 2:* Another of my hobbies is woodworking.
>
> *Rewritten transitional topic sentence 2:* _____
>
> _____
>
> *Topic sentence 3:* Reading is one of my favorite leisure activities.
>
> *Rewritten transitional topic sentence 3:* _____
>
> _____

Support: Using Specific Detail

Support is the heart of any piece of writing. Even a grammatically perfect essay falls flat without strong, specific support. If a thesis or topic sentence is a promise to the reader to discuss a specific topic, then an essay without solid support makes that thesis an empty promise. No matter how good it sounds, there is nothing behind it.

Although few writers deliberately set out to make empty promises, many do so because providing strong support is one of the most difficult dimensions of writing body paragraphs. It takes practice, thought, and the ability to recognize and to construct specific examples and details.

Why It's Hard to Be Specific

Quick, what did you eat for lunch yesterday?

If you are like most people, you answered with a broad term—*fast food, a sandwich, a microwaveable dinner*—rather than with a specific description, such as *a tuna-salad sandwich on rye toast*.

Being specific does not come naturally because the human brain is programmed to think in categories. This ability to lump things together by function saves time. It also gives the brain an orderly way to store the information it receives every day. Without the ability to categorize, a football and a baseball would seem to have as little in common as a dandelion and a Phillips screwdriver. Bits of information would be scattered throughout your brain like confetti, impossible to retrieve.

But the ability to categorize can work against you when you write. Most people would complete the sentence "Harold drove to work in his _____" with the word *car* or *truck*. Few would fill in *beat-up Ford Escort that had seen its best days fifteen years ago* or *ten-year-old Volvo without a single scratch or dent*. Such specific examples do not come to mind easily because the human brain, programmed to categorize, looks first at the big picture.

To write rich, detail-packed paragraphs, train yourself to move beyond general categories and to look for the details. This skill is similar to the one that police officers develop when they learn to observe sharply and to remember details. Police officers, however, receive special training on developing observational skills. Writers are on their own. The exercises in this section are designed to help you move beyond general categories. When you can do that, you will be able to provide examples and details and become a writer who delivers on your promises.

Essay Development Technique 1: Supporting with Specific Examples

Examples are one of the best ways to get a point across because they provide a concrete illustration of the point. If you say your father is sentimental, your reader will get the general idea. If you say he gets teary-eyed over Hallmark commercials, you are giving specific support to the general idea. Examples, then, are specific illustrations, exact instances. Using an example is like making a word or phrase more specific, but on a larger scale, since examples can range in length from a single word to multiple paragraphs. With an example, you are usually giving your reader both the general idea and a specific example of that idea.

An Example in a Word or Phrase

Examples expressed in a word or phrase are usually used when the author wants to illustrate an idea briefly and then move on. Look at the underlined short examples in the following paragraph.

Example of Short Examples in a Paragraph

The Internet gives average people access to an incredible array of free resources that would have been unimaginable a generation or two ago. Thirty years ago, people relied on their physicians for health advice. Today, the family physician's advice is often augmented by that of health-related websites such as WebMD or Mayo Clinic, resources that would have seemed miraculous a generation ago. Fifty years ago, news was served up at regular intervals through print editions of newspapers and scheduled radio or television news broadcasts. Today, news is available on the Internet twenty-four hours a day from news sites such as *CNN*, *MSNBC*, or *Fox*, with updates provided instantly as the news happens. The Internet has also changed our perspective on finances. In the past, people seeking financial advice might go to their banker or to a trusted relative. Today, sites such as *The Simple Dollar* or *Kiplinger* provide comprehensive and detailed advice on saving or spending. Finding health information, news, and financial advice is much easier in the age of the Internet.

EXERCISE 7   **PROVIDING EXAMPLES**

Provide an example of each of the following ideas in a word or a phrase.

1. game

   _____

2. book

   _____

3. luxuries

   _____

4. food

   _____

5. injury

   _____

The Sentence-Length Example

Sometimes, you need more than just a word or phrase to illustrate an idea. In such cases, try giving an example in a sentence or two. The example needs to be a specific, detailed illustration of the general idea you are discussing, not just a vague restatement.

Example 1: Examples in a Sentence or Two

✗ *Idea + vague restatement:* The new disc jockey on the morning show is really obnoxious. He has an unpleasant attitude that makes listening to his show a bad experience.

✔ *Idea + specific example:* The new disc jockey on the morning show is really obnoxious. He tries to humiliate listeners who call in, and his jokes border on the offensive.

Example 2: Examples in a Sentence or Two

X   *Idea + vague restatement:* The new grocery store has added whimsical touches to some of its departments. It's enjoyable to shop in a store that is entertaining.

✔   *Idea + specific example:* The new grocery store has added whimsical touches to some of its departments. In the produce department, thunder rolls and "lightning" flashes above the vegetable bins before the automatic vegetable sprinkler turns on. On the dairy aisle, recordings of mooing cows and clucking hens amuse passing shoppers.

EXERCISE 8	WEEDING OUT VAGUE EXAMPLES

Circle the letter of the sentence that is a general restatement of the idea, *not* a specific example.

1. We needed a break, so we decided to stop and have something to drink.

   a. I ordered coffee, and Marcie had iced tea.

   b. We chose from the restaurant's wide selection of refreshing beverages.

   c. I went to the kitchen and fixed hot herbal tea with honey and lemon.

2. A conflict broke out.

   a. Fists and plates flew as restaurant patrons scuffled over the last yeast roll at the buffet.

   b. Apparently, some sort of disagreement caused an altercation to take place.

   c. John accused Myra of taking his parking place, and the two began to argue.

3. My friends are all trying to be thriftier.

   a. Emily tries to save wherever she can. She knows the value of a dollar.

   b. Tom has decided to bring his lunch instead of eating out every day.

   c. Khara clips coupons and checks grocery store specials before shopping.

4. Charlotte worked hard sprucing up her yard this weekend.

   a. Wearing heavy gloves, she pulled weeds from the flowerbed in front of the house.

   b. She toiled laboriously on the lawn.

   c. Soaked with sweat, she pushed the mower through tall grass for more than an hour.

5. Researchers have found that many of our grandmothers' home remedies really work.

   a. Chicken soup, the all-time favorite home remedy, eases congestion and aids breathing.

   b. Warm milk really does induce sleep.

   c. It seems that Grandma may have known what she was talking about after all.

EXERCISE 9   **PROVIDING SPECIFIC SUPPORT**

For each of the following general ideas, provide a sentence or two of specific support.

1. The kitchen was a mess.

   _____

   _____

2. The police found plenty of evidence that the accident had been Darren's fault.

   _____

   _____

3. The two brands of orange juice are quite different in taste and appearance.

   _____

   _____

4. The package was damaged when it arrived in the mail.

   _____

   _____

5. Litter is becoming a problem on Sanford Road.

   _____

   _____

The Extended Example

Sometimes you may wish to develop an entire paragraph with an extended, paragraph-length example. In this case, your topic sentence will state the general idea, and the rest of the paragraph will provide a detailed example. In this sort of paragraph, it is important to end with a summary sentence that connects the specific example back to the general idea, as in the following paragraph.

Example of Topic Sentence and Paragraph-Length Example

topic sentence
Sometimes, factors totally unrelated to study can interfere

with performance on a test. Test anxiety is an excellent illustra-

tion. It often strikes students who have prepared adequately and

who set high standards for themselves. Test anxiety goes beyond

the mild jitters that plague almost every student the night before a

test. It holds its victims in a paralyzing grip. Typically, the student

extended
example   with test anxiety looks at the first question on the test, and all the

carefully studied material seems to evaporate in a haze of panic.

The student knows the material before entering the examination

room and may recall both questions and answers after the test

has ended, but in the pressure cooker of the test environment,
summary sentence
the answers do not come. As the example of test anxiety shows,

poor test performance is not always an indication that no

studying took place.

EXERCISE 10 **WRITING EXTENDED EXAMPLES**

Write an extended example to support one of the three following topic sentences. Don't forget to write a summary sentence connecting the example back to the idea in the topic sentence.

Topic sentence 1: Instead of hoping that a problem will go away, the best way to deal with it is to confront it head-on.

Topic sentence 2: Sometimes an opportunity comes along at exactly the right time.

Topic sentence 3: Telephone salespersons can be an annoyance.

_____

_____

_____

_____

_____

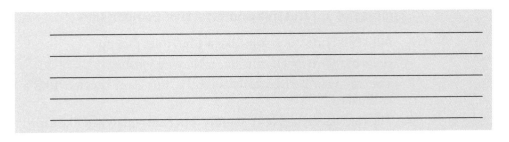

Essay Development Technique 2: Adding Detail through Comparisons

One way to express ideas is by comparing the familiar with the unfamiliar. If your doctor tells you that a centrifuge separates the liquid parts of your blood sample from the solid by centrifugal force, you may not understand. If she says that a centrifuge separates plasma from solid blood components just as a washer on the spin cycle separates water from clothes, then you will understand the concept more readily.

Like an example, a comparison may be brief or extended. Although entire essays are developed using comparison, you may use comparison techniques in any essay to make your writing more specific.

Comparisons Using *Like* or *As*

When you make brief comparisons, you may find the words *like* and *as* useful. A comparison using *like* or *as* is called a *simile*.

Examples of Similes

- ✔ Nina moved across the dance floor like a skater on ice.
- ✔ The car was crumpled like a used tissue.
- ✔ Nina moved across the dance floor as gracefully as a skater on ice.
- ✔ The car was as crumpled as a used tissue.

When you make a comparison, it is usually more useful to compare unlike things than like things. If you say, for instance, "When Billy opened the presents at his eighth birthday party, he looked like a kid at Christmas," the comparison is not very useful. After all, Billy *is* a child and he *is* opening presents, just as he might at Christmas. However, look at what happens if you compare two unlike things: "When Smitty dealt the hand, Jack picked his cards up one by one and arranged them carefully, looking like a kid at Christmas." The comparison reveals two things about Jack that a reader would not know from the rest of the sentence: He has been dealt a good hand, and he is probably not a very good poker player—his face reveals too much.

Examples of Ineffective and Effective Comparisons

✗   Bill's old Ford truck runs like a Chevrolet pickup.

✔   Bill's old Ford truck runs like a Maytag washer.

✗   The car was dented only slightly, but Sam reacted like a typical car enthusiast.

✔   The car was dented only slightly, but Sam squawked like a bird whose baby had fallen from the nest.

EXERCISE 11   MAKING COMPARISONS

Use your own comparisons to complete each sentence.

1.   Throughout the ceremony, the groom looked bored, like a _____

_____.

2.   The small, gray-haired grandmother marched into the mayor's office like

_____.

3.   When the tired-looking server brought my sandwich, it was as tasteless as

_____.

4.   Marcia's old car was as reliable as _____.

5.   Emerging from the dark theater, Brian felt disoriented, like _____

_____.

6.   After Elton's wife left him, he drifted from job to job and from town to town,

like _____.

7.   I hoped the class would have a relaxed atmosphere, but it was as formal as

_____.

8.   Just before final exams, students burst into a frenzy of activity, like _____

_____.

9.   "When I came into this business, I had visions of limos, champagne, and

adoring fans," said the actor. "Instead, I'm working as hard as _____

_____."

10. Looking at the test in front of him, the student sat like _____

_____.

PROGRESSIVE WRITING ASSIGNMENT

Progressive Writing Assignment: Writing Body Paragraphs

If your instructor has assigned the Progressive Writing Assignment, you have already completed your prewriting, your thesis and outline, and your introduction. In this chapter, you will complete your body paragraphs. Recall that each assignment takes you a step further in writing an essay, and by the end of Chapter 7, you will have a complete essay.

Topics and Tips for Writing Body Paragraphs

The Topics

> Topic 1: Discuss three obstacles to your education.
>
> Topic 2: Discuss your short-term goals, long-term goals, or both.
>
> Topic 3: Discuss the values you have learned by observing members of your family.
>
> Topic 4: Discuss your methods of coping with stress.

Tips for Writing Body Paragraphs

THE TOPIC SENTENCE: TIPS FOR DIRECTION

- Make sure that each topic sentence mentions the subject of the paragraph and that each topic sentence links back clearly to the thesis with key words. For example, if you chose Topic 1, "Discuss three obstacles to your education," the key words *education* and *obstacles* (or a synonym such as *barriers)* should appear in each topic sentence. A typical topic sentence might read "One of the obstacles to my education is my financial situation."

TRANSITIONS: TIPS FOR COHERENCE

- Use a transitional word such as *also* or *another* in the topic sentences of body paragraphs 2 and 3. (*Another* of my long-term goals is to start my own business.)
- Make one of the topic sentences a transitional topic sentence. (*After I start my accounting business,* my next long-term goal is to start a family.)
- Check each paragraph to make sure it flows logically and has transitional expressions where needed.

STAYING ON TRACK: TIPS FOR UNITY

- Check each paragraph to make sure that every sentence supports the topic sentence.

EXAMPLES AND DETAILS: TIPS FOR SUPPORT

- Make sure that your language is specific. Have you used words that create pictures by appealing to the reader's sense of sight, hearing, touch, taste, and smell?

- Check to see that you have supported your paragraphs with specific examples. If you are writing on Topic 4, "Discuss your methods of coping with stress," you might use a *specific example* that describes what happened on a particular occasion (Last Tuesday, when I was nervous and worried about a job interview the next day . . .). However, you might also decide to use a *typical example* that describes something that customarily occurs (Every evening when I come home from work, I put on my exercise clothing . . .).

mywritinglab   For support and practice meeting this chapter's goal, log in to www.mywritinglab.com and select Developing and Organizing a Paragraph and The Topic Sentence.

CHAPTER 6

Concluding the Essay

✎ **Chapter Goal:** Write effective conclusions.

True horror
COMING SOON
to an essay near you

Endings are difficult. Courses end with the pressure of exams. Weekends end with Monday mornings. And for many writers, the ending of an essay is the hardest part to write. However, the etiquette of concluding an essay, like that of ending a telephone conversation, is simple: Keep the goodbye short and don't introduce any new information that keeps the other person hanging on too long.

After the specific and detailed support of the body paragraphs, the first sentence or two of the conclusion should take your reader once again to a broad, thesis-level view of the topic. This broader statement may take the form of a summary, a recommendation, or a prediction.

Then comes the closing statement, harder to write but vital because it is the last impression your reader takes away from the essay. The key requirement of a closing statement is that it should *sound* like a closing statement. It should sound as final as the slam of a door.

Focus on Concluding the Essay: Thinking about Endings

Think of the endings to The Shawshank Redemption *and* The Silence of the Lambs. *In* The Shawshank Redemption, *Red (Morgan Freeman) finally gets to the beach in Mexico and to his friend Andy (Tim Robbins), who has successfully—and brilliantly— escaped from prison. The ending of this movie wraps everything up neatly, and the audience gets the sense that the characters will live the rest of their days in relative happiness. Now think of* The Silence of the Lambs. *The vicious and cannibalistic Hannibal Lecter (Anthony Hopkins) has escaped, and he calls FBI agent Clarice Starling (Jodie Foster) to let her know that she will be safe from him. As he hangs up, he casually says, "I'm having an old friend for dinner." The audience knows that when Hannibal Lecter has a friend for dinner, the friend is likely to be on the menu. Nothing is resolved, and Hannibal Lecter roams free to kill again.*

Though these movies have different kinds of endings, each ending works. Audiences are satisfied to see Red and Andy together again and titillated to think of Hannibal Lecter "having a friend for dinner," perhaps with a side of fava beans. The same is true with conclusions in essays; the ending should fit with the content in order to satisfy your audience's expectations.

Reflect on It

Whenever you end something, be it a project or a paper, you want to do it with style. But how do you know when you have the right ending? Try this: Think of a movie you have seen recently, and imagine a totally different ending to it. How does the ending work? Does it feel right, or was the original ending better? Why does a single change make such a big difference? This exercise may illustrate that sometimes you have to "try on" different endings before you get it right. Don't be afraid to experiment!

✐ Methods of Conclusion

To bring your essay to a solid, satisfying close, try one of the following methods of conclusion.

Summary

mywritinglab

Visit MyWriting Lab for additional practice with essay conclusions.

A **summary conclusion** is the simplest and easiest type of conclusion to write. In the first sentence or two, recap the main points of your essay, making sure to use different wording than you used in your thesis and topic sentences. Your final sentence brings the essay to a close.

In the following example, the writer recaps the major points, then ends with a strong, final-sounding statement.

Example of a Summary Conclusion

During my tour of duty with the Air Force, I received hands-on experience in electronics, furthered my education, and developed confidence in my ability to handle my own life. I never piloted a plane while I was in the Air Force, but in many ways, I learned to soar.

EXERCISE 1 **ANALYZING A SUMMARY CONCLUSION**

1. From the above summary conclusion, try to determine the major points of the essay it concludes. In what order were they most likely presented?

   _____

   _____

   _____

   _____

2. Consider the following possible versions of the ending sentence. Which do you think is the strongest? Which is the weakest? Why?

   a. I never piloted a plane while I was in the Air Force, but in many ways, I learned to soar. (original version)

   b. I learned to soar in many ways, although I never piloted a plane while I was in the Air Force.

   c. I never piloted a plane, and while I was in the Air Force, I learned to soar
in many ways.

_____

_____

_____

Recommendation

A **recommendation conclusion** suggests a solution to a problem raised in the
essay. A logical way to end an essay that discusses a problem is to offer a solution or suggest that one is on the horizon.

Example of a Recommendation Conclusion

It does not matter whether the shot is fired in the commission of a
robbery, in the heat of an argument, or by accident. The result is the
same: A life is lost. The logical solution is the one already implemented
by more enlightened countries—to outlaw handguns. Outlawing handguns is a major step toward a safer, saner, less fearful society.

EXERCISE 2 | **WRITING A RECOMMENDATION CONCLUSION**

Imagine that you have written an essay discussing the causes of one of the following social problems. Write a brief conclusion (two to four sentences) making
general recommendations about working toward a solution.

   teenage suicide
   violence in the schools
   poverty among older adults

_____

_____

_____

_____

_____

_____

_____

Prediction

A **prediction conclusion**—a look toward the future—is another good way of ending an essay. In the following example, the writer has discussed society's growing dependence on providers of personal service. The ending is a simple yet effective prediction.

Example of a Prediction Conclusion

A society of graying baby boomers, working parents, and two-income families is becoming increasingly dependent on service providers. In the twenty-first century, hiring help with housecleaning, lawn maintenance, and child care will no longer be a luxury for many Americans, but a necessity.

EXERCISE 3 | **WRITING A PREDICTION CONCLUSION**

You have written an essay suggesting that the solution to reducing the unwanted pet population is to require that every cat and dog be spayed or neutered within five years. Financial help is available for those who cannot afford the procedure, and exemptions are available for pets too old or ill to withstand the operation. Those who wish to breed their animals may purchase a special breeding license at a cost of $500 per animal.

Write a conclusion of two to four sentences predicting the changes that will occur over the next five years as your plan goes into effect.

_____

_____

_____

_____

_____

_____

_____

Full Circle

A **full circle conclusion** incorporates a word or an image from the introduction as a theme in the conclusion, thus bringing the essay full circle to end where it began. This type of conclusion is surprisingly powerful and satisfying.

Example of an Introduction and Full Circle Conclusion

Following is an introduction paired with a conclusion that comes full circle, ending with an image from the introduction.

Introduction

> The photograph in the magazine showed a laboratory rat with a human ear growing out of its back. The strange-looking creature was part of an experiment in the regrowth of human cartilage through genetic engineering. I immediately thought of my neighbor Otis Needham, who lost an ear to cancer. Genetic engineering is a relatively new field, but it promises quantum leaps in organ and tissue replacement, cure of disease, and prevention of birth defects.

Conclusion

> In a laboratory somewhere, a little white rat, burdened with an ear he cannot use, heralds a brighter future for the Otis Needhams of the world. Thanks in part to this little rat and others like him, human beings will live longer and healthier lives through the promise of genetic engineering.

EXERCISE 4   **COMPLETING A FULL CIRCLE CONCLUSION**

Step 1: Read the following introduction.

> I stood in the bookstore line, staring glumly at a green book entitled *Understanding Psychology*. I could not believe my bad luck. Not only was Psychology 1101 the only social science elective left, but I had to take it with Nortenson, the toughest psychology professor on campus. Before the quarter was over, however, I was thankful for the luck that led me to Dr. Nortenson's psychology class.

Step 2: Complete the conclusion by writing a first sentence that brings in the image of the book. Notice that the second sentence, beginning "Every time I look at it . . ." makes a transition that suggests that the book is someplace where you see it often. Perhaps the sentence you write could say where it is.

Conclusion

_____

_____. Every time I look at it, I think

of what I might have missed if I had been able to get the courses I really wanted last fall. Thanks to my bad luck, I discovered an inspiring teacher, a fascinating field of study, and my future career.

Quotation

A **quotation conclusion** can help you bring your point home solidly and effectively. For the strongest effect, make the quotation your closing statement.

Example of a Quotation Conclusion

I had always planned to go to college "someday." But it took a loaded gun to make me realize how much of my life I had squandered behind the counter of the Kwik-Stop #7. The day after the robbery, I gave my notice and filled out a college application. At the time, I had never heard of Cervantes, but his words express a truth I realized that day: "By the streets of someday, one arrives at the house of never."

| EXERCISE 5 | ENDING WITH A QUOTATION |

Write a conclusion that ends in a quotation. Use a topic and quotation of your own choosing, or choose from the list that follows.

_____

_____

_____

_____

_____

_____

_____

_____

_____

_____

_____

_____

_____

_____

Quotations

When poverty comes in at the door, love flies out the window.
>   —Seventeenth-century saying

Our life is frittered away by detail. . . . Simplify, simplify.
>   —Henry David Thoreau, *Walden*

Lost time is never found again.
>   —Ben Franklin, *Poor Richard's Almanac*

It is not the man who has too little, but the man who craves more, who is poor.
>   —Lucius Annaeus Seneca, *Epistles*

Turn your face to the sun, and the shadows fall behind you.
>   —Maori proverb

Life sucks—and then you die.
>   —Bumper sticker, circa 1990

A place for everything, and everything in its place.
>   —Isabella Mary Beeton, *The Book of Household Management*

Have a place for everything and keep the thing somewhere else. This is not advice, it is merely custom.
>   —Mark Twain, *Notebooks*

The cat in gloves catches no mice.
>   —Ben Franklin, *Poor Richard's Almanac*

I have often regretted my speech, but never my silence.
>   —Publius Syrus, *Maxims*

Topics

- In what situations is it most important to be assertive?
- An optimist has been defined as a person who sees the glass as half full, while a pessimist sees it as half empty. Is it wiser to be an optimist or a pessimist?
- Do you consider yourself an organized person?
- What is your biggest regret?
- How important are wealth and material things to you?

Traps to Avoid

Sermonizing

One trap that some otherwise good writers fall into is lecturing a reader who should be assumed to be on their side of the issue. After a thoughtful, well-reasoned essay on why people turn to drugs, for instance, a writer might be tempted to end the essay with a statement such as "Stay away from drugs—you'll be glad you did." Such a statement insults the reader, who should always be counted among the "good guys."

The only type of essay that should end with direct advice to the reader is one in which direct advice is given throughout, such as an essay entitled "How to Shop for a Used Car."

Starched Prose

Writers who speak in a natural voice throughout an essay sometimes stiffen up at the conclusion. They write starched prose such as "As I have proven in this essay by discussing the above-mentioned points. . . ." These writers may simply be feeling the awkwardness of saying goodbye, or they may feel that an announcement of the conclusion is needed. It isn't. Even "in conclusion" is probably too much. Readers know when a writer is concluding because the writer stops developing specific points and begins to look once again at the big picture.

Armed with a set of specific concluding techniques, you can avoid the traps that snare some writers as they go about the difficult task of ending an essay.

PROGRESSIVE WRITING ASSIGNMENT

Progressive Writing Assignment: Concluding the Essay

If your instructor has assigned the Progressive Writing Assignment, you have already completed your prewriting, a thesis and outline, an introduction, and three body paragraphs. In this chapter, you will write your conclusion. Recall that each assignment takes you a step further in writing an essay and that you are now only a chapter away from a complete essay.

Topics and Tips for Concluding the Essay
The Topics

Topic 1: Discuss three obstacles to your education.

Topic 2: Discuss your short-term goals, long-term goals, or both.

Topic 3: Discuss the values you have learned by observing members of your family.

Topic 4: Discuss your methods of coping with stress.

Tips for Concluding Your Essay

- For any of the topics in this assignment, a summary of the main points would be an appropriate concluding strategy, but consider other alternatives, too.
- If you used an anecdote or a particularly striking image in your introduction, consider using a full-circle conclusion.
- Topics 1 and 2 might lend themselves to a prediction conclusion—a vote of confidence that you will overcome the obstacles to your education or will reach your goals.
- Check to make sure that you have not introduced any new material in your conclusion.

mywritinglab   For support and practice meeting this chapter's goal, log in to www.mywritinglab.com and select Essay Introductions, Conclusions, and Titles.

CHAPTER 7

Revising, Proofreading, and Formatting

Chapter Goal: Develop an understanding of the importance of revision and analyze, revise, proofread, and format an essay.

A doggone good revision

Revising, proofreading, and formatting provide a final opportunity to shape your essay into the exact form you want it to take. These three final steps in the writing process can help you close the gap between what your essay is and what you want it to be. Revising helps you capture your ideas more vividly and accurately, while proofreading helps you express them grammatically and with proper punctuation. Finally, formatting gives your essay the visual polish that your readers expect to see.

Focus on Revising, Proofreading, and Formatting: Revision in Real Life

On first seeing the Declaration of Independence *in draft form, some people wonder why the Founding Fathers would put something so important into the hands of a person who made so many mistakes. People see the messiness of the emerging* Declaration *and don't stop to think that Thomas Jefferson, like any other writer, went through multiple drafts.*

The truth is that all writers revise—even Thomas Jefferson. No—make that espe-cially *Thomas Jefferson. After all, when you're doing something as important as building a country, you are not going to rely on the first thing that pops out of your head. The more important the document, the more important it is to think through it and revise it multiple times.*

Reflect on It

Think about something that you do that requires revision, checking and double-checking, or attention to format. For example, you might "revise" an outfit before going out for an important interview. You might "proofread" your appearance in a mirror before you step into the interviewer's office. As you shake the interviewer's hand, it might boost your confidence to notice that your formatting is just right: She is wearing a gray suit, too. What else in your life requires revision, proofreading, or formatting?

Revising

mywritinglab

Visit MyWriting Lab for additional practice with revising the essay.

In your mind, an idea may seem perfect. Yet when you try to get it on paper, it tumbles onto the page like a load of rough gravel. Revising can help you do justice to your ideas and to restore the sparkle that made you want to express them in the first place.

Beyond matters of style, there are practical reasons for revision, reasons that have their roots in the difference between writing and conversation. Conversation is constantly under revision. When your listener says, "What do you mean?" and you explain, you are revising. In conversation, revision is a response to the listener. But in writing, response and revision must take place before your essay meets its reader. Therefore, you must try to see your work through the eyes of a reader.

The word *revise* combines the Latin root meaning *to see* with the prefix meaning *again*. In its most literal sense, to revise means *to see again*, and seeing again is exactly what you need to do as you revise.

To see your work again, you need to create a mental distance between yourself and the work. You can best achieve this mental distance with time. Lay the writing aside for at least twenty-four hours. When you return to it, words that are not precise, sentences that are not clear, and explanations that do not explain enough will be easier to spot.

It may also help to have someone else look at your work. Ask your reader to focus on content and to question any point that does not seem clear. Because the written word carries no facial expression, no gesture, and no tone of voice, it is more open to misinterpretation than face-to-face communication. Discussing your work with a reader can help to close the gap between your intention and your reader's understanding.

In addition to letting your work "cool" for a day or so and enlisting the help of a reader, you can also check your essay point by point to make sure that it fulfills the purpose you had in mind. The revision checklist on the following page will help you go through your essay section by section to make sure each part is doing the job you intend it to do.

Writers on Revising

Books aren't written—they're rewritten.

> —Michael Crichton, author of *Jurassic Park* and winner of an Emmy for screenwriting.

If a teacher told me to revise, I thought that meant my writing was a broken-down car that needed to go to the repair shop. I felt insulted. I didn't realize the teacher was saying, "Make it shine. It's worth it."

> —Naomi Shihab Nye, winner of four Pushcart Prizes for her poetry.

The main thing I try to do is write as clearly as I can. I rewrite a good deal to make it clear.

> —E.B. White, author of *The Elements of Style* and *Charlotte's Web*, winner of an honorary Pulitzer Prize for his entire body of work.

Checklist for Revision

The Introduction

✔ Does the introduction draw the reader in?
✔ Does the introduction provide background information, if needed?

The Thesis

✔ Is the thesis the last sentence of the introduction?
✔ If the thesis does not include points of development, does it state the main idea broadly enough to include all the points you raise in your body paragraphs?
✔ If the thesis lists points of development, does it list three separate and distinct points that do not overlap?

Topic Sentences

✔ Does each topic sentence raise one separate and distinct thesis point?
✔ Is each topic sentence clearly linked to the thesis with a reference to the general subject or to your attitude about the subject?
✔ If your thesis lists points of development, are body paragraphs arranged in the same order as the thesis points?

The Body

✔ Does each body paragraph provide specific detail and examples for each thesis point?
✔ Have you provided enough specific support for each thesis point?
✔ Does each sentence of each body paragraph support the topic sentence?

The Conclusion

✔ Is the first sentence of the conclusion a broad, thesis-level statement?
✔ Is the conclusion short, with no new information introduced?
✔ Is the last sentence satisfying and final-sounding?

Checking Coherence

✔ In the introduction, is there a clear transition between the introductory material and the thesis?
✔ Have you used transitional words or transitional topic sentences to link the second and third body paragraphs to the rest of the essay?
✔ Have you used transitions within the paragraph effectively?

EXERCISE 1	ANALYZING TWO VERSIONS OF AN ESSAY

Read the two versions of each paragraph in the essay "My War on Insects." As you read through each portion of the essay, use the preceding Checklist for Revision as your guide and decide which version of each paragraph is the revision and which is the rough draft.

My War on Insects

Introduction A

    I once read that if a nuclear war wipes out all humanity, insects are the only species that would survive. I believe it. My war on various kinds of insects has shown me that they usually win. Over the years, my battle with insects has caused me to feel disgust, pain, and awe.

Introduction B

    I once read that if a nuclear war wipes out all humanity, insects are the only species that would survive. Over the years, my battle with insects has caused me to feel disgust and pain.

1. The introduction that is a rough draft that needs to be corrected is
   a. introduction A
   b. introduction B

2. In the introduction that you chose as the rough draft, which of the following is missing?
   a. an attention-getting statement and a thesis point
   b. a transition to the thesis and a thesis point
   c. an attention-getting statement and a thesis

First Body Paragraph A

    I fought a battle with the most disgusting insect of all, the cockroach, when I lived in my first apartment. The apartment was the renovated attic of a seventy-five-year–old house. For seventy-five years the house had stood, and for seventy-five years the cockroaches had made it their own. In spite of the landlord's monthly visits with an industrial-sized canister of bug spray, the cockroaches held on tenaciously. My neighbors complained, too, saying that their apartments were overrun with cockroaches. Mrs. Higgins, who lived in the apartment downstairs, said she called the landlord at least twice a month to complain. When I finally moved out of that apartment, I imagined the cockroaches listening from the walls, waiting to reclaim their territory.

First Body Paragraph B

¹I fought a battle with the most disgusting insect of all, the cockroach, when I lived in my first apartment. ²The apartment was the renovated attic of a seventy-five-year–old house. ³For seventy-five years the house had stood, and for seventy-five years the cockroaches had made it their own. ⁴In spite of the landlord's monthly visits with an industrial-sized canister of bug spray, the cockroaches held on tenaciously. ⁵I was embarrassed to invite friends up to the apartment after an evening out. ⁶The first flip of the light switch might reveal the brown insects slithering across the walls of the kitchen into temporary hiding. ⁷The kitchen was so badly infested that I kept all my food in the refrigerator, even bread, and I washed plates and utensils before I used them. ⁸When I finally moved out of that apartment, I imagined the cockroaches listening from the walls, waiting to reclaim their territory.

3. The version of body paragraph 1 that is a rough draft that needs to be corrected is
   a. first body paragraph A
   b. first body paragraph B

4. In the version of the first body paragraph that you chose as a rough draft, which two sentences do not support the paragraph's topic sentence?
   a. sentences 3 and 4
   b. sentences 4 and 5
   c. sentences 5 and 6

Second Body Paragraph A

My next insect battleground had no cockroaches; instead, I fought a painful battle with vicious, stinging wasps. My husband and I moved into an upstairs apartment with a curved iron staircase leading to a postage-stamp yard below. I had visions of planting tomatoes in that small yard. Eagerly, I ran down the steps to examine it. Halfway down the stairs, I was attacked by a horde of stinging wasps. Their painful stings raised red, itchy welts that lasted for weeks. I was reluctant to try those stairs again though my husband had emptied a can of wasp spray on the nests underneath the stairs. I never did plant that tomato garden. Once again, the insects won the battle.

Second Body Paragraph B

My next insect battleground had no cockroaches; instead, I fought a painful battle with vicious, stinging wasps. My husband

and I moved into an upstairs apartment. Under the back stairs, the wasps had found a quiet home. Unfortunately, I disturbed their peace, and the resulting encounter was quite a painful one for me. In spite of my husband's efforts to rid the back stairs of the stinging pests, I never felt comfortable going down those stairs again. Once again, the insects won the battle.

5. The version of body paragraph 2 that is a rough draft that needs to be corrected is

    a. second body paragraph A

    b. second body paragraph B

6. Which problem is corrected in the revised version of body paragraph 2?

    a. Sentences that are off topic are removed.

    b. A lack of specific detail is corrected.

    c. A missing topic sentence is added.

Third Body Paragraph A

The most recent insect conflict has been a war with ants, creatures I can only regard with awe. The sandy soil that our house sits on is honeycombed with ant tunnels, and as long as the ants stay outside, I am willing to coexist peacefully. In recent months, however, they have ventured inside the house in search of food. I am amazed at the way a few scouter ants can become a battalion, marching in a purposeful column toward the food, then retreating with bits of food held like triumphant flags above them. Because I dislike pesticides, I tried using organic remedies such as vinegar and hot sauce around doors and cracks in the wall to repel the ants. But one evening, when I found a twenty-pound bag of cat food transformed into a writhing mass of ants, I decided that the time for more potent weapons had arrived. A pest control agency recommended ant baits, so I purchased a few and laid them out for the ants to find. For now, the ants are gone. I won't say I have won the battle, though, because I have learned that ants are amazingly persistent.

Third Body Paragraph B

Ants are creatures I can only regard with awe. The sandy soil that our house sits on is honeycombed with ant tunnels, and as long as the ants stay outside, I am willing to coexist peacefully. In recent months, however, they have ventured inside the house in search of food. I am amazed at the way a few scouter ants can become a battalion, marching in a purposeful column toward the food, then retreating with bits of food held like triumphant flags above them. Because I dislike pesticides, I at first tried using organic remedies such as vinegar and hot sauce around doors and cracks in the wall to repel the ants. But one evening, when I found a twenty-pound bag of cat food transformed into a writhing mass of ants, I decided that the time for more potent weapons had arrived. A pest control agency recommended ant baits, so I purchased a few and laid them out for the ants to find. For now, the ants are gone. I won't say I have won the battle, though, because I have learned that ants are amazingly persistent.

7. The version of the third body paragraph that is a rough draft that needs to be corrected is
    a. third body paragraph A
    b. third body paragraph B

8. Which problem is corrected in the revised version of body paragraph 3?
    a. A link to the thesis is added in the topic sentence.
    b. Sentences that don't support the topic sentence are removed.
    c. An example that does not fit is removed.

Conclusion A

It seems that anywhere I have lived, I have had to fight insects. I haven't even mentioned the troubles I've had with aphids on my tomatoes and fleas on my cats. It makes me wonder if I should trade in my can of Black Flag for a white flag and simply surrender.

Conclusion B

It seems that anywhere I have lived, I have had to fight insects. I can't help noticing that in most of my battles with them, I am the loser. It makes me wonder if I should trade in my can of Black Flag for a white flag and simply surrender.

9. The version of the conclusion that is a rough draft that needs to be corrected is
    a. conclusion A
    b. conclusion B

10. A problem in the version of the conclusion that you selected as the rough draft is that
    a. it does not start with a broad, thesis-level statement.
    b. it introduces new information.
    c. it is too short.

Proofreading

mywritinglab

Visit MyWriting Lab for additional practice proofreading.

Think about the last time you noticed a misspelling. The minute you saw it, your thoughts moved away from the content of the writer's message and focused on the error. Similarly, errors in your writing take a reader's focus away from your ideas and draw attention to grammar, spelling, or punctuation. Naturally, you want your ideas to stand in the foreground while grammar, spelling, and punctuation remain in the background. Proofreading, then, is an essential last step. Although proofreading is usually a chore, it is a necessary chore.

After you have completed the last revision of your essay, you should proofread it at least twice, once from the top down and once from the bottom up. If you have special problem areas, such as comma splices or subject–verb agreement, you should do at least one extra proofreading focused on your problem areas.

The Top-Down Technique

The first proofreading should go from the top of the essay down. As you proofread from the top down, check to make sure that the connections between your ideas are smooth and solid and that the sentences and paragraphs flow smoothly into one another. Check for parallel structure, clear pronoun reference, and appropriate transitional expressions. After correcting any problems you find in the top-down proofreading, move to the second type of proofreading, the bottom-up proofreading.

The Bottom-Up Technique

The bottom-up proofreading technique is more labor intensive and more focused than top-down proofreading. When you read from the bottom up, you are no longer reading your essay as a single piece of writing but as disconnected sentences that do not flow into one another. Because your focus is on a single sentence, you can look at it closely, as if it is a sentence in a grammar exercise. Read it carefully, correct any errors you find, and then move to the preceding sentence.

The Targeting Technique

If you have a "favorite error"—one that you seem to make more often than any other—try doing an additional proofreading to target that error. Following are some common errors and shortcuts to finding those errors.

mywritinglab

Visit MyWriting Lab for additional practice with targeting subject-verb agreement, comma splices, run-ons, other comma errors, pronoun agreement, and sentence fragments.

As you become more experienced, you will devise your own strategies to target problem areas.

Subject-verb agreement. Check each subject-verb sequence. Look for present-tense verb forms and make sure that they agree with their subjects. Remember that in the present tense, if the subject ends in -*s*, the verb usually does not. If the verb ends in -*s*, the subject usually does not. Exceptions occur when a singular subject ends in -*s* (for example, *boss speaks*) or when a plural subject does not (*children play*).

Comma splices and run-ons. Target long sentences; they are more likely to be run-ons. Target commas, too. If there is a complete sentence on both sides of the comma, you have found a probable comma splice.

Other comma errors. Target each comma and question its reason for being. If you aren't sure why you used it, maybe it doesn't belong. (Check the comma rules in Chapter 24 for further help.)

Pronoun agreement. Look for the plural pronouns *they* and *their*. Make sure that they have a plural, not a singular, antecedent.

Sentence fragments. Using the bottom-up technique, read each sentence to see if it can stand on its own. If you suspect a fragment, check for a subject and a verb. If it lacks either one, it is a fragment.

Proofreading the Computer-Generated Essay

Spelling and grammar checkers can be helpful in proofreading, but they are no substitute for knowledge and judgment. A spelling or grammar checker can find possible errors and suggest possible solutions. However, it is up to you to decide what, if anything, is wrong and how to fix it.

Even when you use spelling and grammar checkers, you should do at least two separate proofreadings. The following sentence, in which all words are spelled correctly, may illustrate the need:

Weather or knot ewe use a spelling checker, you knead too proof read.

Whether to proofread on the screen or to print out a hard copy to proofread is a personal choice. Some writers find it easier to scroll up and down on the computer screen, viewing the essay in small segments. Others swear that they cannot see their errors until they hold the printed copy in their hands. Find out what works best for you.

Group Exercise 1 Proofreading an Essay
Confident? Go solo!

Each of the forty sentences in the following essay contains an error. Form a small proofreading team with two or three of your classmates. Pooling your knowledge, see how many errors you can identify and correct. The first twenty errors are underlined. Record your corrections in the spaces provided or on a separate sheet of paper.

An Urban Legend

[1]Around a carefully tended fire that kept the predators at bay until morning, our cave-dwelling ancestors told <u>tale</u> of the hunt. [2]In the <u>american</u> West, the power of a good yarn drew cowboys around the fire, a circle against the darkness. [3]Today, the folk tale <u>lived</u> on in what is often called the "urban legend." [4]Urban legends are those stories that many <u>has</u> heard but none can verify. [5]<u>Stories of alligators in sewers and narrow escapes in lovers' lanes</u>. [6]One modern folk tale, "Gunshot Wound," exemplifies the urban legend in <u>it's</u> themes of danger, individual power, and reprieve.

[7]Like many urban <u>legend</u>, "Gunshot Wound" plays on modern fears. [8]The story opens in a supermarket parking lot as a female shopper pulls in and notices a woman apparently <u>past</u> out in a car. [9]<u>Afread</u> of the dangers that lurk even in supermarket parking lots, the woman walks on into the store. [10]When she <u>come</u> out, she notices the woman in the car, clutching the back of her head with both hands. [11]The woman's face is etched with <u>terror the</u> shopper offers help. [12]"I've been shot<u>",</u> the woman says, "and I can't open the car door. [13]The back of my skull has been <u>blowed</u> off, and I'm afraid to take my hands away." [14]In horror, the shopper notices the blood on the <u>womans</u> hair and the doughy mass protruding through her tightly clasped fingers. [15]By presenting horror in <u>a</u> ordinary setting, the opening section of this tale brings the listener face to face with the modern nightmare of random violence.

[16]The next part of the tale deals with the power of the individual by showing what <u>1</u> person can do. [17]But in this present-day folk tale, the finger in the dike <u>have</u> been replaced by the finger on the button. [18]The shopper's call to 911 brings <u>ambulances fire</u> trucks, and police cars screaming into the parking lot. [19]"<u>Dont</u> worry, Ma'am," says a police officer. [20]"The Med-Evac chopper <u>is</u> here any minute." [21]In this phase of the tale, a individual's ability

to cope with disaster has been reinforced. [22]It do not matter that, in the tradition of Aladdin, the woman has called on more powerful forces to aid her. [23]Its enough that they come when summoned.

[24]The final phase of the tale deal with rescue and reprieve. [25]a rescue team breaks into the injured woman's car. [26]And carefully removes her. [27]A paramedic bends over her she clutches the spongy, bloody mass at the back of her head. [28]As a chopper appears in the distance, the Paramedic, looking puzzled, pulls what appears to be a metal disk from her head. [29]A spongy mass cling to the disk. [30]Ma'am, he says, are your groceries in the back seat? [31]"Yes", says the woman. [32]The paramedic begin to laugh. [33]"Ma'am, it looks like a biscuit can explodes in your grocery bag. [34]It must of sounded like a gunshot. [35]The metal disk from the can nicked your scalp bad, and biscuit dough and blood covered the back of your head. [36]A superficial wound." [37]To make a long story short and not to beat around the bush, the ending of this urban folk tale provokes relieved laughter. [38]Then a dawning realization that if innocent people were not shot every day, the tale would not be so compelling.

[39]Despite their modern flavor, urban folk tales like "Gunshot Wound" still warn, reassure, and are entertaining. [40]In a way, they transport us too that ancestral fire where we huddle together in temporary safety, a circle against the darkness.

Corrections

1. _____	11. _____
2. _____	12. _____
3. _____	13. _____
4. _____	14. _____
5. _____	15. _____
6. _____	16. _____
7. _____	17. _____
8. _____	18. _____
9. _____	19. _____
10. _____	20. _____

21. _____   33. _____

22. _____   34. _____

23. _____   35. _____

24. _____   36. _____

25. _____   37. _____

26. _____   _____

27. _____   _____

28. _____   _____

29. _____   _____

30. _____   38. _____

_____   39. _____

31. _____   40. _____

32. _____   _____

✐ Formatting

You have heard it all your life: First impressions count. The document you hand to your instructor, the résumé you hand to a prospective employer, or the letter you send to the editor of a newspaper has the ability to present a positive first impression or a negative one. When an instructor sees a computer-generated or neatly handwritten paper, with no smudges, cross-outs or dog-eared edges, the instructor expects that paper to be a good one, written as carefully as it was prepared. In contrast, a hastily scrawled document smudged with eraser marks or heavily laden with correction fluid suggests that the writer did not take the time and the effort to create a good impression—or to write a good paper.

Manuscript format is so important that entire books have been written about it. An instructor who asks you to use MLA style, APA style, or Chicago style is referring to styles outlined in books published by the Modern Language Association, the American Psychological Association, and the University of Chicago, respectively.

If you are given instructions for formatting a document, follow those instructions carefully. If you have no specific instructions, use the guidelines in the following section. They will help you format a document effectively, whether that document is written in class or out of class, by hand or on a computer.

Handwritten Documents

Paragraphs and Essays

For handwritten paragraphs and essays, use lined white 8½ × 11-inch white paper and blue or black ink. Write on one side of the paper only, and leave wide margins.

In the upper left-hand corner of the page, put your name and the date. If you wish, include your instructor's name and the name of the class for which you are preparing the assignment. Center your title, if any, on the first line of the paper, but do not underline the title or put it in quotation marks. Indent each paragraph about three-quarters of an inch. In a handwritten document, do not skip lines unless your instructor specifically requests it. If you make an error, draw a single line through the error, and rewrite your correction above the crossed-out error. Put a single paper clip, not a staple, in the upper left corner to join the pages, unless your professor instructs otherwise.

Essay Tests

When you take an essay test, you may be required to use a "blue book" or to write on the test itself. If you are allowed to use your own paper, use lined paper and write on one side only.

Answers to questions on essay tests should be written in blue or black ink. Because time is too limited for a rough draft, take a moment to organize your thoughts, and then answer the question. Indent each paragraph three-quarters of an inch to one inch. Just as in any paragraph or essay, state your main idea first.

If you misspell a word or make a mistake, cross through it with a single line. Be sure to write clearly and legibly, and if your handwriting is difficult to read, try printing instead.

Computer-Generated Documents

Setting Up Your Document

Choose a font and a font size that are easily readable, such as Times New Roman in a 12-point size. Do not use a bold or italic font.

Margins should be one inch all around. One-inch margins are the default on most word processing programs, so you probably will not have to set the margins at all. Set the software to "double-space." Leave the right edge ragged rather than justifying it. (To justify means to line up in a straight edge, like a newspaper column. Most word processing programs have settings that allow you to justify, but these settings are not commonly used for academic work.)

Formatting the Document

Put your name and the date in the upper right corner of the page. Other information, such as the name of your instructor or the class for which you are preparing the assignment, is optional. Center the title and indent each paragraph as shown in the sample that follows. A title page is not necessary unless your instructor asks for one.

Derek Smith

1 April 2011

Format Reform

  I am ashamed to say that I used to be a format abuser. I used strange fonts such as Adolescence and Space Toaster. I tried to make my papers look longer by using 2-inch margins and a 14-point font. At my lowest point, I turned in a report printed in 15-point Star Trek font on lime-green paper. A caring instructor saw that I had a problem and helped me turn my formatting around. Now, I know how to format a document perfectly.

Printing and Presenting Your Document

When the document has been revised and proofread, print it out on good-quality 8½ × 11-inch white paper. To hold the pages together, place a single paper clip in the upper left corner. Do not staple your document or put it in a report cover unless your professor instructs otherwise.

PROGRESSIVE WRITING ASSIGNMENT

Progressive Writing Assignment: Revising, Proofreading, and Formatting

If your instructor has assigned the Progressive Writing Assignment, you are almost finished. All that remains is to revise the essay, proofread it carefully, and put it in the proper format.

Topics and Tips for Revising, Proofreading, and Formatting

The Topics

>   Topic 1: Discuss three obstacles to your education.
>
>   Topic 2: Discuss your short-term goals, long-term goals, or both.
>
>   Topic 3: Discuss the values you have learned by observing members of your family.
>
>   Topic 4: Discuss your methods of coping with stress.

Tips for Revising, Proofreading, and Formatting

- Ask someone else to look at your essay and to tell you if any point is not clear or if any idea needs further explanation.
- Evaluate your essay using the Checklist for Revision in this chapter.
- Use spelling and grammar checkers, but don't forget to proofread the document at least three times yourself.
- Check the formatting of your essay against your instructor's instructions or against the guidelines in this chapter. Improper formatting can be distracting to a reader, while proper formatting allows your essay to shine.

mywritinglab   For support and practice meeting this chapter's goal, log in to www.mywritinglab.com and select **Revising the Essay** and **Editing the Essay**.

CHAPTER 8

Showing and Telling: Description, Narration, and Example

Chapter Goal: Analyze and write descriptive, narrative, and example essays.

"I was this *far away when the mailman threw his bag at me and started running. All I could see were legs and letters . . ."*

The essays you write and the stories you tell come alive when you use description, narration, and example. Descriptive techniques help you show your reader what you see, hear, smell, touch, or taste. Narrative techniques help you concisely tell the reader a story that makes a point. Examples supply specific illustrations and instances in many types of writing. Description, narration, and example provide the foundations for many other types of essay writing.

Focus on Showing and Telling: The Power of the Narrative

A narrative is a story, and stories are powerful. They stick with us. Do you know the story behind the McDonald's franchise? Behind Coca-Cola? Behind your favorite sports team? Behind your favorite clothing brand? Chances are that such a story will be easy to find.

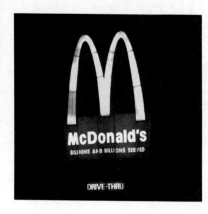

Companies want to share their stories with us, and often, they want us to share our stories with them. The websites of hospitals often feature patients' stories. The advertisements of some companies feature true customer stories. Can you think of any or find any on the Internet? Do you consider such stories advertising? Why do you think companies might ask customers to share their stories?

Reflect on It

Check the website of any of your favorite stores, products, or teams, and see if there is information on the story behind the store or the product or the history behind the team. Read the story. Were you familiar with any of it? How did it affect your attitude toward the story, product, or team?

Description, Narration, and Example in Action

In this chapter, you will have the opportunity to examine and use the techniques of description, narration, and example. To help you become skilled in using these techniques, the text analyzes and explains each one separately. In reality, they are rarely used that way. Instead, authors combine techniques, using the ones that best suit their purpose for writing.

Before looking at description, narration, and example separately, look at how a professional writer uses all three techniques together. The following essay is by Maya Angelou, noted writer, poet, and activist. It is an excerpt from *Wouldn't Take Nothing for My Journey Now,* one of Angelou's several autobiographical books.

The essay embodies all three of the writing techniques featured in this chapter. The predominant technique of the essay is **narration,** or story-telling. Notice how the author highlights her narrative with **dialogue,** or conversation, to help the reader understand the characters she describes.

In the second and third paragraphs, Angelou uses **examples**, exact instances or illustrations of a particular type. Notice how these paragraphs provide specific examples of complainers, showing exactly how they behave.

Finally, the author uses **description** to paint a picture so that the reader can visualize the people in her story. Because humans perceive the world through the senses of sight, hearing, touch, taste, and smell, describing in terms of the five senses is an effective way to make a subject real and concrete to readers.

Complaining

Maya Angelou

When my grandmother was raising me in Stamps, Arkansas, she had a particular   1
routine when people who were known to be whiners entered her store. Whenever she saw a known complainer coming, she would call me from whatever I was doing and say conspiratorially, "Sister, come inside. Come." Of course I would obey.

My grandmother would ask the customer, "How are you doing today, Brother   2
Thomas?" And the person would reply, "Not so good." There would be a distinct whine in the voice. "Not so good today, Sister Henderson. You see, it's this summer. It's this summer heat. I just hate it. Oh, I hate it so much. It just frazzles me up and frazzles me down. I just hate the heat. It's almost killing me." Then my grandmother would stand stoically, her arms folded, and mumble, "Uh-huh, uh-huh." And she would cut her eyes at me to make certain that I had heard the lamentation.

At another time a whiner would mewl, "I hate plowing. That packed-down dirt   3
ain't got no reasoning, and mules ain't got good sense. . . . Sure ain't. It's killing me. I can't ever seem to get done. My feet and my hands stay sore, and I get dirt in my eyes and up my nose. I just can't stand it." And my grandmother, again stoically with her arms folded, would say, "Uh-huh, uh-huh," and then look at me and nod.

As soon as the complainer was out of the store, my grandmother would call   4
me to stand in front of her. And then she would say the same thing she had said at least a thousand times, it seemed to me. "Sister, did you hear what Brother So-and-So or Sister Much to Do complained about? You heard that?" And I would nod. Mamma would continue, "Sister, there are people who went to sleep all over the world last night, poor and rich and white and black, but they will never wake again. Sister, those who expected to rise did not, their beds became their cooling boards, and their blankets became their winding sheets. And those dead folks would give anything, anything at all for just five minutes of this weather or ten minutes of that plowing that person was grumbling about. So you watch yourself about complaining,

Sister. What you're supposed to do when you don't like a thing is change it. If you can't change it, change the way you think about it. Don't complain."

THINKING ABOUT THE ESSAY

1. Examples provide specific instances that help a reader understand a more general point. Look at the two specific examples of complainers: Brother Thomas in the second paragraph and an unnamed whiner in the third paragraph. How do those specific examples help you understand what a whiner does in general? In other words, if you were the proverbial visitor from another planet where whining did not exist, how would you describe a whiner after reading about the two whiners in Angelou's essay?

2. Narration helps essay writers make a point by telling a story. Although the point may become evident as the story unfolds, writers often reinforce the point at the end of the story. Based on the last paragraph, what is the point of Angelou's story? Which character is used to convey the point?

3. Description helps readers understand an essay in the same way that they understand the world: through sight, hearing, taste, touch, and smell. Look at the words used at the beginning of paragraphs 2 and 3 to describe the voices of the whiners. Then, look at the description of the grandmother's body language at the end of paragraphs 2 and 3. What do these descriptions show you about the character of the whiners as opposed to the character of the grandmother, Sister Henderson?

Description

mywritinglab

Visit MyWriting Lab for additional practice describing.

"You can't miss it. It's the big yellow house on the corner."

"Officer, he was bald with a tattoo of a turtle on the top of his head."

"I just asked to borrow a pen, and she gave me a look that would freeze hot coffee on a July day."

Where would we be without description? It is used every day to communicate the essentials of life and to add the embellishments that keep listeners hanging on every word.

In writing, too, description helps readers understand your point and keeps them waiting for the next detail. Descriptive essays often answer questions such as the ones that follow.

- What is your favorite season of the year?
- What one place, for you, is "heaven on earth"?
- Describe a place that causes (or caused) you to feel uncomfortable or unhappy.

Laying the Groundwork for Descriptive Writing

Visualizing

Look at the photograph of the building with the sign "Cocktails" on the front. Then use your imagination to visualize the interior. Is it large and airy or small and intimate? Is the lighting bright or soft? Are the colors warm or cool? How is it furnished and decorated? How are the people dressed? What music would you hear? What kinds of food and drink are served?

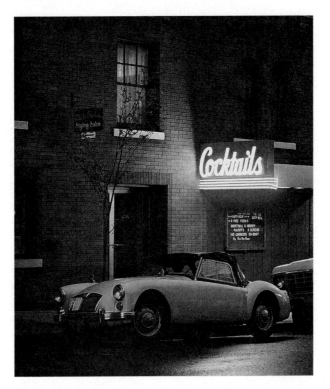

Planning

You have visualized the décor, the people, the music, and the food and beverages that you might find inside the building. Decide which three elements you would include in an essay on this topic. In what order would you place them? Why?

Writing

Write a paragraph about one of the elements you have chosen in the "Planning" section. Your challenge in this assignment is to make everything you describe seem so real that the reader can almost see it, hear it, touch it, taste it, and smell it.

✐ Elements of Descriptive Writing

mywritinglab

Visit MyWriting Lab for additional practice describing.

Effective descriptive writing paints a picture for the reader. Just as artists use canvas, brushes, and paints, writers use the tools of their trade to create a more effective picture. Your tools as a writer of descriptive paragraphs and essays include sense impressions, spatial order, and a dominant impression.

Sense Impressions

Every scrap of information we collect about the world around us comes through our five senses: sight, hearing, smell, taste, and touch. It is logical, then, that descriptions painted using sense impressions present a more vivid picture to your reader.

Sight

In writing, descriptive imagery is most often visual. Visual impressions are strong and lasting. Psychological studies confirm that people are more likely to rely on what they see than on what they hear. For example, you would not be fooled by a clerk's "Thank you" if his facial expression said, "I hate my job." If it is true that seeing is believing, then creating a visual picture for the reader is particularly important in descriptive writing.

Hearing

Our sense of hearing also gives us information about the world around us. We are warned by the blast of a horn, energized by the driving beat of rock or rap, or soothed by the thunder of the ocean. Imagery that appeals to a reader's sense of hearing is an essential dimension of descriptive writing.

Smell

The sense of smell has a powerful connection to memory. The smell of freshly popped popcorn may summon the claustrophobic feel of a dark, crowded movie theater. A whiff of furniture polish can summon memories of an aunt's stately dining room. Using imagery related to smell can help complete the picture you create for your reader.

Touch

The sense of touch is a backdrop for all experience. As you sit reading this, you may feel beneath you the hard surface of a wooden chair or the softness of sofa cushions. You may be aware of the chill of air conditioning or the warmth of sunlight, the scratch of a wool sweater or the cottony feel of an old pair of jeans. Imagery that brings out textures and temperatures adds a special touch to the picture you draw for your reader.

Taste

Taste imagery may play a smaller role in your writing unless you are writing about food. However, used sparingly, references to taste add spice to your descriptive writing.

EXERCISE 1 **RECOGNIZING WORDS OF THE SENSES**

In the following paragraph, underline words and phrases that draw on the senses of sight, hearing, smell, touch, and taste.

Rocking-Chair Saturday

Our screened porch is a peaceful place to read and relax on a Saturday afternoon. Sitting in a creaking wooden rocker, I look through the gauzy wire screen into the backyard. From the top of a pine tree, a mockingbird scolds. In the distance, I hear the sleepy drone of a neighbor's mower. A slight breeze wafts the tempting aroma of grilling hamburgers toward me. Prudence, my calico cat, pads out to join me, stretching out in a warm patch of sunlight near the screen door. I scoop her warm, furry body into my arms as she rumbles her approval. She settles into my lap, content to sit with me and enjoy the peace of the back porch.

EXERCISE 2 **WRITING SENSORY DESCRIPTIONS**

Write a phrase that describes each of the following words in sensory terms. Then note whether you are describing the word through the sense of sight, hearing, smell, touch, or taste. The first one is done for you.

- stone
  a smooth, heavy stone (touch)
- milk

  _____

- wrapping paper

  _____

- sunlight

  _____

- glove

  _____

- coin

  _____

- french fries

  _____

- voice

  _____

- leaves

  _____

- bark (tree or dog's, your choice)

  _____

Spatial Order

Spatial order helps you write about anything that takes up space. Use spatial order to present physical objects in a way that makes sense: bottom to top, left to right, background to foreground, or outside to inside. A partial list of words commonly used when referring to space follows.

above	beyond	near	right
ahead	by	next to	south
around	down	north	toward
behind	east	on	under
beside	in	over	underfoot
between	left	overhead	west

EXERCISE 3   RECOGNIZING EFFECTIVE USE OF SPATIAL ORDER

Look at the following short paragraphs. In which paragraph is spatial order used in a more organized way?

Paragraph A

   The singer looked as if he had just stepped out of the 1960s. His hair, twisted into thick dreadlocks, fell almost to his shoulders. On his feet were chunky leather sandals. A small golden ring pierced his left nostril. His hands, clasped around the microphone in front of his chest, were ringed in silver and turquoise. He wore a faded pair of jeans that flared into a wide bell over his ankles. Over his shirt, he wore a soft leather vest that ended at his waist in a beaded fringe. His shirt, open at the neck, revealed a silver and turquoise necklace. He wore a small golden earring on one ear. He looked as though he belonged on a Woodstock poster.

Paragraph B

   The model walking down the runway looked like a movie actress from the 1940s. Her hair curved under just above her shoulders and dipped across one eye as she turned her head. Her eyebrows were arched and penciled, and her lipstick was a deep red. The jacket of her gray pinstriped suit was padded at the shoulders and nipped in at the waist. Her skirt hugged her hips and legs tightly and flared below the knee. She wore dark stockings with seams up the back, and stiletto heels that looked impossible to walk in. She looked as though she had stepped out of an old black-and-white movie.

The paragraph that uses spatial order more effectively is paragraph _____.

Establishing a Dominant Impression

Description is more than just a tangle of unrelated details. In a descriptive essay, every detail should join in conveying a single **dominant impression.** A dominant impression helps you convey your attitude toward the subject and aids in the unity of your description. If you are writing a description of a house that you pass every day, your description should show more than shutters, bricks, and roofing tiles. What is your overall impression of that house? Is it cheerful? Eerie? Prim? Dignified? The word that you choose to describe the house conveys your dominant impression. As you describe the house, each detail should contribute to the dominant impression.

When you write a descriptive paragraph or essay, it is helpful to include the dominant impression in the topic sentence of your paragraph or in the thesis statement of your essay. Stating the dominant impression helps you keep the paragraph or essay on track by reminding you of the impression that each detail should create. It also lets your reader know what to expect.

If you are describing a house that is eerie, include details designed to send chills up the reader's spine: the loose, creaking shutters and the blankly staring windows. If cheerful dandelions bloom in the yard, let them bloom unseen. Details that do not reinforce the dominant impression do not belong in your description.

The topic sentences below illustrate different ways of stating a dominant impression.

Examples

The classroom was uncomfortably warm.

The car was a joy to drive.

The instructor looked more like a homeless person than a college professor.

The office was obviously a place where serious work was done.

EXERCISE 4   **SUPPORTING THE DOMINANT IMPRESSION**

In each list below, circle the letter of the detail that would not support the dominant impression of the topic sentence.

1. The house on the corner is dignified.
   a. stately columns on the porch
   b. well-trimmed bushes lining the driveway
   c. crumpled beer can on the lawn
   d. dark green shutters framing curtained windows

2. The kitchen was messy.
   a. dirty dishes piled in the sink
   b. cat food spilled on the floor
   c. overflowing trash can
   d. shiny coffeepot stored neatly on a shelf

3. Greta seems studious.
   a. studies in the library every evening
   b. enjoys playing poker
   c. makes good grades
   d. takes good notes in class

4. The garage was a fire hazard.
   a. oily rags and newspapers stacked three feet high
   b. space heater with frayed cord plugged into a wall outlet

c. rusty mower blades and chainsaw blades thrown into an open box

d. boxes of old fireworks, open bags of quick-start charcoal, and dented aerosol cans piled haphazardly on shelves

5. The town seemed prosperous.
   a. many large new homes
   b. new school under construction
   c. boarded-up stores downtown
   d. large manufacturing plant on the outskirts of town

Wordsmith's Corner: Examples of Descriptive Writing

Following are two student examples of descriptive essays. Read each essay and answer the questions that follow.

Descriptive Essay 1

The writer of this essay describes a store's produce department. Notice the imagery appealing to sight, sound, smell, touch, and taste.

A Garden of Temptation

Harry's Farmer's Market is more than just a grocery store. It is a storehouse of temptation. At Harry's, a shopper can find breads and pastries, ethnic delights from a variety of countries, and a selection of candies that would unravel the strongest will. But when it comes to temptation, nothing at Harry's can rival the produce section.

The vegetable bins at Harry's are a feast for the senses. Row upon row of green, musty-smelling cabbages temptingly hint of cabbage rolls and coleslaw to come. Beyond the green cabbages are bins of the purple, curly-leafed variety, piled like basketballs in a sporting goods store. Next come potatoes in all shapes and sizes. Large, long Idahos weigh in the hand like a stone and bake up fluffy and dry. The yellow-fleshed Yukon Golds can be sliced into golden medallions and topped with cheese. Farther along the aisle, carrots beckon like slender fingers, and plump squash nestle comfortably in neat bins. At the end of the aisle, mountains of waxy purple eggplant lie in lush array. The vegetable bins at Harry's provide a feast for the eyes as well as for the taste buds.

Beyond the vegetables lie the fruits in a patchwork of geographic and seasonal variety. Bananas, pineapples, mangoes, and limes flaunt tropical hues. Their exotic aromas hint of balmy breezes, marimba bands, and sweet summer nights. Across the aisle, the season is fall.

Apples, crisp as a New England day, stir the air with the fragrance of autumn. Their red and yellow colors and even their names—Crispin, Pippin, Granny Smith, Ginger Gold—suggest brisk autumn days, the crunch of leaves underfoot, and a cozy hearth. Farther on, yellow grapefruit, bright as the California sun, suggest a return to summer. Beside them, giant navel oranges add a hint of citrus to the air. In this section of Harry's, time and place blend in a fruit-basket turnover.

For customers who can't wait until they are out of the store to sample the delights of Harry's fruits and vegetables, the juice bar offers instant gratification. Thirsty shoppers can drink in the tartness of a California grapefruit or taste the sweetness of freshly squeezed orange juice. For something different, customers can sample apricot juice in hues of rich dusky amber or exotic papaya flavored with coconut milk. Vegetable lovers can sip a cool, pale celery drink, rich red tomato juice, or carrot juice so brightly orange that many shoppers swear their eyesight improves just by looking at it. There's no better way to end a trip through Harry's produce department than by drinking it in.

Grocery shopping can be a chore, but at Harry's, it is more often a delight. A trip through the produce department is a tempting tour through a garden where every vegetable is in season and no fruit is forbidden.

Questions

1. What is the dominant impression of the essay?

   _____

2. The introduction of the essay is
   a. an anecdote
   b. broad to narrow
   c. narrow to broad
   d. quotation

3. Write the thesis statement on the line below. Are the points listed?

   _____

   _____

4. Write the topic sentence of each body paragraph on the lines that follow.

   _____

   _____

   _____

_____

_____

5. Underline the sense impressions in the essay. Can you find images related to all five senses? Write five images below that evoke each of the senses.

   a. sight _____

   b. hearing _____

   c. smell _____

   d. touch _____

   e. taste _____

Descriptive Essay 2

An unusual museum exhibit inspired this essay. Notice how the writer moves the reader through the exhibit.

Juke Joint

I hear a rising laugh, like notes played on a piano, as I approach the doorway marked "Little Grocery." By day, the Little Grocery sold milk, bread, cereal, and cigarettes—the stuff of everyday life. At night, under a pungent haze of smoke, the jukebox played "Slip Away" or "Mr. Big Stuff" to the clink of bottles of illegal liquor. But I am not worried about a police raid, for I am in the Tubman African American Museum, looking at artist Willie Little's re-creation of his father's North Carolina juke joint. The setting, the music, and the life-size figures are nostalgic reminders of an earlier era.

As I enter the doorway, I step into a setting from the past. The sawdust-covered floor leads to an old-fashioned glass-topped counter. On the counter, beside a gallon jar of pickled pig's feet, sits an empty bottle labeled "Sun-Drop Golden Cola—As Refreshing as a Cup of Coffee." Behind the glass are old-fashioned bottles of White Rain shampoo and a half-filled box of individually wrapped Moon Pies. A card offers "Mystery Edge Razor Blades, 4 blades 10¢." To the left of the counter, a sawdust trail leads to a large yellow cooler emblazoned with the words "Royal Crown Cola" in red. Above the cooler, a rectangular metal sign advertises "Viceroy Filter Tip Cigarettes—Filtered Smoke with the Finest Flavor." Beside the cooler sits a jukebox.

The old-fashioned jukebox pulses with light and music, taking me back to the sixties. I walk toward it, passing a tall thin figure whose upraised fingers, the color of mahogany, look as though they are holding an invisible harmonica. As I move closer, I can make out the name "Wurlitzer Zodiac" on the front of the jukebox. I look at the selections. If I had a quarter, I could hear "Jimmy Mack" by Martha and the Vandellas, "Mercy, Mercy Me" by Marvin Gaye, or Aretha Franklin's "Respect." A museum employee walks by, opens the jukebox, and presses a button. I hear the machine clicking through the selections, and more music fills the air. "How Sweet It Is to Be Loved by You" is followed by "Midnight Hour" and "Mr. Pitiful," songs that must have once filled the smoky air in "Mr. Charlie's" juke joint.

The artist has also brought the past to life with re-creations of the people who danced, drank, and laughed in his father's juke joint. Beside me, a slim, chocolate-colored figure in jeans dances with outstretched arms, her head a mass of pink curlers. Across from the jukebox, a sad-looking figure of a man with a goiter sits on an old church pew, his hat resting on his knee, his tie undone. Beside him, a female figure, an unlit cigarette clenched between her lips, extends an empty pack of Pall Malls. Her polyester pantsuit is pink and glittery, her blouse a satiny sky blue. Beyond them, a figure labeled "Sara Carroway" holds a parasol above her head. She is wearing soiled Keds, and stockings are knotted under her knobby knees. Despite her shabby attire, her bearing is formal and prim. As I look more closely, I see that her tight, pressed curls are created with round seed pods. In a shadowed corner at the back of the exhibit, two figures embrace. A long-haired figure of a woman in harlequin glasses stands against the wall, her short skirt hiked around her hips. Her lover, a light-skinned, impassioned-looking male figure, stretches out his hand as if to reach under her skirt. Feeling like an intruder, I back away. As I leave, I notice the male's pants, unbuckled and falling below slim hips.

As I leave the exhibit, I hear again the rising laughter. It comes from a small group of students touring the museum. Yet it seems to me to echo the laughter that once floated above the haze of cigarette smoke in the Little Grocery in the 1960s.

Questions

1. Which two senses does the essay emphasize most strongly?

   _____

2. Write the thesis statement on the following line. Does it list the points to be discussed in the essay?

   _____

   _____

3. What is the dominant impression? Is it stated in the thesis and topic sentences?

   _____

4. List the topic of each body paragraph.

   _____

   _____

   _____

5. Underline the sense impressions in the essay. Can you find imagery of all five senses?

   a. sight _____

   b. hearing _____

   c. smell _____

   d. touch _____

   e. taste _____

TOPICS FOR DESCRIPTIVE WRITING

Small Scrawls: Imaginative Short Writings

What is a Small Scrawl? A "scrawl" is something written quickly. In this case, it is a page or so of quick writing that allows you to practice a particular type of writing, in this case, descriptive writing. Have fun with it!

Small Scrawl 1: Mosquito's-Eye View

You are a mosquito, seeking human flesh on which to feed. As you buzz along, you see the ocean and a stretch of sand on which people seem to be grilling themselves just for your dining pleasure. These human beings come in all sizes and shapes, but what they have in common is large expanses of exposed flesh, gleaming with suntan oil and sunscreen. Describe what you see, focusing on your five senses.

Small Scrawl 2: A Walk Outside

Go outside and take a short walk around. Take notes on what you see, hear, smell, and touch. Look at everything. Then focus on one thing, area, or person and write about that, using the other information you have collected to fill in the background.

Small Scrawl 3: An Ordinary Object

Find an ordinary object in your pocket or bag or in the room you are in. It can be an ordinary object such as a coin, wallet, book, pen, key ring, or piece of paper. It may be ordinary, but you will describe it in an extraordinary way. Experience it with all your senses. Touch it, noting its weight, texture, and temperature. Listen to the sound it makes as you hold it, shake it, or drop it on the desk in front of you. Look at its color, its dimensions, and its shape. Smell it, noting whether the smell is pleasant or unpleasant, strong or faint. Then write about it, incorporating your sensory impressions into your description.

Essay Assignments

Descriptive Essay 1: Describing a Place

Write an essay describing a place. It can be a store, office, nightclub, park, beach, street, parking lot, church sanctuary, stadium, or any place of your choosing. In your thesis statement, state the dominant impression in one word, choosing a word from the following list or thinking up your own word. Make sure all the details of your description reinforce that dominant impression. *Hint:* Your thesis statement will follow this pattern:

The __(place)__ was/is __(dominant impression)__ .

cheerful	colorful	filthy	orderly
cluttered	disgusting	spotless	chaotic
serene	dull	crowded	lonely
bleak	gloomy	eerie	noisy
messy	elegant	exciting	calm
shabby	depressing	impersonal	cozy

Descriptive Essay 2: Describing a Person

Write an essay describing a person. It can be someone you know well, such as a friend or relative, or someone you see often but don't really know, such as a library worker or a fellow student. Be sure that you state a dominant impression in your thesis; a few possibilities are listed below. Make sure that all the details in your essay support the dominant impression. Focus on sense impressions, details that can be expressed through sight, hearing, smell, touch, and taste. Don't simply *say* that someone has bad breath; let your reader *smell* it: "His breath reeked with the sour, sharp odor of cigarettes, unbrushed teeth, and onions he had eaten the night before."

arrogant	easygoing	graceful	neat
dignified	elegant	gruff	unhappy
disorganized	forbidding	messy	upbeat

Descriptive Essay 3: Vacation in Paradise

What is your idea of the perfect vacation spot? Describe the spot, including details such as the climate and the landscape; the hotel, campsite, or cabin you would stay in; and the attractions you would visit.

Descriptive Essay 4: Essay-Based Topic

Re-read Maya Angelou's essay, "Complaining," at the beginning of this chapter. Sister Henderson, Angelou's grandmother, was obviously a strong influence in her life. Write an essay describing an adult who influenced you when you were a child. Focus on the traits of character and personality in your role model that helped to make you the person you are today. Try, as Angelou does, to show the character of the person you describe through the person's actions and words.

Description in the Real World: Secret Shopper

Many times, people ask how writing essays will help them in the "real world." This real-world assignment gives just one example of how descriptive writing might be used outside the classroom.

Stores or restaurants often hire "secret shoppers" who are asked to write reports about their experiences in a particular store or restaurant. The reports focus first on the store or restaurant environment: Is it clean, neat, and inviting? Next come the employees: Are you greeted immediately? Are employees friendly and professional? Next, what about the merchandise or the food? If it is merchandise, is it logically and invitingly arranged? Can you find what you want easily? If the establishment is a restaurant, is the food invitingly presented? Is it hot and fresh? How does it taste?

For this assignment, choose a store or restaurant—it may be the college bookstore or cafeteria if you wish—and pretend you are a secret shopper hired to evaluate the place from a customer's point of view.

✍ Narration

---

mywritinglab

Visit MyWriting Lab for additional practice with narration.

Narration is the art of storytelling. You know already that every story has a beginning, a middle, and an end, but there are several other characteristics of a successful story. First, it emphasizes details that are central to the story's point and downplays those that are not. Next, it is usually told in chronological order. It most often involves a conflict, and it may include dialogue. Finally, it makes a point. Though every good narrative may not have every one of these characteristics, you will find them in stories that delight you. Incorporating them into your own writing helps you delight your own readers.

Narrative essays typically address topics similar to the ones that follow.

- Write about an experience that changed your life.

- Describe an experience that was frightening or embarrassing when it occurred but is funny now when you look back on it.

- What is the bravest thing you have ever done?

Laying the Groundwork for Narrative Writing

Visualizing

Look at the photograph of two women. What is happening in this picture? What are the women discussing?

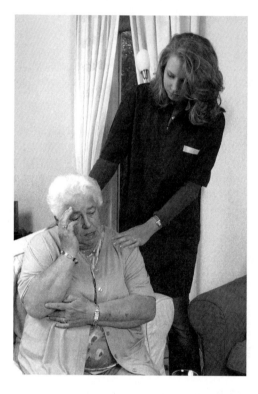

Planning

If you could write about this photograph using only the words spoken by the two women, how would you reveal important information about what had happened beforehand?

Writing

Write a narrative about the moment shown in the picture. Use dialogue to show what is said and description to show who speaks and how others react during the conversation. Here's a special challenge: Make sure that in your narrative, the conversation is short but that it shows through dialogue what happened before the conversation took place and what might happen afterward.

Techniques for Successful Narration

Emphasize Important Details

In a successful narrative, important details are emphasized, and unimportant ones are de-emphasized or omitted entirely. If you are writing about the time you performed the Heimlich maneuver to save a fellow-restaurant patron from choking to death, you will not go into detail about what was on the menu, how the traffic was on the way to the restaurant, or the quality of the service. You will focus on those few minutes of crisis when you noticed that someone was choking, remembered your training, and went into action. Details of those few minutes—the worried faces of the man's family, your feeling that time had slowed down, the eyes of the restaurant patrons turning toward you, and the choking man's desperate, frightened eyes—may all have a place in your narrative as you lead up to the moment when a small chunk of steak flew from the man's throat and landed on the carpet.

EXERCISE 5   CHOOSING RELEVANT DETAILS

Imagine that you are writing a narrative about accidentally locking yourself out of your house and having to convince a passing police officer that you are not a burglar. Which of the following details would you include in your narrative? Put a checkmark beside details that you would include and an X beside those you would not. Then compare your list with a classmate's and see how closely you agree.

_____ 1. The phone rang just as I was going out the door, so I set my keys on the counter.

_____ 2. When my car pool arrived, I hung up the phone and hurried out the door.

_____ 3. The lettuce on the sandwich I ate for lunch was wilted.

_____ 4. After work, my car pool dropped me off in front of my house.

_____ 5. I waved goodbye to my car pool and reached into my pocket for my keys.

_____ 6. I realized I had forgotten them.

_____ 7. I thought I remembered leaving an upstairs window unlocked.

_____ 8. I took a ladder from an unlocked storage room just off the carport.

_____ 9. I covered my neat shirt and tie with an old black sweatshirt I had left in the storage room.

_____ 10. My house is painted blue.

_____ 11. I placed the ladder against the house and began to climb.

_____**12.** Just as I reached the top of the ladder, I heard a polite but firm voice ask, "Are you the homeowner?"

_____**13.** I looked down and saw a uniformed officer.

_____**14.** The officer asked if I had any identification.

_____**15.** Luckily, I was carrying my wallet and my driver's license, which bears my photo and address.

_____**16.** The picture on my license is unflattering and does not capture my good looks.

_____**17.** As the officer watched suspiciously, I descended the ladder, then showed her my license.

_____**18.** She thanked me and explained that she was keeping a close watch because of the recent burglaries.

_____**19.** Crimes of all types are rising across the United States.

_____**20.** It felt strange to be a suspect, if only temporarily.

Use Chronological Order

Most stories are best told in the order in which they happen, with background details near the beginning of the narrative. Chronological order helps your story unfold in a way that is logical to your reader.

Center on Conflict

Most successful narratives center around conflict. People overcome difficulties or difficulties overcome people. The conflict may be an inner conflict, such as the one involved in deciding whether to attend a college near home or one far away. It may be a conflict with another person. It may be a conflict with an impersonal outside force, such as a declining job market. It may be a conflict with a combination of forces. When the conflict ends, the story ends, too.

Show, Don't Tell

Significant moments in your narrative should be slowed down and observed closely. At these times, you want to _show_ what is happening rather than simply reporting it. Instead of telling your readers that your friend was angry, show his narrowed eyes and let them hear his sharp words. Another way of showing is through dialogue, letting your readers hear the exact words of the people you write about. Use dialogue sparingly and at significant moments for the strongest effect.

Building CONNECTIONS

Descriptive writing skills can also be incorporated into narrative writing. Your narrative becomes even stronger when you present it in terms of sight, sound, touch, taste, and smell.

Example of Telling versus Showing

Telling

As I drove down the highway in the snow, I saw a terrible accident. A small black pickup truck passed me, and just a few moments later, I saw that same truck roll off the highway and come to rest in a ravine. I pulled off to the side of the road to call 911, wondering if the young man driving the truck was alive. Other cars pulled off, too, and their drivers got out to help. Soon, someone told me that the young man was still breathing. I drove off feeling very relieved.

Showing

A light snow fell silently as I drove down the highway, making me feel at peace. Suddenly, a small black pickup truck shot past me at a dangerous speed. I could see that the driver was very young. "Idiot," I thought. Seconds later, I watched in horror as the speeding truck fishtailed across the snowy highway. In what seemed to me like slow motion, the truck rolled end over end across the highway and into a deep ravine. As I pulled to the side of the road to dial 911, several other cars pulled over, and three men scrambled down the ravine. After a few worried minutes, I saw one of the men running toward me. "He's still alive," the man said. "Have you called

911?" I said that I had, and, feeling that I could be of no more help, decided to be on my way. As I pulled onto the highway, I heard the welcome sound of sirens screaming in the distance.

Make a Point

The purpose of the story is its reason for existence, the reason that you find it worth telling. If no change takes place, if nothing significant happens, your reader will say impatiently, "What is the *point?*" Having a point does not mean that your story needs to have a moral, like an Aesop's fable. It simply means that you should know why you are telling it. As with any type of essay or paragraph, you should be able to state your point in one sentence: your thesis statement or topic sentence.

Wordsmith's Corner: Examples of Narrative Writing

Below are two student examples of narrative writing. Read each essay and answer the questions that follow.

Narrative Essay 1

For the writer of this essay, a lesson learned on the first day of class was a painful one that had nothing to do with astronomy.

What I Learned in Astronomy 101

It was the first day of class. I got up early, threw on a pair of jeans, a sweatshirt, and a ball cap and hurried off to my 8:00 A.M. class, Introduction to Astronomy. I have always been interested in astronomy, so I took a seat in the front row. But the lesson I learned that day was not on the syllabus. I discovered how quickly a mean-spirited professor could dampen my desire to learn.

When Dr. Laster walked in and thumped his books on the desk, the classroom was packed, and several students were standing along the walls. The professor looked around the room until his eyes stopped on me. He did not look pleased. "Young man," he said, "where are your manners?" I looked around and saw some female students standing while I sat. Embarrassed, I rose and gestured for one of them to take my seat. "Sit down," snapped the professor. "I'm sure these ladies can stand for a few more minutes. Do you and these other gentlemen always wear your hats indoors?" I felt a flush creeping slowly up my neck, and as

I whipped my cap from my head, I saw stealthy movements as others quickly removed theirs. During the rest of the class, I hid my embarrassment by pretending to read the syllabus and take notes.

By the time class was over, I had decided that one crusty old professor was not going to keep me from taking a class that genuinely interested me. I headed for the bookstore, but the astronomy books were sold out. That's when I had an idea. I would drop by the professor's office to let him know that the bookstore was out of books. That small courtesy, I reasoned, might help me to get back on the right track with him.

When I got to the professor's office, the door was open and he was sitting at his desk reading. I knocked softly on the door frame and said, "Professor Laster? I just came by to let you know that the bookstore is out of astronomy textbooks." Instead of being pleased that I had come by, he looked annoyed. "That's not my problem," he said. "It's the bookstore's problem, and it's your problem. And it does not excuse you from reading the chapter or turning in the assignment." I was speechless. "Will that be all?" said Professor Laster. I wanted to offer an explanation or stand up for myself in some way, but I was so astonished by his hostility that I could not think of a reply. "Yes, sir," I finally stammered, then turned to leave.

I dropped the class that afternoon. I will never know why Dr. Laster behaved as he did. I do know that his petty, arrogant behavior cheated me out of a class I wanted to take and cheated him out of a good student who wanted to learn. All Dr. Laster taught me was to be a bit less trusting, a bit more cynical and, next time, more willing to stand up for myself.

Questions

1. Circle the letter of the statement below that best conveys the writer's main point.
   a. I have always been interested in astronomy, so I took a seat in the front row.
   b. I discovered how quickly a mean-spirited professor could dampen my desire to learn.
   c. I wanted to offer an explanation or stand up for myself in some way, but I was so astonished by his hostility that I could not think of a reply.
   d. I dropped the class that afternoon.

2. Write one sentence of dialogue from the essay that reflects the professor's attitude.

   _____

   _____

3. Write one sentence from the essay that incorporates description into the narrative.

_____

_____

_____

Narrative Essay 2

The writer of "Running from Trouble" tells of a decision that was easy to make but hard to forget.

Running from Trouble

Several years ago, my boyfriend Paul and I packed up our small orange Datsun and moved to the town where he had answered an ad for an experienced copier technician. Things went fine for a while; then Paul lost his job. My part-time job checking groceries barely brought in enough money for food and gas, and we got behind on our bills. Soon, creditors began harassing us with angry phone calls. Two months later, we made a decision that has haunted me ever since. We decided to run from our debt.

It was a Friday night, and I had just gotten paid. My check came to $145.82, not enough to make a dent in the electricity bill and one month's back rent. We sat at the small kitchen table of our furnished apartment with our pitiful store of cash and the remains of a frozen pizza between us. Paul looked at me with dull, discouraged eyes and said, "Why don't we just leave? We can start fresh." I nodded numbly, too tired to think or reason out the consequences. I had been raised in a family that paid its debts and met its problems head-on, so there should have been a voice in me somewhere telling me to find another way. But there was no voice, just empty silence. As Paul left to gas up the car, I cleared the dishes from the table and began to pack.

I had our clothes packed and our dishes boxed when I heard the Datsun pull around to the back. I wondered why Paul had gone to the back instead of parking in our space out front, so I went to the kitchen door that looked out on a wooded area behind our apartment. Paul had pulled the Datsun onto the strip of grass that bordered our small concrete patio. In the twilight, he was spray-painting our bright orange car a dull, flat black. My senses suddenly went on alert. I heard the loud rattle of the ball inside the can as Paul shook it. I smelled the sharp odor of the paint on the crisp November air. I saw the fine mist of paint in the air. In that moment of clarity, I also saw that what we were doing was illegal. We owed money, and we were skipping out. I pictured myself being arrested and fingerprinted. I imagined a future in which Paul and I moved from town to town, staying long enough to get in debt, leaving soon enough to dodge the repo man. Still, I felt detached from the whole process. I turned from the door and continued to pack.

When four aerosol cans of paint had been emptied onto the car, we loaded our possessions into the trunk and the back seat, careful to avoid touching the still-wet paint. As I went back for the last box, I saw a curtain twitch at a back window of the apartment next door. Had our neighbor seen us? I put the box in the car, got in, and closed the door with a soft slam. We pulled out into the night, our headlights off until we were safely past the resident manager's unit and onto the street. We drove through deserted streets and finally joined the ribbon of headlights on the interstate. I felt a sudden wild joy. "We're free!" I shouted to Paul. We exchanged high-fives as we headed toward a new and unencumbered life.

I no longer live with Paul, but I live with our decision every day of my life. It has left a blank spot in my work history and on forms that ask for previous addresses. It is a nagging guilt that plagues me sometimes in the night, a stalking shadow that may still overtake me one day. When I hear of hit-and-run drivers or criminals whose past has caught up with them, I feel a tug of kinship. I, too, know the hunted feeling of running from trouble.

Questions

1. Circle the letter of the statement below that best conveys the writer's main point.
   a. It is a nagging guilt that plagues me sometimes in the night, a stalking shadow that may still overtake me one day.
   b. In that moment of clarity, I also saw that what we were doing was illegal.
   c. Two months later, we made a decision that has haunted me ever since.
   d. "We're free!" I shouted to Paul, and we exchanged high-fives as we headed toward a new and unencumbered life.

2. What conflicts are present in the narrative? Which conflict is most important to the writer?

   _____

   _____

   _____

3. Give an instance of one specific place in the essay where the writer follows the principle, "Show, don't tell."

_____

_____

_____

TOPICS FOR NARRATIVE WRITING

Small Scrawls: Imaginative Short Writings

What is a Small Scrawl? A "scrawl" is something written quickly. In this case, it is a page or so of quick writing that allows you to practice a particular type of writing, in this case, narrative writing. Have fun with it!

Small Scrawl 1: Wake-up Call

You wake to the sound of the radio tuned to an unfamiliar station. As you open your eyes, you realize something is wrong. This is not the room you fell asleep in last night. As you reach to change the station on the radio, you freeze, transfixed by the sight of your outstretched arm. This is not the body you fell asleep in. Write the story.

Small Scrawl 2: Living Small

Write a one-page story about living in this house.

Small Scrawl 3: Stories in Art

Write a one-page story about what is happening in one of the paintings below.

Nighthawks by Edward Hopper

The Arnolfini Wedding by Jan van Eyck

Essay Assignments

Narrative Essay 1: Treat or Mistreat

In an essay, write about a time when someone treated you in one of the following ways:

> misjudged you
>
> gave you praise or credit you did not deserve
>
> encouraged you
>
> ridiculed you
>
> treated you with unexpected kindness
>
> treated you unfairly

Narrative Essay 2: A Significant "First"

Write a narrative essay about a significant "first" in your life. Some possibilities include your first date, first day of school, first day on a job, or first trip away from home without your parents. Make sure that the incident you choose is one that will fit into an essay. It would be hard, for instance, to write a narrative that fully discussed your first marriage or your first job (unless it lasted only a day or two!).

Narrative Essay 3: An Uncommon Encounter

Imagine that you have the opportunity to meet and converse with anyone, living or dead, for an hour. It may be a famous person, a historical figure you have always admired, or a relative or ancestor you have never met. Write a narrative describing your imaginary meeting. In describing your encounter, you may want to include details such as what the person says to you, the questions you ask, the person's appearance, and the setting in which the meeting takes place.

Narrative Essay 4: Essay-Based Assignment—A Teachable Moment

Review Maya Angelou's essay, "Complaining," at the beginning of this chapter. The author tells a story in which her grandmother, using the people who come into her store as examples, teaches a lesson about life. Situations and incidents that offer an opportunity for one person (usually an adult) to teach an important lesson to another person (usually a child) are called "teachable moments." Write a narrative describing a time in your life when someone caught you at a "teachable moment." Before you write, re-read Angelou's narrative carefully. Notice how vividly she describes her grandmother and the complainers who came into the store. Try to present the characters in your narrative, as well as the lesson you learned, in a vivid and memorable way.

Narration in the Real World: Observation Skills

Many times, people ask how writing essays will help them in the "real world." This real-world assignment gives just one example of how narrative writing might be used outside the classroom.

People in many professions are required to develop keen powers of observation. Those in security or police work need to be observant and to know what is going on around them. For medical personnel, keen observation of patients can make the difference between life and death. In fact, just about anyone can benefit from observing more about his or her environment.

Your assignment is to go to a place, observe what happens for a set period of time—say, fifteen minutes—and write it up as a narrative, with events described in chronological order.

Part of your job as an observer is not to be caught observing. Go to a place where your pen and paper will not seem out of place—a library, a cafeteria, a coffee shop, a bench on the campus somewhere—and sit down. Be careful not to stare or to make your observation of anyone seem more than casual. You might try opening your book and placing it on the table as if you are doing an assignment—and you are!

Your narrative should give the reader a clear idea of the place you are in and of the people and activities in the place.

Example

mywritinglab

Visit MyWriting Lab for additional practice using examples.

Examples give your reader a specific illustration of an idea. A good example is never a generalization but a crisp and specific picture that shows exactly what the sentence it illustrates means. An example is a shortcut, providing a vivid and direct way to get your meaning across to your reader. Because examples are used to illustrate a point, they often include narration or description.

Examples can be used in almost any type of essay. However, essays supported by examples alone might be used to answer questions such as the ones that follow.

- What would cause you to end a friendship?
- Discuss some of the ways that an individual can help the environment.
- How has attending college affected your eating habits?

Building CONNECTIONS

You have seen the way brief anecdotes—small narratives—can be used to introduce an essay. Anecdotes can often serve as examples, too. For instance, if you need an example of rude behavior to illustrate an essay, tell a story. Maybe you recently encountered a gum-chewing clerk in a convenience store who talked on a cell phone during your entire transaction. Perhaps a rude driver cut you off in traffic. A supporting anecdote can add life to your example essay.

Laying the Groundwork for Writing Using Examples

Visualizing

Look at the photograph of the "Beach Closed" sign; then use your imagination to generate several examples of dangers that might have forced the closure of this beach.

Planning

Plan a paragraph discussing the closure of the beach pictured. Choose between one and three examples of dangers that could cause the closure of a beach.

Writing

Write a paragraph discussing two or three hypothetical examples or reasons this beach might have been closed, or, if you wish, take just one of your examples and write it out in detail, describing all of the circumstances that led to the closure of the beach.

EXERCISE 6 USING EXAMPLES EFFECTIVELY

To get an idea of how examples help you get your meaning across, look at the following paragraphs. Which presents a clearer picture?

Paragraph A

A person who visits another country should be prepared for more than just differences in climate and language. Even such a simple thing as taking a drive can result in culture shock if a tourist is not prepared for the different driving customs in the country he is visiting. Nothing can prepare a person for some of the strange driving customs of other countries. Not everyone drives the way we do in the United States. Even though road signs are supposed to be international in meaning, driving customs are not. An American visiting another country may put himself in danger or, at the very least, risk confusion simply by taking a drive. For their own safety and that of others, tourists to other countries should become familiar with driving customs before getting behind the wheel.

Paragraph B

A person who visits another country should be prepared for more than just differences in climate and language. Even such a simple thing as taking a drive can result in culture shock if a tourist is not prepared for the different driving customs in different countries. In the United Kingdom, for example, a car's steering wheel is on the right side of the car, and people drive on the left-hand side of the road. An American used to driving on the right-hand side may put himself in danger or, at the very least, risk confusion simply by taking a drive. In Cairo, Egypt, drivers navigate the city's streets at night with their lights off. Like bats flying into the dusk, these drivers steer by sound, tooting their horns every few minutes to warn approaching drivers of their presence. Driving with the lights on, it is widely believed, will drain a car's battery whether the car is running or not. Is maneuvering a car down dark streets and highways dangerous without headlights? Perhaps it is. But in that city, it might be even more dangerous to turn headlights on and risk blinding other drivers on the dark, noisy streets. For their safety and that of others, tourists to other countries should become familiar with driving customs before getting behind the wheel.

The paragraph that makes its point more clearly through examples is paragraph ___.

EXERCISE 7   SHORT AND EXTENDED EXAMPLES

As you saw in Chapter 5, a paragraph may be supported by a series of short examples or by one long, extended example. Look at the following paragraphs. Which is supported by a series of examples and which by an extended example?

Paragraph A

My roommate Charlotte is excessively neat. She makes her bed up military style, with the covers so tight she could bounce a battalion of quarters from the taut surface. If I shower after her, it is as if I am the first one in the bathroom. The shower stall and mirrors are wiped dry. Her wet towel has been whisked into the hamper, and a dry towel, neatly folded, hangs from the towel rack. Her hair dryer hangs neatly on its hook, and her toothbrush stands soldierlike in its holder. Of course, the cap is back on her toothpaste tube, which is neatly rolled up from the end, not squeezed in the middle. In her closet, skirts and jackets, as fresh as if they had just been brought from the dry cleaner, fall neatly from hangers spaced exactly one inch apart. Her CDs are arranged in alphabetical order, as are the books on her shelves. I admire neatness; I even strive for it. But Charlotte takes neatness a step too far.

Paragraph B

Social service agencies sometimes do more harm than good. A recent story in the local newspaper provides a good example. A young woman went to a hospital's emergency room because of complications from the recent birth of her child. Because she had no one to keep the child, she brought him with her to the emergency room. When a decision was made to admit her to the hospital, she told hospital personnel that she had no family in the United States, and there was no one to take care of her baby. Trying to help her, hospital officials called a state social services agency to get temporary care for the child. When the child's mother was released from the hospital five days later, she was told that she would have to prove she was a fit mother before regaining custody of her child. The woman was angry and did not understand why her fitness as a mother was being questioned. A spokesperson for the social services agency said its personnel were simply following procedure. In this case, the agency did more harm than good, making the woman a victim instead of giving her the help she needed.

The paragraph that is supported by a series of examples is paragraph ____.

The paragraph that is supported by a single extended example is paragraph ___.

Wordsmith's Corner: Examples of Writing Supported by Example

Below are two student essays supported by example. Read each and answer the questions that follow.

Example Essay 1

It's on the dinner plate now, but what was its life like before? The writer of this essay shows the reader through examples.

Cruel Portion

My grandmother was nine years old when her pet chicken, Belle, showed up on the table at Sunday dinner or, to be more precise, *as* Sunday dinner. Grandma did not eat chicken that Sunday or for many Sundays thereafter. These days, most of us have no such intimate contact with our food before we eat it. Chicken comes from the Colonel or from the Shop-Rite down the street. We have lost touch with the way that animals are treated before they reach our plate. All too often, animals raised for food are treated cruelly—like crops instead of creatures.

While chickens in Grandma's time were allowed to flap, squawk, and strut around the chicken yard until that fateful dinner invitation came, today's chickens lead unnatural lives. They are born in hatcheries, raised in cages on special diets, then crated like cantaloupes and trucked to the processing plant. Who has not seen those trucks, with chickens huddled several to a cage, and cage piled upon cage? Feathers fly as the truck ferries its terrified cargo down the highway, and by the time it reaches its destination many chickens are already dead. Why should we worry when the chickens are going to die anyway? We should worry because we have, it seems to me, a minimal ethical responsibility to give any animal we use for food a decent life.

Some farm animals seem to have decent lives, but often we do not see the whole picture. Cattle graze peaceably in fragrant pastures and gather under trees to escape the summer sun. Yet many cattle never see those fragrant pastures. Some dairy cows are kept permanently in stalls, their engorged udders rubbed raw by the milking machine. The white flesh of veal is the flesh of calves that are deliberately weakened and kept in cages their entire short lives, calves that never rise on unsteady legs to follow their mothers through the clover. These animals live their lives behind barn doors, where no one can see their plight.

Finally, consider the lobster, perhaps the worst-treated of all our food. Once caught, it is doomed to spend the rest of its life in a small fish tank in the fluorescent-lit seafood department of a grocery store. Its claws are closed with heavy rubber bands, and it is crowded together with its fellows at the bottom of the tank. Is it fed, I wonder, or does it slowly starve as it waits to be eaten? Peered at by children, ignored by adults until it is finally bought, it ends its miserable life being boiled alive. Isn't there a more humane way to keep it and to cook it?

After the hunt, the Cherokee had a custom of thanking an animal for its sacrifice. They did not forget that it was a fellow creature, that it had the right to walk the earth and roam the forests. We, too, owe a debt to the animals we raise for food. At the very least, we can treat them like creatures and not like crops.

Questions

1. Write the thesis statement and each of its topic sentences in the following space.

   Thesis statement:_____

   _____

   Topic Sentence 1: _____

   _____

   _____

   Topic Sentence 2: _____

   _____

   _____

   Topic Sentence 3: _____

   _____

2. Which body paragraph uses two short examples rather than an extended example? _____

3. What type of introduction does the essay have?
   a. broad to narrow
   b. anecdote
   c. narrow to broad

4. Write two descriptive details from the essay that appeal to the reader's sense of sight.

   _____

   _____

_____

_____

Example Essay 2

Who are the heroes of today? One student writer provides three examples.

Quiet Heroes

Movie stars and athletes are often held up as heroes and role models because they lend their names to a cause or visit a child in the hospital, followed, of course, by a convoy of reporters. These "heroes" are showered with media attention and admiration. But in every community, there are also quiet heroes. I know several of these quiet heroes, ordinary people of all ages who work to make their community a better place.

One of my heroes is Deb, an outgoing grandmother of three who works with Habitat for Humanity. Deb can wield a hammer with the best of them, but it is her talent for feeding people that makes her contribution special. Deb spends the morning chopping, slicing, and mixing in a kitchen filled with delicious aromas. By 11:30 A.M., she is on the road to the construction site. In winter, she may bring hot vegetable soup or Brunswick stew. On warm days, lunch may be homemade pimento cheese sandwiches, fruit, and iced tea. But day after day, Deb uses her money, time, and talent to keep the Habitat crew going.

Then there is Pete, an accountant, who uses his clear, expressive voice to share the joys of reading. He is a member of the Rolling Readers, a group that visits elementary schools to interest children in reading. Pete reads every week to a class he has adopted. To keep the children reading over the summer, he gives each child a book furnished by the Rolling Readers program. Pete also shares his love of reading by volunteering for the Radio Reading Service for the blind and the print-handicapped. Once a week, he gets up at 6:00 A.M. and drives to a small recording studio. He takes the morning paper and selects the articles he will read from each section of the paper, judging from experience when he has enough to fill the hour. Then, he goes into a recording booth and reads, editing out mistakes as he goes along. By reading to others, Pete manages to turn what is usually a solitary activity into a shared joy.

Another hero is Andrea, a high school junior who has organized a "Friendship Brigade" to serve senior citizens. The Friendship Brigade mows lawns, runs errands, and does chores for low-income senior citizens that it has "adopted." The brigade has also sought business sponsorship to provide for various needs such as wheelchair ramps and smoke detectors. Andrea says that her reward is knowing that she and her friends are helping older people live more independent lives.

   To me, a hero is not necessarily a movie star who jets in for a personal appearance accompanied by a hair stylist, a personal trainer, and an appointment secretary. More often, heroes are ordinary people who, without fanfare, work to improve their community and their world.

Questions

1. Write the thesis statement and each of its topic sentences below.

   Thesis Statement: _____

   _____

   Topic Sentence 1: _____

   _____

   Topic Sentence 2: _____

   _____

   Topic Sentence 3: _____

   _____

2. How many examples of "quiet heroes" does the writer provide?_____

3. What type of introduction does the essay have? Circle the correct answer.
   a. broad to narrow
   b. anecdote
   c. contrast

4. What type of conclusion does the essay have? Circle the correct answer.
   a. full circle
   b. recommendation
   c. prediction

TOPICS FOR WRITING WITH EXAMPLES

Small Scrawls: Imaginative Short Writings

What is a Small Scrawl? A "scrawl" is something written quickly. In this case, it is a page or so of quick writing that allows you to practice a particular type of writing, in this case, writing supported by examples. Have fun with it!

Small Scrawl 1: Henry the dog

Write a small scrawl using Henry the dog, below, as an example of a particular trait in a dog (i.e., loyal, protective, friendly, mischievous, active, lazy.) Give detailed examples of Henry's behavior to convince your reader that Henry exemplifies the trait you have chosen. Use your imagination!

Small Scrawl 2: Facebook Faux Pas

Social networking sites are popular and enjoyable, but people have been fired over posts and photos on social networking sites. Some employers look at social networking sites before hiring a person and base their decision in part on what they see on an applicant's Facebook page. Write a Small Scrawl supplying several detailed examples of the kinds of things that a job seeker would be wise not to post on his or her Facebook page.

Small Scrawl 3: Follow the Leader

To borrow the plot of an uncounted number of movies, you have a friend who looks human but just happens to be an alien from a distant galaxy. Your job is to keep him safe and undetected until he is able to return home. You have already explained away his very limited use of English by saying he is from another country. But tonight, he must accompany you to dinner at the home of one of your distant relatives, who is also a top government scientist. It is essential that your friend the alien escape detection. Will he eat the centerpiece? Use a fine china plate as a Frisbee? Not if you provide the right example. Write a narrative that starts with your knock at your host's door. Provide specific examples of the things you do to guide your alien friend through this dinner party undetected. Have fun!

Essay Assignments

Example Essay 1:

Computer programs are often described in terms of their user-friendliness. What about your college campus? Is it a student-friendly place to acquire an education? Support your answer with specific examples that prove your point.

Example Essay 2: (S)hopping Mad!

When you shop, what are your pet peeves? Provide extended examples or a series of short examples of the things that make shopping a pain. A few suggestions are provided to get your thoughts flowing.

> the customer ahead of you in line who can't find her checkbook, pen, or credit card
>
> the clerk who is too busy with a phone conversation to wait on you
>
> the salesperson who follows you as if she has just seen your picture on the FBI's "Ten Most Wanted" list
>
> the shopping cart sitting in the middle of the parking place where you would like to park
>
> the grocery store shopper who waits until the total has been rung up and then says, "Oh, I have coupons here . . . somewhere"
>
> the clothing store with locked dressing rooms and no one on duty to open them

Example Essay 3: Essay-Based Assignment—It Takes All Kinds

In her essay, "Complaining," featured at the beginning of this chapter, Maya Angelou wrote about one type of person she observed while helping her grandmother in a store. Write an essay about one type of person that you have observed in a particular situation and would or would not want to emulate. Like Angelou, you will be giving multiple examples of a single type. You may have observed this type of person at work, at school, or in a social situation. Reread Angelou's essay to see how she uses language and narrative to make her examples vivid and real.

Some adjectives that describe people's attitudes are listed below to start you off:

optimistic	grumpy
pessimistic	amiable
considerate	timid
rude	brave
efficient	lazy
inefficient	hardworking

Examples in the Real World: Safety Measures

Many times, people ask how writing essays will help them in the "real world." This real-world assignment demonstrates how writing with examples might be used outside the classroom.

You are the director of security for a large mall. Many employees leave after dark, and recently, a female store manager was the victim of a carjacking as she left alone, late at night. You want to remind all employees of the mall, both male and female, of basic safety procedures they can follow to stay safe from carjackings and other types of crimes. You want to mention and give examples of such safety measures, which might include using a buddy system, going to one's car with a security guard, being observant, having keys ready and cell phone dialed to security, and other measures you might think of.

Consider the tone of your message. You do not want employees to be unduly alarmed, but you wish them to be cautious and to watch out for themselves and one another.

Building CONNECTIONS

Methods of development are tools of a writer's trade. Like a carpenter's hammer, saw, and sander, they each do a specific job. Which one should you use? It depends on the job you have to do. Some pieces of writing will require just one method, but most will require you to use more than one of the tools of your trade.

TOPICS FOR COMBINING METHODS OF DEVELOPMENT

Description, narration, and example are methods of showing or telling a reader exactly what you mean. Combining the methods adds even more power to your writing. The assignments that follow ask you to combine two or more of the methods of development discussed in this chapter.

Mixed Methods Assignment 1: Strong at the Broken Places

Essay: Narration and Example

Popular wisdom holds that adversity makes people stronger, that it is only in hard times that a person's inner strength comes through. Write a narrative and example essay describing how hard times have made you (or someone you know) a stronger person.

You may wish to make the essay primarily a narrative of a difficult time in your life, supported by examples of the way you (or the person you are writing about) became stronger. Alternatively, you may wish to write an example essay showing three different tough situations that made you (or the person you are writing about) stronger. If your essay is primarily an example essay, then at least one of your examples should be an anecdote, a brief story that demonstrates your point.

Mixed Methods Assignment 2: A Day in the Life

News Story: Narration, Description, and Example

You are a newspaper reporter. Your editor has assigned you to write a human interest story on a day in the life of a person whose life or job is difficult—a homeless person, a single parent, a person with Alzheimer's disease, a firefighter, a fast-food worker—the choice is yours. Your job in this human interest story is to allow your reader to get to know the person through narration, description, and example. You may write about someone you know or you may simply use your imagination to create a day in the life of a fictional person.

A human interest story is structured differently from an essay. The first paragraph is an introduction that tells who, what, when, and where. Since you are writing about a day in a person's life, the basic structure of your essay will be narrative, but you will also describe the person and give examples of problems that he or she encounters as the day goes on.

A human interest story should be immediate and fresh, so journalists often write them in the present tense.

Consider using an opening like the one that follows.

> Crossing the living room, Charlotte McCabe shuffles to the door in her bedroom slippers. Her shoulders are hunched, and her thin white hair is cut short. Clutching her robe around her with one hand, she tries the doorknob with the other. Her daughter looks at me and whispers apologetically, "I have to keep it locked. She wanders if I don't." Charlotte McCabe is 78 years old, and a day in her life is filled with the confusion and frustration of Alzheimer's disease.

Mixed Methods Assignment 3: Movie Time

Movie Review: Description, Narration, and Example

You are a movie critic. Your assignment is to write a review describing the best or worst movie you have ever seen. You may describe the acting, the music, the plot, or any other aspect of the movie that you particularly like or dislike. At least one of your paragraphs should contain a narrative example (a retelling) of one of the scenes in the movie.

mywritinglab   For support and practice meeting this chapter's goal, log in to **www.mywritinglab.com** and select **Essay Development: Narrating, Essay Development: Describing,** and **Essay Development: Illustrating.**

CHAPTER 9

Limiting and Ordering: Definition, Classification, and Process

> ✍ **Chapter Goal:** Analyze and write definition, classification, and process essays.

4,362 of a kind

As a writer, you have probably found that your ideas are sometimes hard to pin down—they prefer to roam free. Writing an essay can be a bit like herding sheep into a pen—finding ideas that go together, separating them from their natural environment, and confining them within the fences of an essay. The techniques of definition, classification, and process will help you to fence in your ideas—to limit and order information and to answer the questions *What is it? How many different types exist?* and *How does it work?* Although this chapter presents each technique in isolation, you may eventually find yourself using the three techniques together to define an idea, show its different variations, and describe how it works.

157

Focus on Limiting and Ordering: Thinking about Definition, Classification, and Process

Who is the man in the photo? As the police officer searches his pockets, he has the resigned look of someone who has been through it all before. Is he a career criminal?

A gangster? No, he is Lenny Bruce, a comedian who was arrested repeatedly during the 1960s for the content of his comedy act. Like many comedians today, Bruce considered any topic fair game for comedy, and his act was often raunchy and profane.

Society was less tolerant then, and Bruce was charged with obscenity in a trial that became famous in the 1960s. Celebrities testified on his behalf and newspapers reported every detail. Ultimately, Lenny Bruce was convicted of obscenity.

Lenny Bruce's trial provides a real-world example of the use of the writing techniques outlined in this chapter: definition, classification, and process. First, prosecutors had to define obscenity. Next, material from Lenny Bruce's act had to be reviewed to see if it could be classified as obscene. Finally came the process of laying out the evidence in a courtroom trial.

Reflect on It

Every profession limits and orders the work of its members in some way. Think about your own profession. What part of your job might require you to define something, classify something to show how it fits into a larger picture, or explain a process?

Source: http://en.wikipedia.org/wiki/Lenny_Bruce

Definition, Classification, and Process in Action

In this chapter, you will have the opportunity to examine and use the techniques of definition, classification, and process. In this text, each technique is explained separately, although writers seldom use them in isolation. Just as an aspiring tap dancer would learn and practice the ball change, the shuffle-flap, and the hop-step separately before employing them together to do the Shim Sham Shimmy, so is it useful for writers to learn and practice techniques of writing separately before using them together in a composition.

Before looking at definition, classification, and process separately, examine the way that a professional writer uses all three techniques together. The following essay is by Letty Cottin Pogrebin, writer, founding editor of *Ms.* magazine, and activist in feminist and Jewish causes.

The essay embodies all three of the writing techniques featured in this chapter. Mainly, the essay shows the **process** through which the author acquired her superstitions and passed them on to the next generation. Notice how Pogrebin moves through the process in chronological order, starting with her childhood and ending with an anecdote about her own child.

The author also employs **definition** in her essay. In the first paragraph, Pogrebin makes it clear that her definition of her topic will be a personal one. Notice that Pogrebin cites examples of traditional superstitions before moving on to a discussion of her own brand of superstition, a common technique in definition essays.

In the third through sixth paragraphs, the author employs **classification** as she outlines the various types of behavior that might allow the "Evil Eye" to inflict harm. Writers often use examples to illustrate classification. Notice Pogrebin's clear and sharp examples as she discusses forbidden behaviors.

Superstitious Minds

Letty Cottin Pogrebin

I am a very rational person. I tend to trust reason more than feeling. But I also   1
happen to be superstitious—in my fashion. Black cats and rabbits' feet hold no power for me. My superstitions are my mother's superstitions, the amulets and incantations she learned from her mother and taught me.

I don't mean to suggest that I grew up in an occult atmosphere. On the con-   2
trary, my mother desperately wanted me to rise above her immigrant ways and become an educated American. She tried to hide her superstitions, but I came to know them all: Slap a girl's cheeks when she first gets her period. Never take a picture of a pregnant woman. Knock wood when speaking about your good fortune. Eat the ends of bread if you want to have a boy. Don't leave a bride alone on her wedding day.

When I was growing up, my mother would often tiptoe in after I seemed to   3
be asleep, making odd noises that sounded like a cross between sucking and spitting. One night I opened my eyes and demanded an explanation. Embarrassed, she told me she was exorcising the "Evil Eye"—in case I had attracted its attention that day by being especially wonderful. She believed her kisses could suck out any envy or ill will that those less fortunate may have directed at her child.

By the time I was in my teens, I was almost on speaking terms with the Evil   4
Eye, a jealous spirit that kept track of those who had "too much" happiness and zapped them with sickness and misery to even the score. To guard against this mischief, my mother practiced rituals of interference, evasion, deference, and above all, avoidance of situations where the Evil Eye might feel at home.

This is why I wasn't allowed to attend funerals. This is also why my mother hated **5** to mend my clothes while I was wearing them. The only garment one should properly get sewn into is a shroud. To ensure that the Evil Eye did not confuse my pinafore with a burial outfit, my mother insisted that I chew thread while she sewed, thus proving myself very much alive. Outwitting the Evil Eye also accounted for her closing window shades above my bed whenever there was a full moon. The moon should only shine on cemeteries, you see; the living need protection from the spirits.

Because we were dealing with a deadly force, I also wasn't supposed to **6** say any words associated with mortality. This was hard for a 12-year-old who punctuated every anecdote with the verb "to die," as in, "You'll die when you hear this!" or "If I don't get home by ten, I'm dead." I managed to avoid using such expressions in the presence of my mother until the day my parents brought home a painting I hated and we were arguing about whether it should be displayed on our walls. Unthinking, I pressed my point with a melodramatic idiom: "That picture will hang over my dead body!" Without a word, my mother grabbed a knife and slashed the canvas to shreds.

I understand all this now. My mother emigrated in 1907 from a small Hungar- **7** ian village. The oldest of seven children, she had to go out to work before she finished the eighth grade. Experience taught her that life was unpredictable and often incomprehensible. Just as an athlete keeps wearing the same T-shirt in every game to prolong a winning streak, my mother's superstitions gave her a means of imposing order on a chaotic system. Her desire to control the fates sprang from the same helplessness that makes the San Francisco 49ers' defensive team more superstitious than its offensive team. Psychologists speculate that this is because the defense has less control; they don't have the ball.

Women like my mother never had the ball. She died when I was 15, leaving me **8** with deep regrets about what she might have been—and a growing understanding of who she was. Superstitious is one of the things she was. I wish I had a million sharp recollections of her, but when you don't expect someone to die, you don't store up enough memories. Ironically, her mystical practices are among the clearest impressions she left behind. I honor this matrilineal heritage—and to symbolize my mother's effort to control her life as I in my way try to find order in mine—I knock on wood and do not let the moon shine on those I love. My children laugh at me, but they understand that these tiny rituals have helped keep my mother alive in my mind.

A year ago, I awoke in the night and realized that my son's window blinds had **9** been removed for repair. Smiling at my own compulsion, I got a bed sheet to tack up against the moonlight and opened his bedroom door. What I saw brought tears to my eyes. There, hopelessly askew, was a blanket my son, then 18, had taped to his window like a curtain.

My mother never lived to know David, but he knew she would not want the **10** moon to shine upon him as he slept.

1. A personal definition is often quite different from a traditional definition. In what ways does Pogrebin's definition of superstition vary from a more traditional definition?
2. When writers describe a process, they use sequential or chronological order. As Pogrebin describes how she acquired her superstitions, she uses chronological order. Look at the essay and identify three stages of Pogrebin's life that were touched by superstition.
3. Classification of ideas deals with types or kinds. In the essay, Pogrebin outlines various types of behavior that allowed the Evil Eye to operate. What types of behavior does she mention? What do they have in common?

📝 Definition

mywritinglab

Visit MyWriting Lab for additional practice with definition.

When you think of definitions, you probably think of the dictionary. If you want to know the definition of *curmudgeon* or the difference between an *ectomorph* and an *endomorph,* you turn to the dictionary for definitions. Similarly, when you want to define an idea or concept in detail, you may write a definition essay.

A dictionary entry provides a good example of a definition. Examine the sample dictionary definition of the word *burden,* and then answer the questions that follow.

Sample Dictionary Definition

bur'den (ber'dan) *n.* **1,** something carried; a load. **2,** something borne with difficulty, as care, grief, etc. **3,** an encumbrance. **4,** a main theme; a refrain.

(from The New American Webster Handy College Dictionary, New Third Edition)

Questions

1. Would you characterize the definition as brief or extended?
2. Does the entry provide any clue about how the person writing the entry felt about the subject, or is it strictly factual?
3. Does the dictionary definition include any examples?

As you may have noticed, a dictionary definition is extremely brief and entirely factual. However, there are two very brief examples in definition 2—*care* and *grief.*

A definition essay is like a dictionary definition in some ways. For example, a definition essay, like a dictionary definition, attempts to capture the essence of something—an object, a feeling, or a task—in words.

However, unlike the writer of a dictionary definition, you have the luxury of using many words in your definition essay. Instead of a four-word definition, you may have a four-hundred-word definition.

A definition essay might answer questions like the following:

- What is a status symbol?
- What are the characteristics of a leader?
- What does the word *duty* mean to you?

Laying the Groundwork for Writing a Definition
Visualizing

Look at the photograph of the couple with the "Just Married" sign attached to their car. Think about the images and experiences that help you define what marriage is. Then think about how you would define marriage. Do you believe that your definition is different from the couple's definition?

Planning

Before you write a definition of marriage, consider other definitions. How would the state define marriage? How would the church define marriage? How do those definitions differ from one another and from your personal definition?

Writing

In a paragraph, write your personal definition of marriage.

Using Examples in Definition Essays

Were you surprised that the dictionary entry for *burden* included an example? Dictionary entries often contain examples. Examples work well in definitions because they take an abstract idea, such as *devotion,* and make it into a concrete illustration such as *My family tells me that my dog Lucky waits for hours at the window and barks with joy when he sees me on the front walk.* Definitions tend to be general, and examples help to add the specificity that readers of both dictionaries and essays appreciate. Like the writer of the dictionary entry, you may decide to use an example to illustrate your definition. Instead of an example in a single word, however, you may provide an example in one or two sentences or even a whole paragraph.

Building CONNECTIONS

In writing, using one method of development to support another is a common technique. Examples are often used to support and illustrate definitions. The more methods of development you know how to use, the more useful tools you will have in your writer's toolbox.

Subjective and Objective Definitions

As you examined the sample dictionary entry, you may have noticed that it was strictly factual, that it did not reflect its writer's opinion. Such factual definitions are called **objective definitions.** When you define something objectively, your task is relatively simple. An objective definition is a factual definition. You define a person, place, thing, or idea by providing facts such as physical characteristics, function or use, how it works, and its history. To define a mosquito objectively, for instance, you might say it is a winged insect that draws blood from humans and animals and sometimes spreads disease. An objective definition is the type that you would write when answering an essay question or writing a research paper.

Real-World Writing: Is Subjectivity Bad?

How often have you heard people say, "Oh, that's just an opinion," as if opinions don't count? Such statements give subjectivity a bad reputation.

True, there are some forms of writing in which subjectivity is not appropriate—factual reports, encyclopedia entries, and scientific experiments, for example.

However, subjectivity is perfectly appropriate in many types of writing—letters to the editor, personal essays, and journal entries, to name a few. The best subjective writing is backed up by facts, so it's not "just" an opinion—it's a well-supported, well-thought-out opinion.

A **subjective definition**, on the other hand, is a personal definition—one that reflects your attitude toward your subject. It may still follow the same general pattern as the objective definition, but it goes beyond the merely factual. If you were defining a mosquito subjectively, you might say that it is a pesky insect that spoils summer evenings by hovering around its innocent victims, waiting for an opportunity to suck their blood.

A subjective definition, the kind found in personal essays and paragraphs, always reflects the writer's feelings about the subject. In a personal definition, a new parent might define love as a feeling that is overwhelmingly tender, yet fierce and protective. In contrast, someone who has recently been disappointed in romance might define love as a risky game that too often ends in disappointment.

EXERCISE 1	OBJECTIVE AND SUBJECTIVE DEFINITIONS

Read the following paragraphs and answer the questions that follow.

Paragraph A

Denial is a type of psychological defense mechanism that allows a person to cope with a disturbing event by refusing to believe that it exists. For instance, a parent confronted with evidence that his child is using drugs might refuse to believe it. A person diagnosed with a serious illness, such as cancer, might believe that she is really healthy and that she has been misdiagnosed. When a loved one dies, the first reaction is often disbelief. Denial does not solve a problem, but it temporarily reduces the psychological discomfort that it causes.

Paragraph B

    To some, pottery may be simply a craft, but to me, it is a kind of therapy. When I sit at my potter's wheel, I am in control. A lump of wet clay turns on the wheel and, under my hands, takes shape as a bowl or a vase. As I shape the clay, life seems once again within my control. If I can shape clay into a pot, I can handle a difficult boss or a deadline at work. When I look at the lopsided pots and homely pitchers I made when I first started, then see the symmetrical urns and large, graceful bowls I now make, I have hope that whatever situation I am facing, whether it is a problem with my health or with a relationship, will improve. If practice can make me so much better at pottery, then practice will also help me handle difficult times with grace and humor. Pottery always helps restore my optimism and my sense of control.

- Which paragraph contains an objective definition? _____
- List an example used in each paragraph.

_____

_____

_____

_____

Wordsmith's Corner: Examples of Writing Developed by Definition

Two student essays developed by definition follow. Read each and answer the questions that follow.

Definition Essay 1

The writer of this essay takes an old subject—manners—and gives the reader an updated definition.

Manners for the Twenty-First Century

    When the older man let the door swing shut behind him, I thought he did not see the woman entering the health club behind him. She caught the door before it shut and went through, holding it so I could enter behind her. As I walked into the men's locker room behind him, he said, "I don't hold doors for women anymore. These days, women will tell you off if you try to hold a door for them." I just looked at him, amazed. For most people, a changing world does not alter the need to be polite. The man's narrow-mindedness prompted me to construct my own definition of good manners for the twenty-first century.

First of all, politeness in the twenty-first century does not reinforce stereotypes. The "helpless woman" stereotype that may have once prompted men to hold doors for women is gone, but courtesy lives on. As a man, I should not hesitate to open the door for a woman, but it's also appropriate if she opens it for me. Stereotypical ideas about people with disabilities need to be revised, too. They are not helpless, nor are they invisible. My friend Miko, who uses a wheelchair, says she appreciates it when people hold an elevator door for her. But she wishes they would look at her, not at the floor or at her companion. And while stereotypes about rank, race, or age might at one time have determined who was considered worthy of politeness, that is no longer the case. In the twenty-first century, everyone—from the bank president to the homeless person on the street—is worthy of the effort of being polite.

Politeness in the twenty-first century also means considerately sharing space in a crowded world. Having good manners means not smoking in crowded public places where second-hand smoke might be offensive to others. Increasingly, politeness has also come to include not wearing strong aftershave or cologne to the office or the theater. Similarly, loud, boneshaking car stereos are usually enjoyed only by those who play them. Consideration for others means keeping noise at a moderate level. While politeness might have once meant enjoying a conversation with a seatmate on a plane, now it often means leaving her alone to work on her laptop computer. The more crowded the world becomes, the more it is necessary to share space considerately.

Communications technology in the twenty-first century has brought a whole new set of rules. Texting or talking on a cell phone in a theater or a classroom is considered bad manners, as is hanging up on someone's voicemail after the beep has sounded. Email requires new rules, too. Sending email without a subject line or trying to sell an exercise bike through company email can waste people's time and is therefore considered a breach of etiquette. In email messages or on social networks, typing in all-capital letters is considered "shouting." The technology may be fairly new, but the basic principle of consideration for others has not changed.

 Manners are not dusty relics of a former age. They change with the world and must be tailored for each new century. Manners for the twenty-first century, as in previous centuries, are simply rules that help the world run more smoothly.

Questions

1. Which introductory technique does the writer use? Circle the correct answer.
   a. broad-to-narrow
   b. narrow-to-broad
   c. anecdote

2. Write the thesis statement on the line below. Does the writer's thesis indicate that his definition will be subjective or objective?

   _____

   _____

   _____

3. Write each topic sentence in the space provided.

   _____

   _____

   _____

   _____

   _____

4. Write in the following space each example that supports the topic sentence in the second body paragraph.

   _____

   _____

   _____

Definition Essay 2

The writer of this essay defines foot binding, a custom practiced for hundreds of years in China among the upper classes. The practice was officially banned by the Chinese government in 1911.

Bound by Tradition

As I lay nursing painful heel spurs that made the kitchen and the oatmeal raisin cookies my husband had baked seem impossibly far away, I began to reflect on the ancient Chinese custom of foot binding. When I first heard about it back in grade school, I was fascinated. It was, we were told, an ancient custom for Chinese girls to have their feet bound so that they would remain small. I pictured women in kimonos tottering merrily on tiny, delicate feet and wished that I had feet so small. Over the years, however, I have found an adult understanding and a darker definition of this ancient custom.

Binding the feet was a painful way to acquire what was then considered beauty. When, as a teenager, I read of a young girl who wept each time her feet were bound, it dawned on me for the first time that preventing the growth of a body part involved pain. Though some modern practices may seem strangely similar—torturing our feet into four-inch-high heels or starving ourselves to pencil thinness, for example—at least we have a choice. An upper-class Chinese girl of that era had no alternative. Custom decreed that her feet be bound, and so her toes were folded under and her feet tightly wrapped in soaked bandages that shrank as they dried. The girl's parents believed they were ensuring her future, for no young man of good family could be expected to marry a woman with large peasant's feet.

Bound feet were also testament to a woman's aristocracy and marriageability. They served as public evidence that she was from a good and wealthy family. But there was a darker, more private reason that men liked bound feet: They were considered erotic. The bound foot was kept under wraps for the husband alone, to be admired behind closed doors. Well those doors might be closed, for the bindings concealed what to modern eyes would seem a shameful secret. Foot binding did not simply make feet small; it deformed them. The toes were folded permanently underneath the foot, making it misshapen and difficult to walk on. But at that time and in that place, the bound foot was considered more beautiful than the foot as nature created it.

The most horrible aspect of this ancient custom is that it deprived these supposedly privileged women of freedom. They never knew the childish pleasure of stomping through piles of crackling leaves just to hear the noise they made. As young women, they did not dance to the music of a lute under the full moon or romp through a sunlit garden with their dogs and children. It is doubtful that these women so much as walked to the kitchen for almond cookies and tea. As women of privilege, they were brought whatever they needed and were carried by servants wherever they wanted to go. If they were independent-minded women, if they would have preferred to range over the hills alone or to wander so far along a dry creek bed that they could no longer hear the bickering of servants or the shouting of children, it did not matter. They were carried, or they did not go.

As I reflected on that bitter bygone custom, I suddenly needed to feel my feet under me. My walk to the kitchen for the oatmeal raisin cookies was slow and painful, but I was thankful to walk on feet that would again dance, again hurry me forward on matters of no particular urgency, again run for joy. The cookies were plump and packed with raisins. I savored every bite.

Questions

1. Which two introductory techniques does the essay's introduction combine?
    a. broad-to-narrow and quotation
    b. narrow-to-broad and historical
    c. anecdote and historical
    d. anecdote and broad-to-narrow

2. In the space below, write the thesis statement of the essay.

    _____

    _____

3. In the space below, write the topic sentence of each supporting paragraph.

    _____

    _____

    _____

    _____

    _____

    _____

4. In the topic sentence of the third body paragraph, the word *most* indicates that the author is using
    a. chronological order.
    b. emphatic order.
    c. sandwich order.

5. Though the definition is partly subjective, revealing the writer's opinion, it also includes much objective detail. Circle the letter of the detail that is subjective.

   a. Foot binding involved wrapping the feet in soaked bandages that shrank as they dried.

   b. The toes were folded permanently underneath the foot, making it misshapen and difficult to walk on.

   c. The deliberate deforming of the foot is shameful.

   d. At that time, having bound feet made a woman more marriageable.

6. What type of conclusion does the essay have?

   a. prediction

   b. recommendation

   c. full circle

TOPICS FOR WRITING USING DEFINITION

Small Scrawls: Imaginative Short Writings

What is a Small Scrawl? A "scrawl" is something written quickly. In this case, it is a page or so of quick writing that allows you to practice a particular type of writing, in this case, definition. Have fun with it!

Small Scrawl 1: It's for Your Own Good

You are the owner of Rowf, a mixed-breed dog. You become convinced that neutering Rowf is the best thing to do. It's best for Rowf, best for you, and best in terms of the pet population. Write a definition of neutering based on these beliefs.

Small Scrawl 2: It's Unnecessary Surgery

You are Rowf, from the assignment above. Define neutering from the canine point of view. (Cat lovers—feel free to substitute a cat for Rowf.)

Small Scrawl 3: Happiness Is . . .

"Happiness is a warm puppy."
  —Charles Schultz
"Happiness is nothing more than good health and a bad memory."
  —Albert Schweitzer
"Happiness is having a large, loving, caring, close-knit family . . . in another city."
  —George Burns
"Happiness is a warm gun."
  —Lennon/McCartney song

Happiness is defined differently by different people. How do you define it? Write a Small Scrawl defining what happiness is for you.

Essay Assignments

Definition Essay 1: Definition of a Role

Write a definition essay about a role that you play in your life. It may be the role of student, friend, son or daughter, mother or father, husband, wife, or other significant other. It may be a work role, such as restaurant server, bank teller, or paramedic. Your definition will be a subjective one because you will infuse into it your enjoyment or dislike of the role and your attitudes toward it.

Definition Essay 2: Defining an Activity

Write a definition essay on an activity that you enjoy, such as fishing, dance, aerobics, reading, or shopping.

Definition Essay 3: What Is a Hero?

Write an essay giving your definition of a hero.

Begin by prewriting to generate a list of the characteristics of a hero. You will use these characteristics as a basis for your three body paragraphs. Then, make a list of people who possess these characteristics. These may be actual people (your sister; Dr. Martin Luther King, Jr.) or general categories (caregivers; firefighters). The people will serve as examples in your paragraphs.

Your thesis, then, will list the characteristics of a hero, and your paragraphs will illustrate those characteristics with specific examples.

Definition in the Real-World: Job Description

Many times, people ask how writing essays will help them in the "real world." This real-world assignment demonstrates how writing a definition might be used outside the classroom.

Occasionally, employees will be asked to write (or to update) their job descriptions so that management will have a clear idea of what everyone does. Invariably, these employees find that their jobs are much more complex than they ever imagined.

When you write a job description, you are, in essence, writing a definition of that job. You may support that definition with specific examples of the tasks that you perform on the job.

Write a job description of the job you now hold or the job you aspire to.

✐ Classification

mywritinglab
Visit MyWriting Lab for additional practice with division/classification.
Whether you know it or not, **classification** comes naturally to you. From the time you are born, you explore. You discover that some things are pleasurable and others are painful, that some things are edible and others are not. Those are your first lessons in classification.

By the time you reach adulthood, you divide people, articles of clothing, words, teachers, and ways of behaving into different types or categories so automatically that you are barely aware of it. When you answer a classmate's question, "What kind of teacher is Dr. Burton?" or reply to a friend who asks what kind of day you have had, you are classifying.

Writing a classification essay allows you to use your categorizing skills to answer questions like the ones that follow.

- What kinds of extracurricular activities benefit students most?
- What types of students do you least enjoy having as classmates?
- How would you classify the fans that you see at a football game?

Laying the Groundwork for Writing Classification Papers

Visualizing

Look at the photograph of the dangerous curve in the road. Imagine cars going around that curve. Some drivers are cautious, others speed; some clutch the steering wheel with a death grip, others casually drape one hand across it. Look at the drivers in your mind; see their faces, anxious or relaxed or gleefully demonic.

Planning

Think about the drivers you have visualized and other kinds of drivers you have encountered. What different types are there? What specific term would you use for each?

Writing

In a paragraph, describe how two of the types of drivers you have listed might approach the dangerous curve at night.

Establishing a Basis for Classification

In the following list, which item does not belong?

Kinds of Teachers

a. the drill sergeant

b. the comedian

c. the sociology teacher

If you chose *c,* you are right. You have recognized, consciously or subconsciously, that the first two have the same basis for classification—teaching style. The third item has a different basis for classification—subject matter.

Building CONNECTIONS

Classifications, especially those that are your own invention, may often begin with a definition. For example, if you classified "teacher" into three groups—the drill sergeant, the comedian, and the prima donna—you might begin each body paragraph with a definition: "The drill sergeant is a professor who runs the classroom as if it were boot camp."

When you write a classification essay, it is important that your classification have a single basis or underlying principle. If it does not, then your categories of classification may be so close that they overlap or so far-flung that they seem to have no connection with one another.

In the example above, "sociology teacher" overlaps all three categories since sociology teachers have a variety of teaching styles. A single basis for classification ensures that your categories of classification are separate and distinct.

Categories of classification that are too diverse can be illustrated with a different example. A writer who has listed "airplane" and "bus" under the heading "types of transportation" would not be likely to add "camel" to the list, even though a camel can be a mode of transportation in some parts of the world. The other two types are modern forms of mass transportation, so "camel" does not fit in.

EXERCISE 2 | CLASSIFYING ITEMS IN A LIST

Fill in the blanks with the appropriate words to classify each list of items.

1. Kinds of _____   Basis for classification: _____
   a. Dalmatian
   b. Labrador retriever
   c. cocker spaniel
   d. poodle

2. Kinds of _____   Basis for classification: _____
   a. French
   b. Italian
   c. ranch
   d. blue cheese

3. Kinds of _____   Basis for classification: _____
   a. heavy metal
   b. rap
   c. country
   d. pop

4. Kinds of _____   Basis for classification: _____
   a. carving
   b. fillet
   c. steak
   d. pocket

5. Kinds of _____   Basis for classification: _____
   a. rocky road
   b. Neapolitan
   c. fudge ripple
   d. coffee

6. Kinds of _____   Basis for classification: _____
   a. pepperoni
   b. sausage

    c. cheese

    d. mushrooms

7. Kinds of _____   Basis for classification: _____

    a. dining

    b. coffee

    c. end

    d. card

8. Kinds of _____   Basis for classification: _____

    a. skim (fat-free)

    b. 1%

    c. 2%

    d. 4%

9. Kinds of _____   Basis for classification: _____

    a. rollerball

    b. ballpoint

    c. felt-tip

    d. fountain

10. Kinds of _____   Basis for classification: _____

    a. bow tie

    b. elbow

    c. angel hair

    d. twist

EXERCISE 3 FINDING A BASIS FOR CLASSIFICATION

Part 1: Circle the letter of the item that does not belong in the following lists. Then write the basis for classification of the other items in the blank.

1. Cars   Basis for classification: _____

    a. Ford

    b. Mazda

    c. sports car

    d. Nissan

2. Cats   Basis for classification: _____

    a. tiger

    b. tabby

    c. snow leopard

    d. cheetah

3. Restaurants   Basis for classification: _____

    a. Mexican

    b. Italian

    c. Thai

    d. fast food

4. Schools   Basis for classification: _____

    a. fewer than 200 students

    b. 201–500 students

    c. high school

    d. 501–1000 students

5. Dances   Basis for classification: _____

    a. tango

    b. Macarena

    c. senior prom

    d. electric slide

Part 2: As entry *d* in each list, add one item that fits the basis for classification.

6. Drugs

    a. caplet

    b. liquid

    c. patch

    d. _____

7. Games

    a. solitaire

    b. hearts

    c. go fish

    d. _____

8. Books

    a. geography

    b. biology

    c. history

    d. _____

9. Tools
   a. trowel
   b. shovel
   c. hedge clippers
   d. _____

10. Hair
   a. brown
   b. black
   c. red
   d. _____

| EXERCISE 4 | FINDING THE POINT THAT DOES NOT FIT |

The following paragraph contains one point that is on a different basis for classification than the other two. Read the paragraph, and then answer the questions that follow.

Kinds of Exercisers

At the gym where I work out, three types of exercisers stand out from the crowd. The first type, the struggler, breaks into a sweat just at the sight of an exercise bike. Strugglers walk five laps around the track and then stop, huffing and puffing, to rest on a bench before attempting another few laps. In contrast to strugglers are the fashion plates, who always have the latest in exercise wear. Exercising in front of the mirror, fashion plates can admire their colorful leotards, smartly cut shorts, or new athletic shoes. Even when they exercise, fashion plates never have limp, straggly hair or sweat-stained clothing. They always look their best. Finally, there are the athletes, who do not mind working up a sweat and are dedicated to fitness. In a Zumba class, they step wider and shake more vigorously than anyone else, even after an hour on the treadmill. Before they leave, they may swim a few laps in the pool just to cool off. Whether they are suffering strugglers, self-absorbed fashion plates, or dedicated athletes, these exercisers are fun to watch as I struggle through my own workout.

1. Which type of exerciser is not classified on the same basis as the others?

   _____

2. What is the basis for classification of the other two points?

   _____

Wordsmith's Corner: Examples of Writing Developed through Classification

Following are two student essays developed through classification. Read each and answer the questions that follow.

Classification Essay 1

Drawing on observation and her own experience as a shopper, this writer divides shoppers into different categories.

Kinds of Shoppers

"Why do women love to shop?" my husband asks. I point out that it's a strange question from a man who, when it comes to pulling out a credit card, is quicker on the draw than a gunslinger in the Old West. I am convinced that men, despite their protests to the contrary, enjoy shopping as much as women do. But as a woman, I know female shoppers and I believe I know what motivates them. Some are bargain hunters, some are pleasure seekers, and others are social shoppers.

For bargain hunters, shopping is a game of strategy and skill, and saving money is the motivation. My friend Renee is a perfect example of a bargain hunter. She never shops without a plan. Her motto is, "Never pay full price for anything." This past October, when the breeze picked up and the temperature dropped, we went shopping. I watched her bypass the tables of long-sleeved shirts and racks of dresses in deep colors with names like "pumpkin" and "eggplant." On a clearance table, she found marked-down shorts and tank tops in tropical colors. Then we went to the men's department, where she expertly searched through a picked-over display of short-sleeved shirts and khaki pants to find her husband's sizes. Buying clothes at the end of the season, she says, lets her buy twice the clothes at half the price.

Unlike the bargain hunter, a pleasure seeker shops because it feels good. Shopping is therapy, celebration, and comfort. I admit to being a pleasure seeker. If I am feeling down, the cure is a trip to the mall for aromatherapy at Lotions and Potions. Placing strawberry-guava shower gel, cucumber-mint facial masque, or mango-honey lip pomade into a wicker shopping basket, I feel my mood lift, and by the time I present my Visa card at the register, I am feeling downright cheerful. Celebrations call for a soft velour dress or just the right pair of earrings. Even an ordinary Saturday becomes special if I can pick up a novel or a few magazines and stop by

Candyland for a treat to enjoy as I read. Shopping is always a mood enhancer for me.

For the last type of shopper, shopping is a social act. Social shoppers travel in pairs or threes or even groups of five or six. Laughing and chatting, they flit through the stores, fingering cashmere, modeling hats, and spritzing colognes on one another. Since the purpose of the trip is mainly social, making purchases is optional. One subgroup of the social shopping group, however, shops seriously, usually in pairs. These shoppers don't need a mirror; they have one another. Their voices ring through the dressing room: "Lydia, what do you think of this peach color on me?" "Mom, does this bathing suit make me look fat?" "Ooo-wee, girl, that skirt looks good on you!" If the shopping trip is fruitful, so much the better. If not, the social shopper is undaunted. There is, after all, a food court and a sit-down restaurant that serves yummy pumpernickel croutons with its salad. The social shopper almost never has a shopping trip she doesn't enjoy, unless she has to shop alone.

Why do so many women love to shop? The reasons are as varied as the individuals themselves. As long as money, pleasure, and companionship motivate humans, the bargain hunter, the pleasure seeker, and the social shopper will keep the cash registers humming at shopping centers everywhere.

Questions

1. What type of introduction does this essay have?
   a. narrow-to-broad
   b. historical
   c. anecdote
   d. contrast

2. In the space below, write the thesis statement of the essay and the topic sentence of each body paragraph.

   _____

   _____

   _____

   _____

   _____

   _____

3. What is the basis for classification in this essay on types of shoppers?
   a. amount of money spent
   b. motivation for shopping
   c. type of merchandise bought
   d. type of store visited

4. Which body paragraph begins with a transitional topic sentence?

   _____

5. What type of conclusion does the essay have?
   a. prediction
   b. recommendation
   c. summary
   d. quotation

Classification Essay 2

The writer of this essay explores people's attitudes toward life.

Attitudes Toward Life

I have always heard it said that people are the same under the skin, and in many ways it's true. People have similar impulses, hopes, and dreams. However, people vary widely in their attitudes toward life.

A person with a negative attitude puts a pessimistic twist on life, even when good things happen. If she has a front-row center seat at the concert, she complains that her neck hurts from sitting so close or that the music is too loud. If he has a new job, he complains that the hours are too long and the benefits inadequate. When I congratulated my friend Tim on his new job, his response was typically negative. "It's okay, I guess," he said, "but the money and the chances for advancement aren't that great. I'm just biding my time until something else comes along." Negative people can turn even good fortune into bad luck.

A positive person, on the other hand, can find the good in almost anything. My coworker Mario always says, "Something good is going to happen today." At first, I thought Mario's good cheer was just a false front. But I have worked with him for a while now and I have begun to see that there is nothing fake about his optimism. He really does look for good things to happen, and he sees failure as an incentive to work harder. Any doubt I had about Mario's attitude evaporated when he confided that his wife has cancer. "It's made me realize what's important in my life," he said, "and it's made me closer to her than ever before." Even tragedy has its positive side to a positive person like Mario.

The person with a wait-and-see attitude withholds judgment on everything. If you ask him how he is today, he may cautiously reply, "So far, so good." He sees no point in committing himself when unexpected disaster or great good fortune may befall him at any time. My elderly neighbor is a classic example of the wait-and-see person. The last time I saw her, I asked about her children and grandchildren. She told me that her daughter and son-in-law had just celebrated their twenty-fifth wedding anniversary. When I commented on how long their marriage had lasted, my neighbor shrugged. "Yes, I guess it's a good marriage," she said. "Time will tell."

Attitudes toward life shape the way we see the world. A negative person finds the bad in everything, while a positive person looks for the good. And the person with a wait-and-see attitude, like someone watching a play, sits back and waits for the next act to unfold.

Questions

1. What two techniques are used in the introduction?
   a. narrow-to-broad and contrast
   b. quotation and contrast
   c. anecdote and quotation
   d. anecdote and contrast

2. In the following space, write the thesis statement of the essay and the topic sentence of each body paragraph.

   _____

   _____

   _____

   _____

   _____

   _____

3. What basis does the author use to classify people's attitudes?
   a. gender of the person
   b. how the attitude was acquired
   c. type of attitude.
   d. age of the person

4. Which body paragraph contains three short examples?
   a. body paragraph 1
   b. body paragraph 2
   c. body paragraph 3

TOPICS FOR WRITING USING CLASSIFICATION

Small Scrawls: Imaginative Short Writings

What is a Small Scrawl? A "scrawl" is something written quickly. In this case, it is a page or so of quick writing that allows you to practice a particular type of writing, in this case, classification. Have fun with it!

Small Scrawl 1: Kinds of People

Write a Small Scrawl classifying and describing one of the following categories of people.

gum chewers	doughnut eaters	cell phone users
coffee drinkers	texters	grocery shoppers

Small Scrawl 2: Funny Food Classification

Usually, we classify food on the basis of nutrition or taste. Just for fun, classify your foods according to color (i.e., red, brown, purple, green) or shape (i.e., round, square, cylindrical, spherical).

Small Scrawl 3: Treasure Trunk

You find that you have inherited an old trunk from great-uncle that you never knew you had. It is a large trunk containing an intriguing assortment of items. Do some prewriting to imagine what those items are; then classify the items into three groups which have a common basis for classification. For example, if you were classifying them according to value, your groups might include items with no value, items with sentimental value, and items with monetary value. Or you might imagine you have found a trunk full of sports memorabilia and classify the items according to sport (i.e., baseball, football, and basketball). Use your imagination and have fun!

Essay Assignments

Classification Essay 1: Relationship in Ruins

Discuss the kinds of problems that can ruin a relationship. It is up to you to decide what the relationship is—it may be a romance, a friendship, a marriage, a student-teacher relationship, a relationship with a coworker, or a relationship with a neighbor. Choose the type of relationship that you wish to discuss, then write an essay about the types of problems that might ruin it.

Classification Essay 2: Classy Classification

Write an essay classifying one of the following items having to do with classes.

assignments	tests
desks	schedules
professors	textbooks
classmates	note takers

Classification Essay 3: It Takes All Kinds

Write a classification essay categorizing one of the types of people below.

pet owners	parents
drivers	neighbors
dates	sports fans
friends	coworkers
teachers	classmates

Classification Assignment: Real-World Topic— Designing a New Program

Many times, people ask how writing essays will help them in the "real world." This real-world assignment demonstrates how writing using classification might be used outside the classroom.

You are part of a human resources team at a medium-sized company. Profits have been so good that the company has set aside five million dollars to fund a program that will benefit employees and the company. Each team member has been asked to come up with ideas about the kinds of programs that might be offered. The only restrictions are that both the company and the employees should benefit from the programs. For example, wellness programs such as exercise, weight loss, or stop-smoking clinics would benefit both the employee, who would be healthier, and the company, which would theoretically benefit because healthier employees would use less sick leave and incur lower health insurance costs. Incentive programs offering rewards for increased productivity would similarly benefit both the rewarded employees and the company, which would benefit from the increased productivity.

Write an essay describing three types of programs that might be developed. Give examples of how each program would work and describe how it would benefit both the employees and the company.

Process

mywritinglab

Visit MyWriting Lab for additional practice with process.

When you write a **process** essay, you describe how something is done or how it works. Process writing surrounds you. Recipes, instruction manuals, and any of the many self-help books that offer advice on how to become fit, lose weight, save money, or lead a more satisfying life are all examples of process writing. A chapter in your American government text that tells you how a bill becomes a law, the page in your biology text on the life cycle of the fruit fly, and the fine print on the back of your credit card statement that explains how interest is applied are also examples of process writing.

Process essays typically answer questions like the ones that follow.

- What is the best way to handle a broken relationship?
- What is your recipe for an enjoyable vacation?
- Describe an effective process for setting and reaching goals.

Laying the Groundwork for Process Writing

Visualizing

Look at the photograph of the young man and woman. What is happening in the photograph? How might it end?

Planning

What process are these two individuals engaged in? What are the steps in this process? Do the steps usually occur in a different order, or is the order the same every time? Which stage of the process is the couple in?

Writing

In a paragraph, list the steps in the process in a logical order, giving a one-sentence explanation of what happens in each step.

Organizing the Process Essay

Some processes are **fixed** processes—that is, ones in which the order of the steps cannot vary. If you tell someone how to change the oil in a car, for instance, you can't place the step "add new oil" before the step "drain old oil." If you explain how a bill becomes a law, you can't place "goes to the president for signing or veto" before "approved by both houses of Congress." If you are describing a fixed process, list the steps in chronological order or step-by-step order.

Other processes are **loose** processes. They have no fixed, predetermined order. Loose processes include such things as handling money wisely or becoming physically fit. In describing these processes, it is up to the writer to choose the most logical order.

Imagine that you are writing a paper on handling money wisely. You decide that the steps involved include paying down debt, developing a spending plan, and saving for the future. Developing a spending plan seems logical as a first point, but you can't decide whether to place "saving" or "paying down debt" next in the order. You may say, "It's impossible to save any meaningful amount until debts are paid. Therefore, paying off debt before saving is logical." Or you may reason like this: "Most people stay in debt for most of their lives. If it's not a credit card, it's a car loan or a mortgage. The important thing is to pay yourself first, no matter what." Either order is logical. What is important is that you have thought about it and chosen the order that best suits your own philosophy.

Building CONNECTIONS

As you analyze the process you plan to write about, you will find yourself breaking the process into pieces in a way that feels a lot like classification. Process and classification have a lot in common and can often be combined. An essay titled "The Road to Alcoholism," for instance, might mainly describe the process by which someone became an alcoholic. However, it would probably also break the process into definite stages—a form of classification.

One important point to remember when organizing the "how-to" process paper is that many processes require tools or must be done under certain conditions. Ideally, a "how-to" paper should be written so clearly and logically that the reader could carry out the process on the first read-through. Usually, then, the first step of your process will direct the reader to gather tools and make preparations. Whether you're telling your reader how to make a pastry or how to defuse a bomb, no reader will appreciate being led to a crucial point and then being instructed to use a tool that isn't handy.

Introducing the Process Essay

If you are explaining a process with wide appeal to readers, almost any of the types of introduction discussed in Chapter 4 will serve your purpose. However, if you are writing about a process of more limited interest, you may find it useful to motivate a specific audience and explain the value of or reason for the process.

When you are motivating a specific audience, think about who might find your process useful. If you are writing about study strategies, your target audience would be students. If your topic is "choosing a day-care center," your target audience would be parents of young children. Once you have identified your audience, think about how the process will benefit that audience. Readers are more likely to be motivated to read your essay if you can show them that the process has value for them.

Example of Introduction to Motivate

Choosing the right day care for your child can mean the difference between a happy child who looks forward to the fun and friends at day care and a child who hangs back in the mornings, reluctant to leave the house. A child's attitude toward day care is often a precursor to his or her attitude about school. Because the choice of day care is so vital, it pays to know what to look for in a day-care center.

Concluding the Process Essay

The conclusion of a process paper should answer the question, *What is the value of the process?* If your paper is a "how-to" process paper, the answer to the question may motivate the reader to carry out the process. If the paper is an explanation of how something works, the conclusion serves as a reminder of the value of or reason for the process.

Example of Conclusion to Motivate

Getting your finances in order is hard work. But consider the rewards. You will no longer be feeding money into the black hole of credit card debt to pay for long-forgotten purchases. And when you get mail from the bank, it will be your savings statement, not an overdraft notice.

Example of Conclusion to Explain the Value of the Process

As the hatchlings make their way instinctively toward the sea, some are plucked from the sand and eaten by hungry gulls. Turtles that survive that crucial journey to the sea may one day return to this very beach to deposit their eggs and begin the cycle of life anew.

Wordsmith's Corner: Examples of Process Writing

Following are two student process essays. Read each and answer the questions that follow.

Process Essay 1

This essay describes a process of self-discovery as the writer confronts a learning disability.

Discovering My Abilities

On my report cards, my teachers used to write, "Erica doesn't apply herself" or "Erica lacks motivation." When I decided to go to college, I thought I had the motivation I needed. But I still had trouble finishing what I started, and I always felt frustrated, disorganized, and ten steps behind the rest of the class. In desperation, I visited the college's counseling center and began a process of self-discovery that turned my life around.

My journey to self-discovery began the day I walked into the counseling center. I came in shyly, just planning to pick up a few brochures. But the counselor, Dr. Fordham, invited me into her office and asked me about my study problems. I told her that I would start writing an essay and find myself playing solitaire on the computer. I would get most of the work done on a term paper, and then resistance would set in and I would find excuses not to finish. I habitually lost assignment sheets, syllabi, and library books. I was my own worst enemy. After we had talked a bit longer, Dr. Fordham said that some of the habits I mentioned could be symptoms of attention deficit disorder, or ADD. I told her I did not have a learning disability; I was just lazy and disorganized. Dr. Fordham did not press, but along with the study skills brochures she gave me an information sheet on ADD.

The next step in my process of self-discovery involved overcoming denial. When I read the brochure, I recognized myself immediately. However, I was not about to be labeled "learning disabled" at my age. But I reasoned that getting more information could not hurt, so I searched the Internet. Along with other information about ADD, I found an adult ADD checklist. The checklist said that experiencing twenty or more of the symptoms could indicate a tendency toward ADD. I had checked forty-six of them. It was becoming harder for me to deny that I had a problem.

The most difficult step in the process was getting up the courage to be tested. I finally talked to my parents. "So what if you have a learning disability?" my practical mother said, "It's not going to change who you are." My father did some research, and told me that Einstein had a learning disability. Finally, I overcame my reluctance and went to an ADD center that Dr. Fordham recommended. The tests confirmed that I had ADD. Somehow, knowing the truth lifted a weight from my shoulders. Now I was ready to do something about my problem. When a doctor at the center suggested Ritalin, I was doubtful. I had always thought it was some sort of tranquilizer for unruly kids. Dr. Sims told me it was actually a stimulant that helped many people with ADD to focus. After talking with Dr. Sims, I agreed to try it. I also scheduled a visit with a counselor to learn coping techniques. Accepting my learning disability and finding ways of coping was the last step in my process of self-discovery.

Now, dealing with school is much easier. Last term, for the first time, I made the dean's list. It is as if I have discovered my abilities, not my disability. I know that I am not lazy and unmotivated, but a smart and determined person. Now, though, I'm able to show it.

Questions

1. In the space below, write the thesis statement of the essay.

    _____

    _____

2. In the space below, write the topic sentence of each body paragraph.

    _____

    _____

_____

_____

_____

_____

3. What were the steps the writer followed in accepting her disability?

_____

_____

_____

Process Essay 2

A job in a bakery, an ambition to start a business, and a bit of observation helped the writer of this essay to learn about the process of pleasing a customer.

A Lesson in Customer Service

As a full-time college student majoring in business administration, I have hopes of owning my own business someday. As a part-time worker in a bakery, I see what a hassle owning a business can be. Business owners have to worry about making a profit and keeping employees happy and productive. Most of all, they have to worry about keeping customers, even when they can't always deliver what the customer wants. The other day, I watched Herschel, our bakery manager, deal with a difficult customer. Herschel's behavior showed me how to handle a customer complaint.

The first thing that Herschel did was to accept full responsibility. The customer had been told that there were no angel food cakes. The last two had been thrown out that morning because they were out of date. She was upset. Why hadn't they been marked down? My answer would have been, "Sorry, it's company policy." Herschel took responsibility. He said, "When you buy a cake, I want you to have the freshest one available. If I sell merchandise that is out of date, I know I'm not giving you my best." The woman was still not happy. "Other stores sell out-of-date products at a reduced price," she said. "If I get it for a reduced price, I don't expect it to be as fresh."

As I watched, I was getting a little irritated with the woman, but Herschel explained his position patiently. He spoke of his pride in his products and his belief that every customer was entitled to quality. He spoke calmly and casually, as if the customer were a friend. He leaned forward, his body language saying that their conversation was of great interest. "If you take home a cake or a loaf of bread and you don't eat any for four days," he said, "it should still be good when you open it." The customer said, "Okay, I understand," and started to leave.

I would have probably shrugged and let her walk away, but Herschel took a little extra time to make her feel important. He walked with the woman around the bakery, squeezing loaves of bread and chatting. He pointed out fat-free muffins and raisin bread and told her how much he liked the carrot cake. It was trivial conversation, but the point was not what he said. The point was that his willingness to take time with her suggested that she was a valuable customer. When she left, she was smiling and carrying a loaf of raisin bread with her.

Instead of taking the easy way out, Herschel accepted responsibility for company policies, took the time to explain, and made the woman feel like a valued customer. I believe he won a customer for life. As for me, I received a lesson in customer service that I will remember when I am running my own business.

Questions

1. In the space below, write the thesis statement of the essay.

    _____

2. In the space below, write the topic sentence of each body paragraph.

    _____

    _____

    _____

    _____

    _____

3. What are the steps involved in handling a customer complaint, according to the writer?

    _____

    _____

TOPICS FOR PROCESS WRITING

Small Scrawls: Imaginative Short Writings

What is a Small Scrawl? A "scrawl" is something written quickly. In this case, it is a page or so of quick writing that allows you to practice a particular type of writing, in this case, writing about a process. Have fun with it!

Small Scrawl 1: An Everyday Task

Write a Small Scrawl telling your reader how to do a simple, everyday task. Describe it so well and so completely that a reader could complete the process based on your directions alone. Be sure to include at the beginning of the paper any tools that the reader will need. A few suggestions follow.

tying shoelaces	putting on and buttoning a shirt
brushing teeth	feeding a pet
making toast	putting on makeup
making coffee	shaving
starting a car	reading a newspaper

Small Scrawl 2: How It's Done

Describe a process that you observe often but do not do yourself. For instance, you might know exactly how the barista in the coffee shop makes a latte or how your instructor begins class every day. You might know how your dog fetches a stick or shows you she is hungry. Describe one of these processes or one of your own in a Small Scrawl.

Small Scrawl 3: Picture This!

In each of the pictures below, someone is doing something, perhaps humorously and not very well. For this Small Scrawl, you have two options. Either describe the process as it is shown in the picture, from beginning to end (not just what is going on in the moment captured in the photo or drawing) or describe the process from beginning to end the way that it should be done.

Essay Assignments

Process Essay 1: The Way You Do the Things You Do

Write an essay telling your reader how to do something that you do well. It might be a physical skill, such as pitching a baseball, driving a car, or doing an aerobic exercise routine. It might be a social skill, such as making people feel comfortable or mediating an argument. Or it might be a practical skill or a craft, such as getting the most for your money at the grocery store or making a stained-glass window.

Process Essay 2: The Process of Change

Change can be difficult, and the process of coping with it is not always easy. Think of a change or transition that was difficult for you and describe in a five-paragraph essay your process of coping with it.

Process Essay 3: The Right Start

Write an essay directed at someone who is just getting started in one of the following processes.

> starting a physical fitness program
>
> beginning college
>
> setting up a budget
>
> trying to lose or gain weight

Process Assignment: Real-World Topic— Performing a Job-Related Task

Describe one of the tasks involved in your job. Describe it step by step, so well that someone who had the necessary tools and knowledge could do the job from your description.

Consider your audience. Will you describe this task for a person who possesses job skills and knowledge similar to your own, or will you write it for someone who is not familiar with the terminology of your field? Consider your tone. Descriptions of a task convey much more than the bare bones of the task itself, they convey your attitude toward it.

TOPICS FOR COMBINING METHODS OF DEVELOPMENT

Definition, classification, and process are methods of showing the limits of a topic—the borders that define it—and of ordering it into steps, stages, or types. The following assignments ask you to combine one or more methods of development.

Mixed Methods Assignment 1: Stress

Essay: Definition and Classification

In this essay, your job is to define the term *stress* and to divide it into types. Your definition must be broad enough to cover all the types of stress that you explore in your essay. As a suggestion for organizing your essay, try defining the broad term *stress* in the introduction. Then, list and define each type of stress in a topic sentence. Since classification essays often incorporate examples, you may wish to support your body paragraphs with examples that give the reader a clear picture of each type of stress.

Mixed Methods Assignment 2: Problems and Solutions

Consultant's Report: Definition, Classification, and Process

You are a consultant. A large organization—it could be a school, a shopping center, a grocery store, a church, or some other organization that serves many people—has hired you to look at its problems and determine how the organization can fix those problems. It is up to you to choose the organization and define and classify its problems. Just to give some examples, a shopping center might find that many people with handicaps have trouble moving freely about within the center. They can't navigate the sidewalks easily, the aisles in some of the stores are too narrow, and restaurant tables are too close together. You might classify these as "mobility problems." That same shopping center might find that teenagers, who traditionally have high disposable incomes, are not spending their money. Instead of making the shopping center profitable by buying clothing, DVDs, or video games, they are hanging out in outdoor areas with friends or flirting with other teenagers. How can the shopping center lure these teenagers into the stores to spend money? These problems might be classified as "profitability problems." Or perhaps existing parking is not adequate, and there is no land available adjacent to the shopping center to create more parking—a parking problem. Your first task, then, is to decide on the organization you want to write about and to define and classify its problems.

Once you have listed the problems and classified them into groups, your job is to come up with a process by which the organization can solve its problems.

This report can easily be organized like a traditional essay. The thesis will state the problems faced by the organization, and each body paragraph will define and classify a problem and suggest a process for solving it.

Mixed Methods Assignment 3: What It Is, How It Works

Essay: Definition and Process

Everyone develops ways of doing things—of completing everyday processes—that work for them. Some people even name their systems—Andrea's Clothing Coordination System, Raoul's Never-Fail Approach to Getting a Date, Betty's Efficient Grocery Shopping Method. What's your system? In this essay, your job is to define a process that works well for you, pointing out its advantages over conventional methods. Then, describe the process, step by step, so that a reader could easily follow your directions and use your process.

mywritinglab For support and practice meeting this chapter's goal, log in to **www.mywritinglab.com** and select **Essay Development: Definition**, **Essay Development: Division/Classification**, and **Essay Development: Process**.

CHAPTER 10

Examining Logical Connections: Comparison-Contrast, Cause-Effect, and Argument

Chapter Goal: Analyze and write comparison-contrast, cause-effect, and argument essays.

Back to back
Not eye to eye,
We disagree
And don't know why.

We are the same,
Yet poles apart,
Perhaps my words
Can touch your heart.

Focus on Examining Logical Connections: Thinking about Logic

Look at the sign pictured here. Is it illogical under the circumstances?

Evidence of illogical thinking is everywhere. Often, that lack of logic comes from forced comparisons, faulty cause-effect relationships, or ill-formed arguments. It's not enough just to compare two things or say that an effect happened or to argue without evidence. It's also necessary to show the logical connections between the two things that are being compared, explain how an effect clearly stemmed from a cause, or provide evidence that supports an argument.

Reflect on It

Find a sign somewhere that you think has some sort of logical flaw. Describe your sign (or better yet, take a picture of it), and explain why it is logically flawed.

When you compare one alternative with another, when you look for causes and effects, or when you argue for a particular course of action, you are using logic to explore connections between ideas. If your logic is thin or your connections weak, your reader will notice it. The methods in this chapter call for rational thought and careful planning. The skills that go along with these methods of development—pinpointing differences and similarities, discovering reasons, predicting results, and arguing an issue logically—are essential. These higher-order tools of thought can help you in the college classroom and beyond.

Comparison-Contrast, Cause-Effect, and Argument in Action

In this chapter, you will have the opportunity to examine and use the techniques of comparison-contrast, cause-effect, and argument. The text explains the techniques separately so that you can become thoroughly familiar with them and learn to use them successfully. Later, you will mix techniques to suit your purpose for writing.

Before looking at definition, classification, and cause-effect separately, look at how a professional writer uses all three techniques together. The following essay is by Liz Pulliam Weston, a personal finance writer for MSN.com and author of two books on personal finance.

The essay embodies all three of the writing techniques featured in this chapter. The first technique that the writer incorporates is **comparison-contrast**.

Mainly, the essay compares the ways that people spent money in the 1970s with the way they spend it today. We could also say that the essay *contrasts* the ways that people spent money in the 1970s with the way they spend it today and be just as correct. The term *comparison* also includes contrast; that is, we may compare two things and find them similar, or we may find them quite different. The term *contrast,* however, always suggests that a difference will be found.

The author also uses **cause-effect** to suggest the effect that emulating the spending of the 1970s might have on the reader's overall spending. After comparing the areas of spending in the two decades, Weston tells us exactly how much money might be saved by reverting to the spending habits of the 1970s.

Finally, the entire essay constitutes an **argument** for dialing back spending a few decades. Argumentation, sometimes called *persuasion* or *persuasive writing,* comes in all strengths, from "gentle nudge" to "baseball bat over the head." Weston's argument is on the gentler end of the scale. How can we tell? First, touches of humor spice the essay throughout with gentle jabs at the 1970s. In addition, Weston's tone is helpful rather than dictatorial; that is, she presents her ideas as helpful suggestions. She is considering her audience, which consists of people who have chosen to read her personal-finance column and are therefore predisposed to accept what she says. Although Weston does not suggest that her readers give up modern conveniences (she even admits that she would not give up her iPod), she does suggest that a pullback toward an earlier decade would help to fatten the reader's wallet.

Save Big with the Flashback Budget

Liz Pulliam Weston

Last week's innovation becomes yesterday's luxury, which quickly becomes today's necessity.

Just think of air conditioners. Or televisions. Or microwave ovens. Or personal computers.

Each started as a novelty. Now each is considered a requirement of daily living by a majority of Americans, according to a recent Pew Research Center survey. (Cell phones almost made the necessity list; 49% considered them so.)

Percent of adults polled who rate the following items as necessities:

Car	91%	Home computer	51%
Clothes washer	90%	Cell phone	49%
Clothes dryer	83%	Dishwasher	35%
Home air conditioning	70%	Cable/satellite TV	33%
Microwave	68%	High-speed Internet	29%
TV set	64%	Flat-screen TV	5%
Car air conditioning	59%	iPod	3%

Source: Pew Research Center, December 2006

But clearly, people lived rich, fulfilling, functional lives before any of these gadgets came along. So we here at MSN Money thought it would be fun to dial the Way Back Machine to one of those times, to see how much money we could save.

Those were the days . . . of "Muskrat Love"

We picked the 1970s—era of Watergate and disco, "The Brady Bunch" and pet rocks, streaking and "Muskrat Love" (if you have to ask, you really, really don't want to know). It's the era when I grew up, and I have photos of the frizzy, Barbra-Streisand-in-"A-Star-Is-Born" perm to prove it.

And here's what we found:

We were living small

The average new home in 1970 took up less than 1,500 square feet. Today, new homes average more than 2,400 square feet, and there are fewer people living in them (about one person fewer, compared with the 1970s). Smaller homes cost less to buy, insure, heat, cool, and maintain. Since the typical American household spent $15,167 on shelter and related costs in 2005, trimming even 10% of that bill would save you more than $1,500 a year. (If you could actually save a proportional amount—1970s homes were about 40% smaller—that would be about $6,000 in savings.)

We drove smaller, too

The 1973–74 oil crisis led to lines at the gas pumps and a new interest in fuel-efficient vehicles. But most households didn't have multiple tanks to fill. At the start of the 1970s, only 31% of households had more than one car, according to the U.S. Census Bureau; more than a quarter had no vehicles at all. By 1995, 60% of households had more than one car and only 8% were carless. The AAA tells us the average car costs about $7,800 a year to finance and operate, so one fewer vehicle could save you a tidy sum.

We ate at home

Food in general used to take up a lot more of our budgets. Food costs declined from 20.2% of the average family's expenditures in 1960 to 16.3% in 1972 to 12.8% in

2005. But even as food costs have dropped, the portion of our budgets we spend on eating out has grown considerably. That jibes with my family memories; eating out used to be a fairly rare treat. Eating out just one less night a week could save a whopping $1,560 a year (and that's in today's dollars).

We vacationed closer to home, too

U.S. airlines weren't deregulated until 1978, and before then flying was a pricey proposition. Most of my family's vacations were camping trips to national forests within a day's drive of our Washington State home, with an occasional train trip to visit relatives in the Midwest or (O glorious day!) Disneyland in California. You don't need to give up Southwest Airlines for the Greyhound bus—for all I know, Southwest is cheaper—but if you skipped just one flight a year, you'd save $300 to $400 a person.

Phones and entertainment

"We don't care. We don't have to. We're the phone company."

If you got that reference, then you remember Lily Tomlin's obnoxious Ernestine the Operator character from the hit show "Laugh-In," which ran from 1968 to 1973. (She reprised the character for "Saturday Night Live" a few years later.) The joke was on us, since back then we all rented our telephones from one big monopoly—AT&T—and paid through the nose, especially for long-distance calls. A federal judge ordered the breakup of AT&T in 1984, and clearly life is better now that we can choose from several phone companies that don't care. I wouldn't suggest returning to Ma Bell era, but you could realize some savings if you recreated the days when families had one phone number, rather than half a dozen. Figure $360 or so in savings for every line you drop.

Entertaining yourself

As one of the 3% who consider iPods necessities (or at least close to it), I wouldn't dream of telling you to swap yours for an eight-track player. There are some sacrifices no one should have to make. But downsizing your expectations as far as your television could save you some serious bucks. Back then, a 27-inch screen was considered huge, and most of us watched three (count 'em, three) network channels with maybe a public broadcast station thrown in. TV was free; most people picked up stations with an antenna attached to the roof. Cable television didn't really take off until the late 1970s, and it wasn't until the 1990s that most folks paid for TV. VCRs weren't introduced until the late 1970s, either, although we did have video games like Pong and Tank (ask your grandpa, kids). I won't insist you get a black-and-white set, since by 1972 half of U.S. homes had a color television. I'll just note that ours wasn't one of them; I didn't realize the "Star Trek" crew had different-colored uniforms until I was in college. Anyway, unplug cable for a year and you'd save $600 or so.

Had enough? I certainly have. Living through the '70s once was more than enough. And now I can't get "Muskrat Love" out of my head.

THINKING ABOUT THE ESSAY

1. Why do you think the author compares the budgets of the 1970s with today's budgets, rather than simply advising her readers to budget for items as if it were the 1970s? In other words, why does she show us in such detail how our usage of various items has changed?

2. This essay shows the effects of cutting back a household budget to resemble a 1970s budget. Name one area in which 1970s budgeting would have an effect. What would such budgeting do, according to Weston's article? The essay also describes changes that have taken place over the decades since 1970. Name one of these changes. What has been the result?

3. Weston argues that taking a household budget back to the 1970s is a way to save money. Does she base her argument on fact or opinion? Give an example.

🖉 Comparison-Contrast

mywritinglab

Visit MyWriting Lab for additional practice comparing and contrasting.

One of the most effective ways of describing an unfamiliar situation or object is by comparing or contrasting it with something familiar. When you make a **comparison**, you show how two things are similar. If a friend asks you about a class you are taking, you may describe it by comparing it to a class that the two of you have taken together. When you **contrast** two things, you show how they are different. If you are asked on a political science exam to discuss the legislative and judicial branches of the government, you may find yourself contrasting the ways each branch shapes the country's laws. In an English class, you may find yourself using both comparison and contrast to show how two writers develop similar themes in different ways. Used alone or used together, comparison and contrast are useful tools for any writer.

Comparison-contrast techniques are useful in answering questions such as those that follow.

- What are some of the differences between high school and college classes?

- Discuss the similarities and/or differences between your values and those of your parents.

- A line from the movie *Forrest Gump* says, "My mama always said life was like a box of chocolates. You never know what you're going to get." A line from an old song says, "Life is just a bowl of cherries." Now it's your turn to fill in the blank: Life is like a _____. Discuss three ways in which life is like the word or phrase you chose.

Laying the Groundwork for Comparison-Contrast Writing

Visualizing

Look at the photograph of the homeless man and his dog. Think about a day in the life of this dog. How might this dog's life be different from the life of a dog that lives in a house? How might it be the same? How might the relationship between the man and his dog be different from the relationship of a home-owner and her dog? How might it be the same?

Planning

List three points of comparison or contrast between a dog owned by a homeless person and a dog owned by a person who has a home.

Writing

Write a paragraph comparing or contrasting the lives of two dogs: one belong-ing to a homeless person and one belonging to a homeowner. Use one of the two beginnings that follow, or make up your own. Note that in the second opening, the dogs are named. It takes a sentence to establish the names, but cumbersome repetition is avoided.

Opening 1: A homeless person's dog lives much like any other dog.

Opening 2: Banjo and Cadet are mixed-breed dogs who are much loved by their owners. But the similarity ends there because Banjo travels the open road with his homeless owner, while Cadet lives with his family in a three-bedroom ranch house with a yard.

Setting Up a Comparison-Contrast Paper

The first step in setting up a comparison-contrast composition is to choose your points of comparison or contrast and decide whether to compare or contrast. One way to decide is to prewrite. That way, you can see whether your primary focus is on comparison or on contrast. Following is a sample brainstorming for a paragraph or essay.

Brainstorming—Two Teachers

<u>Kimball</u>	<u>Bettman</u>
extremely good teacher	excellent teacher
liked by students	liked by students
✔ funny but disorganized	✔ organized lectures—hints about lectures, test questions
✔ multiple-choice tests	✔ essay tests
✔ group project assignment	✔ research paper
easy to talk to	approachable and friendly

Though there are several points of comparison, the contrasting points "lectures," "tests," and "assignments" may make a more interesting paragraph than the points of comparison. These points will also be more valuable to a reader who is trying to decide which class to take.

The next step in planning the comparison-contrast paper is to decide whether to use a point-by-point pattern or a block pattern to discuss the points.

Point-by-Point Outline for a Comparison-Contrast Essay

In a point-by-point pattern, each point of comparison or contrast is considered separately. Following is a **point-by-point outline** that could be developed into a paragraph or essay:

Point 1: Lectures

Kimball: Humorous but disorganized
Bettman: Organized, gives hints

Point 2: Tests

Kimball: Multiple choice, tricky questions
Bettman: Essay questions require creative thought

Point 3: Outside Projects

Kimball: Group presentation
Bettman: Research paper

Block Outline for a Comparison-Contrast Essay

In a block pattern, information about one subject is presented in one big block, followed by information about the other subject in a second big block. A **block outline** is shown here:

Kimball: Point 1: Delivers humorous but disorganized lectures
                 Point 2: Gives tricky multiple-choice tests
                 Point 3: Assigns a group project
Bettman: Point 1: Delivers organized, hint-packed lectures
                 Point 2: Gives essay exams that require creative thought
                 Point 3: Assigns a term paper

EXERCISE 1   **RECOGNIZING COMPARISON-CONTRAST PATTERNS**

Following are two paragraphs written from the outlines above. Read each paragraph and decide which is the point-by-point paragraph and which is the block paragraph.

Paragraph A

    Mr. Kimball and Dr. Bettman are both excellent sociology teachers, but they are different in the way they lecture, test, and make assignments. Mr. Kimball makes jokes during class and throws out silly puns that make the class groan. He speaks quickly, so taking accurate notes can be difficult. Sometimes he gets sidetracked and forgets what he was talking about. Dr. Bettman does not tell jokes, but she is extremely organized. Her lectures are practically in outline form, and as she lectures, she gives hints about what might be on the test. The testing styles of the two teachers are also different. Mr. Kimball's tests are multiple choice, and he words questions so that students must read carefully. Dr. Bettman's tests are in essay format, and she expects students to use their knowledge in new and creative ways. The two instructors also differ in their assignment of outside projects. Mr. Kimball requires a group project and presentation. He asks for a typed list of references but no formal paper. Dr. Bettman, on the other hand, requires a research paper complete with a bibliography. Both are able instructors, but each approaches lecturing, testing, and outside projects in a different way.

Paragraph B

Mr. Kimball and Dr. Bettman are both excellent sociology teachers, but they are different in the way they lecture, test, and make assignments. During his lectures, Mr. Kimball makes jokes and throws out silly puns that make the class groan. He speaks quickly, so taking accurate notes can be difficult. Sometimes he gets sidetracked and forgets what he was talking about. His tests are multiple choice, and he words questions so that students must read carefully. Mr. Kimball requires a group project and presentation at the end of the term rather than a traditional term paper. In contrast, Dr. Bettman's style and classroom requirements are quite different. She does not joke during class, and she is extremely organized. Her lectures are almost in outline form, and she gives little hints about what might be on the test. Dr. Bettman's tests are in essay format, and she expects students to use their knowledge in new and creative ways. At the end of the term, she requires a research paper, complete with a bibliography. Both Mr. Kimball and Dr. Bettman are able instructors, but each approaches lecturing, testing, and outside projects in a different way.

1. The paragraph organized in point-by-point format is paragraph _____.

2. The paragraph organized in block format is paragraph _____.

3. Look at the two paragraphs. In which paragraph do you find more transitions?

_____

Why?

_____

_____

Building CONNECTIONS

When you make comparisons or draw contrasts, *examples* are often useful in making the similarities or differences clear to your reader.

Wordsmith's Corner: Examples of Writing Using Comparison-Contrast

In the following essays, see how two student writers use comparison-contrast. Read each essay and answer the questions that follow.

Comparison-Contrast Essay 1

This essay contrasts home ownership and apartment living. At what point in the essay are you certain which one the writer prefers?

The Advantages of Apartment Living

The other day, a friend asked, "When are you going to buy a house?" When I told him that my wife and I were happy in our apartment, he shook his head. "You don't know what you're missing," he said. I think I do. Natalie and I have talked about buying a house, but we always come to the same conclusion. Apartment living offers many advantages over home ownership.

First of all, apartment living gives us luxuries we could never afford if we owned a home. If we bought a home, it would be a small home in a modest neighborhood. We would be lucky to have a postage-stamp yard for recreation. Our security system would probably consist of a deadbolt lock on the door. Any home in our price range would certainly not have lighted tennis courts, a pool, and 24-hour security. In our apartment complex, we have all of those things. Anytime I like, I can go over to the courts for a set or two of tennis. Afterward, I can cool off in the clear blue water of our apartment complex's swimming pool. At night, I can sleep well, knowing that if thieves or vandals venture into the complex, there is on-site security to take care of them. Only apartment living can give me so many luxuries for such a small price.

As apartment dwellers, we are also more mobile than homeowners. If Natalie and I owned a home and one of us were offered a dream job in a distant city, we would have to put our home on the market and worry about whether it would sell. If it had not sold by the date of our move, we could entrust it to a real estate agent, or one of us could stay behind and try to sell it. In any case, it would be a burden to us until someone else bought it. Living in an apartment, we have none of those worries. The worst that could happen is that we would have to forfeit our deposit if we did not give adequate notice. If we had to move, we could leave right away and focus on settling into a new job and a new community.

Perhaps most important, apartment living frees us from the chores of home ownership. If the water heater, the air conditioner, or the refrigerator in our apartment breaks down, I don't pull out the owner's manual and call the parts store. I call the resident manager, who sends over a repair person. If the roof develops a leak or the outside of the building needs a coat of paint, I don't risk my neck climbing a shaky ladder, as a homeowner might. I know that the apartment complex will hire a roofer or painter to take care of the problem. And on Saturdays, when my home-owning friends are mowing lawns, cleaning gutters, or trimming shrubbery, I am relaxing in front of the television or enjoying a game of tennis. For an apartment dweller, routine chores are handled by the apartment complex's maintenance staff.

Some people enjoy home ownership in spite of the hassles that go along with it. But I prefer the luxury, mobility, and freedom from chores that apartment living offers.

Questions

1. In the following space, write the thesis statement of the essay.

   _____

2. In the following space, write the topic sentence of each paragraph.

   Topic sentence 1: _____

   _____

   Topic sentence 2: _____

   Topic sentence 3: _____

   _____

3. Does the essay compare or contrast? What is being compared or contrasted?

_____

_____

_____

4. In this essay, two of the three body paragraphs are in block format.

   Which paragraph is presented point by point?

_____

Comparison-Contrast Essay 2

The writer of this essay uses comparison-contrast to show the world of work, past and present.

Working—Then and Now

When a reader wrote to the advice columnist Ann Landers saying he could not find a job in spite of a college degree and work experience, Ann suggested that perhaps the man's attitude was to blame. An avalanche of mail told Ann that she was behind the times. In the decades since Ann Landers began writing her column, the job market has undergone a mixed bag of changes. Today's workplace is more diverse, more demanding, and less secure than the workplace of the 1960s.

The most positive change in the workforce is that it has become more diverse. In the 1960s, executive jobs went mostly to white males, while women and minorities were steered toward secretarial or janitorial jobs. Today, an ever-widening crack in the door to the executive suite is admitting all ethnic groups and both genders. Minorities have moved from the mail room to the board room, and females from the typing pool to the executive suite. There is likewise a diversity in mindset. Once, the "corporation man" was esteemed because his values and his ideas were likely to be in line with those of upper management. Now, however, employees are no longer expected to be yes-men or yes-women. Corporations now have become more creative and competitive, so the employee with a different slant on things is useful. Greater diversity has made today's workplace stronger and more vital.

Today's workplace also makes more demands on its workers' time than the workplace of the sixties. In those days, "nine to five" was the rule rather than the exception, and if a worker took an hour for lunch, the true workday was only seven hours long. The work week spanned Monday through Friday, and weekends were for rest. Today, split shifts, extended shifts, and brown-bag lunches at the desk are common. The downsized workforce of today means that the average worker simply has more to do, even if that work has to be done on weekends or after hours.

The most profound change in today's workplace is a change in the level of job security. When a college graduate from the class of 1965 went to work for a company like IBM, he expected to retire thirty-five years later with a gold watch and a fat pension. He could be assured that if he did his job reasonably well, he would not be fired. Today, however, the first job after college is seldom a permanent one. It is an item for the résumé, a stepping-stone to other jobs. Pensions have changed as well. Once totally financed by employers, pensions have evolved into 401(k)s and IRAs that are at least partially financed by employees themselves. The worst aspect of today's workplace is that good employees with many years of service have no guarantee of keeping their jobs. If the company downsizes to cut costs, the worker's job may be eliminated regardless of years of service.

Since the 1960s, the job market has changed drastically. Today's workers face a workplace that is more diverse, more demanding, and much less secure.

Questions

1. In the space below, write the thesis statement of the essay.

   _____

   _____

2. In the space below, write the topic sentence of each paragraph.

   Topic sentence 1: _____

   _____

   Topic sentence 2: _____

   _____

   Topic sentence 3: _____

   _____

3. Does the essay compare or contrast? What is being compared or contrasted?

   _____

   _____

4. In this essay, two of the three body paragraphs are in block format. Which paragraph is presented point by point?

_____

_____

Topics for Comparison-Contrast Writing

Small Scrawls: Imaginative Short Writings

What is a Small Scrawl? A "scrawl" is something written quickly. In this case, it is a page or so of quick writing that allows you to practice a particular type of writing, in this case, comparison and contrast. Have fun with it!

Small Scrawl 1: It's Like This

Choose one of the following questions and write a small scrawl comparing the two items in the questions. Use your imagination and have fun!

How is a person you don't know like an unopened gift?

How is getting a divorce like getting fired?

How is losing a game like failing an assignment in school?

How is a first date like a job interview?

How is life like a game?

How is your life like a puzzle?

Small Scrawl 2: Suitable for Framing

Look at the pictures below. Choose one picture and contrast the two things or animals pictured in it.

Small Scrawl 3: This and That

Write a Small Scrawl contrasting one of the following pairs:

two brands of pizza   two times of day or days of the week

two classrooms   two sports teams

Essay Assignments

Comparison-Contrast Essay 1: Optimism and Pessimism

In an essay, discuss the differences in the way an optimist and a pessimist might approach life. It might help to select three areas such as work, school, relationships, finances, or religion and write a paragraph comparing and contrasting each point.

Comparison-Contrast Essay 2: School Days

Write an essay explaining some of the differences between high school and college.

Comparison-Contrast Essay 3: Today and Tomorrow

In five years, how will your life be different from the way it is today? In this essay, be sure to contrast the present and the future rather than simply discussing your plans for the future.

Comparison-Contrast Assignment 4: Essay-Based Topic—Budgeting by the Decade

Re-read Liz Pulliam Weston's essay on page 197 of this chapter. Then pick three of the six spending areas (homes, cars, food, vacations, telephones, and entertainment) that she discusses in her essay. Compare or contrast your own spending in that area to the spending of today's consumer or to the spending of a 1970s consumer, as described in Weston's essay.

Comparison-Contrast Assignment 6: Real-World Topic—Going the Extra Mile

You are applying for a small-business startup grant for the business of your choice. The application asks you to compare your business to other, similar businesses and show how yours meets a need or needs in the community that are not filled by other businesses in the same category. In other words, if you are opening a dry cleaning shop, how is it different from all the others? Do you deliver to meet the needs of senior citizens or busy working people? Are your hours extended to meet a need that other dry cleaners do not meet? Do you offer some other service that other dry cleaners do not? Dry cleaning is just an example; choose any business you wish, and write an application for the grant.

✍ Cause-Effect

mywritinglab

Visit MyWriting Lab for additional practice with cause and effect.

When you look for the **causes** of an event, you are looking for the reasons it happened. In other words, you are looking for answers to "why" questions. Why did your last romantic relationship end badly? Why is your Uncle Leroy's car still humming along at 150,000 miles? Why are so many high schools plagued by violence?

When you look for the **effects** of an action, you are looking for its results. You are answering the question "What would happen if . . .?" What would happen if every community had a Neighborhood Watch? What would happen if you decided to devote just one hour a day to an important long-term goal? What is the effect of regular maintenance on an automobile?

When you explore both **cause and effect**, you look at both the reason and the result. You may explore actual cause and effect, as in "Uncle Leroy performs all scheduled maintenance on his car and changes the oil every 3,000 miles; as a result, his car is still going strong at 150,000 miles." You may also explore hypothetical cause and effect, as in "Many members of my generation are bored and cynical because everything—material possessions, good grades, and even the respect of others—has come to them too easily."

A cause-effect essay might be written in response to any of the following questions.

What are the causes of violence in schools?

What are the major effects of stress?

What are some of the reasons that people fear growing old?

Laying the Groundwork for Cause-Effect Writing

Visualizing

Look at the following photograph of a burning house. Visualize the flames inside, licking at furniture and consuming the belongings of a family.

Planning

Write down four possible causes of the fire. If you were writing a paper, how would you develop a paragraph about those causes? Would you use examples? Would you explain a process?

Next, think about the effects of the fire. How many different people or groups might it affect? List them. If you were writing a paper about the effects of the fire, how would you set it up?

Writing

Write a paragraph on the causes or effects of a house fire. If you wish, you may focus on just one cause or just one effect in your paragraph.

Identifying Causes and Effects

A cause is a *reason*. If you are asking a "why" question, the answer is probably a cause. Why do toilets flush in a counterclockwise spiral north of the equator and in a clockwise spiral south of it? Why did I do so poorly on my history test? Why did the chicken cross the road? From the scientific to the silly, these "why" questions can be answered by finding reasons or causes.

An effect is a *result*. If you ask "What will happen if . . ." or "What were the results of . . .," then your answer is an effect. What would the results be if the speed limit were lowered by ten miles per hour? What would happen if I set aside an hour a day to exercise? What would happen if I threw these new red socks into the washer with my white underwear? When you answer these and other "what if" questions, your answer is an effect.

EXERCISE 2	CAUSES OR EFFECTS?

For each topic listed, indicate whether an essay or paragraph on the topic would involve a discussion of causes (reasons) or effects (results).

_____ **1.** Why do so many people enjoy watching action-adventure films?

_____ **2.** What would the results be if private ownership of automobiles were phased out over a ten-year period?

_____ **3.** Why are so many American children overweight?

_____ **4.** Describe your reasons for attending college.

_____ **5.** What would happen if so-called recreational drugs were made legal for adult use and regulated in the same way as alcohol?

_____ **6.** What would happen if private ownership of handguns were banned?

_____ **7.** What bad habit have you broken lately? Why did you decide to break it?

_____ **8.** Do you recycle? Why or why not?

_____ **9.** What would be the effects of a mandatory parenting course for every first-time parent?

_____ **10.** What would be the effect if all nonviolent, first-time criminals had the option of performing community service and undergoing counseling as an alternative to prison?

Wordsmith's Corner: Examples of Writing Using Cause and Effect

Following are two examples of student writing dealing with causes and effects. Read each essay and answer the questions that follow.

Cause-Effect Essay 1

Our movement toward a twenty-four-hour society provided inspiration for the writer of this essay.

Open All Night

There was a time when the world woke with the sun and slept when darkness fell. In some places it is still that way, but in modern America, the line between night and day is becoming blurred. In the trend toward a twenty-four-hour society, the average American is being caught up in a cycle of unceasing activity.

For most Americans, the movement toward a twenty-four-hour society means that "nine to five" is no longer the rule at work. As factories install expensive technology that must run twenty-four hours a day to be cost effective, many workers find themselves pulling the night shift, twelve-hour shifts, or even split shifts. They become exhausted trying to maintain family relationships, attend school functions with their children, and catch a few hours' sleep during the day. The problem does not occur only among shift workers. Executives who used to leave their work behind them at the office now are given the mixed blessing of laptop computers, cell phones, and home fax machines that keep them in constant touch and make it harder to leave work behind. Americans increasingly complain that they are giving more and more of their lives up for work.

As America moves toward a twenty-four-hour society, people of all ages are playing harder and longer than ever before. A greater awareness of fitness means that many people get up before dawn to struggle to 6:00 A.M. yoga or head for the gym for an evening tai chi class. For those seeking entertainment, the search can continue around the clock. All-night restaurants, skating rinks, movie houses, and miniature golf courses light up the night. Even child's play no longer stops at dusk. Little League fields are lighted for night games that sometimes start as late as 8:00 or 8:30 P.M. and last long past the time when children used to be in bed. Midnight basketball, which arose in cities as a way to keep teens off the streets and out of trouble, has become increasingly popular.

With the movement toward a twenty-four-hour society, there is also more to do at home than ever before. Decades ago, television and radio stations went off the air at midnight, but even at 3:00 A.M., today's couch potatoes can choose from a performance of Handel's *Messiah,* a Three Stooges film, or a rerun of *Green Acres.* No matter what time it is, there is no reason to put off Christmas shopping or filing income taxes. Catalog companies often have twenty-four-hour order lines, and the Internet is open twenty-four hours a day for shopping or downloading tax forms. And why shouldn't a homeowner go grocery shopping or start a painting project at 2:00 A.M.? The grocery store and the discount store are open twenty-four hours a day.

Now that the world never shuts down for rest, many people feel they must constantly seek some pleasurable or productive activity. These days, more Americans are living faster and enjoying it less.

Questions

1. In the space below, write the thesis statement of the essay.

   _____

   _____

2. In the space below, write the topic sentence of each paragraph.

   Topic sentence 1: _____

   _____

   Topic sentence 2: _____

   _____

   Topic sentence 3: _____

   _____

3. Does the essay emphasize causes or effects?_____
4. Identify the cause(s) and effect(s) discussed in the essay.

   _____

   _____

   _____

   _____

Cause-Effect Essay 2

In this essay, the writer discusses the burden of perfectionism.

The Effects of Perfectionism

Some people urge themselves to better performance with slogans like "Practice makes perfect." However, I am a perfectionist, and I have to remember another slogan: "Sometimes good is good enough." I stay away from proverbs that urge perfection. Over the years, I have noticed that the effects of perfectionism are mostly negative.

First of all, my perfectionism makes me anxious about high-pressure situations. In school, I worry about taking tests. The pressure is on because there is no way to go back or change my performance. As I enter the classroom on test day, I feel my hands becoming clammy and I worry that I will forget everything I have studied. Socially, I worry when I have to go to parties or meet new people. I am afraid that I will be dressed too casually or too formally, that I will forget someone's name, or that I won't be able to make small talk. Before I met my girlfriend's parents, I spent a week worrying about what I would say and how I would act. First impressions count, and with my perfectionistic nature, it was important to me make a good impression.

Trying to do things perfectly often means that I do not do them quickly enough. Once, my perfectionism cost me my summer job at a car wash. On my first day, I was issued a T-shirt with a slogan on the back: "If you can read this, I'm moving too slowly." My job was to detail the cars after they came out of the automated washer. I would wipe the water from the car and polish the tires and rims, while my partner, Grady, cleaned the inside of the windows, polished the dash, and vacuumed the seats. Grady always finished before I did and had to help me with the rims and tires. When the manager thought we weren't working quickly enough, he would yell, "Hustle it up, guys!" But hurrying meant that dirt was left on the rims, watermarks on the car, and gray streaks on whitewalls, and my perfectionistic nature shrank from doing less than my best. I was forced to turn in my T-shirt before the month was over.

Perfectionism also makes me my own worst critic. I know that others do not see me as negatively as I see myself. To my teachers, I seem like a serious student who usually does well.

To my friends and acquaintances, I am a funny, likeable guy, and to their parents, I am a well-mannered young man. Even my boss at the car wash could not deny that I worked hard. But I see only my failures. I see the question I missed on a test, not the ones I answered correctly. I notice my social blunders, not the times when I handle myself well. Perfectionism magnifies my faults and shrinks my good qualities. It means that no matter how hard I try or how well I do, there is one person that I can never please—myself.

Perfectionism affects my performance in high-pressure situations, the speed of my work, and the way I see myself. It may be true that nobody is perfect, but unfortunately, that has not stopped me from trying.

Questions

1. In the space below, write the thesis statement of the essay.

   _____

2. In the space below, write the topic sentence of each paragraph.

   Topic sentence 1: _____

   _____

   Topic sentence 2: _____

   _____

   Topic sentence 3: _____

3. Does the essay emphasize causes or effects? _____

4. Identify the cause(s) and effect(s) discussed in the essay.

   _____

   _____

5. What two introductory techniques are used in this essay?
   a. anecdote and quotation
   b. quotation and contrast
   c. broad-to-narrow and quotation

TOPICS FOR PRACTICING CAUSE-EFFECT WRITING

Small Scrawls: Imaginative Short Writings

What is a Small Scrawl? A "scrawl" is something written quickly. In this case, it is a page or so of quick writing that allows you to practice a particular type of writing, in this case, cause-effect. Have fun with it!

Small Scrawl 1: Effects

Look at the pictures below. Choose one picture and describe the possible effects of the item or situation depicted. If you wish, be imaginative and write it in story form, but be sure to show a clear cause and effect.

Small Scrawl 2: Tell Me Why

Look at the pictures below. Choose one picture and describe the possible causes of the situation depicted. If you wish, be imaginative and write it in story form, but be sure to show a clear cause and effect.

Small Scrawl 3: Just Causes

In a Small Scrawl, discuss the causes of one of the following problems.

suicide among the elderly   homelessness

shoplifting   rudeness

stress or burnout   distrust between generations

Cause-Effect Essay 2: A Milestone

Write an essay discussing the effects of an important event in your life. Some possibilities include the addition of a family member, the death of someone close to you, or a surprising discovery about yourself or someone you love.

Cause-Effect Essay 3: A Painful Decision

Write an essay discussing the reasons for a painful decision in your life. A decision to divorce, to have an abortion or to give up a child for adoption, to break off a friendship, or to quit a job are some possibilities.

Cause-Effect Essay 4: Healthful Effects

Write an essay describing the effects of exercise on a person's health, energy level, and self-esteem.

Cause-Effect Essay 5: Essay-Based Topic—The Necessities of Life

Look at Liz Pulliam Weston's essay on page 197 of this chapter. She identifies several items that at least some percentage of the population identified as necessities. The list includes the following items:

car   home computer

washer   cell phone

dryer   dishwasher

home air conditioner   cable/satellite TV

microwave   high-speed internet

TV set   flat screen TV

car air conditioner   iPod

From this list or from your own experience, choose three items that you would classify as necessities. These should be technology-based items that were not available in an earlier era. Write an essay showing why these items are necessities in your life. In other words, show the effects that these items have on your everyday life that make you consider them necessary.

Cause-Effect Assignment 6: Real-World Topic—Ending Unprofessional Conduct

You are the manager of a resort hotel, part of a large chain. Recently, in a guest poll covering the entire chain, your hotel was cited among the rudest. Guests reported desk clerks hanging up on them, screaming matches between employees in the hall, and housekeeping employees who rudely shoved towels at them and stalked off down the hall. The hotel chain regards this very seriously, and though no one has said so, you feel your job may be on the line. Your supervisor has asked you to write an action plan that will turn your employees from surly to polite and improve your hotel's image. The action plan is to be very specific, with each action described in detail along with its expected result. For instance, if you say that you plan to train employees, describe specifically what you plan—role-playing games in which employees act out handling problems with customers, punitive actions or conferences with problem employees, or whatever—and then describe the expected result and why you think it will work. The more specific and detailed your plan is, the safer your job will likely be.

Argument and Persuasion

mywritinglab

Visit MyWriting Lab for additional practice with argument and persuasion.

Argument and persuasion are related techniques of writing in which you take a side on an issue and defend your position. Much of the writing you do on the college level will require you to provide evidence to defend a position, and will thus require argument or persuasion. **Argument** involves taking and defending a position on an issue, whereas **persuasion** imposes the added burden of trying to win others over to your side.

Argument and persuasion answer questions such as the ones that follow.

- Is television a harmful influence on children?

- Should courses in consumer finance be required in high school?

- Is capital punishment an appropriate sentence for serious crimes?

Aristotle's Influence on Argument and Persuasion

Much of what we believe today about effective persuasion and argument comes to us from the ancient Greek philosopher Aristotle. Aristotle identified three elements of an argument: ethos, pathos, and logos. Look at these ideas one by one to see what an ancient Greek philosopher has to say about your writing in the twenty-first century.

Ethos (*eeth-ahse* or *eeth-ohse*), according to Aristotle, involves the reputation and image of the writer. *Ethos* is the root of the English words *ethics* and *ethical*. What does this have to do with writing in the modern world? Everything. Readers want to know that your reputation and the reputation of any sources you use as references are ones (or one) of honesty and reliability. That is why it is important to write honestly and not twist your words or anyone else's to suit your purpose. That's why it's important, when you research a topic, to choose sources carefully rather than just grabbing the first few sources that come up in an Internet search. The stronger the reputation of your sources, the stronger your paper will be.

Ethos also has to do with the image you project as a writer, the way you present yourself. Writers project a poor image when they don't proofread or when they use poor grammar and careless spelling. Their images suffer when they try to cover up lack of knowledge and understanding with long words or when they do not put sufficient thought into their writing. Your reader's acceptance of you as a credible writer will strengthen if you put the necessary thought into your writing and if you construct a paper that does not distract the reader with poor grammar and careless errors.

Pathos (*payth-ahse* or *payth-ohse*), in Aristotle's framework, has to do with persuading your reader with appeals to emotion and feeling. The Greek word *pathos* is at the root of the English words *sympathy* and *empathy,* both of which deal with a feeling of connection between people. Here are three ways to connect with your reader more easily.

Know your reader. When you write an essay, it's good to know who your intended audience is. How much are they likely to know about your subject? What is their position likely to be? For example, if you are writing about using a designated driver, your primary audience is probably people who drive to destinations where alcohol is served. However, anyone who shares the same roads or who has loved ones who drive will be a secondary, and supportive, audience. Knowing your audience makes it easier to persuade your audience.

Remember that tone is important. Have you ever heard someone say, "It wasn't so much what he said; it was the way he said it"? People take offense if they feel they are being talked down to or lectured to. Your goal is to make your tone conversational, peer-to-peer, as though you are talking to someone you know and like.

Engage your reader with anecdotes and examples. Stories and examples can liven your writing and draw your reader in. Here is where you provide specific examples, real or hypothetical, to back up and drive home your argument.

Logos (*low-gahse* or *low-gohse*), or logic, according to Aristotle, is the final element in argument or persuasion. The Greek word *logos* is at the root of English words such as *logic* and *logical.* Logic is extremely important on making an argument or persuading an audience. No matter how strong the other elements of your writing are, they will count for nothing if your argument does not make sense.

Signs of Flawed Logic in Argument

Here are some danger signs that may signal flawed logic:

Painting with too broad a brush. If you say "Older people are *usually* bad drivers because their reflexes have slowed and their reaction time is poor," you are generalizing, or painting an entire group of people with a single brushstroke. On the one hand, words like *usually*, *never*, and *always* increase your responsibility to make sure that what you are saying is absolutely accurate. On the other hand, words like *often*, *can*, and *may* allow you to make a point without using too broad a brush. Saying "Older drivers *may* lose their ability to react quickly as they age" is much more realistic.

Staying on the surface. If you find yourself repeating generalizations instead of analyzing, providing strong support, and giving examples, your argument is a surface argument. Look at the two paragraphs that follow to see the difference between a paragraph that remains on the surface and one that goes into more depth.

Paragraph A

A living will is a document that states your wishes about life-prolonging treatments should you be unable to make decisions for yourself. When you make a living will, you are letting your doctors and your family know your wishes, even though you are unable to express them at the time. Your family will not have to guess, they will know exactly what your instructions are because those instructions will be explicitly stated in the living will. Your doctors will not have to wonder what you would want them to do because your living will speaks for you. A living will is not costly to prepare, but it can bring your family great peace of mind in the event that you are near death and unable to speak for yourself.

Paragraph B

A living will is a document that states your wishes about life-prolonging treatments should you be unable to make decisions for yourself. If you are comatose and dying in a hospital, do you want to be kept alive by machines or do you want nature to take its course? You may trust your family to decide, but do you want to give them the burden of guilt they will bear if they have to decide to allow you to die? Most families, given a choice, want to do everything possible to keep their loved one alive, no matter how much it costs or how many doctors are saying that there is no hope for recovery. Your living will can bring your family great peace of mind in the event that you are near death and unable to speak for yourself.

Making exaggerated claims. Have you seen ads that make claims like this?

"Have the body of your dreams in just ten minutes a day!"
"Make $100,000 a year from home in your spare time!"
"Attract the person of your dreams with our phenomenal pheromone spray!"
"Call our psychics now to find out what the future holds for you. They already know you are going to call!"

Advertisements like these probably make you skeptical, even if they tempt you just a bit. And you are right to be skeptical, because the claims of those ads are clearly exaggerated. In an argument essay, you are expected to take a position and support it, but that does not mean you want to exaggerate. Think through your topic thoroughly, and be aware of the complexity of the problem you are discussing.

Look at the two sample introductions that follow. Though they are almost alike, one takes an exaggerated approach that is likely to turn a reader off, while the other is more moderate and thus more believable. The differences in the two introductions are underlined.

Sample Introduction 1

The number of children who are overweight and obese is steadily increasing in our society. Public health officials are increasingly searching for solutions to this problem, fearing that overweight children will become unhealthy adults. Childhood obesity is a <u>growing</u> problem, but there are ways to <u>stop it in its tracks.</u> Educating children and their parents, providing healthy school lunches, and incorporating physical activity into every school day <u>will soon make childhood obesity a thing of the past.</u>

Sample Introduction 2

The number of children who are overweight and obese is steadily increasing in our society. Public health officials are increasingly searching for solutions to this problem, fearing that overweight children will become unhealthy adults. Childhood obesity is a <u>complex</u> problem, but there are ways to <u>combat it.</u> Educating children and their parents, providing healthy school lunches, and incorporating physical activity into every school day <u>are steps that will help make childhood obesity a thing of the past.</u>

The differences between these two paragraphs are small but significant. Just a few small changes turn the exaggerated essay opening into one that does not promise too much.

Laying the Groundwork for Writing an Argument or Persuasion Essay

Visualizing

Look at the photograph of the young woman using a mobile phone underneath a sign forbidding the use of mobile phones. What is she talking about? Is her conversation urgent or casual? Is she aware that she is breaking a rule?

Planning

Make a list of reasons that some places ban the use of cell phones. Then make another list of reasons, this time a list of arguments a cell phone user might use to support her right to use a cell phone.

Writing

Write a paragraph arguing for or against a person's right to use a cell phone in most public places.

Taking Sides

It has been said that there are two sides to every argument. Your essay, however, should favor just one side. In an argument essay, it is important to make your position clear and not waffle. Starting on the "pro" side of an argument and switching to the "con" side will not work. If you feel it is necessary to acknowledge the other side of the argument, try doing so in the introduction.

Introducing an Argument or a Persuasive Essay

An introduction to an argument or a persuasive essay can be a **historical introduction** that provides background for your argument. It might also be a **contrast introduction** in which you briefly summarize the opposing view and then present your own. (See Chapter 4 for examples.) A third type of introduction that works well for an argument essay is the **concession**, or "yes-but" introduction. In a yes-but introduction, you acknowledge the opposition's strong points before bringing in your own argument. This type of introduction makes your essay seem fair and balanced. In the following example, the writer concedes the strong points of the opposition's argument and then states his own thesis.

Example: Concession or Yes-But Introduction

Many a reluctant student is pulled from a warm bed for an eight o'clock class by a college attendance policy that limits the number of absences a student may accumulate. Such policies have the advantage of ensuring that the professor is not talking to an empty room at 8:00 A.M. on a frosty Monday morning. They also help many marginal students make it through a class. But these policies do more harm than good by treating college students like kindergartners, forcing students who know the material to sit in class anyway, and unfairly penalizing students who may be absent for legitimate reasons.

Fact or Opinion?

Opinions are statements that, in an essay, need to be supported by facts or examples. It is important to be able to distinguish fact from opinion. **Fact** can be defined as a statement that is ultimately provable. In other words, you can look it up in an encyclopedia, you can observe it for yourself, or you can measure it against some objective standard.

However, you can expect even facts to be slippery because of differences in people's perceptions. Any police officer who has taken down eyewitness statements can describe the immense differences in the accounts of people who have all witnessed the same event. Facts can also be slippery because of the differences in the way people see the world. Does the sun rise in the east every morning, travel across the sky, and set in the west? While most of us might say yes, a scientist or a literal-minded person might remind us that the sun does not travel at all, but instead remains fixed while the earth moves. In other words, while facts may be ultimately provable (or disprovable), they are not indisputable.

Group Exercise 1

Individually, write down three facts and three opinions. Mix them up and do not label them. In groups of three, trade papers and mark each statement as F (fact) or O (opinion). If there are any differences of opinion, write the disputed statement on a sheet of paper and hand it to the instructor for discussion by the entire class.

| EXERCISE 3 | **FACT OR OPINION?** |

In the blank to the left of each statement, mark each statement as fact (F) or opinion (O).

_____ 1.   The walls in the classroom are ugly.

_____ 2.   The walls in the classroom are green.

_____ 3.   The walls in the classroom are an ugly green.

_____ 4.   The president of the United States is doing a good job.

_____ 5.   The president promised in a campaign speech that he would not raise taxes.

_____ 6.   The school café needs to add more menu choices.

_____ 7.   The school café serves no salads and only two kinds of sandwiches.

_____ 8.   Killing another human being is never justifiable.

_____ 9.   Private ownership of handguns should be outlawed in the United States.

_____ 10.   Locking away firearms is one way of preventing tragic accidents.

_____ 11.   According to historians, Abraham Lincoln's Gettysburg Address was not really written on the back of an envelope.

_____ 12.   Martin Luther King, Jr.'s "I Have a Dream" speech was delivered in Washington, D.C.

_____ 13.   King's "I Have a Dream" and Lincoln's Gettysburg Address are two of the greatest speeches ever delivered in the United States.

_____ 14.   Writing essays is the only way to become a better thinker and writer and to express oneself more effectively.

_____ 15.   One way to diet is to cut carbohydrates.

_____ 16.   The death penalty for murder is always justified in cases where the victim is a child or a police officer.

_____ 17.   It is fair to charge overweight passengers for two airline tickets if they take up two seats.

_____ 18.   Some airlines charge overweight passengers for two tickets if they take up two seats.

_____ 19.   The justice system in the United States is fair.

_____ 20.   The level, two-mile trail can be walked in less than an hour by anyone who is in reasonably good physical condition.

Supporting an Opinion Essay

A good opinion essay is always a mixture of fact and opinion. Factual support for opinions can take the form of examples, facts, and even anecdotes. The opinions themselves are not only supported by facts, they are logically connected to the facts. In other words, a person in possession of only the facts might logically draw the same conclusion from them that the writer does—and the key word is *might*. Again, facts can be slippery, and the same facts can often be used to support two different conclusions. For example, look at the following set of facts about the parking situation at a hypothetical school.

1. There are three types of parking: red zone parking (closest to the classroom buildings, for faculty only); green zone parking (near classroom buildings, for commuter students); and blue zone parking (near on-campus housing, for students who live on campus).
2. Each automobile is issued a red, blue, or green numbered sticker to indicate where it is to be parked.
3. Shuttle buses take students who live on campus from housing to classroom buildings.
4. Many people pay no attention to the parking regulations—students park in faculty spaces, and on-campus students park in commuter spaces.
5. Tickets are given when security staff can be spared to patrol the parking lots.
6. No penalty is assessed for those who do not pay the fines.

Opinion 1, from a Commuter Student

Obviously, the current system is not working. We have three clearly marked parking zones, but people park wherever they choose, and security staff patrol only when they have nothing else to do. The school needs to hire someone full time to patrol the parking lots. If fines are collected, perhaps people will obey the rules. If fining does not work, stiffer penalties need to be enforced. The parking regulations themselves need no change. It is fair that faculty park close to the classroom buildings, and students housed on campus, who have the benefits of a shuttle to the campus buildings, park farthest away if they choose to drive.

Opinion 2, from a Student Who Lives on Campus

Obviously, the current system is not working. The three parking zones are a joke, since no one is ever fined and security rarely patrols. In fact, security personnel have more important things to do than to patrol the parking lots, and this petty task should be removed entirely from their duty roster. The parking regulations themselves are the problem. Faculty and commuter students get privileged parking, while those of us who pay extra to live on campus get the leftovers. The system is inherently unfair. A first-come, first-served parking system would be fair to everyone.

Opinion 3, from a Faculty Member

Obviously, the current system is not working. Students complain about faculty having special parking privileges, but they don't realize that we may have day and evening classes, meetings in the afternoon, and all manner of class materials to bring from our vehicles. It is only fair that we get the spaces closest to the classroom buildings. However, since the current system is not enforced, faculty members need a gated parking lot that can be entered only with a key card.

The three previous examples make it clear that the facts can lead different people to different conclusions. The only thing that all parties agree on in the previous examples is that change is needed. Because the same facts can be used to support more than one conclusion or more than one opinion, a good opinion paper usually contains both fact and opinion, skillfully woven together.

Look at the following paragraph. Fact and opinion are woven together in it to make a convincing argument.

opinion   opinion
Professor Smith is not a good teacher. His lectures are
                                                    fact
impossible to understand because he stands with his head in

his notes and mumbles at the lectern instead of talking to the
                opinion   fact
class. He always seems to be in a hurry, rushing through his

notes and speaking rapidly, making it difficult to take notes.
[*opinion* over "difficult to take notes"]

When one student asked him to go more slowly, he said, "Sorry,
[*fact* over "asked him to go more slowly"]

we have to get through this material." Personally, I would rather
[*opinion* over "I would rather"]

cover less material and understand it more. He also does not
[*opinion* over "does not"]

like to respond to questions. When students ask questions,

he asks us to save them until the end of the period, but he
[*fact* over "he asks us to save them until"]

never stops lecturing early enough for us to ask questions.

His tests are also clearly unfair. When it was time for us to take
[*opinion* over "clearly unfair"] [*fact* over "it was time for us to take"]

the midterm exam, we had covered only chapters 1–10, but the
[*fact* over "we had covered only chapters 1–10"]

midterm covered chapters 1–12. He told us we would just have
[*fact* over "midterm covered chapters 1–12"]

to read chapters 11 and 12 on our own because he had already
[*fact* over "to read chapters 11 and 12 on our own because he had already"]

made out the midterm. I would not advise anyone to take a class
with Professor Smith.

| **EXERCISE 4** | **RECOGNIZING FACT AND OPINION** |

Underline and label the fact and opinion in the following paragraph:

Dr. Greentree is an excellent teacher. Her lectures are clear and are supplemented by PowerPoint outlines that help the class take notes. She knows how to keep the class's attention by injecting humorous stories into her lectures and varying the pitch of her voice. She helps us understand by asking questions frequently and encouraging us to ask questions. In addition, she cares about students who may be falling behind. She maintains office hours and encourages class members to come by if they have questions or concerns. I would advise anyone to take a class with Dr. Greentree.

Will You Change Anyone's Mind?

A good argument is aimed at changing people's views. On some topics, a convincing argument may change someone's mind. On other topics, though, you will find it next to impossible to sway an opinion that may have been molded by a lifetime of experience. Particularly on such hot-button issues as abortion, assisted suicide, and the death penalty, the best you can realistically hope for is to open a window to your viewpoint. In this case, success means coaxing your reader to look through that window long enough to say, "I see what you mean, and I understand your point of view."

Building CONNECTIONS

Arguing a point often involves *contrast* and *cause-effect*. Making an argument sometimes involves contrasting one side with another. An argument favoring a particular course of action (for example, making handgun ownership illegal) often involves examining the positive effects of that action.

Wordsmith's Corner: Examples of Writing Using Argument

Following are two student essays that argue a point. Read each essay and answer the questions that follow.

Argument Essay 1

Is it time to bench college athletes and let the scholars take the field? In this essay, one student speaks out.

Giving Academics the Edge

College athletic programs offer obvious benefits. Games bring money and recognition to the school. Athletic teams promote school pride and unity, and going to games can be fun. In spite of these benefits, the attention given to athletics shortchanges the majority of the students and forces scholarship to take a back seat. It is time for colleges to take the spotlight away from athletics and give academics the edge.

Special treatment for athletes sends the wrong message to other students. At some colleges, athletes are given their own dorms and a separate dining hall that provides special meals to help them reach the peak of physical condition. Coaches and staff watch over them carefully. If their grades lag, they are given tutoring and encouragement. These special privileges send the wrong message. College should be about academics, not athletics. If there are special dorms, they should be for students who are on academic scholarships. If there are special dining halls, they should serve "brain food" to students on the dean's list. And colleges should have a way of watching over every student. If an ordinary "C" student begins to lag behind, help and encouragement should be as immediate for her as it would be for a star athlete. The special privileges athletes enjoy should be spread among all students.

Expensive athletic facilities and equipment should not be used only by the teams. At the college level, sports should stress fitness and the joy of competition and should include everyone. It's time to open the basketball courts, unlock the weight rooms and saunas, and bring out the track and field equipment for everyone to enjoy. If students are to focus on academics, they need a healthy outlet for their energy. Encouraging every student—even the clumsy or the overweight, even the couch potatoes and the party people—to use these facilities for exercise would contribute to healthier bodies and minds for the whole student body.

Perhaps the worst consequence of shining the spotlight on athletics is that it takes the focus away from scholarship. Many talented students write computer programs, conduct experiments in physics or psychology, or write poems, stories and plays. The attention, however, is not on these students, but on the few who manage to move a pigskin-covered ball a few yards down a green field or who use their height and coordination to dunk a ball through a hoop. A focus on academics would give bright, successful students the attention they deserve. Then other students, seeing the recognition that scholarship brought, would be inspired to make the most of their own intellectual talents.

Sports programs have their place. However, when a school is more recognized for its athletic program than its academics or when athletes are seen as heroes by fellow students while scholars are dismissed as geeks and nerds, something is wrong. It's time for colleges to draft a new game plan, one that places the focus on academics.

Questions

1. In the space below, write the thesis statement of the essay.

_____

_____

2. In the space below, write the topic sentence of each paragraph.

Topic sentence 1: _____

_____

Topic sentence 2: _____

_____

Topic sentence 3: _____

_____

3. The type of introduction used is
   a. contrast.
   b. concession (yes-but).
   c. broad-to-narrow.

4. List the three arguments that the writer makes against college athletic programs.

   _____

   _____

5. Do you agree or disagree with the writer's argument? If you agree, what further points could you make in support of it? If you disagree, what arguments would you make against it?

   _____

   _____

   _____

Argument Essay 2

The writer of this essay is willing to share the road, but thinks that truckers—and their rigs—should be held to a higher standard.

Curbing the Trucking Industry

Truckers have been called "the knights of the road," and for the most part, it's true. Drivers of the big rigs will usually change lanes to let a car onto the interstate, radio for help for a stalled car, or flash lights in a friendly warning that a speed trap lies ahead. Yet trucks cause problems, too. The trucking industry and the government should join forces to curb unsafe drivers, control pollution, and keep truckers away from residential areas.

The keys to controlling unsafe drivers are education and enforcement. Education for truckers should go beyond load limits and gear ratios. It should stress professional conduct. Most automobile drivers know the terror of having twenty tons of steel and cargo inches from their bumper, and quite a few have seen sleep-deprived truckers driving erratically. Education is one way to eliminate such dangerous behavior. For those who will not be educated, enforcement is the answer. Heavier penalties for speeding and reckless driving should be enacted and enforced. Truck drivers who drive under the influence of drugs or alcohol should face a mandatory minimum license suspension of one year and mandatory counseling. Those who repeat the offense should never be allowed behind the wheel of an eighteen-wheeler again. Education and enforcement will put dangerous truckers out of business and help the image of those who are already safe and courteous drivers.

Measures also need to be taken against two types of truck pollution: air pollution and ear pollution. Automobile emissions are strictly regulated, but "truck yuck" continues to pollute the air over interstates and cities. Like automakers, truck manufacturers should be required to develop and install better pollution control devices. Trucks that do not belch clouds of black, foul-smelling diesel smoke will be much more welcome on the road. Noise pollution is another problem that should be controlled. Many cities are filled with the deafening roar of large trucks, and the low rumble of an interstate highway is audible for miles in some places. Noise barriers around interstates and the development of quieter engines are two possible ways to mute the deafening roar of large trucks.

Finally, truck traffic through residential areas needs to be strictly limited. As cities and towns become more spread out and roads become better, trucks are encroaching on residential areas. They move cargo over roads that are not built for heavy vehicles. Their noise and pollution disturb the peace of the neighborhood, and their speed endangers children who play or ride their bikes in the streets. Laws are needed to preserve the peace of residential neighborhoods by keeping heavy trucks on the interstates and major roadways that are built to withstand truck traffic.

The trucking industry is essential, but like any other industry, it must be regulated to preserve safety, prevent pollution, and preserve the peace of residential neighborhoods.

Questions

1. In the space below, write the thesis statement of the essay.

_____

_____

2. In the space below, write the topic sentence of each paragraph.

Topic sentence 1: _____

_____

Topic sentence 2: _____

_____

Topic sentence 3: _____

_____

3. What three changes would the writer like to see in the trucking industry?

_____

_____

4. What type of introduction does the writer use?
   a. anecdote
   b. historical
   c. concession (yes-but)

TOPICS FOR WRITING USING ARGUMENT

Small Scrawls: Imaginative Short Writings

What is a Small Scrawl? A "scrawl" is something written quickly. In this case, it is a page or so of quick writing that allows you to practice a particular type of writing, in this case, argument and persuasion. Have fun with it!

Small Scrawl 1: A Worthwhile Act

Write a small scrawl persuading someone to join you in performing one of the following worthwhile acts:

Becoming an organ donor

Donating blood

Donating your hair to make wigs for children with cancer

Walking to raise money for a cause

Collecting canned goods for a food bank

Small Scrawl 2: Do You Have What It Takes?

You apply for a car sales job. Your interview goes well, but the interviewer tells you that there is one more test to see if you have what it takes to sell cars. You have to write a persuasive ad that will make someone want to buy the car pictured in the following photo.

Small Scrawl 3: Opposing Argument

Choose any controversial issue that you feel strongly about. Then, as an exercise in objectivity, write a Small Scrawl supporting the opposing viewpoint.

Argument Essay 1: Dangerous Drugs

In an essay, support your position on one of the following issues.

1. Should physicians be allowed to prescribe lethal doses or combinations of drugs to assist terminally ill patients in suicide?
2. Should the growing of marijuana for medical or personal use be legal?

Argument Essay 2: School Days, Rule Days

Does your school have a policy or rule that makes you angry? If so, write an essay giving your reasons why the policy is unwise. Some students object to policies limiting the number of absences, while others fret at library policies that say a book may be checked out for only two weeks. Still others object to exams that all students must pass before graduating: Sometimes these are tests of reading and writing ability, and at other times they are senior comprehensive exams in a student's major field. Brainstorming with other students will help get your thoughts focused on your school's policies.

Argument Essay 3: At Liberty

What is the most important freedom you have? Why is it important to you? Some of the freedoms that people in the United States take for granted are freedom to practice the religion of their choice; freedom to speak their mind, even against their government; freedom to move from place to place; and freedom to pursue any career they wish. Discuss in your essay one of these freedoms or any other that you value.

Argument Essay 4: Essay-Based Assignment—Living in the Past

Look at Liz Pulliam Weston's essay on page 197 of this chapter. She argues that budgeting as if it were the 1970s can be financially beneficial. Would changing our lifestyle to that of an earlier era be beneficial in other ways, too? Write an essay in which you argue that living as if it were the 1970s (or any decade of your choice) would be beneficial, or, alternatively, argue that it would be harmful. Think of specific examples that help your argument and use them as support.

Argument Assignment 5: Real-World Assignment—The Next Step Up

You are one of several paraprofessional teacher's aides in an elementary school. You have the opportunity to apply for a full scholarship to a college of education to become a teacher. (Feel free to alter the occupation, but make sure that the scholarship provides a step up in the profession—licensed practical nurse to registered nurse, and so on.) You must write a letter to the scholarship committee detailing your experience and accomplishments as a teacher's aide as well as other experiences with children in the community (scout leader, coach, and so on). You are being judged on what you have already done, not on what you plan to do, so give concrete and specific examples of your accomplishments.

TOPICS FOR COMBINING METHODS OF DEVELOPMENT

Comparison-contrast, cause-effect, and argument are methods of looking at the logical connections between ideas. How are they alike? How do they differ? How does one affect another, and what logical arguments can be made for or against an idea? The following assignments ask you to combine one or more methods of development.

Mixed Methods Assignment 1: Transportation

Essay: Contrast and Argument

Imagine that you are faced with one of the following decisions regarding transportation:

- Should I buy or lease a car?
- Should I buy a used car or a new car?
- Should I buy a car, or should I use public transportation?

First, choose one of the three questions as the basis for your essay. Contrast the two alternatives and make a recommendation (an argument) for the best alternative.

As you write each body paragraph, you may find advantages and disadvantages to each alternative. For example, in terms of monthly payment, leasing a car is better than buying. However, buying a car may cost less in the long run, since you own it when the payments are finished. If you have mixed results such as these, your conclusion will be a "decision paragraph" in which you weigh the arguments for and against each alternative and make a recommendation.

Mixed Methods Assignment 2: Argument For or Against Legalizing Marijuana

Argument before the State Senate: Argument, Comparison-Contrast, and Cause-Effect

You are a state senator. One of your fellow legislators has placed a bill before the state senate advocating the legalization of marijuana for personal use. You are preparing a speech to argue for or against this proposal. In your argument, you may also want to compare or contrast marijuana with alcohol, a legal substance with similar effects. You may also wish to discuss the effects that legalizing marijuana may have on the people of your state.

Organize your paper as a speech, with an introduction mentioning the proposal to legalize marijuana and stating your position for or against the legalization of marijuana. The body of your speech will contain your arguments for or against the proposal. You should provide at least three strong arguments. Conclude by strongly urging your fellow senators to vote for or against the proposed law.

Mixed Methods Assignment 3: Poor Child, Poor Adult

Report: Comparison-Contrast, Cause-Effect, and Argument

Is it harder to be poor as a child or to be poor as an adult? In this essay, you will answer the question with an argument—that is, your thesis will state that it is harder to be poor as a child or that it is harder to be poor as an adult. Although the larger structure of the essay will be one of argument, you will also explore the effects of poverty on children and adults and contrast them to see which group would probably find poverty more difficult, thus bringing cause-effect and comparison-contrast techniques into your essay.

This is a surprisingly complex topic with strong arguments to be made for both sides. Before you write, prewrite thoroughly to explore the differing ways in which adults and children might experience poverty.

mywritinglab   For support and practice meeting this chapter's goal, log in to www.mywritinglab.com and select Essay Development: Comparing and Contrasting, Essay Development: Cause and Effect, and Essay Development: Argument.

CHAPTER 11

Writing a Summary

> ✐ **Chapter Goal:** Summarize and paraphrase the work of others appropriately and write effective summary reports.

It usually takes a long time to find a shorter way.

—Author Unknown

Although the saying above is probably intended as a warning against short-cuts, it could just as easily apply to writing a summary. Summarizing is a painstaking process. It involves fully understanding the material to be sum-marized, determining the most important ideas, and condensing those ideas in your own words. A summary may be a shorter way of saying something, but writing one is a time-consuming process.

Focus on Writing a Summary: Looking at the Summary

Think of the last movie you saw. In a sentence or two, what was it about? If someone were to ask you, for example, to explain what Avatar *was about, would you simply say,*

"It was a great movie" or "Don't bother seeing it"? No. You would describe the events of the movie as concisely as possible.

You are constantly summarizing information. You may replay your day to a significant other, describe movies or TV shows to friends, or explain situations to your boss. The better you are at summarizing, the greater the chances that your significant others will actually listen, that your friends will be entertained, and that your boss will think you do your job well.

Reflect on It

Think of your favorite movies, and choose one to summarize in no more than four sentences. Your first sentence should give the movie's title and general subject. The next two sentences should present the movie's central problem and how it is solved. The final sentence should summarize the movie's overall message. With a limit of four sentences, you will need to emphasize only the major details and leave out minor ones. It's not as easy as it may seem!

Writing a Summary

mywritinglab

Visit MyWriting Lab for additional practice with summary writing.

A **summary** condenses and presents information, often from a single source. When you write a summary, your goal is to concisely present information from an essay, article, or book so that your reader understands the main points. A summary ordinarily presents the author's ideas objectively, without criticism or evaluation. At the end of your summary, if the assignment calls for it, write a brief evaluation of the essay or article you are summarizing.

Five Steps in Writing a Summary

The following section shows you the steps in summarizing an essay or article.

Step 1: Choose a Topic and Find Sources of Information

Your instructor may assign a topic or area of investigation or you may be asked to choose your own. Choose a topic that interests you and about which information is readily available.

Articles on your topic may be found in periodicals, databases, or on Internet sites. An overview of each type of information source follows.

Periodicals are publications such as newspapers, magazines, and scholarly journals that are published on a regular basis—daily, monthly, or quarterly, for example. Newspapers and magazines are written for the general public, while journals are written for scholars in a particular field.

Subscription and CD-ROM Databases

Periodical articles are also available through subscription databases or CD-ROM databases. Most college libraries subscribe to databases such as ABI/INFORM, Academic Search Premier, ERIC, and Research Library. These databases may contain full-text articles from journals, newspapers, or magazines, or they may contain article abstracts. **Full-text articles** are complete articles, presented exactly as originally published. **Article abstracts** are summaries intended to help you decide if a particular article is appropriate for your purposes. If it is, you will need to find the original article in the periodical in which it originally appeared.

What Does the Suffix of an Internet Site Mean?

An Internet site's suffix can tell you a bit about the person or group behind the site. Here's a key to decoding Internet suffixes.

.org: A nonprofit organization

.edu: A college or university

.gov: A U.S. government site

.com: A business or a private individual

Internet Sources

Some websites may contain articles previously published in print sources; others may contain articles written for and published on the Internet. Internet sources vary widely in quality; it is up to you to evaluate the credibility of each site you visit.

Step 2: Evaluate Sources of Information

Once you have found articles on your chosen topic, evaluate them to make sure that they are suitable for your summary. Use the following criteria for evaluation to find suitable articles.

- *Length.* If an article summary covers all the major points in the article, it will probably be 25 to 50 percent of the length of the article. Therefore, if you are assigned a five-hundred-word summary, choose an article of between one thousand and two thousand words. These figures are only an approximation. The idea is not to choose an article so short that a few sentences can summarize it or one so long that you cannot summarize the entire article.

- *Readability.* In any article that you choose, expect to find unfamiliar terminology and concepts that are new to you. After all, the purpose of research is to learn something new. However, some articles are written for experts in the field and may be hard for a layperson to understand. If you read the article three times and still feel as though you are trying to comprehend ancient Egyptian hieroglyphics, choose another article.

- *Publication date.* A publication date helps you to evaluate the timeliness of the source. In fields where change is rapid, such as medicine or computer technology, finding up-to-date sources is essential.

- *Author.* Is the author an authority in the field? If not—if the author is a journalist, for example—does the author consult and quote credible, authoritative sources? These questions will help you evaluate the authority and credibility of your source.

Step 3: Read the Article Thoroughly

Before taking any notes, read the article through once or twice. Then, with a highlighter in hand, look for the following information.

- *Main and major ideas.* Read through the article, highlighting main and major ideas. Remember, main ideas are often found at the beginning of an article and repeated at the end. Major ideas are often stated at the beginning of a paragraph or after a headline, and they are often supported by examples. Don't worry if finding and highlighting main and major ideas takes more than one reading.

- *Examples and supporting details.* Once you have found the main and major ideas, go back and highlight the supporting details and examples that most directly support those ideas. A summary contains a minimum of the detail that fleshes out the main ideas, so be selective and choose only necessary and important details.

- *Information for the Works Cited list.* The final step in taking notes from your source is to write down the information you will need for your Works Cited list. In a summary of a single article, you have only one work to cite, but it is important to cite it correctly. A list of information needed for your Works Cited list follows.

For all sources

- Author
- Title of article
- Title of the magazine, journal, or newspaper in which the article was published
- Date of publication
- Volume and issue number of periodical, if available
- Page numbers

Additional information for online sources:

- Date of access
- The URL (Universal Resource Locator, or complete Web address) of an article from a website
- The name of the database for articles accessed from subscription databases through a college (or other) library.

Step 4: Draft Your Summary

Drafting a summary report is similar to drafting an essay. Your draft should contain the following elements:

- *Introduction.* The introduction includes the author's name, the title of the article, and the central idea of the article.

Sample Introduction to a Summary

For many, the Internet is an increasingly vital part of everyday life. Senior citizens, however, are often less willing to embrace technology and reap the benefits the Internet might provide. In her article, "Bringing the Internet to Seniors," Ima Wizzard argues that an Internet connection can make a vast difference in quality of life for many senior citizens.

- *Body Paragraphs.* The body paragraphs outline the most important points in the article. The topic sentence of each body paragraph should state the idea that the paragraph will develop and incorporate a reference to the author.

Sample Topic Sentence in a Body Paragraph of a Summary

✔ Wizzard points out that the Internet can connect seniors to a larger community.

✔ For many seniors, Wizzard stresses, an Internet connection can mean the difference between loneliness and a sense of community.

The inclusion of the author's name in each topic sentence makes it perfectly clear to the reader that you are still discussing the ideas of another person rather than your own ideas.

The body paragraph itself will paraphrase the author's ideas; that is, you will state the ideas in your own words. Quoting the author is also permissible, but use quotations sparingly. Most of the summary should be in your own words.

Sample Body Paragraph of a Summary

The Internet can also connect seniors to a world of information. Wizzard names many websites designed specifically for senior citizens. For many seniors, Wizzard stresses, an Internet connection can mean the difference between loneliness and a sense of community. The Internet can provide connections to family and friends through email.

- *Conclusion.* The conclusion sums up the author's ideas and presents your evaluation of or reaction to the article. Placing your evaluation in the conclusion is a way of clearly separating your reaction to the article from the summary, but if your evaluation is lengthy, you may place it in a final body paragraph before beginning the conclusion.

Step 5: Format, Proofread, and Cite Your Source

The final draft of your paper will include proper formatting and a Works Cited page. Use the documentation style recommended by your instructor. (Brief guides to APA style and MLA style are provided in Chapter 12.) Your instructor may also ask you to provide a copy of the article you are summarizing.

✎ Paraphrasing: An Essential Skill

One of the most difficult tasks of writing a summary is to convey an author's ideas in your own words. When you **paraphrase**, you capture an idea using your own sentence structure and your own words. Here are some pointers to help you when you paraphrase:

- It's always permissible to repeat key terms. If the author uses the term "geriatric medicine," there's no need to rephrase it as "medical care of the elderly."
- Unusual phrasings should be reworded. If the author refers to a spider web as "a spider's gossamer trap," a paraphrase should simply call it a spider web.
- The sentence structure of a paraphrase should vary from that of the original material.

EXERCISE 1   RECOGNIZING EFFECTIVE PARAPHRASES

For the numbered items below, circle the letter of the better paraphrase.

1. Original material:

   From retail buying to bargain hunting, the Internet has revolutionized shopping. Shoppers used to be limited to the retail stores in their area; now, online stores across the country or even across the world are open to them if they have an Internet connection and a credit card. Shoppers can find items that are not available locally and can compare prices to get the best deal. Bargain hunters no longer have to get up early and spend a Saturday morning scouring area yard sales. Now they can sign on to eBay or similar auction sites to find secondhand items in a variety of places, from Alaska to Nebraska and beyond. Both buyers and sellers have benefited from the availability of online shopping.

   a. Because of the Internet, shoppers are no longer limited to stores within driving distance. Online shopping has made a wider range of goods available to both retail shoppers and bargain hunters. Online stores and auction sites have benefited both buyers and sellers.

   b. The Internet has revolutionized shopping from retail buying to bargain hunting. Shoppers are not limited to items that can be bought locally. From Alaska to Nebraska, online shoppers can get better deals from eBay, other auction sites, as well as from online retail stores the world over.

2. Original material:

   The feline eye is different from the human eye in several respects. The first and most obvious difference is the shape of the pupil as it contracts. The pupil in the human eye is round, and when exposed to light, it contracts, retaining its circular shape. The round pupil of the feline eye, in contrast, contracts from each side to form an ellipse. Unlike the human eye, the feline eye shines in the dark. A cat's eye contains a reflective layer of cells that picks up and reflects available light, enhancing the vision of these nocturnal animals. A final feature that distinguishes the feline eye from the human eye is the nictitating membrane, an inner eyelid that serves to clean and protect the cat's eye.

   a. The feline eye is different from the human eye in the shape of the pupil as it contracts. The pupil in the human eye retains its circular shape when it contracts, but the round pupil of the feline eye contacts from each side to form an ellipse. Unlike the human eye, the feline eye shines in the dark. Finally, a cat's eye has a nictitating membrane, an inner eyelid that cleans and protects the cat's eye.

   b. Though they perform the same function, the feline eye and the human eye are different in some ways. While the pupil of the human eye remains round as it contracts, a cat's pupil becomes elliptical. A cat's eye also reflects light in the dark, something the human eye cannot do. In addition, cats' eyes possess a protective inner eyelid called the nictitating membrane.

Making the Switch to Academic Writing

As you move from personal writing to academic writing, you need a new set of strategies. Here are five helpful strategies for academic writing.

A Learning Approach

While personal writing allows you to write about the things you are familiar with, academic writing requires a willingness to read, understand, and evaluate the ideas of others.

Objectivity

Personal writing is *subjective*—that is, it allows you to express your own feelings and opinions. Academic writing, on the other hand, is *objective*. It requires you to put aside your own opinions and to look without bias at the ideas of another person—even if you disagree with those ideas.

Knowledge of Key Terms

When you read and write about academic subjects, understanding key terms is essential. Make an effort to learn the meanings of unfamiliar terms. This essential step will help your comprehension of the article you are reading and will help you use the terms knowledgeably in your writing.

Use of the Third Person

When you write from personal experience, you often use the *first-person* pronouns *I, me,* or *my*. In academic writing, *third person* is preferred, even when you are expressing your own opinion. Thus you would write, "Several of Emily Dickinson's poems reflect an obsession with death," not "I think that Emily Dickinson's poetry reflects an obsession with death."

Careful Acknowledgment of Others' Work

If you are quoting or using the ideas of other writers, it is important to acknowledge your sources both informally within the text of your paper and formally through parenthetical references and a Works Cited page. Failure to acknowledge sources is called plagiarism and is considered cheating.

EXERCISE 2   **PARAPHRASING SHORT PASSAGES**

Paraphrase the following short passages.

Passage 1

Aggressive driving is characterized by the tendency to view driving as a competition rather than as a means of getting from one place to another. While most drivers are content to move along with the flow of traffic, aggressive drivers weave from lane to lane, seeking any advantage that will place them ahead of others. Aggressive drivers are also more likely to tailgate and honk the horn in an effort to intimidate other drivers or simply to move them along faster. When confronted with heavy traffic, aggressive drivers often engage in dangerous behaviors such as passing on the right, using utility or turn lanes as driving lanes, and ignoring traffic signals. Paradoxically, aggressive drivers often pride themselves on their skill. They see other, more cautious drivers as the problem, not themselves.

_____

_____

_____

_____

_____

_____

Passage 2

  The National Academies' Institute of Medicine now recommends an hour per day of total physical activity such as walking, stair-climbing, or swimming. Many Americans fall far short of reaching this goal. Some are still trying to catch up to the previous guidelines of thirty minutes of activity five days per week. A century ago, Americans would have found it easier to exercise for an hour per day. Without cars, people walked more, and without modern labor-saving devices, life required more physical exertion. Today, however, many Americans sit at a desk all day and come home to sit in front of a TV or computer. Even those who make an effort to exercise often find that they lack the time.

_____

_____

_____

_____

_____

_____

EXERCISE 3 **SUMMARIZING A PASSAGE**

In a paragraph, summarize the following longer passage. Use your paraphrasing skills to condense the ideas in the original material.

Developing Focus

  One of the most valuable skills a student can develop is focus. *Focus* is the ability to concentrate on one thing for an extended period, shutting out everything else. The person who is focused has no trouble with homework; her mind is on the task until it is finished. The focused person has no trouble concentrating during a test. She does not even notice the voice of the lecturer in an adjacent classroom, the tapping pencil of the student two rows over, or her instructor's squeaking chair.

  People differ widely in their ability to concentrate. Some seem capable of laserlike focus on any job until it is completed. Others are easily distracted, jumping up from homework to do a hundred small but suddenly urgent tasks as the homework gets pushed further into the background. Like any other skill, the ability to focus can be learned and reinforced through practice. To improve your ability to concentrate, start by establishing a set time and place to study. If possible, study at the same time and in the same place every day. Establishing a routine gives study the importance it deserves and helps make studying a habit. Then, to keep yourself on task, set a small timer as you begin studying. Start by setting the timer to go off after fifteen minutes. Until the timer goes off, give studying your full attention. If your mind wanders—and it will—pull it back to the task. Then reward yourself with something small: five minutes of solitaire on your computer or a trip to the refrigerator for a glass of iced tea. Time your reward, too—about five minutes should be sufficient. Then set the timer for another fifteen minutes.

As concentration becomes a habit, that habit will spill over into the classroom, too. You will be better able to focus on your instructor's words or on the test you are taking. If extraneous noises during the test still distract you, invest in a pair of earplugs to shut out noise as you take your test.

The ability to concentrate is a necessary skill. Fortunately, it is a skill that can be improved with effort.

_____

_____

_____

_____

_____

_____

_____

_____

_____

_____

A Model Summary Report

For her summary report, Anna chose an article dealing with the effects of a college student's diet, sleeping habits, and drinking or smoking habits on memory and learning. The article follows, along with Anna's highlighting and annotations and the final draft of her summary report.

The Perils of Higher Education

Steve Kotler

We go to college to learn, to soak up a dazzling array of information intended to prepare us for adult life. But college is not simply a data dump; it is also the end of parental supervision. For many students, that translates into four years of late nights, pizza banquets and boozy weekends that start on Wednesday. And while we know that bad habits are detrimental to cognition in general—think drunk driving—new studies show that the undergrad urges to eat, drink and be merry have devastating effects on learning and memory. It turns out that the exact place we go to get an education may in fact be one of the worst possible environments in which to retain anything we've learned.

Main idea

Dude, I Haven't Slept in Three Days!

Normal human beings spend one-third of their lives asleep, but today's college students aren't normal. A recent survey of undergraduates and medical students at Stanford University found 80 percent of them qualified as sleep-deprived, and a poll taken by the National Sleep Foundation found that most young adults get only 6.8 hours a night.

All-night cramfests may seem to be the only option when the end of the semester looms, but in fact getting sleep—and a full dose of it—might be a better way to ace exams. Sleep is crucial to declarative memory, the hard, factual kind that helps us remember which year World War I began, or what room the French Lit class is in. It's also essential for procedural memory, the "know-how" memory we use when learning to drive a car or write a five-paragraph essay. "Practice makes perfect," says Harvard Medical School psychologist Matt Walker, "but having a night's rest after practicing might make

Procedural and declarative memory— major point

Support—
Harvard
study

you even better. <u>Walker taught 100 people to bang out a series of nonsense sequences on a keyboard—a standard procedural memory task. When asked to replay the sequence 12 hours later, they hadn't improved. But when one group of subjects was allowed to sleep overnight before being retested, their speed and accuracy improved by 20 to 30 percent. "It was bizarre," says Walker. "We were seeing people's skills improve just by sleeping."</u>

For procedural memory, the deep slow-wave stages of sleep were the most important for improvement—particularly during the last two hours of the night. Declarative memory, by contrast, gets processed during the slow-wave stages that come in the first two hours of sleep. "This means that memory requires a full eight hours of sleep," says Walker. He also found that if someone goes without sleep for 24 hours after acquiring a new skill, a week later they will have lost it completely. So college students who pull all-nighters during exam week might do fine on their tests but may not remember any of the material by next semester.

Walker believes that the common practice of back-loading semesters with a blizzard of papers and exams needs a rethink. "Educators are just encouraging sleeplessness," says Walker. "This is just not an effective way to force information into the brain."

Who's Up for Pizza?

Walk into any college cafeteria and you'll find a smorgasbord of French fries, greasy pizza, burgers, potato chips and the like. On top of that, McDonald's, Burger King, Wendy's and other fast-food chains have been gobbling up campus real estate in recent years. With hectic schedules and skinny budgets,

Diet—major
point

students find fast food an easy alternative. A recent Tufts University survey found that 50 percent of students eat too much fat, and 70 to 80 percent eat too much saturated fat.

Diet—
major point

But students who fuel their studies with fast food have something more serious than the "freshman 15" to worry about: They may literally be eating themselves stupid. Researchers have known since the late 1980s that bad eating habits contribute to the kind of cognitive decline found in diseases like Alzheimer's.

Since then, they've been trying to find out exactly how a bad diet might be hard on the brain. Ann-Charlotte Granholm, director of the Center for Aging at the Medical University of South Carolina, has recently focused on trans fat, widely used in fast-food cooking because it extends the shelf life of foods. Trans fat is made by bubbling hydrogen through unsaturated fat, with copper or zinc added to speed the chemical reaction along. These metals are frequently found in the brains of people with Alzheimer's, which sparked Granholm's concern.

USC study— support   → To investigate, she fed one group of rats a diet high in trans fat and compared them with another group fed a diet that was just as greasy but low in trans fat. Six weeks later, she tested the animals in a water maze, the rodent equivalent of a final exam in organic chemistry. "The trans-fat group made many more errors," says Granholm, especially when she used more difficult mazes.

When she examined the rats' brains, she found that trans-fat eaters had fewer proteins critical to healthy neurological function. She also saw inflammation in and around the hippocampus, the part of the brain responsible for learning and memory. "It was alarming," says Granholm. "These are the exact types of changes we normally see at the onset of Alzheimer's, but we saw them after six weeks," even though the rats were still young.

NIA study— support   → Her work corresponds to a broader inquiry conducted by Veerendra Kumar, Madala Halagaapa and Mark Mattson of the National Institute on Aging. The researchers fed four groups of mice different diets—normal, high-fat, high-sugar and high-fat/high-sugar. Each diet had the same caloric value, so that one group of mice wouldn't end up heavier. Four months later, the mice on the high-fat diets performed significantly worse than the other groups on a water maze test.

The researchers then exposed the animals to a neurotoxin that targets the hippocampus, to assess whether a high-fat diet made the mice less able to cope with brain damage. Back in the maze, all the animals performed worse than before, but the mice that had eaten the high-fat diets were most seriously compromised. "Based on our work," says Mattson, "we'd predict that people who eat high-fat diets and high-fat/high-sugar diets are not only damaging their ability to learn and remember new information, but also putting themselves at much greater risk for all sorts of neurodegenerative disorders like Alzheimer's."

Welcome to Margaritaville State University

It's widely recognized that heavy drinking doesn't exactly boost your intellect. But most people figure that their booze-induced foolishness wears off once the hangover is gone. Instead, it turns out that even limited stints of overindulgence may have long-term effects.

Alcohol—major point

Less than 20 years ago, researchers began to realize that the adult brain wasn't just a static lump of cells. They found that stem cells in the brain are constantly churning out new neurons, particularly in the hippocampus. Alcoholism researchers, in turn, began to wonder if chronic alcoholics' memory problems had something to do with nerve cell birth and growth.

UNC study—support

In 2000, Kimberly Nixon and Fulton Crews at the University of North Carolina's Bowles Center for Alcohol Studies subjected lab rats to four days of heavy alcohol intoxication. They gave the rats a week to shake off their hangovers, then tested them on and off during the next month in a water maze. "We didn't find anything at first," says Nixon. But on the 19th day, the rats who had been on the binge performed much worse. In 19 days, the cells born during the binge had grown to maturity—and clearly, the neurons born during the boozy period didn't work properly once they reached maturity. "[The timing] was almost too perfect," says Nixon.

While normal rats generated about 2,500 new brain cells in three weeks, the drinking rats produced only 1,400. A month later, the sober rats had lost about half of those new cells through normal die-off. But all of the new cells died in the brains of the binge drinkers. "This was startling," says Nixon. "It was the first time anyone had found that alcohol not only inhibits the birth of new cells but also inhibits the ones that survive." In further study, they found that a week's abstinence produced a twofold burst of neurogenesis, and a month off the sauce brought cognitive function back to normal.

What does this have to do with a weekend keg party? A number of recent studies show that college students consume far more alcohol than anyone previously suspected. Forty-four percent of today's collegiates drink enough to be classified as binge drinkers, according to a nationwide survey of 10,000 students done at Harvard University. The amount of alcohol consumed by Nixon's binging rats far exceeded intake at a typical keg party—but other research shows that the effects of alcohol work on a sliding scale. Students who follow a weekend of heavy drinking with a week of heavy studying might not forget everything they learn. They just may struggle come test time.

Can I Bum a Smoke?

If this ledger of campus menaces worries you, here's something you really won't like: Smoking cigarettes may actually have some cognitive benefits, thanks to the power of nicotine. The chemical improves mental focus, as scientists have known since the 1950s. Nicotine also aids concentration in people who have ADHD and may protect against Alzheimer's disease. Back in 2000, a nicotine-like drug under development by the pharmaceutical company Astra Arcus USA was shown to restore the ability to learn and remember in rats with brain lesions similar to those found in Alzheimer's patients. More recently Granholm, the scientist investigating trans fats and memory, found that nicotine enhances spatial memory in healthy rats. Other researchers have found that nicotine also boosts both emotional memory (the kind that helps us not put our hands back in the fire after we've been burned) and auditory memory.

There's a catch: Other studies show that nicotine encourages state-dependent learning. The idea is that if, for example, you study in blue sweats, it helps to take the exam in blue sweats. In other words, what you learn while smoking is best recalled while smoking. Since lighting up in an exam room might cause problems, cigarettes probably aren't the key to getting on the dean's list.

Nonetheless, while the number of cigarette smokers continues to drop nationwide, college students are still lighting up: As many as 30 percent smoke during their years of higher education. The smoking rate for young adults

Margin notes:

Major point—smoking

Support—nicotine aids memory

Support—state-dependent learning

between the ages of 18 and 24 has actually risen in the past decade. All this news makes you wonder how anyone's ever managed to get an education. Or what would happen to GPAs at a vegetarian university with a 10 p.m. curfew. But you might not need to go to such extremes. While Granholm agrees that the excesses of college can be "a perfect example of what you shouldn't do to yourself if you are trying to learn," she doesn't recommend abstinence. "Moderation," she counsels, "just like in everything else. Moderation is the key to collegiate success."

Recommendation—moderation

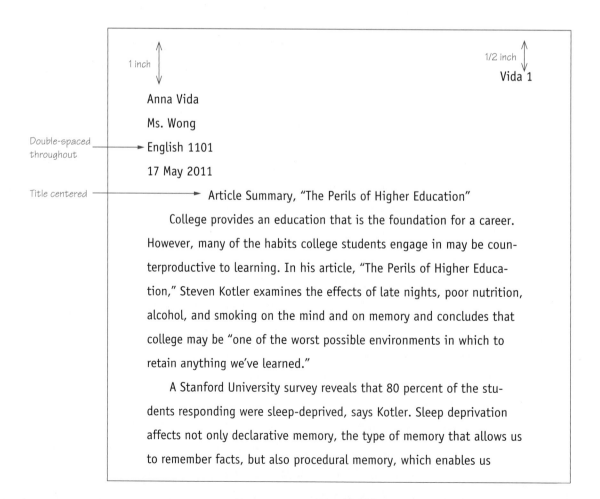

1 inch

1/2 inch

Vida 1

Anna Vida

Ms. Wong

Double-spaced throughout → English 1101

17 May 2011

Title centered → Article Summary, "The Perils of Higher Education"

College provides an education that is the foundation for a career. However, many of the habits college students engage in may be counterproductive to learning. In his article, "The Perils of Higher Education," Steven Kotler examines the effects of late nights, poor nutrition, alcohol, and smoking on the mind and on memory and concludes that college may be "one of the worst possible environments in which to retain anything we've learned."

A Stanford University survey reveals that 80 percent of the students responding were sleep-deprived, says Kotler. Sleep deprivation affects not only declarative memory, the type of memory that allows us to remember facts, but also procedural memory, which enables us

Vida 2

to carry out processes such as driving a car. Sleep is necessary for processing both kinds of memory, and in fact, procedural memory actually improves after sleep, according to one Harvard study.

Fast-food eateries on college campuses combined with the fatty foods in the college cafeteria serve to ensure that 50 percent of students, according to a Tufts University survey, eat diets that are too high in fat. High-fat diets have been shown to impair brain function in mice and rats. In particular, hydrogenated fats, or trans fats, produced changes in a rat's brain that were comparable with those found in the early stages of Alzheimer's disease.

A University of North Carolina study showed that rats given large doses of alcohol and tested over a period of weeks began to perform worse on a water maze test after the nineteenth day—enough time for neurons born during the time the alcohol was ingested to mature. Scientists have found that not only do brain cells produced during a time of heavy alcohol ingestion perform worse, they also die off more quickly. Though abstinence can bring normal brain function back within two months—in rats, anyway—students who binge on weekends may have a harder time academically than they would if they stayed sober.

The list of diseases attributed to smoking is long and well documented, but the nicotine in cigarettes actually improves memory and may help prevent Alzheimer's disease. However, recall of material learned while smoking is state-dependent, other studies show. In other words, if a student learns material while smoking, it is easier to recall it while smoking, an impossibility under most testing conditions.

Vida 3

Steven Kotler's article provides much food for thought. As college students are preparing for the adult world of work and career, the knowledge they acquire becomes increasingly important. At the same time, many want to try out habits forbidden at home or go along with the crowd in drinking alcohol or smoking. Is there a middle ground? Anne-Charlotte Granholm, UNC researcher and author of a study on fats, provides hope. "Moderation," she says, "is the key to collegiate success."

Vida 4

Centered ———————————▶ Works Cited

First line is flush with left margin; any subsequent lines are indented one-half inch.

Kotler, Steven. "The Perils of Higher Education." *Psychology Today* 38.2 ▶ (2005): 64-65. *General OneFile*. Web. May 2011.

SUMMARY REPORT ASSIGNMENTS

Summary Report Assignment 1: Summarizing an Article about Your Career or Major

Write a summary of an article that deals with some aspect of your chosen career or major. The article may be one about job opportunities in your field, or it may focus on a particular issue central to your field. Follow the step-by-step process outlined in this chapter to find your article, evaluate it, read it to find the main ideas, and write your summary.

Summary Report Assignment 2: Summarizing an Article That Solves a Problem

Write a summary of an article that helps you solve a problem in your life. Whether you are trying to find ways to save more money, impress an interviewer, organize your time, choose an automobile, or eat more nutritiously, dozens of articles await you in the library or on the Internet. Because articles of this type vary widely in length, be sure to choose an article substantial enough to lend itself to summarizing. Follow the step-by-step process outlined in this chapter to find your article, evaluate it, read it to find the main ideas, and write your summary.

Summary Report Assignment 3: Summarizing an Article That Explores a Social Issue

Write a summary of an article that explores a current social problem. You will find articles on homelessness, drug abuse, domestic violence, school violence, and many more issues of current concern in the library or on the Internet. Articles may vary in length, so be sure to choose an article substantial enough to lend itself to summarizing. Follow the step-by-step process outlined in this chapter to find your article, evaluate it, read it to find the main ideas, and write your summary.

mywritinglab   For support and practice meeting this chapter's goal, log in to www.mywritinglab.com and select Summary Writing.

CHAPTER 12

Writing a Research Paper

✎ **Chapter Goal:** Conduct academic research and write research-based essays.

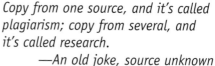

Copy from one source, and it's called plagiarism; copy from several, and it's called research.
—An old joke, source unknown

If you have ever written a research paper, you know that it involves much more than "copying from several sources." If you have written only personal essays, you will find that incorporating outside sources into a research paper is a challenge. First, you must find the right sources; then you must carefully incorporate those sources and acknowledge their authors. However, a research paper is structurally similar to a personal essay, with an introduction that provides background and presents a thesis, body paragraphs that support the thesis, and a conclusion. It embodies all of the qualities of good writing—direction,

Focus on Writing a Research Paper: Thinking about Research

www.benitaepstein.com

© Benita Epstein 1996

"I already wrote the paper. That's why it's so hard to get the right data."

The man in the cartoon wrote his paper before finding the data. Now he has a problem. When researching, you will usually begin with a general idea of what you want to say and then do the research. This method leaves room for at least a few surprises. If you want to learn something about a topic such as the life of someone you admire or the history of a company you want to work with, you usually have a little knowledge to begin with and a lot more knowledge after searching credible sources for information.

Reflect on It

Think of how often you research in any given day. What kind of information do you search for online? How many times in one day (or one week) do you look for information in order to verify something you were unsure of or learn something you didn't know?

unity, coherence, and support. As you write a research paper, you follow the familiar steps in the writing process. Prewriting and planning take longer with a research paper because research is now a part of those preliminary steps. Drafting takes longer because each source must be acknowledged and a Works Cited page prepared. Revision and proofreading are, as always, the final steps in the process. The research paper provides new challenges, but the methods remain the same.

This chapter discusses the five steps in writing a research paper: creating a research question, finding and evaluating information, outlining and note taking, drafting, formatting the paper, and citing sources. It provides discussion and practice of two essential research skills, summarizing and paraphrasing. The chapter ends with a brief guide to APA (American Psychological Association) and MLA (Modern Language Association) styles of writing research papers and a sample paper written and documented in MLA style.

Six Strategies for Academic Writing

Academic essays differ in several ways from personal essays and therefore require different strategies. Six strategies are listed below.

A Learning Approach

Whereas personal writing allows you to write from your own experience, academic writing requires you to understand and evaluate the ideas of others. Therefore, academic writing requires a willingness to learn and to research.

Objectivity

Personal writing is *subjective*—that is, it allows you to express your own feelings and opinions on a topic. Academic writing, on the other hand, is *objective*. It requires you to put aside your own opinions and to look without bias at the ideas of another person—even if you disagree with those ideas.

Knowledge of Key Terms

Understanding key terms is essential in any field. When writing about a short story, for example, you might be asked to comment on *setting, character,* or *point of view,* while your paper in psychology might discuss *internal* versus *external locus of control.* When you write about a particular field, be willing to learn and use its key terms.

Use of the Third Person

In personal writing, you often use the *first person*—the pronoun *I.* In academic writing, the *third person* is preferred even when you are expressing your own opinion. Thus you would write, "Several of Emily Dickinson's poems reflect an obsession with death," not "I think that Emily Dickinson's poetry reflects an obsession with death."

Analysis, Not Summary

In a research paper, it is usually not enough to simply summarize the ideas in an essay, article, or book. A research paper usually involves manipulating information: comparing, contrasting, categorizing, analyzing, or showing a progression through time. When you write a research paper, impose your own order on the material. Analyze, don't simply summarize.

Careful Acknowledgment of Others' Work

When you quote sources or paraphrase the ideas of other writers, it is important to carefully acknowledge your sources. Failure to do so is called **plagiarism** and is considered cheating.

✍ Five Steps in Writing a Research Paper

Step 1: Find a Topic and Create a Research Question

mywritinglab

Visit MyWriting Lab for additional practice with the research process.

Your instructor may assign a topic or area of investigation, or you may be asked to choose your own topic. Within the range of choices you are given, choose something that interests you. Once you have selected a topic, your next job is to narrow it by formulating a research question. In a personal essay, you would formulate a thesis at this point. However, research deals with a question to be answered, not a thesis to be proven, so writing a thesis at this point would be premature.

Just as a thesis statement provides direction for your essay, a research question provides direction for your research. For example, let's say that you decide your topic will be the Internet. When you look for articles on such a broad topic, you may find too much information. You will find information on the Internet as a business tool, a research tool, and a communication tool. You will find information on the history of the Internet and the future of the Internet. You will find articles on Internet addiction, the Internet and pornography, and the Internet and education. A research question will help you narrow your search to articles in one specific area.

Suppose you decide on the research question, *How can the Internet be made safer for children?* Now you have direction. You can focus your search on articles dealing with children and the Internet and on Internet safety. However, remember that your research question is tentative. If you find a more interesting angle on your topic, don't be afraid to alter your question. If you cannot find enough information to answer your question, write a whole new question. It is easier to change the question or alter your angle of investigation before you have researched than it is later in the process.

Step 2: Find and Evaluate Information from Various Sources

Sources for information may include encyclopedias, books, periodicals, databases, and Internet sites. Once you have found source material, you will evaluate the material and determine its relevance to your research question.

Sources for Research

Different sources have different strengths and weaknesses. Some provide the latest information, some go into depth, and some provide a broad overview. Knowing the characteristics of various types of sources will help you select the right ones for your project.

General encyclopedias provide broad, general, factual information. They provide a broad overview and thus may be a helpful source of background information. However, they do not go into much depth and may not provide the latest information. Examples of general encyclopedias include *Encyclopedia Britannica, Compton's Encyclopedia, Funk and Wagnalls New World Encyclopedia,* and *World Book Encyclopedia.*

Subject encyclopedias focus on one specific area and go into greater depth than general encyclopedias. Examples of subject encyclopedias include the *Encyclopedia of Social Work,* the *Encyclopedia of Educational Research,* the *AMA Encyclopedia of Medicine,* and the *Encyclopedia of the Vietnam War.*

Books go into great depth and may be written by authorities in a particular field. Unless the books have been recently published, however, they may not contain the most recent information.

Periodicals are publications such as newspapers, magazines, and scholarly journals that are published on a regular basis—daily, monthly, or quarterly, for example. Newspapers and magazines are written for the general public, while journals are written for scholars in a particular field. Recent periodicals of all types will contain current, up-to-date information.

Subscription and CD-ROM Databases

Most college libraries offer students access to subscription databases and CD-ROM databases from vendors such as EBSCOhost, GaleNet, FirstSearch, and ProQuest. Some of the more widely used databases, which may be available from one or more of the vendors, include *ABI/INFORM, Academic Search Premier, ERIC, Medline,* and *Research Library.* These databases may contain full-text articles from journals, newspapers, magazines, and encyclopedias, or they may contain article abstracts. **Full-text articles** in a database are exactly the same articles you would find in a periodical, so there is no need to locate the original periodical. **Article abstracts** are summaries of articles that appear in periodicals. To access the complete text of an abstracted article, locate a copy of the periodical in which it originally appeared.

Internet Sources

Internet sources vary widely in quality, so it is necessary to be aware of the type of site you are visiting. If the site has the suffix *.gov,* it is an official government site. The suffix *.org* indicates a nonprofit organization. The *.edu* suffix is reserved for colleges and universities. Sites with this suffix may contain faculty and student home pages, official college information, and community outreach sites. The *.com* suffix denotes a commercial site, and anyone may set up a site with the suffix *.com.* It is up to you to evaluate the credibility of each site you visit.

Evaluating Sources: Four Questions to Ask

The four questions that follow will help you evaluate an article or book that you are thinking of using in your research.

- *When was it published?* A publication date helps you evaluate the timeliness of the source. In fields where change is rapid, such as medicine or computer technology, finding up-to-date sources is essential.

- *Who wrote it?* Is the author an authority in the field? If not—if the author is a journalist, for example—does the author consult and quote credible, authoritative sources? These questions help you evaluate the authority and credibility of your source.

- *Is the coverage in-depth or is it an overview?* While an overview may provide good background information, you also need articles and books that cover your topic in depth.

- *Does it provide an answer to my research question?* Just because an article is on the topic you have decided to research does not mean that it answers the question you are asking. *Hint:* If, after reasonable effort, you can't find articles that answer your question, ask a different question. Use the articles you have already scanned to help uncover other interesting research questions.

After evaluating your sources, you will have narrowed the choices to the articles, books, or websites that are most helpful to you. Check out books and photocopy or print items that cannot be checked out. Although you can take notes while you are in the library, it is a better idea to read through your sources, live with them for a while, and absorb the material before taking notes.

Step 3: Outline Your Paper and Take Notes from Your Sources

Once you have evaluated your sources and thoroughly read your source material, you are ready to organize your paper. Make a brief outline of the points you will make and the source or sources you will use to support each point. Then, take notes from your sources, choosing the material that most effectively supports the point you are making in your paragraph.

The first step in taking notes from your sources is to write down the information you will need for your Works Cited list. There is no more painful experience for a researcher than to discover, after the paper is written, that this basic information on the source has somehow disappeared. A list of information needed for your Works Cited list follows on p. 267.

Advice for Online Researchers

Get Ready to Go Online

Research used to mean poring through stacks of books and periodicals. Today, it usually means sitting in front of a computer screen. Even print sources must be located through online catalogs, indexes to periodicals, and databases. Even if you are comfortable using a computer, these resources may seem alien to you at first. But don't feel intimidated. Everyone has to start somewhere—even librarians who are experts at finding information on the computer were beginners once. If you need help, do not hesitate to ask questions. As a researcher, part of your job is to ask questions and to seek help when you need it.

Find a Friend

It's a good idea to find someone in class who will agree to be your research partner. You don't need an expert; nor do you need someone who is working on the same topic. All you need is someone who is willing to go through the process with you. The two of you can work side by side and handle the rough spots together.

Ask a Librarian

Librarians are experts in finding information, and they are there to help. If you and your research partner need help, ask. Explain your project and the kind of information you are looking for, and the librarian will help you find it.

Print the Information

When you find useful articles online, print them so that you will not have to look for them again. Just taking notes may not be sufficient. Documentation of online sources requires that you acknowledge the database you used and the date you accessed the information. That information will be on your printout. The library may charge a minimal amount for printing, to cover the costs of paper and ink.

Be Patient

Be patient with yourself and with the process of finding information. Finding information always takes longer than you think it will, and you may need to make several trips to the library before you have everything you need.

For all sources

- Author
- Title (If the source is contained within a larger work, make a note of both titles. For example, if your source is an article in a magazine, note the title of the article and the title of the magazine.)
- Date of publication
- Volume and issue numbers for periodicals
- Month, day (if available), and year for magazines or newspapers
- Page numbers

Additional information for online sources:

- Date of access
- The URL (Uniform Resource Locator, or complete Web address) of an article from a website
- The name of the database (for example, Academic Search Premier or Lexis-Nexis Academic Universe) for articles accessed from subscription databases through a college library.

The next step is to take careful notes from your sources. As you note the information, also note whether you are directly quoting the material or paraphrasing it. Direct quotations should be used sparingly and only to highlight the most important points. Most of your paper should be in your own words. When you paraphrase, recheck your paraphrases to make sure your wording is not too close to that of the original material.

Real-World Writing: Is research easier because of the Internet?

Yes. According to *The Chronicle of Higher Education,* first-year college students are becoming increasingly Internet-savvy and are thus finding libraries and research less intimidating.

Step 4: Draft Your Paper

Drafting a research paper is quite similar to drafting a personal essay. Your draft should contain the following elements:

- An **introduction** that provides necessary background to the issue you have researched. The introduction should end in a thesis statement that directly answers the research question you have asked.

- Several **body paragraphs** beginning with **topic sentences** that state the point that the paragraph will support. Support in your body paragraphs will come from the sources that you found during your research. As you write the draft, make a note of sources and page numbers beside each paragraph.

- A **conclusion** that sums up your paper. A summary conclusion is always appropriate, but other possibilities include suggesting avenues for further research or proposing solutions to a problem.

Step 5: Format Your Paper and Cite Your Sources

The final draft of your paper will include proper formatting, parenthetical references, and a Works Cited page. Citing sources is considered so important that various academic disciplines have adopted their own methods of formatting papers and acknowledging sources. Fields such as psychology, sociology, nursing, and criminal justice generally use the **APA** style of documentation, as outlined in the *Publication Manual of the American Psychological Association*. Scholars in literature and the humanities often use the **MLA** style of the Modern Language Association, as outlined in the *MLA Handbook for Writers of Research Papers*. When you are assigned a paper, use the documentation style recommended by your instructor. The brief guide to MLA style that appears later in this chapter may be used unless your instructor specifies another style.

🖌 Paraphrasing and Summarizing: Essential Research Skills

mywritinglab

Visit MyWriting Lab for additional practice with summary writing.

One of the most difficult tasks of writing a research paper is to convey an author's ideas in your own words. When you *paraphrase*, you rephrase a sentence or paragraph using your own sentence structure and your own words. A *summary* involves exactly the same skills—capturing ideas in your own words—but with a longer piece of source material. You would normally paraphrase a sentence or a short paragraph but summarize a longer paragraph, a section of an article, or a chapter in a book. A paraphrase can usually capture an idea a bit more closely. When you have only a sentence or a short paragraph to paraphrase, you can express the author's idea fully in your own words. A summary of a chapter or of a long section of an article will be more general and will leave out the details. Both a paraphrase and a summary must be properly referenced as containing ideas from someone else's work.

Paraphrasing

A **paraphrase** captures an idea expressed in a short piece of writing, such as a sentence or a paragraph. It is an author's idea expressed in your own words. Here are some pointers to help you when you paraphrase:

- It is always permissible to repeat key terms. If the author uses the term *geriatric medicine*, there is no need to rephrase it as "medical care of elderly people."
- Unusual phrasing should be rephrased. If the author refers to a spider web as "a spider's gossamer trap," a paraphrase should simply call it a spider web.
- A paraphrase is usually a bit shorter than the source material, but it captures the entire idea.
- The sentence structure of a paraphrase should vary from that of the original material.

| EXERCISE 1 | PARAPHRASING SHORT PASSAGES |

Paraphrase the following passages.

1. Many workers no longer receive a paycheck. Instead, their employers issue a plastic card that looks something like a credit card. Each payday, the employee's pay is made available electronically through any ATM.

   _____

   _____

   _____

2. Though the custom of "giving away" the bride is strictly symbolic now, among the ancient Romans it had a legal purpose. A Roman patriarch literally owned a daughter for a lifetime, even after she was married, unless he chose to formally transfer her and her possessions to her husband. To moderns, the ceremony may seem to symbolically exchange one kind of bondage for another, but ancient Romans probably saw it as liberating a daughter to live her own life as a married woman.

   _____

   _____

   _____

   _____

   _____

   _____

Summarizing

A **summary** is a statement of the main idea of a longer portion of a work. Like a paraphrase, your summary should restate the author's idea in your own words. Unlike a paraphrase, your summary does not need to capture the details of the paragraph or section of the work that you are summarizing. Therefore, a paragraph summary might be just a sentence or two, and a summary of a chapter might be just a paragraph or two.

EXERCISE 2	SUMMARIZING SHORT PASSAGES

Summarize the following passages in a sentence or two.

1. Migraine researchers have recently confirmed what many *migraineurs,* or migraine sufferers, have known all along: Weather can affect migraines. Specifically, falling barometric pressure can trigger a migraine in many people. People who possess what one sufferer terms a "weather head" often feel symptoms as a thunderstorm rolls in and the barometric pressure begins to fall. "I should have been a weather forecaster," jokes one longtime migraine sufferer. "I always know when a storm is coming."

    _____

    _____

2. What is the scientific method? The scientific method is a process of gathering and testing information. The four steps in the scientific method are observation, formulation of a hypothesis, prediction, and experimentation. The first step, observation, involves observing a particular phenomenon, usually over a period of time. In the second step, the scientist constructs a hypothesis that explains something about the phenomenon. In the third step, the hypothesis is then used to make a prediction about the phenomenon, an "educated guess" that the scientist must prove through the fourth step, experimentation. The experiment must be set up so that it can be repeated by the same scientist or by others to verify the results. If the experiment confirms the prediction consistently, the hypothesis becomes a theory, an assumption about the way the phenomenon works.

    _____

    _____

    _____

✍ Using Documentation Styles

mywritinglab

Visit MyWriting
Lab for additional
practice with
documentation.

When you write a college research paper, you will likely be asked to use one of two documentation styles: APA (American Psychological Association) style or MLA (Modern Language Association). In general, MLA style is used in the fields of English language and literature, media studies, and cultural studies. APA style is used in the fields of psychology, sociology, business, economics, nursing, and criminal justice.

Why Use a Documentation Style?

Documentation styles help you document, or cite, sources that you use in your research. One reason to cite sources properly is to avoid accidentally plagiarizing. But the use of documentation styles goes beyond the need to avoid plagiarism. Documentation styles have their own methods of formatting, titling, and spacing.

The driving force behind documentation styles is the need for consistency. If a journal or other publication in, for instance, the field of economics receives ten papers to be reviewed for publication, it is important that those papers all be in the same format and use the same method of documenting sources. That way, editors (and later on, readers) will not get bogged down worrying about why Professor X used in-text citations and Professor Y used footnotes. They can direct their focus to the content of the papers.

In the same way, by requiring you to use a particular format for your papers, your professors are ensuring that style remains a background issue and content occupies the foreground. Imagine if spelling were as inconsistent today as it was in Shakespeare's day, when even Shakespeare's name had several variants, including "Shakspear" and "Shaxberd." It would be easy to become sidetracked wondering about the different spellings of a word or name and to lose sight of the content entirely.

In addition, when your instructors require you to use a particular style or format, they are preparing you for a time when you might be a writer in a particular field yourself and be required to use those styles. At the very least, your instructors are preparing you for a time when you will be required to adapt your writing to a particular style or format used in your workplace. Every workplace has a format for writing memos, letters, and reports. Again, consistency keeps the focus on the content of those documents. In addition, just as academic writing has certain conventions that must be followed, workplaces, too, have particular writing styles. A police report would never say, "The low-down slimeball tried to get away from me, so I grabbed the sucker and got him in a headlock." Instead, an officer would choose factual, unemotional words, such as "The subject attempted to escape and was restrained."

In addition to a particular format, each documentation style requires a list of sources. The list of sources is an important part of your research paper.

Ideas are the currency of the academic community, and a list of references in a standardized style makes it easier to share those ideas. You list sources so that other researchers in your field can go back to the original sources, read them, and form their own conclusions.

Using Online Sources

You will probably do much of your research on the Internet through various academic databases. Accessing online sources allows you to search beyond the print holdings of your college's library. It also allows you the convenience of researching from a remote location through your college library's website.

Documenting online sources is more complex than documenting print sources. The content of a print source will not change, but online sources often change and evolve. When a website is updated, its previous content may disappear forever. A site may move to a new server and change its Web address entirely, or a library may drop its subscription to one database and pick up another. Because of these complexities, extra documentation is necessary for online sources of information.

The online researcher needs to document when and where source material was viewed. The date that the material was accessed, the name of the library that was used to access a subscription database, and the address of a website are necessary for the Works Cited list. For that reason, printing out all the material accessed online is strongly recommended. The date, the database used, and most other relevant information will be on the printed copy for easy reference.

Many databases provide the convenient option of mailing a full-text article to yourself. In addition, you often have the option of copying or sending yourself a citation in the style you wish to use for your Works Cited page or the References page. Two words of caution are necessary. First, if you use the citation option, be sure that you select the correct style from the drop-down menu. That seems obvious, but it is easy to forget. Second, be aware that automatic citation formatters may vary sightly from database to database and may not be up to date. It's always a good idea to check the citation against this text or against another reliable source.

Guide to APA (American Psychological Association) Style

The following section outlines some of the basic principles of APA style. For complete information on APA style, consult the *Publication Manual of the American Psychological Association,* available in most college libraries and bookstores.

Formatting Your Paper

- Use 8 ½ × 11 inch paper.
- Preferred fonts are 12-point Times Roman and 12-point Courier.
- Double-space the paper, including the References page.
- Use one-inch margins all around.
- Indent paragraphs one-half inch.

Preparing the Title Page

The title page will include a page header in the upper left corner, a page number in the upper right corner, and the title, author, and affiliation centered and double spaced in the upper half of the page, as illustrated below.

The words "Running Head" are dropped after the first page. → Running Head: IN THE ZONE 1 ← Page number

In the Zone: Achieving Peak Performance

in Physical and Mental Activities ← Title

Author → Michael Law

Referencing Sources within Your Paper

Within your paper, references to your sources are **parenthetical references**, not footnotes. APA style calls for brief references enclosed in parentheses and placed immediately after the author's name, after the referenced idea, or at the end of the sentence that contains the idea. For each work cited within the text of your paper, you will place a bibliographic reference in a separate section called References.

One thing to consider as you write your paper is whether to mention an author's name in the text of your paper or to put it in a parenthetical reference. A good rule of thumb is to use the author's name in the text of your paper if you are discussing that author's original research or ideas. If the author is reporting a fact, as in a reference book, an interview, or a news story, put the author's name in a parenthetical reference.

The following examples show the APA style of reference.

A Work by a Single Author

If you have already used the author's name in the sentence or paragraph where the parenthetical reference occurs, use the year as a reference.

Example

✔ Jurgen Frembgen (2006) writes that in Southwest Asia, bats are considered part of the demonic realm because of their strange "anatomy" and nocturnal activities.

If you have not used the author's name in the sentence or paragraph, place the author's last name and the year in parentheses after the quote or a paraphrase of the author's words. A comma is used to separate the author's name and the year.

Example

✔ In Southwest Asia, bats are considered part of the demonic realm because of their strange anatomy and nocturnal activities (Frembgen, 2006).

A Work by Two Authors

As with a single author, if the authors are already mentioned in the sentence or paragraph in which you discuss their work, the page number alone serves as the reference. If you have not mentioned the author's names, your parenthetical reference should include their last names separated by an ampersand (&) along with the page number. Use the ampersand only in the parenthetical reference, not in a reference within the text.

Examples

✔ Skybo and Buck (2007) found that children's anxiety about proficiency testing and their use of coping strategies actually decreased over the course of the school year.
✔ One study found that children's anxiety about proficiency testing and their use of coping strategies actually decreased over the course of the school year (Skybo & Buck, 2007).

A Work by Three or More Authors

When a reference forms an essential part of a sentence, the first reference within the text to three, four, or five authors should cite all authors by last name.

Example

✔ Budnitz, Shelab, Kegler, and Richards (2007) attribute 90 percent of emergency room visits by older adults for adverse drug reactions to three classes of drugs: antidiabetic drugs, oral anticoagulants, and narrow therapeutic index drugs.

Later citations within the text would be in the form "Budnitz et al. (2007)" for the first mention in a paragraph, and "Budnitz et al." for subsequent references within the same paragraph. Note that the abbreviation "et al." (meaning "and others") is not italicized and that a period is placed after "al." Parenthetical references to a work by more than three authors should include the lead author's name and the abbreviation "et al."

Example

✔ Ninety percent of emergency room visits by older adults for adverse drug reactions could be attributed to three classes of drugs: anti-diabetic drugs, oral anticoagulants, and narrow therapeutic index drugs (Budnitz et al., 2007).

Groups as Authors

For works authored by corporations, government agencies, or other organizations, write out the name each time it appears in the text. If the name is one with a familiar abbreviation (i.e., IRS for Internal Revenue Service), the name of the group or organization may be abbreviated in the text after the first reference.

Examples

✔ Prevent Child Abuse America (2004) lists six warning signs that a child may be involved with an online sexual predator, including telephone calls from strangers or unexplained gifts or cash.

✔ Warning signs that a child may be involved with an online sexual predator include telephone calls from strangers or unexplained gifts or cash (Prevent Child Abuse America, 2004).

A Work with No Author Listed

Some works, such as editorials, reports, brochures, Web pages, and encyclopedia articles, may have no author listed. Each parenthetical reference should include the first few words of the title (unless it is *a, an,* or *the*) and the year. Shortened book titles are italicized (or underlined if your instructor prefers); article titles are put in quotation marks. If the work's author is listed as "Anonymous," treat "Anonymous" as you would the name of a single author.

Examples

✔ The Student Search Service, operated by the College Board, sells names and basic information to colleges looking to recruit students ("Colleges," 2006).

✔ Protein powders are not just for bodybuilders; they also help in weight-loss programs by helping dieters shed fat, increase muscle, and reduce cravings. ("Take it off," 2008).

Personal Communication

In APA style, personal communications such as interviews or emails are cited in the text only, not in the list of references, and are called "personal communications" regardless of the method used.

Example

✔ P. Borck said that the library is one of the best places to get help with a research paper (personal communication, February 9, 2011).

The References List

In APA style, your References list, or Bibliography, is double-spaced on a separate sheet headed "References." Use the following model entries as a guide to preparing your References list. When there are two examples, the first is from an online source, the second from a print source.

Articles that can be accessed online are now documented in the reference list with a DOI, or digital object identifier, when one is available. The DOI is found on the first page of the article itself or in the database citation. If you do not see a DOI, go to www.crossref.org, and using the Guest Query feature, enter the title of the article and the first author's last name. If you cannot find a DOI, use the alternate "Retrieved from" citation shown in the first example below. For more information on digital object identifiers and their proper use, see http://www.apastyle.org/learn/faqs/what-is-doi.aspx

One Author

Davis, J. (2008, January). Refer madness. *ABA Journal, 94*(1), 24–24. Retrieved from http://www.ebscohost.com/academic/business-source-complete

Collins, J. (2011, January). Reaching out to Latinos. *Business & Economic Review, 54*(2), 12–15.

Rast, P. (2011, May). Verbal Knowledge, working memory, and processing speed as predictors of verbal learning in older adults. *Developmental Psychology. 94*(5), 1163–1184. doi: 10.1037/a0023422

Multiple Authors up to Seven

Diehl, S., Mueller, B., & Terlutter, R. (2007). Consumer responses towards non-prescription and prescription drug advertising in the US and Germany. *International Journal of Advertising, 27*(1), 99–131. Retrieved from http://www.ebscohost.com/academic/business-source-complete

Strachan, J., & Pavie-Latour, V. (2008). Food for thought. *International Journal of Market Research, 50*(1), 13–27.

In APA style, when an article has two to seven authors, all authors are listed.

More than Seven Authors

Schlooz, W., Hulstijn, W., Broek, P., van der Pijll, A., Gabreëls, F., van der Gaag, R . . . Rotteveel, JJ. (2006, December). Fragmented visuospatial processing in children with pervasive developmental disorder. *Journal of Autism & Developmental Disorders, 36*(8), 1025–1037. doi:10.1007/s10803-006-0140-z

Tzimos, A., Samokhvalov, V., Kramer, M., Ford, L., Gassmann-Mayer, C., Lim, P., . . . Eerdelems, M. (2011, February). Safety and tolerability of oral paliperidone extended-release tablets in elderly patients with schizophrenia: A double-blind, placebo-controlled study with six-month open-label extension. *American Journal of Geriatric Psychiatry, 16*(1), 31–43.

When an article has more than seven authors, the first six are listed, followed by an ellipses (. . .) and the final author.

Magazine Article

Zimmer, E. (2007, February). Taming the gypsy in her soul. *Dance Magazine, 81*(2), 62–66. Retrieved from http://www.ebscohost.com/uk-eire-schools/advanced-placement-source

Clark, J. (2002, July). As seen on TV. *Kiplinger's,* 98–105.

Newspaper Article

Neuharth, A. (2002, July 19). Can we curb rude cellphone manners? *USA Today*, A–13.

Unsigned Encyclopedia Entry

Conservation. (2008). In *Encyclopaedia Britannica.* Retrieved from http://search.eb.com/eb/article-272704.

Book by a Single Author

Schlosser, E. (2002). *Fast food nation: The dark side of the all-American meal.* New York, NY: HarperCollins.

Book by Two Authors

Halfacre, R., & Shawcroft, A. (1997). *Landscape plants of the Southeast.* Raleigh, NC: Sparks.

Personal Interview

In the APA style, personal interviews are cited only in the text in parentheses, not in the list of references.

Article on a Website

Sahadi, J. (2004, October 24). The ideal budget. *CNN/Money.* Retrieved from http://money.cnn.com.

Guide to MLA (Modern Language Association) Style

The following section outlines some of the basic principles of MLA style. For complete information on MLA style, consult the *MLA Handbook for Writers of Research Papers,* available in most college libraries and bookstores.

Formatting Your Paper

- Double-space the paper, including the Works Cited page.
- Use one-inch margins.

- Indent paragraphs one-half inch.

- Do not use a title page. Instead, put your name, your instructor's name, your course name, and the date at the top of the first page, each on a separate line, each line flush with the left margin. Center the title above the first paragraph. This material, like the rest of your paper, should be double-spaced.

Referencing Sources within Your Paper

Within your paper, references to your sources are **parenthetical references**, not footnotes. MLA style calls for very brief references that interfere as little as possible with the flow of the text.

One thing to consider as you write your paper is whether to mention an author's name in the text of your paper or to put it in a parenthetical reference. A good rule of thumb is to use the author's name in the text of your paper if you are discussing that author's original research or ideas. If the author is reporting a fact, as in a reference book, an interview, or a news story, put the author's name in a parenthetical reference.

The following examples show the MLA style of reference.

A Work by a Single Author

If you have already used the author's name in the sentence or paragraph where the parenthetical reference occurs, use the page number(s) alone as a reference.

Example

✔ According to Merlin Stone, early societies were matrilineal because humanity had not yet figured out the role of men in producing children. To our earliest ancestors, females were the sole givers of life (10–11).

If you have not used the author's name in the sentence or paragraph, place the author's last name and the page number in parentheses after the quote or paraphrase of the author's words. Position the parenthetical reference as close to the end of the sentence as possible, but before the period that ends the sentence. No punctuation is needed between the author's name and the page number.

Example

✔ A thirty-minute organizing session every Friday afternoon is recommended as a way to keep an office functioning smoothly (Morgenstern 109).

A Work by Multiple Authors

As with a single author, if the authors are already mentioned in the sentence or paragraph in which you discuss their work, the page number alone serves as the reference. If you have not mentioned the author's names, your parenthetical reference should include their last names separated by *and* along with the page number.

Examples

✔ Light waves from an advancing light source become shorter and take on a blue tint, while light waves from a retreating body become longer and have a red tint (Jones and Wilson 507).

✔ Because people tend to lose lean body mass as they age, older adults may become increasingly susceptible to the effects of alcohol (Blow, Oslin, and Barry 50–54).

Parenthetical references to a work by more than three authors should include the lead author's name and the abbreviation *et al.,* which means "and others."

Example

✔ Unless parents are involved and patients are motivated, medical professionals may have little success in treating childhood obesity (Story et al. 210).

A Work with No Author Listed

Some works, such as editorials, reports, Web pages, and encyclopedia articles, may have no author listed. Each parenthetical reference should include the first word of the title (unless it is *a, an,* or *the*) and the page number(s), if any. Shortened book titles are italicized; article titles are put in quotation marks.

Examples

✔ In the wake of corporate accounting scandals, a ruling requiring company executives to certify the accuracy of their company's financial records may help to restore public confidence ("First" 6A).

✔ While early versions of the electronic pacemaker worked continuously, newer versions react to the patient's heartbeat and turn on only when they are needed ("Pacemaker").

Quote from an Interview or Reference to Another Author's Work

Use the abbreviation *qtd. in* (for *quoted in*) if you are quoting or paraphrasing someone who has been quoted in an interview. Also use *qtd. in* when you paraphrase or quote one author's paraphrase of another author's ideas, but only if you cannot obtain the original source. In other words, if Author A writes an article that paraphrases the ideas that Author B has written about, find Author B's article and use it as your source.

The example below is a paraphrase of an idea expressed by Holly Shimizu, executive director of the United States Botanic Garden, in an interview with Cassandra M. Vanhooser.

Example

✔ Holly Shimizu, the executive director of the United States Botanic Garden, believes that Congress's willingness to fund a renovation of the Washington, D.C., garden sends a message that plants are important (qtd. in Vanhooser).

The Works Cited List

The Works Cited list is double-spaced and alphabetized according to the last name of the author (or if no author is listed, by the first word of the title). The first line of each entry is flush with the left margin while subsequent lines are indented one-half inch. The last item in an entry is the medium of the source, for example, "Print," "Web," or "Film." Impermanent sources such as unstable websites, an interview, or a live performance include the date of access.

Journal Article

Cassady, Jerrell C., and Ronald E. Johnson. "Cognitive Test Anxiety and Academic Performance." *Contemporary Educational Psychology* 27.2 (2002): 270–295. Print.

Newham, David. "Outside In." *Nursing Standard* 24.12 (2009): 26. *Academic Search Complete.* Web. 9 Feb. 2008.

Magazine Article

Clark, Jane B. "As Seen on TV." *Kiplinger's* Jul. 2002: 98–105. Print.

Zedillo, Ernesto. "2008: Year of Reckoning?" *Forbes* 7 Jan. 2008: 21+. *Academic Search Complete.* Web. 9 Feb. 2008.

Newspaper Article

Neuharth, Al. "Can We Curb Rude Cellphone Manners?" *USA Today* 19 Jul. 2002: A-13. Print.

Anna Gorman. "Making for easier assimilation; Through a task force, a booklet and a website, the U.S. government is helping immigrants learn English and integrate into society." *Los Angeles Times*. LATimes.com, 7 Feb. 2008. Web. 7 Feb. 2008.

Encyclopedia Entry

"Post-traumatic Stress Disorder." *Gale Encyclopedia of Medicine.* 2nd ed. 2001. Print.

Book by a Single Author

Schlosser, Eric. *Fast Food Nation: The Dark Side of the All-American Meal.* New York: HarperCollins, 2002. Print.

Note: If more than one city is listed for the publisher, include only the first one mentioned.

Book by Two Authors

Halfacre, R. Gordon, and Anne Shawcroft. *Landscape Plants of the Southeast.* Raleigh: Sparks, 1997. Print.

Personal Interview

Borck, Pat. Personal Interview. 22 August 2008.

Article on a Website

Sahadi, Jeanne. "The Ideal Budget." *CNN/Money.* Cable News Network, 27 Oct. 2004. Web. 13 Feb. 2011.

This citation includes the author's name, article title, website name, organization responsible for website, date of article, medium of publication, and date of access.

Article on a Website, No Author Listed

"Ten Tips for Public Speaking." *Toastmasters International.* Toastmasters International, n.d. Web. 11 Feb. 2011.

Because no author is listed, this citation includes the article title, website name, organization that holds the website's copyright, the abbreviation "n.d." to indicate that the article is not dated, medium of publication, and date of access.

A Model Research Paper

Witt 1

Lilly Witt

Psychology 1101

Dr. Nemec

3 April 2011

Double-spaced throughout

Title centered.

The Purpose of Dreams

Since ancient times, people have wondered about the scenes that play themselves out in the sleeping mind. What are dreams? Ancient cultures saw them as prophecies, as sources of inspiration, or as ways to heal the body or mind (Winson 54). Modern psychologists and biologists are also intrigued by the nature and purpose of dreams. Over the last century, dream research has evolved from Sigmund Freud's view of a dream as wish fulfillment to today's widely varying ideas about the practical role of dreams in human existence.

Factual reference; author's name in parenthetical reference.

Thesis statement. Reference to original ideas; author's name mentioned in paragraph.

The most important early work on dreams was Sigmund Freud's *The Interpretation of Dreams*. First published in 1900, Freud's book debunked the idea that dreaming was merely a physical process (65). Instead, a dream was a mental process of wish fulfillment. The idea of a dream as the fulfillment of a wish was clear, Freud wrote, when a thirsty person dreamed of water or a hungry person of food. But how could anxious and unpleasant dreams fulfill a wish? In Freud's system, even nightmares concealed wishes carefully hidden from the dreamer by the unconscious mind. For Freud, the purpose of dreams was to allow the dreamer's wishes to come true, if only in sleep, while at the same time hiding and disguising wishes that might not be acceptable to the conscious mind (98–123).

Witt 2

Since Freud's early work, much research has been done on dreams. A breakthrough came in 1953 with the discovery of REM (rapid eye movement) sleep, the stage of sleep in which the most vivid dreams occur (Fernald 166). Rather than rely on a sleeper's morning memories of dreams, today's sleep researchers work in sleep laboratories, where sensitive equipment alerts researchers when a sleeper falls into REM sleep. One point of agreement that most modern researchers share with Freud is that most dreams are prompted by events that occur during the day. In other words, dreamers process the day's events through dreams (Fernald 169). There, however, the agreement stops, and modern theories vary widely.

Many researchers believe that dreams play a role in learning. Stephen LaBarge of Stanford University's Sleep Disorder Clinic believes that one role of dreams is to move information from short-term memory to long-term memory. His studies show that people who are deprived of REM sleep find it difficult to "learn new skills, remember, or concentrate" (qtd. in Beaubien). Researcher J. Allan Hobson suggests that the information-processing function of REM sleep may include comparing old information with new and storing only what is new and different. Old information that is already in the memory is not stored again (295).

Paradoxically, it has also been proposed that the purpose of dreams is to help the dreamer forget. Biochemist Francis Crick, whose work on the structure of DNA won a Nobel Prize, has worked with Graeme Mitchison to discover why people dream. According to Crick and Mitchison, memory is stored in a "neural net" within the brain, a system that allows a memory to be accessed from many different pathways instead of just one. The neural net has limited capacity, and the only way to keep it working properly is to flush out unneeded memories. It is through dreams and REM sleep that this process of "reverse learning"

Factual reference; author's name in parenthetical reference.

The abbreviation qtd. in is used with information from a published interview.

Witt 3

occurs (229–237). The reverse-learning theory is supported by observations of two mammals that lack REM sleep, the dolphin and one species of anteater. These two mammals, Crick and Mitchison state, have unexpectedly large brains for their body size. It is possible, then, that the function of dreaming and REM sleep is "to make advanced brains more efficient and, in particular, to allow these brains to have a smaller size than they would otherwise have" (244).

Some of the most recent studies raise the possibility that dreams regulate moods. Rosalind Cartwright of the Sleep Disorder Service and Research Center believes that dreams help people to work through emotional problems. Dreams tend to be more negative than positive, providing "emotional homework" that allows a dreamer to work through problems. Dealing with negative emotions at night helps the sleeper to wake up in a better, more positive mood (qtd. in Beaubien).

The idea that dreams regulate mood is confirmed by Milton Kramer and Mark Barasch. According to their studies, two possible scenarios may play out as a sleeper confronts emotional issues in dreams. The first scenario is similar to the one described by Cartwright. Dreams become progressively more positive as, dream by dream, the sleeper works through a problem. The sleeper awakes refreshed and in a positive mood. Sometimes, however, the dreams simply repeat the conflict again and again. In this case, the sleeper may wake up more irritable and depressed than he was when he went to sleep.

Why do dreams improve the moods of some people and worsen the moods of others? One of Rosalind Cartwright's studies points to an answer. The study compared clinically depressed people with people who were not depressed. Those who were not clinically depressed showed a normal pattern of mood improvement as dreams became more positive

Information from a published interview.

Omission of page number indicates that entire article is referenced or that a previously published article is published without page numbers on a website.

Witt 4

throughout the night. Most depressed patients, however, showed the opposite pattern: their dreams became less positive and their moods became progressively worse as morning drew near. However, one subset of depressed patients showed a normal pattern. Significantly, those were the ones whose depression was cured (qtd. in Neimark).

If dreams have such a powerful effect on mood, can they be used deliberately to help people work through emotional issues and problems? The D.R.E.A.M.S. Foundation of Canada reports that it is possible to use dreams deliberately through a process called "dream incubation." The process involves focusing on the question before sleeping and forming the intention to have a dream that will shed light on the problem. Dreams may produce an obvious answer or they may require some interpretation. According to the Foundation's website, a trust in the process and a willingness to act on the insights that dreams provide will help to make the process work. The foundation reports that dreams may also be useful in solving creative and professional problems. For example, the Beatles' tune "Yesterday" and Samuel Taylor Coleridge's poem "Kubla Khan" were inspired by dreams, and it is said that the golfer Jack Nicklaus worked out a problem with his golf swing in a dream ("Dreams").

Most researchers agree that dreams have a purpose, but few can agree on what that purpose is. Dream research has moved away from Freud's idea that a dream is the mind's fulfillment of a wish. Modern researchers view the dream both as a way of learning and as a type of reverse learning that helps the brain purge unneeded memories. More recent research shows the dream as a regulator of moods, perhaps even as a tool that can be used deliberately to enhance mood and creativity. Whatever the purpose of dreams, they continue to be a source of fascination and speculation.

Information from a published interview.

First word of title is given for a page on a website with no author listed.

Conclusion sums up the paper's content.

Works Cited page is separate, but numbering continues from previous pages.

Witt 5

Works Cited

First line is flush with left margin; subsequent lines are indented one-half inch.

Beaubien, Greg. "In Your Dreams." *Natural Way for Better Health*

Nov./Dec. 1995: n. pag. *Alt HealthWatch*. Web. 8 May 2003.

Name of database.

Crick, Francis, and Graeme Mitchison. "REM Sleep and Neural Nets."

Journal of Mind and Behavior 7.2–3 (1986): 229–49. Print.

"Dreams—How to Apply and Benefit from Them." *D.R.E.A.M.S. Founda-*

tion. D.R.E.A.M.S. Foundation, n.d. Web. 30 Mar. 2011.

Fernald, Dodge. *Psychology*. Upper Saddle River, NJ: Prentice Hall, 1997.

Print.

Volume and issue numbers of a journal.

Freud, Sigmund. *The Interpretation of Dreams*. Trans. Joyce Crick. New

York: Oxford UP, 1999. Print.

Hobson, J. Allan. *The Dreaming Brain*. New York: Basic Books. 1988.

Print.

Kramer, Milton, and Mark Barasch. "Dreamspeak." *Psychology Today*

Sep./Oct. 2000, 56–61. *Academic Search Premier*. Web. 7

Mar. 2011.

Month and year of magazine.

Neimark, Jill. "Night Life." *Psychology Today* Jul./Aug. 1998, 30-35.

Academic Search Premier. Web. 3 Mar. 2011.

Winson, Jonathan. "The Meaning of Dreams." *Scientific American Special*

12.1 (2002): 54–61. Print.

Volume and issue number of journal.

ASSIGNMENTS FOR WRITING A RESEARCH PAPER

Choose one of the following research assignments. Follow the step-by-step process outlined in this chapter to complete the steps in writing a research paper: choosing a topic and creating a research question, finding and evaluating sources, outlining your paper and taking notes, drafting your paper, and finally, formatting your paper and citing your sources.

Research Assignment 1: Exploring an Issue in Education

Following the steps in research outlined in the chapter, explore and write about a current issue in education. Use one of the topics listed below or a topic of your own choosing. You may write about issues in higher education (at the college level), or you may choose to focus on an issue in secondary or elementary education. Focus your research on a single problem or issue within your chosen topic. For example, if you choose "disabilities," you might narrow your focus to a specific learning disability or to methods of making study materials more accessible to students with visual or hearing impairments.

Bilingual education	Gender equity
Disabilities	Nontraditional students in college
College access and admissions policies	Technology in education

Research Assignment 2: Exploring a Social Issue

Following the steps in research outlined in the chapter, explore and write about a current social issue. Use one of the topics listed below or a topic of your own choosing. Focus your research on a single problem or issue within your chosen topic. For example, if you choose drug abuse as your topic, your research question might focus on the problem of limited opportunities for rehabilitation and the possible solutions to that problem. If you choose domestic violence, your research question might focus on the effectiveness of services provided by domestic violence hotlines and "safe houses" for victims of abuse.

Alcoholism	Gangs	Drug abuse
Domestic violence	Poverty	Prisons

Research Assignment 3: Exploring an Issue in Health and Wellness

Following the steps in research outlined in the chapter, explore and write about an issue in health and wellness. Use one of the topics listed below or a topic of your own choosing. Be sure that your research question is issue-oriented. For example, rather than focusing on defining breast cancer, an issue-oriented paper would address a question such as which of several treatments works best.

Alternative medicine	Pets and health
Diet	Weight training (or another form of exercise)
Breast cancer (or another disease)	
Mental health	

mywritinglab For support and practice meeting this chapter's goal, log in to www.mywritinglab.com and select **Research Process**.

CHAPTER 13

Verbs and Subjects

✍ **Chapter Goal:** Recognize subjects, verbs (including action, linking, and irregular verbs), and prepositional phrases and use them appropriately.

A Journalist's Questions
~~Who?~~
~~What?~~
When?
Where?
Why?

If there were no verbs or subjects, the top two items in the list of traditional journalist's questions would be eliminated. Verbs tell *what* was done, while subjects tell *who* or *what* the sentence is about.

The **verb** of a sentence carries the action, if any, and directs that action to and from the other words in the sentence. Some verbs, called **linking verbs**, function as connectors of related words.

A **subject** is what the sentence is about. It is usually a noun or a pronoun. It is probably not the only noun or pronoun in the sentence, but it is the only one that enjoys such a direct grammatical connection to its verb. If you ask,

"Who or what _____?" putting the verb in the blank, the answer to your question is always the subject of the sentence.

Action and Linking Verbs

mywritinglab

Visit MyWriting Lab for additional practice with action and linking verbs.

Verbs work in two ways within a sentence. Some verbs show the action, physical or mental, of the subject of the sentence. These verbs are called *action verbs*. Other verbs link the subject with other words in the sentence. These verbs are called *linking verbs.*

Action Verbs

Action verbs show physical or mental action performed by a subject. Look at the following action verbs, highlighted in italic font.

Examples of Action Verbs

✔ Rachel *drove* to the doughnut shop. (physical action)

✔ She *bought* a dozen doughnuts and *ate* two on the way home. (physical action)

✔ She *wondered* why she found sweets irresistible. (mental action)

PRACTICE 1   RECOGNIZING ACTION VERBS

Underline the action verbs in the following sentences twice.

1. The judge's decision sparked controversy in the small community.
2. The twins' vivid red hair draws everyone's attention.
3. James worried about Monday's history test.
4. The cat leaped to the safety of the tree's lower branches.
5. The old car puttered along like a windup toy.

Linking Verbs

A linking verb links its subject with a word that describes it. The most common linking verb in English is the verb *to be,* in all its various forms: *is, are, was, were, has been, will be, could have been,* and so on. Look at the following examples to see how the verb *to be* functions as a linking verb.

Examples of Linking Verbs

✔ The dog *is* hungry.

The verb *is* links the subject, *dog,* with an adjective describing it.

✔ Ann *has been* a police officer for ten years .

The verb *has been* links the subject, *Ann,* with a phrase, *police officer,* that tells more about her.

✔ Tomorrow *will be* the last day to drop a class without penalty.

The verb *will be* links the subject, *tomorrow,* with a noun, *day,* that tells more about it.

Other common linking verbs include the verbs *to seem, to appear, to grow,* and *to become.* Verbs of the senses, such as *to smell, to taste, to look, to sound,* and *to feel,* can be action or linking verbs, depending on how they are used.

Examples of Verbs That Can Link or Show Action

L   The gym socks *smelled* terrible. (*Smelled* is a linking verb—the socks are performing no action.)

A   Monica *smelled* the perfume sample. (The verb *smelled* shows Monica's physical action.)

L   The pumpkin pie *looks* tasty. (The verb links *pie* with the adjective *tasty.*)

A   The dog *looks* forlornly at every passerby, hoping for a handout. (The verb shows the dog's physical action.)

The Linking Verb Test

To find out if a verb is a linking verb, see if you can substitute *is* or *was* in its place. If the substitution works, the verb is probably a linking verb.

Examples of the Linking Verb Test in Use

?   The crowd *grew* quiet as the conductor stepped onto the podium.

L   The crowd ~~grew~~ *was* quiet as the conductor stepped onto the podium.

The above substitution makes sense; therefore, *grew* is used as a linking verb.

?   The vines *grew* until they covered the cottage.

A   The vines ~~grew~~ *were* until they covered the cottage.

The previous substitution does not make sense; therefore, *grew* is used here as an action verb.

?   Michael stayed home from work because he *felt* sick.

L   Michael stayed home from work because he ~~felt~~ *was* sick. (linking verb)

?   Barbara *felt* the stress of the day dissolve as she stepped through the door of her apartment.

A   Barbara ~~felt~~ *was* the stress of the day dissolve as she stepped through the door of her apartment. (action verb)

PRACTICE 2   RECOGNIZING ACTION AND LINKING VERBS

Underline the verbs in the following sentences twice. In the blank to the left of each sentence, write *A* if the verb is an action verb, *L* if it is a linking verb.

_____ 1.   Sharon is in a sour mood today.

_____ 2.   Emilio smelled the container to determine its contents.

_____ 3.   The bologna smells spoiled.

_____ 4.   The terrier leaped with joy as Nancy entered the house.

_____ 5.   Kim studied her sociology notes carefully before the test.

_____ 6.   The committee decided to postpone its meeting until Wednesday at noon.

_____ 7.   The small post office branch handles a large volume of mail.

_____ 8.   The ground is parched from lack of rain.

_____ 9.   The advertisement seems appealing.

_____ 10.   Too many drivers fail to use turn signals.

_____ 11.   Hisako grew tomatoes in a container on the patio.

_____ 12.   The audience grew restless when the singer was late.

_____ 13.   Yesterday Rozell tasted tiramisu, a layered Italian dessert, for the first time.

_____ 14.   The dessert tasted creamy and delicious.

_____ 15.   The burglar fled with over two thousand dollars in cash.

_____ 16.   Bernard felt sleepy all afternoon.

_____ 17.   Alanna pounded loudly on the door.

_____ 18.   The baker felt the silky texture of the flour between her fingers.

_____ 19.   On the upper right-hand corner of the envelope, Alex carefully pasted the stamp.

_____ 20.   Sandra looked through the tiny window at the front of the house.

Recognizing Verbs and Subjects

Finding the Verb

mywritinglab

Visit MyWriting Lab for additional practice with subjects and verbs.

Finding the subject and verb of a sentence is easier if you look for the verb first. Here are some guidelines to help you spot the verb in a sentence.

1. **A verb may show action.**

   ✔ The ancient elevator <u>groaned</u> to a stop on the second floor.

   ✔ Larry <u>wondered</u> if he should take the stairs.

2. **A verb may link the subject to the rest of the sentence.**

   ✔ The inspection sticker <u>was</u> three years out of date.

   ✔ The old lion <u>looked</u> sleepy.

3. **A verb may consist of more than one word. Some verbs include a main verb and one or more helping verbs.**

   ✔ Jemal <u>has been taking</u> flute lessons for six years.

   ✔ Katherine <u>has not found</u> the keys she lost yesterday.

   ✔ Gwen <u>might have been going</u> to the library when we saw her this morning.

4. **Some verbs are compound verbs. Some subjects have more than one verb. When more than one verb goes with the same subject, the verb is called a compound verb.**

   ✔ The meteorologist <u>pointed</u> to a low-pressure system on the weather map and <u>predicted</u> rain.

   ✔ The teller <u>counted</u> the bills twice and <u>handed</u> them to the customer.

   ✔ I <u>ate</u> the asparagus and avocado casserole but <u>did</u> not <u>like</u> it.

5. **An infinitive (*to* + present tense verb) cannot act as a verb in a sentence.**

   ✘ Paulo wanted <u>to accept</u> the award on his brother's behalf.
   The phrase *to accept* is an infinitive and cannot be the main verb of the sentence. The verb in this sentence is *wanted*.

   ✔ Paulo <u>wanted</u> to accept the award on his brother's behalf.

6. **A verb form ending in *-ing* cannot act as a verb in a sentence unless a helping verb precedes it.**

   ✘ The <u>setting</u> sun sank below the horizon.
   Setting cannot be the verb because a helping verb does not precede it. The verb in this sentence is *sank*.

   ✔ The setting sun <u>sank</u> below the horizon.

   ✔ A crowd <u>was gathering</u> at the scene of the accident.

The verb in the previous sentence is *was gathering* (helping verb main verb).

✔ James <u>has been thinking</u> about changing his major.

The verb in this sentence is <u>*has been thinking*</u> (helping verb main verb).

PRACTICE 3   FINDING VERBS

Underline the verbs in each of the following sentences twice.

1. A strong breeze filled the sails of the small boat, pushing it toward the shore.
2. On her next computer, Joy wants a touch screen and face recognition sign-on.
3. Iced tea tastes refreshing on a hot day.
4. Mrs. Binks sat on her porch and waited for the mail to arrive.
5. I have been listening to the radio, hoping to hear my favorite song.
6. A person has a better chance of being struck by lightning than of winning the lottery.
7. Maud wondered why she had bought the black T-shirt with an image of tarantulas on it.
8. Every morning, Anthony reads the comics page of the paper first.
9. Grandpa said the baby looked like him—bald and toothless.
10. Inch by inch, the tiny kitten climbed up the side of the bed.

Finding the Subject

Now that you can find the verb of a sentence, you can more easily find the subject of the verb. The easiest way to find the subject of a sentence is to find the verb first and work from there.

A subject answers the question "Who or what _____?" The verb fills in the blank. Be sure that the words *who or what* are stated before the verb, or you may find the object of the verb rather than its subject.

✔ The telephone <u>rang</u>, startling Raoul.

Who or what rang? The <u>telephone</u> rang. *Telephone* is the subject of the verb *rang*.

✔ The tour group <u>will fly</u> to Toronto on the 6:00 P.M. flight.

Who or what will fly? <u>The tour group</u> will fly. *Group* is the simple subject of the verb *will fly*. (The words *the* and *tour* are modifiers and are part of the complete subject.)

✔ Cedric and Joseph <u>sat</u> on the bench waiting for their mother.

Who or what sat? <u>Cedric and Joseph</u> sat. *Cedric and Joseph* is the compound subject of the verb *sat*.

✔ Carefully, Sandra <u>measured</u> the cinnamon and raisins and <u>folded</u> them into the bread dough.

Who or what measured? <u>Sandra</u> measured. *Sandra* is the subject of the verb *measured*. Who or what folded? <u>Sandra</u> folded. *Sandra* is the subject of the verb *folded*.

✔ Carefully, Sandra <u>measured</u> the cinnamon and raisins, and Brian <u>folded</u> them into the bread dough.

Who or what measured? <u>Sandra</u> measured. *Sandra* is the subject of the verb *measured*. Who or what folded? <u>Brian</u> folded. *Brian* is the subject of the verb *folded*.

PRACTICE 4   RECOGNIZING VERBS AND SUBJECTS

Find the verb in each sentence below and underline it twice. Then find the subject by asking "Who or what _____?" Underline the subject once.

1. *Casablanca* is Adrienne's favorite movie.
2. Exhaustion showed in Hank's face.
3. Ophelia's college diploma hung on the wall of her office.
4. Dust clung stubbornly to the computer screen.
5. Tracy drove to the post office and mailed her package.

Recognizing Prepositional Phrases

A subject will not be part of a prepositional phrase. In many sentences, prepositional phrases intervene between subject and verb.

✔ The rim *of the glass* is chipped.

When we pick out the subject of the verb by asking "What is chipped?" it is tempting to say, "The glass is chipped." But *glass* cannot be the subject of the verb in this sentence. Grammatically, it already has a job: It is the object of the preposition. The subject of this sentence is *rim*. To avoid mistakes in picking out the subject of the sentence, cross out prepositional phrases before picking out the subject and the verb.

Famous Prepositional Phrases

The following prepositional phrases have been used as titles for songs, television shows, movies, and books. How many do you recognize? Can you think of others?

Above Suspicion	In Living Color
Against the Wind	Of Mice and Men
Around the World in Eighty Days	On Golden Pond
At Long Last Love	On the Waterfront
At the Hop	Over the Rainbow
Behind Closed Doors	Behind Enemy Lines
Beneath the Planet of the Apes	Beyond the Sea
Beyond the Sea	Up on the Roof
In Cold Blood	Up the Down Staircase

- **Prepositional phrases always begin with a preposition.** Prepositions are often short words like *of, to, by, for,* or *from.* They are often words of location, such as *behind, beside, beneath, beyond,* or *below.* A list of common prepositions follows.

Frequently Used Prepositions

about	beneath	in	to
above	beside	into	toward
across	between	like	under
after	beyond	near	underneath
along	by	next to	until
along with	down	of	up
around	during	off	upon
at	except	on	with
before	for	outside	within
behind	from	over	without

- **Prepositional phrases always end with a noun or a pronoun.** The object of a preposition, always a noun or a pronoun, comes at the end of a prepositional phrase: of the *mongoose,* beside a sparkling *lake,* with *them,* to *James and Harlow,* within five *minutes.*

- **Prepositional phrases often have a three-word structure.** Often, prepositional phrases have a three-word structure: preposition, article (*a, an,* or *the*), noun. Thus phrases like *of an employee, under the car,* and *with a gift* are easy to recognize. But prepositional phrases can also be stretched with modifiers and compound objects: *beside Katie's bright blue dance shoes and pink-and-purple designer leotard.* More often, though, the three-word pattern prevails.

PRACTICE 5 **ELIMINATING PREPOSITIONAL PHRASES**

Cross out the prepositional phrases in the following sentences.

1. The vivid colors of the flowers in the blue bowl on the table brighten the room.
2. Outside the office, on the busy street, swarms of happy vacationers were leaving for weekend trips.
3. The point of Mr. Smith's remarks to the class was lost on Kendall, who dozed peacefully in the back row.
4. For dessert, I'll have a cup of coffee and a slice of that gooey, rich pecan pie.
5. The smell of freshly brewed coffee and frying bacon wafted through the open door of the small restaurant on the corner of Poplar and Main.

Real-World Writing: Is It Okay to End a Sentence with a Preposition?

How else would you say, "Will you pick me up?" or "I feel left out"? People who object to prepositions at the end of sentences are often really objecting to awkward or redundant constructions. The sentence "Where are you at?" will bring a scowl to any English teacher's face—not because it ends with a preposition, but because it is redundant: "where" and "at" are both doing the same job—indicating location.

But by all means, say "I have nothing to put this in" or "The dog wants to go out." Except in the most formal writing, ending sentences with prepositions is something almost everyone can live with.

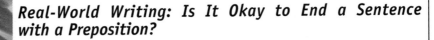

Regular and Irregular Verbs

mywritinglab

Visit MyWriting Lab for additional practice with regular and irregular verbs.

Regular verbs follow a predictable pattern in the formation of their **principal parts**. Every verb has four principal parts: the present-tense form, the past-tense form, the past participle (used with helping verbs), and the present participle (the *-ing* verb form used with helping verbs). Regular verbs add *ed* to form their past tense and past participles. Some examples of regular verbs follow.

Examples of Regular Verbs

Present	Past	Past Participle	Present Participle
add	added	(have) added	(are) adding
change	changed	(have) changed	(are) changing
pull	pulled	(have) pulled	(are) pulling
walk	walked	(have) walked	(are) walking

Irregular verbs, on the other hand, follow no predictable pattern in their past and past participle forms. Sometimes a vowel changes: *sing* in the present tense becomes *sang* in the past tense and *sung* in the past participle. Sometimes an *n* or *en* will be added to form the past participle: *take* becomes *taken*, *fall* becomes *fallen*. Some verbs, such as the verb *set*, do not change at all. Others change completely: *buy* in the present tense becomes *bought* in the past and past participle forms.

Some common irregular verbs and their principal parts follow. If you are unsure about a verb form, check this list or consult a dictionary for the correct form.

Principal Parts of Common Irregular Verbs

Present	Past	Past Participle	Present Participle
be (am, are, is)	was (were)	(have) been	(are) being
become	became	(have) become	(are) becoming
begin	began	(have) begun	(are) beginning
blow	blew	(have) blown	(are) blowing
break	broke	(have) broken	(are) breaking
bring	brought	(have) brought	(are) bringing
burst	burst	(have) burst	(are) bursting
buy	bought	(have) bought	(are) buying
catch	caught	(have) caught	(are) catching
choose	chose	(have) chosen	(are) choosing
come	came	(have) come	(are) coming
cut	cut	(have) cut	(are) cutting
do	did	(have) done	(are) doing
draw	drew	(have) drawn	(are) drawing
drink	drank	(have) drunk	(are) drinking
drive	drove	(have) driven	(are) driving
eat	ate	(have) eaten	(are) eating

Present	Past	Past Participle	Present Participle
fall	fell	(have) fallen	(are) falling
feel	felt	(have) felt	(are) feeling
fight	fought	(have) fought	(are) fighting
find	found	(have) found	(are) finding
fly	flew	(have) flown	(are) flying
freeze	froze	(have) frozen	(are) freezing
get	got	(have) gotten (or got)	(are) getting
give	gave	(have) given	(are) giving
go	went	(have) gone	(are) going
grow	grew	(have) grown	(are) growing
have	had	(have) had	(are) having
hear	heard	(have) heard	(are) hearing
hide	hid	(have) hidden	(are) hiding
hold	held	(have) held	(are) holding
hurt	hurt	(have) hurt	(are) hurting
keep	kept	(have) kept	(are) keeping
know	knew	(have) known	(are) knowing
lay (put)	laid	(have) laid	(are) laying
lead	led	(have) led	(are) leading
leave	left	(have) left	(are) leaving
lend	lent	(have) lent	(are) lending
lie (recline)	lay	(have) lain	(are) lying
lose	lost	(have) lost	(are) losing
put	put	(have) put	(are) putting
ride	rode	(have) ridden	(are) riding
rise	rose	(have) risen	(are) rising
run	ran	(have) run	(are) running
see	saw	(have) seen	(are) seeing
set (place)	set	(have) set	(are) setting
sing	sang	(have) sung	(are) singing
sit (be seated)	sat	(have) sat	(are) sitting
speak	spoke	(have) spoken	(are) speaking

Present	Past	Past Participle	Present Participle
swim	swam	(have) swum	(are) swimming
take	took	(have) taken	(are) taking
tear	tore	(have) torn	(are) tearing
throw	threw	(have) thrown	(are) throwing
write	wrote	(have) written	(are) writing

PRACTICE 6   USING THE CORRECT FORM OF IRREGULAR VERBS

Fill in the blank with the correct form of the verb shown to the left of each question. For help, consult the list of irregular verbs above.

(become)   **1.**   James has _____ an accomplished pianist.

(break)   **2.**   Latanya hopes she has not _____ her MP3 player.

(drink)   **3.**   The dog _____ all the water in her bowl before we came home.

(eat)   **4.**   Have you _____ dinner?

(go)   **5.**   James has _____ to pick up his daughter.

(lead)   **6.**   The mother duck _____ her ducklings across the busy intersection.

(lend)   **7.**   The bank _____ Miguel the money to buy a car.

(run)   **8.**   Alisha _____ across the street, hoping to catch the bus.

(see)   **9.**   When Greg _____ his test grade, he felt relieved.

(swim)   **10.**   When Tamiko had _____ for half an hour, she got out of the pool.

Puzzling Pairs

Some irregular verbs are easily confused with other words. The following section will help you make the right choice between *lend* and *loan, lie* and *lay,* and *sit* and *set.*

Lend and Loan

Lend is a verb meaning *to allow someone to borrow,* as in "*Lend* me ten dollars until payday," or "She *lent* her book to another student." *Loan* is a noun meaning *something borrowed,* as in "He went to the bank for a mortgage *loan.*"

Correct and Incorrect Examples of *Lend* and *Loan*

✗   I was not sure the bank would *loan* me the money.

✔   I was not sure the bank would *lend* me the money.

✗   Mrs. Timmons *loaned* her son the money for tuition.

✔   Mrs. Timmons *lent* her son the money for tuition.

Real-World Writing: Lend? Loan? Who Cares!

People who care about English also care about the distinction between *lend* and *loan*. Though the use of *loan* as a verb is widespread, it is not considered acceptable by careful writers and speakers of English.

  Therefore, it's best to avoid such constructions as "Loan me a quarter for the telephone," or "He loaned me his car."

PRACTICE 7   USING *LEND* AND *LOAN*

In each sentence, underline the correct word.

1.   I promised my grandmother I would pay back the (lend, loan), but she said, "Consider it a gift."
2.   Derek tries not to (lend, loan) books he wants to keep.
3.   Shakespeare wrote, "Friends, Romans, countrymen, (lend, loan) me your ears."
4.   Amy is irresponsible with money; she needs a (lend, loan) before each payday.
5.   Would you mind (lending, loaning) me a hand?

Lay and *Lie*

Lay and *lie* are often confused, partly because their forms overlap. The present tense of the verb *lay* and the past tense of *lie* are both the same: *lay.* Look at the following chart to see the different forms of each verb.

Present	Past	Past Participle	Present Participle
<u>lay</u> (put)	laid	(have) laid	(are) laying
lie (recline)	<u>lay</u>	(have) lain	(are) lying

•   The verb *lay* means *to put* or *to place.* It always takes an object; that is, there will always be an answer to the question "Lay what?"

Examples of Correct Uses of *Lay*

✔ Horace <u>lays</u> his work <u>problems</u> aside before he walks into his house.
  (verb: lays, object: problems)

✔ Jessica <u>laid</u> her <u>duffel bag</u> on a bench in the locker room.
  (verb: laid, object: duffel bag)

✔ Spiros <u>has laid</u> the <u>brick</u> for his patio, and he promised he would help me with mine.
  (verb: has laid, object: brick)

✔ Preston and I <u>are laying</u> the <u>groundwork</u> for our project.
  (verb: are laying, object: groundwork)

- The verb *lie* means *to recline*. It does not take an object.

Examples of Correct Uses of *Lie*

✔ Since Anna broke her ankle, she <u>lies</u> around watching soap operas all day.
  (verb: lies)

✔ The turtle <u>lay</u> upside down in the middle of the highway, unable to right itself.
  (verb: lay)

✔ I <u>have lain</u> on that soft couch for too long; now my back is aching.
  (verb: have lain)

✔ The flashlight <u>was lying</u> on the mantel where Kaya had left it.
  (verb: was lying)

PRACTICE 8   USING *LAY* AND *LIE*

Underline the correct verb forms in the following paragraph.

Before the sun rose, Martin went out to pick up the newspaper that was [1](laying, lying) in his driveway. Because it was dark, he did not even see the small shape that [2](laid, lay) in the street just past his mailbox. Inside the house, he [3](lay, laid) the paper on the kitchen counter, fixed a bowl of cereal for himself, and opened a can of food for his golden retriever, Bart. But when he went to the back door to call Bart, the dog did not come. "He must have jumped the fence again," Martin thought. "I'll have to [4](lay, lie) down the law to that crazy dog." But when Martin pulled out of his driveway to go to work, he saw Bart [5](laying, lying) beside the road. The dog [6](lay, laid) so still that Martin thought he was dead. As he bent down, Martin heard a soft whine, so he picked the dog up and gently [7](lay, laid) him in the back seat of the car. At the vet's office, Dr. Jordan said, "I'll have to [8](lay, lie) it on the line. Bart's injuries are serious, and it will be twenty-four hours before we can make any real predictions." That night, Martin [9](lay, laid) awake for a long time. When he called Dr. Jordan the next morning,

the vet said, "Bart's a strong dog. I think he's going to make it." As he
[10](lay, laid) the telephone receiver back in its cradle, Martin breathed a
sigh of relief. It would not be a day for goodbyes.

Sit and Set

The verb *sit* means *to take a seat* or *to be located.* It does not take an object.

Examples of Correct Uses of *Sit*

✔ The house <u>sits</u> on a hill overlooking the lake.

✔ Phooey <u>sat</u> beside her bowl wearing a look that said, "Feed me."

✔ The children <u>have sat</u> in front of the television for too long.

✔ The Arnolds' car <u>is sitting</u> in the driveway, so they must be at home.

Set means *to put* or *to place.* The verb *set* always takes an object; that is, you will always find an answer to the question "Set what?"

Examples of Correct Uses of *Set*

✔ <u>Set</u> the <u>groceries</u> on the counter.

✔ On New Year's Eve, Janis <u>set</u> her <u>goals</u> for the year.

✔ I believe I <u>have set</u> the <u>tomato plants</u> too close together.

✔ The students believe the teacher <u>is setting</u> <u>standards</u> that they cannot meet.

PRACTICE 9   USING SIT AND SET

Underline the correct verb forms in the following sentences.

1. The cat (sits, sets) in the window, entertained for hours by the sparrows outside.

2. The letter carrier (sat, set) the package beside the door.

3. While the grownups were (sitting, setting) on the porch, Billy scrawled abstract designs on the living room wall.

4. (Sitting, setting) at the table, Bonita (sat, set) her goals down in writing.

5. Craig's bread machine has (set, sat) on the shelf ever since he bought it.

Review Exercises

Complete the Review Exercises to see how well you have learned the skills described in this chapter. As you work through the exercises, go back through the chapter to review any of the rules you do not understand completely.

REVIEW EXERCISE 1	FINDING SUBJECTS AND VERBS

Cross out prepositional phrases in the following sentences. Then underline the subject once and the verb twice.

1. In many homes, the kitchen is the hub of family activity.
2. The television has been blaring loudly in the living room almost all day.
3. The kite sailed majestically upward, then spiraled to earth.
4. The coffee in this pot tastes bitter and strong.
5. The meeting of the planning committee might be rescheduled.
6. The dog has been drinking from your glass of water.
7. The lack of space in my office may force me to dispose of some of my books.
8. Anita longed for a new car to replace her unreliable old clunker.
9. Computers were supposed to create a "paperless office."
10. Instead, they generate even more paper.

REVIEW EXERCISE 2	FINDING SUBJECTS AND VERBS

Cross out prepositional phrases in the following sentences. Then underline subjects once and verbs twice.

1. The sleeping cat woke when Mattie went into the kitchen.
2. Some of the leftovers in this refrigerator should be thrown out.
3. The dictionary's cover was tattered and worn.
4. The sound of the gong reverberated throughout the auditorium.
5. Selenium is believed to play a role in cancer prevention.
6. Tim glanced in the mirror at his shaggy hair and decided to get a haircut after work.
7. The company's apology came too late for Claire.
8. Jake and Mike are fraternal twins and do not look much alike.
9. The melon, grown in poor, sandy soil, barely reached the size of a baseball.
10. The witness could not recollect the color of the robber's shoes.

| REVIEW EXERCISE 3 | PUZZLING PAIRS |

Choose the correct form of the following verbs.

1. (Sit, Set) down and make yourself comfortable.
2. In the summer, Kristen enjoys (laying, lying) on the beach.
3. James was sorry he had (lent, loaned) his circular saw to Matt.
4. Pablo has promised to (lend, loan) his expertise when we paint the set.
5. A shining ribbon of discarded cans (lay, laid) alongside the road.
6. The rivals shook hands and (lay, laid) their differences aside.
7. Barbara has (laid, lain) in the sun too long.
8. Joan called and asked, "Are you busy, or are you just (sitting, setting) around?"
9. Can you (loan, lend) me a pencil?
10. The video games, removed from their cases, were (laying, lying) on the table.

| REVIEW EXERCISE 4 | USING IRREGULAR VERBS |

Fill in the blank with the correct form of the verb shown to the left of each question. For help, consult the list of irregular verbs in this chapter.

(lie)   1. Nicole walked along the stretch of sand, occasionally stopping to pick up one of the shells that _____ scattered along the shoreline.

(burst)   2. The child stood in the supermarket aisle, crying because his balloon had _____.

(fly)   3. The nest was deserted; the nestlings had long since _____ .

(put)   4. Howard brought the groceries in and ____ them away immediately.

(fall)   5. When Alison _____ on the track, everyone rushed over to ask her if she was hurt.

(begin)   6. It is distracting when people enter the theater after a performance has _____.

(tear)   7. An hour ago, the cat _____ out of the house, and I haven't seen him since.

(spend)   8. I _____ $35 and left the grocery store with just one small bag.

(fight)   9. When they were young, the sisters _____ continually.

(throw)   10. Quinton _____ the ball too hard and pulled a shoulder muscle.

| REVIEW EXERCISE 5 | USING IRREGULAR VERBS |

Fill in the blank with the correct form of the verb shown to the left of each question. For help, consult the list of irregular verbs in this chapter.

(bring)   **1.** After she was hired, the new manager _____ a measure of stability to the department.

(rise)   **2.** After the dough had _____, Mary shaped it into loaves.

(ride)   **3.** Mr. Smith said he had not _____ a bicycle since he was a child.

(see)   **4.** Yesterday I _____ a wasp's nest in our garage.

(drink)   **5.** Who _____ all the diet cola?

(lay)   **6.** Harriet _____ a blanket across the sleeping child.

(break)   **7.** The company _____ with tradition by adding athletic shoes to its line.

(go)   **8.** Betty _____ to work before the sun rose.

(lose)   **9.** Adam has _____ the combination to the safe.

(drive)   **10.** Four police cars have _____ past within the last hour.

mywritinglab   For support and practice meeting this chapter's goal, log in to www.mywritinglab.com and select **Subjects and Verbs**.

CHAPTER 14

Subject-Verb Agreement

Chapter Goal: Identify and correct problems with subject-verb agreement.

Singular with singular
Will need no referee,
And plural paired with plural is
In perfect harmony.

In grammatical relations,
Achieve tranquility
By using combinations
That never disagree.

In Standard English, subjects and verbs must always agree. This does not necessarily mean that they shake hands, as in the drawing that opens this chapter. In grammatical terminology, **agreement** always means that singular is paired with singular and plural with plural. All of the rules for subject-verb agreement presented in this chapter have the same idea behind them: **A singular subject requires a singular verb, and a plural subject requires a plural verb.**

✐ The Basic Pattern

mywritinglab

Visit MyWriting Lab for additional practice with subjects and verbs.

Because most subject-verb agreement problems occur in the present tense, let's begin by looking at a present-tense verb as it moves through the first, second, and third person.

	Singular	Plural
First person	I walk	we walk
Second person	you walk	you walk
Third person	he, she, it walks	they walk

PRACTICE 1 CONJUGATING A VERB

All regular verbs follow the pattern above. Using the sample above as a model, fill in the forms of the verb *sing* in the spaces below.

	Singular	Plural
First person	I _____	we _____
Second person	you _____	you _____
Third person	he, she, it _____	they _____

Did you remember to put the *s* on the third-person singular form? Notice that it is only in the third person that the singular form is different from the plural form. Notice, too, that the third-person verb pattern is exactly the opposite of the pattern you see in nouns. When you look at the noun *cat*, you know that it is singular and that the plural form is *cats*. But verbs in the third person, present tense work in exactly the opposite way. The third-person singular form of the verb ends in *s*, not the plural form. When you see the verb *walks*, you know it is singular because it ends in *s*.

Examples of Subject–Verb Agreement in the Present Tense, Third Person

A third-person singular subject and verb usually follow the pattern shown below:

✔ The *cat walks.* (The singular noun does not end in *s*; the singular verb does end in *s*.)

A third-person plural subject and verb usually follow this pattern:

✔ The *cats walk.* (The plural noun ends in *s*; the plural verb does not end in *s*.)

Memory Jogger

If you have trouble with third-person verbs, remember the following verse.

The Singular S
When verbs are in the present tense,
You never need to guess.
The singular third-person verb
Always ends in *s*.

PRACTICE 2   CONJUGATING VERBS

On a sheet of paper, fill in the first-, second-, and third-person forms of the following regular verbs: *inspire, locate, dance, resist, type*. Remember to add the *s* to the third-person singular form.

Verbs Ending in *s*

Look at the regular verb *confess* in the present tense. Here, when the verb already ends in *s*, the third-person singular form also changes, adding *es*.

	Singular	Plural
First person	I confess	we confess
Second person	you confess	you confess
Third person	he, she, it confess**es**	they confess

Using Third Person

Third person is sometimes confusing. One reason is that it is the only person for which the verb form changes. The biggest reason, however, is that third person includes much more than just the pronouns *he, she, it,* and *they*. Third-person singular also includes any noun or pronoun that can be replaced by *he, she,* or *it. James, Ms. Smith, cat, table, child, one, bank teller,* and *Abraham Lincoln* are all third-person singular. Thus, each requires a present-tense verb ending in *s* or *es*.

Any noun or pronoun that can be replaced by *they* is third-person plural. The *Joneses, both, washer and dryer, beds, automobiles,* and *several* are words that can be replaced by *they*. Thus, all are third-person plural and require a present-tense plural verb, the form that does not add *s* or *es*.

The Verb *to be*

Now look at the most common irregular verb, the verb *to be*.

	Singular	Plural
First person	I am	we are
Second person	you are	you are
Third person	he, she, it is	they are

Notice that the pattern still holds: The third-person singular form of the verb always ends in *s* or *es*.

A Fundamental Rule

Knowing the pattern that present-tense verbs follow should make it a bit easier to apply the fundamental rule of subject-verb agreement:

A singular subject requires a singular verb, and a plural subject requires a plural verb.

Examples of Singular and Plural Subjects and Verbs

    S   V

<u>Susan</u> *takes* a walk every morning before leaving for work. (singular subject, singular verb)

      S   V

A <u>hurricane</u> *spins* in a huge spiral around a central eye. (singular subject, singular verb)

         S V

Ice cream <u>shops</u> *do* most of their business during the summer months. (plural subject, plural verb)

                   S   V

In the kitchen of the new restaurant, <u>crates</u> of dishes and glassware *<u>wait</u>* to be unpacked. (plural subject, plural verb)

PRACTICE 3   MAKING SUBJECTS AND VERBS AGREE

Underline the correct verb form in each of the following sentences.

1. Roberto (insists, insist) on biking every day, rain or shine.

2. If Karen (impress, impresses) the interviewer, she will have a good chance of getting the job.

3. The cuckoo clock (squawks, squawk) loudly on the hour and half hour.

4. The names of Trevor's goldfish (is, are) Moe, Larry, and Curly.

5. The speckled jellybeans (tastes, taste) like buttered popcorn.

6. The cat had found the jellybeans, and they (was, were) scattered across the floor.

7. An airline's reputation (suffers, suffer) when one of its planes crashes.

8. Because the sisters (is, are) so busy, they rarely see one another.

9. Ms. Roberts (quiz, quizzes) her students on grammar every week.

10. For breakfast, Lauren (insist, insists) on eating sugary cereal with multicolored marshmallows.

Problems in Subject-Verb Agreement

mywritinglab

Visit MyWriting Lab for additional practice with subject-verb agreement.

Prepositional Phrase between Subject and Verb

One problem in subject-verb agreement occurs when a prepositional phrase comes between a subject and a verb, making it easy to make mistakes. Crossing out prepositional phrases will help you remember this important rule:

The subject of a verb is not found in a prepositional phrase.

Example 1

Consider the following problem in subject-verb agreement:

✔ The members of the softball team (practices, practice) every afternoon until five.

Which verb is correct? If you look for the subject by asking the question, "Who or what *practices* or *practice*?" it might seem logical to say, "The *team* practices, so *team* is the subject of the sentence and *practices* is the verb." However, *team* cannot be the subject of the sentence because it already has a job: It is the object of a preposition, and *the subject of a sentence is never found in a prepositional phrase.*

Incorrect Solution

✗   The members of the <u>softball team</u> <u>practices</u> every afternoon until five.

Correct Solution

Cross out prepositional phrases to find the subject.

✔   The <u>members</u> ~~of the softball team~~ (practices, <u>practice</u>) every afternoon until five.

Example 2

✔   The <u>color</u> ~~of the draperies~~ <u>matches</u> the stripe woven ~~into the fabric of the sofa~~.

The verb agrees with its subject, *color,* not with the object of the preposition.

PRACTICE 4   ELIMINATING PREPOSITIONAL PHRASES
_____

In the following sentences, cross out the prepositional phrases to find the subject of the sentence. Then, underline the subject and double-underline the correct verb.

1.   The hands on the clock (seems, seem) to have stopped.
2.   The layers of grime on the old desk (obscures, obscure) its beautiful finish.
3.   The loudness of the music in the cardio room of the fitness center (makes, make) Yolanda's head ache.
4.   As the stairs of the escalator (disappears, disappear) into the floor, a child stands watching in amazement.
5.   The computers in the library of the college (attracts, attract) many students.

Indefinite Pronouns as Subjects

Problems in subject-verb agreement are also likely to occur when the subject is an **indefinite pronoun,** a pronoun that does not refer to a specific person or thing. The following indefinite pronouns are always singular and require singular verbs.

each	everybody	everyone	anything
either	nobody	one	everything
neither	somebody	someone	nothing
anybody	anyone	no one	something

Memory Jogger

Remember the singular indefinite pronouns more easily by grouping them:

Each, either, neither

All the bodies (anybody, everybody, somebody, nobody)

All the ones (anyone, everyone, someone, one, no one)

All the things (anything, everything, something, nothing)

Examples of Singular Verbs Used with Singular Indefinite Pronouns

✔ If <u>no one</u> <u>comes</u> to their yard sale, Pat and Amy will donate the goods to charity.

The subject *no one* is singular, as is the verb *comes.*

✔ <u>Each</u> ~~of the party guests~~ <u>has been asked</u> to bring an inexpensive gag gift.

The singular verb *has been asked* agrees with the singular subject *each.* The plural object of the preposition, *guests,* does not affect the verb.

PRACTICE 5   MAKING VERBS AGREE WITH INDEFINITE PRONOUNS

In each of the following sentences, cross out prepositional phrases, and underline the verb that agrees with the indefinite pronoun subject.

1. Neither **of the contestants** (was, were) prepared to lose.
2. Everybody **on the street** (pass, passes) the homeless man **without a backward glance.**
3. No one **in any of my classes** (has, have) taken a class from Dr. Mason.
4. Something **on the bottom of Sidney's shoes** (makes, make) them stick **to the floor** as he walks.
5. Everything **on the table** (looks, look) good to me.

Subject Following the Verb

Problems in subject-verb agreement are also likely to occur when a subject follows the verb. In most English sentences, the subject comes before the verb. However, the subject follows the verb in these situations:

1. when the sentence begins with *here* or *there*

2. when the sentence begins with a prepositional phrase that is immediately followed by a verb

3. when the sentence is a question

Examples of Subject-Verb Agreement When the Subject Follows the Verb

✔ There <u>are</u> no more <u>tissues</u> left in the box.

The plural subject *tissues* requires the plural verb *are.* The word *there* is not the subject of the sentence.

✔ On top of the refrigerator <u>sit</u> my lost <u>keys.</u>

The prepositional phrases *on top* and *of the refrigerator* are immediately followed by a verb. Because the subject is never found in a prepositional phrase, it must be located somewhere after the verb. The plural verb *sit* agrees with the plural subject *keys.*

✔ What <u>was</u> the <u>answer</u> to the first question?

The singular subject *answer* follows the singular verb *was.*

✔ What <u>were</u> the <u>answers</u> to the first two questions?

The plural subject *answers* follows the plural verb *were.*

PRACTICE 6   MAKING VERBS AGREE WITH SUBJECTS THAT COME AFTER VERBS

Cross out prepositional phrases in each of the following sentences. Then underline the subject and double-underline the correct verb.

1. Nestled **in the little valley** (was, were) a cluster **of houses.**

2. Why (is, are) Trevor's parents moving **to Detroit?**

3. Here (is, are) the study guides you asked for, Jonathan.

4. (Does, Do) Angelica know that her paper is due **on Friday?**

5. There (wasn't, weren't) any newspapers left **at the bookstore.**

Compound Subjects

Compound subjects, subjects joined by *and, or, either/or,* or *neither/nor,* may also cause confusion in subject-verb agreement. The rules for subject-verb agreement with compound subjects are outlined in the sections that follow.

Compound Subjects Joined by *and*

Because *and* always joins at least two elements, compound subjects joined by *and* require a plural verb. Remember this rule:

Compound subjects joined by *and* require a plural verb.

Look at the following sentence:

✔ Keisha and her brother (is, are) scheduled to arrive today.

If you look at the sentence and ask *how many* will arrive, subject-verb agreement should be easy. *More than one* will arrive, so the logical choice is the plural verb *are*.

✔ <u>Keisha</u> and her <u>brother</u> <u>are</u> scheduled to arrive today.

Examples of Plural Verbs with Compound Subjects Joined by *and*

✔ A good <u>book</u> *and* a warm <u>fire</u> <u>are</u> ideal companions on a winter night.
✔ <u>Patience</u> *and* <u>persistence</u> <u>pay.</u>
✔ A bent <u>umbrella,</u> an old <u>chair,</u> *and* a discarded <u>mop</u> <u>sit</u> forlornly beside the trash can.
✔ Tall <u>pines</u> *and* scrub <u>oaks</u> <u>dot</u> the landscape.

PRACTICE 7   MAKING VERBS AGREE WITH SUBJECTS JOINED BY *AND*

Cross out prepositional phrases; then underline the verb that agrees with each compound subject and double-underline the verb.

1. A bright-eyed Raggedy Ann doll and a tattered bear (adorns, adorn) the bookshelf **in Kim's room**.
2. Cold pizza and a moldy scrap **of cheese** (was, were) the only food **in Foster's refrigerator**.
3. A bowl **of cold ice cream** and a hot bath (awaits, await) Kim **at the end of the day**.
4. Two plates **of spaghetti with meatballs**, two salads, a glass **of iced tea**, and one cup **of coffee** (costs, cost) less than ten dollars **at the Coffee Cup Cafe**.
5. A monster truck show and a trip **to the drive-through window of a fast food restaurant** (was, were) not Gayle's idea **of a good time**.

Compound Subjects Joined by *or, either/or,* or *neither/nor*

When subjects are joined by *or, either/or,* or *neither/nor*, it is not always possible to use logic to determine whether the verb will be singular or plural. Therefore, one rule applies to all compound subjects joined by *or, either/or,* or *neither/nor*.

When a compound subject is joined by *or*, *either/or*, or *neither/nor*, the verb agrees with the part of the subject closer to it.

Consider the following sentence:

✔ Keisha or her brother (is, are) scheduled to arrive today.

How many will arrive today? *Just one* will arrive: either Keisha *or* her brother, so using the singular verb *is* makes logical sense. The singular verb *is* also agrees with *brother*, the part of the subject closer to the verb.

✔ <u>Keisha</u> or her <u>brother</u> <u>is</u> scheduled to arrive today.

Now, let's change the sentence a bit.

✔ Keisha's brothers or her parents (is, are) scheduled to arrive today.

How many will arrive? In this sentence, *more than one*—either *brothers* or *parents*. It makes sense, then, to use a plural verb. The plural verb *are* also agrees with *parents*, the part of the subject closer to the verb.

✔ Keisha's <u>brothers</u> or her <u>parents</u> <u>are</u> scheduled to arrive today.

The next two sentences do not lend themselves to logical examination.

✔ Keisha or her parents (is, are) scheduled to arrive today.
✔ Keisha's parents or her brother (is, are) scheduled to arrive today.

How many will arrive? There is no way to tell. Simply follow the rule and make the verb agree with the part of the subject closer to it.

✔ Keisha or her <u>parents</u> <u>are</u> scheduled to arrive today.
✔ Keisha's parents or her <u>brother</u> <u>is</u> scheduled to arrive today.

Examples of Subject-Verb Agreement with *or*, *either/or*, and *neither/nor*

✔ A term <u>paper</u> *or* an oral <u>report</u> <u>is</u> required ~~in Mr. Hanson's class~~.
✔ A term <u>paper</u> *or* two oral <u>reports</u> <u>are</u> required ~~in Mr. Hanson's class~~.
✔ *Either* two oral <u>reports</u> *or* a term <u>paper</u> <u>is</u> required ~~in Mr. Hanson's class~~.
✔ *Neither* the <u>cats</u> *nor* the <u>dog</u> <u>shows</u> any interest ~~in the parakeet~~.
✔ ~~Among the requirements~~ <u>was listed</u> an associate's <u>degree</u> *or* <u>five years</u> ~~of experience~~.

PRACTICE 8   MAKING VERBS AGREE WITH SUBJECTS JOINED BY *OR, EITHER/OR, OR NEITHER/NOR*

Cross out prepositional phrases; then underline the verb that agrees with each compound subject.

1. Garlic bread or dinner rolls (is, are) served **with the meal**.
2. Either the neighbors or my mother (watches, watch) my house while I am **on vacation**.
3. Neither Ms. Pitts nor Mr. Shaw (possesses, possess) the qualities that the personnel director looks for **in a manager**.
4. A thunderstorm or a hailstorm (is, are) expected later this afternoon.
5. Neither going **to a movie** nor eating **at a trendy restaurant** (appeal, appeals) to Jenae.

Review Exercises

Complete the Review Exercises to see how well you have learned the skills introduced in this chapter. As you work through the exercises, go back through the chapter to review any of the rules you do not understand completely.

REVIEW EXERCISE 1   MAKING VERBS AGREE WITH THEIR SUBJECTS

Underline the correct verb in each of the following sentences.

1. The persistent ringing of the alarm clock (wakes, wake) Shawn every morning at six o'clock.
2. Books from the library (is, are) an inexpensive form of entertainment.
3. Each of the kittens (has, have) found a good home.
4. Neither of the witnesses to the crime (tells, tell) the same story.
5. The shampoo and the conditioner (smells, smell) good, but neither is worth five dollars.
6. The flowers and the grass (has, have) dried out in the dry weather.
7. Neither Benjamin nor his professors (was, were) told that he would receive the award.
8. In an emergency, salt or baking soda (substitutes, substitute) for toothpaste.
9. How (does, do) Angela and Dennis get away with being late every day?
10. There (is, are) few students remaining on campus after exams are over.

RECOGNIZING CORRECT AND INCORRECT SUBJECT-VERB AGREEMENT

Write *correct* in the blank if the italicized verb agrees with its subject. If the verb is incorrect, write the correct form in the blank.

_____ 1. The icy surface on the trails *make* skiing at Mount Smith tricky for beginners.

_____ 2. Because of its flashbacks and frequent changes of scene, the movie's plot *was* unclear to the audience.

_____ 3. One of my friends *are* holding a seat for me in the crowded cafeteria.

_____ 4. No one from her family *have* graduated from college.

_____ 5. Mondays and Tuesdays *are* my only days off from work.

_____ 6. Dinner and homework assignments *was* the only things on David's agenda for tonight.

_____ 7. Suzanne and Carlos's boss always *schedule* extra shifts for them when they need more money.

_____ 8. The science textbook or the two math textbooks *belongs* to Sam.

_____ 9. Why *has* the game *been canceled* today?

_____10. Here *is* the schedule for the next two weeks.

FINDING AND CORRECTING SUBJECT-VERB AGREEMENT ERRORS

In each set of sentences, cross out the two verbs that do not agree with their subjects. Then write the correct verb forms on the lines provided.

1. The two quizzes in math class **was** not difficult, but the test was very hard. However, the last two problems on the test **was** for extra credit.

   Sentence 1: _____   Sentence 2: _____

2. Not one of the animals in that pet shop **look** very healthy. An animal adopted through the Humane Society **cost** much less, and spaying or neutering is included in the fee.

   Sentence 1: _____   Sentence 2: _____

3. Neither Tanya nor her friends **was** able to find a job as a grocery store cashier. Neither of the grocery stores **were** hiring.

   Sentence 1: _____   Sentence 2: _____

4. A college diploma or a technical school certificate **are** required by most employers these days. As a result, people of all ages **is** attending these schools.

   Sentence 1: _____   Sentence 2: _____

5. "Why **is** the lines always so long in this grocery store?" Stephanie complained. "There **is** just not enough cashiers to help all of the customers."

   Sentence 1: _____   Sentence 2: _____

| REVIEW EXERCISE 4 | FINDING AND CORRECTING SUBJECT-VERB AGREEMENT ERRORS |

In each set of sentences, cross out the two verbs that do not agree with their subjects. Then write the corrected verbs on the lines provided.

1. One of the purposes of children's games **are** to teach. I sometimes wonder what the violence in so many video games **teach** children.

   Sentence 1: _____   Sentence 2: _____

2. Keith and Valerie always **budgets** carefully and cut out coupons from the Sunday paper to save a few extra dollars. But it seems as if bills or an unexpected emergency **take** whatever they manage to save.

   Sentence 1: _____   Sentence 2: _____

3. Our neighborhood used to be quiet and peaceful, but now that there **is** a gas station and a shopping center two miles down the road, traffic has increased. Why **have** the city's zoning board approved commercial development so close to quiet residential districts?

   Sentence 1: _____   Sentence 2: _____

4. When an outbreak of influenza occurs, attendance at elementary schools always **drop**. Some parents keep their kids at home just to ensure that the children **doesn't** come in contact with anyone who is infected.

   Sentence 1: _____   Sentence 2: _____

5. Neither the cat nor the dog **have** been fed this morning. What **is** the chances of running out of cat food and dog food at the same time?

   Sentence 1: _____   Sentence 2: _____

| REVIEW EXERCISE 5 | EDITING FOR CORRECT SUBJECT-VERB AGREEMENT |

Find and correct the ten subject-verb agreement errors in the following paragraph

¹My friend Brittany **believe** that she is addicted to shopping. ²She says that whenever she feels depressed or disappointed, the

neon lights and large department stores of the local mall **seems** to draw her right in. [3]As she wanders around the department stores, displays of stylish clothing **catches** her eye, and she starts to forget her problems. [4]On the racks in front of her **hang** the answer to her problems. [5]By the time one of the salesclerks **offer** to show her to a dressing room, her mood has improved considerably. [6]As she tries on clothing, she begins to feel that a new dress or a pair of jeans **are** just what she needs. [7]Before she knows it, she is standing at the register with an armload of clothes, and there **are** a charge slip or a check in front of her waiting to be signed. [8]As she walks to her car, pleasure and satisfaction **washes** over her, and everything is right with the world. [9]But by the time she gets home, the logical part of her mind **have** begun to take over. [10]She realizes she has bought unnecessary items and **know** she will be back at the store tomorrow to return them.

1. _____   6. _____

2. _____   7. _____

3. _____   8. _____

4. _____   9. _____

5. _____   10. _____

mywritinglab   For support and practice meeting this chapter's goal, log in to www.mywritinglab.com and select **Subject-Verb Agreement.**

CHAPTER 15

Coordination and Subordination

> ✐ **Chapter Goal:** Connect ideas and control emphasis through coordination and subordination.

It's good to have choices.

✐ Writing Effective Sentences

Imagine a world without choices. What if everyone were named John or Jane? What if everyone ate oatmeal for breakfast, wore green clothing, and drove a white Chevrolet? What if every sentence had to start with the subject and one verb and contain only one idea? Here's a paragraph from that world.

> My name is Jane. I got up this morning. The sky was blue. The sun was shining. I put on my green slacks. I put on my green shirt. I put on my green shoes. I ate oatmeal. I ate it for breakfast. I drove my white Ford. I drove it to school.

Fortunately, the real world is abundant with choices in names, foods, cars, and sentence structure. Here's what it really looks like.

> Hi, I'm Isabella. When I got up this morning, the sun was steaming through my window from a clear blue sky. I threw on a pair of jeans, a pink sweater, and a pair of gray athletic shoes. My stomach was rumbling, so I sliced a ripe banana into a bowl, poured milk over it, and ate it standing at the counter. Then I stepped into the sunlight, cranked up my silver Toyota, and headed for school.

When you learned to write, you started by expressing one idea per sentence. Now, your ideas are more complex. Your sentence structure, too, has become more sophisticated in order to handle those complex ideas. This chapter will help you polish your sentence structure with the tools of **coordination** and **subordination** and may even help you add a few new tricks to your repertoire.

Connecting Ideas through Coordination

mywritinglab

Visit MyWriting Lab for additional practice connecting ideas through coordination.

Often, ideas expressed in short, simple sentences can be joined to make a more effective sentence. One way to connect sentences is called *coordination*. Coordination can be done in two ways: by using a comma and a FANBOYS conjunction, or by using a semicolon and a joining word.

Comma and FANBOYS

FANBOYS conjunctions, more commonly called *coordinating* conjunctions, are used with a comma to connect two independent clauses. Remember that a **clause** is a grammatical unit that contains a subject and a verb and that an **independent clause** can stand alone as a sentence. The acronym FANBOYS stands for the seven coordinating conjunctions: **for, and, nor, but, or, yet, so.**

Following is the pattern used when a FANBOYS conjunction is used with a comma to connect two independent clauses. The comma goes before the FANBOYS conjunction.

<u>Independent clause</u>, and <u>independent clause</u>.

Example of Sentences Connected with a Comma and FANBOYS

     S   V

✔ <u>Luis</u> <u>scanned</u> the small auditorium. (independent clause)

     S   V   V

✔ <u>He</u> <u>did</u> not <u>see</u> his friend Katie. (independent clause)

The preceding two independent clauses can be connected with a FANBOYS and a comma:

✔   Luis scanned the small auditorium, **but** he did not see his friend Kathy.

PRACTICE 1   **CONNECTING SENTENCES WITH FANBOYS**

Connect each of the following sentence pairs with a comma and a FANBOYS.

1. In the quiet classroom, a cell phone began to ring.
   Someone quickly silenced it.

   _____

   _____

2. Austin's girlfriend tells him that he is lazy.
   Austin says he's just an expert at conserving energy.

   _____

   _____

3. Cars packed the parking lot of the new restaurant.
   A long line of customers waited to get in.

   _____

   _____

4. Vanessa's family used to travel as far as they could on vacation.
   Rising gas prices have compelled them to vacation closer to home.

   _____

   _____

5. Shane hopes to move out of his parents' house and into his own place.
   He works and saves as much as possible.

   _____

   _____

Semicolon and Joining Word

Another method of coordination is using a semicolon and a joining word. As with a comma and FANBOYS conjunction, a complete sentence (an independent clause) will appear on both sides of the semicolon.

<u>Independent clause</u>; therefore, <u>independent clause</u>.

Example of Sentences Connected with a Semicolon and a Joining Word

✔ Shakira thought she would have money left over at the end of the month.

✔ She did not anticipate having to buy a new tire.

The two separate sentences can be combined with a semicolon and a joining word.

✔ Shakira thought she would have money left over at the end of the month; **however,** she did not anticipate having to buy a new tire.

The joining words also function as *transitional expressions,* underscoring the relationship between the two clauses.

A list of joining words commonly used with semicolons follows.

Joining Words Used with a Semicolon

accordingly	furthermore	meanwhile
also	however	nevertheless
as a result	in addition	of course
besides	in fact	on the other hand
finally	instead	therefore

PRACTICE 2   CONNECTING SENTENCES WITH A SEMICOLON AND A JOINING WORD

Connect each of the following sentence pairs with a semicolon, a joining word from the preceding list, and a comma.

1. Mallory knew her paper was due on Friday.
   She resisted the temptation to go out shopping with her friends.

   _____

   _____

2. Diego agreed to help Clara move to her new apartment.
   He did not know she had so much furniture.

   _____

   _____

3. The woman who sat next to DeShawn on the plane insisted on telling him her life's story.
   He pretended to go to sleep to avoid her chatter.

   _____

   _____

4. Snow swirled against the windshield, obscuring Natalie's view.
    She slowed down and drove with extreme caution.

    _____

    _____

5. Vehicles in the southbound lanes of the highway crawled to a halt because of
    an accident ahead.
    Traffic in the northbound lanes flowed smoothly and quickly.

    _____

    _____

    _____

Connecting Ideas through Subordination

Another way of connecting ideas is through **subordination**. Placing a **dependent word** such as *because, although, if, when,* or *after* in front of an independent clause makes it a **dependent** or **subordinate clause**, one that can no longer stand on its own as a sentence. It must be connected to another idea that is stated as a complete sentence. It will then *depend on* the sentence it is attached to and can no longer be separated from it. Two examples are shown here using the dependent word *because*.

Example 1

✔ The fuel gauge in Rashid's car was broken.
✔ He never knew for certain when he was running low on gas.

   If the dependent clause acts as an introductory clause, a comma follows it.
   Because <u>dependent clause</u>, <u>independent clause</u>.

✔ Because the fuel gauge in Rashid's car was broken, he never knew for certain when he was running low on gas.

Example 2

✔ The weathercaster told her audience to break out the barbeque grills and the sunscreen.
✔ The weekend would be sunny and hot.

   <u>Independent clause</u> because <u>dependent clause.</u>

✔ The weathercaster told her audience to break out the barbeque grills and the sunscreen **because** the weekend would be sunny and hot.

A list of dependent words follows.

Dependent Words

after	even though	what
although	if	whatever
as	once	when
as if	since	whenever
as long	so that	where
as soon as	that	wherever
as though	though	which
because	unless	while
before	until	who

PRACTICE 3   CONNECTING SENTENCES WITH DEPENDENT WORDS

Choosing from the preceding list of dependent words, connect each sentence pair using the following pattern:

Dependent word <u>dependent clause</u>, <u>independent clause</u>.

The first one is done for you.

1. Ruth searched through her purse for her debit card.

    The customer in line behind her sighed dramatically.

    As Ruth searched through her purse for her debit card, the customer in line

    behind her sighed dramatically.

2. Movies and television have romanticized the excitement and danger of detective work.

    Police detectives say their work is ninety-five percent routine and five percent terror.

    _____

    _____

    _____

3. Thomas Edison invented the electric light bulb in 1879.

    He paved the way for society to function 24 hours a day instead of stopping at sunset.

    _____

    _____

4.   The holiday weekend promised beautiful weather.
     The lake was crowded with picnickers, boaters, sunbathers, and swimmers.

     _____

     _____

5.   Jake sat on a park bench eating his lunch.
     Bold pigeons strutted and pecked around his feet, hoping to share his meal.

     _____

     _____

PRACTICE 4   CONNECTING SENTENCES WITH DEPENDENT WORDS

Choosing from the preceding list of dependent words, connect each sentence pair using the following pattern:

<u>Independent clause</u> dependent word <u>dependent clause.</u>

The first one is done for you.

1.   Security was tight at the university's graduation.
     The vice-president of the United States was expected to give the commencement address.

     Security was tight at the university's graduation because the vice-president of the

     United States was expected to give the commencement address.

2.   Maria had just sat down to eat.
     The doorbell rang, causing her to sigh with impatience.

     _____

     _____

3.   Jason watched in dismay.
     The cup of coffee he had just bought slipped from his hand and fell to the floor, splashing coffee on his pants.

     _____

     _____

4.   Susan's muscles were sore and tired.
     She had spent the afternoon swimming laps in the campus pool.

     _____

     _____

5. Ashley changed her mind about teaching young children.
    She spent a week assisting with a preschool class.

    _____

    _____

Creating Emphasis through Subordination

Dependent words also act as transitional words, showing the relationships between ideas. Using dependent clauses helps downplay one idea while emphasizing another. Usually, the idea expressed in the independent clause is of greater importance, while the idea in the dependent clause is of lesser importance.

Examples of Creating Emphasis through Subordination

✔   emphasis on the pay
    Although police work is important and often dangerous, the pay is surprisingly small.

                        emphasis on the danger
✔   Police work is important and often dangerous although the pay is surprisingly small.

                     emphasis on the cheer
✔   A cheer went up from the crowd as the home team scored the winning run.

                   emphasis on the run
✔   The home team scored the winning run as a cheer went up from the crowd.

PRACTICE 5   USING DEPENDENT WORDS TO EMPHASIZE IDEAS

Choosing from the preceding list of dependent words, connect each sentence pair. The idea that is given less emphasis should be introduced by a dependent word. The first one is done for you.

1. Valerie could barely cover her monthly expenses.
    She decided to look for a second job. ✔ *Emphasize this idea.*
    Because Valerie could barely cover her monthly expenses, she decided to look for
    a second job.

2. Orlando looked forward to having an entire week off. ✔ *Emphasize this idea.*
    He had no money for a vacation.

    _____

    _____

3. The endless expanse of blue sky passed by the plane's window unnoticed.
   Sameera headed back to India for her father's funeral. ✔ *Emphasize this idea.*

   _____

   _____

4. The flowers were already shedding their petals all over the kitchen table.
   ✔ *Emphasize this idea.*
   Julia had picked them from her garden just yesterday.

   _____

   _____

5. James was celebrating his twenty-first birthday.
   He broke his leg in a Jet Ski accident. ✔ *Emphasize this idea.*

   _____

   _____

Review Exercises

REVIEW EXERCISE 1   **CONNECTING SENTENCES USING COORDINATION**

Connect each sentence pair using *coordination.* Use a comma and a FANBOYS *or* a semicolon, a joining word, and a comma.

1. Alonzo put his portable music player on shuffle.
   He began to jog though the park, listening to his favorite tunes.

   _____

   _____

2. Roxanne knew that traffic would be heavy in Phoenix.
   She had not bargained for drivers who were speeding, weaving in and out of traffic, and following an inch from her bumper.

   _____

   _____

3. Heavy winter clothing was crowded onto the rod in the closet.
    The entire rod eventually fell under its weight.

    _____

    _____

4. The rich, warm sound of the violin used to be produced by strings made of sheep's intestines.
    Today's synthetic strings stay in tune longer and produce a sound that is just as rich.

    _____

    _____

    _____

5. People used to have to wait for a daily paper or for the six o'clock news program for a news update.
    News is now available twenty-four hours a day on the Internet and on television.

    _____

    _____

    _____

REVIEW EXERCISE 2   CONNECTING SENTENCES USING SUBORDINATION

Connect the two sentences using *subordination*.

1. Tina does her grocery shopping after most people have gone to bed.
    The store is never crowded late at night.

    _____

    _____

2. Kim's children were bored.
    She took them to the miniature golf course on Saturday morning.

    _____

    _____

3. Sanjay carefully removed the casserole dish from the oven.
    It slipped from his fingers and shattered on the floor.

    _____

    _____

4. Nick had always wanted to try carpentry.
   He signed up for a woodworking class.

   _____

   _____

5. The applicant seemed charming and capable at the job interview.
   She proved to be undependable and careless.

   _____

   _____

REVIEW EXERCISE 3   **CONNECTING SENTENCES USING COORDINATION OR SUBORDINATION**

Connect each sentence pair using *coordination* or *subordination*.

1. Many people filtered into the movie theater.
   The previews were playing.

   _____

2. The author originally thought of her book as a children's story.
   She was surprised by the number of adult fans of her work.

   _____

   _____

3. Marcos wanted to ski the mountain's most difficult trails by the end of winter.
   He failed to master many of the necessary skills and had to stick to the
   bunny slope.

   _____

   _____

   _____

4. Aline wanted a pet.
   Her landlord wouldn't allow them.

   _____

5. Matt didn't understand the assignment.
   He visited his instructor during office hours.

   _____

   _____

| REVIEW EXERCISE 4 | CONNECTING SENTENCES USING COORDINATION OR SUBORDINATION |

There are eighteen sentences in the paragraph. Connect them using *coordination* and *subordination,* so that you have no more than nine sentences when you are through. Be sure to use both techniques.

[1]Most people know that "getting onto one's soapbox" means giving a heartfelt opinion. [2]Fewer people are familiar with the origin of the term. [3]The term dates back to a time when large wooden crates were used to ship soap. [4]It comes from a practice that was popular in the 1800s and early 1900s. [5]A person who wanted to express an opinion publicly would first find a public park or street corner. [6]He would find an improvised platform, often a large, sturdy soapbox. [7]Standing on the box, he would speak his mind. [8]An audience was not guaranteed. [9]If his oratorical skills were good, he might gather a crowd. [10]If they were poor, he might be heckled or have no audience at all. [11]Audiences cheered speakers that they agreed with. [12]Speakers they disagreed with met a less pleasant fate. [13]Audiences showed their displeasure by throwing tomatoes or fruit, preferably rotten, at the speaker. [14]He would end his speech quickly and leave, humiliated and covered in tomato juice. [15]Today, getting on one's soapbox has been made easier by the Internet. [16]Anyone can post a blog on one of the many free sites set up for just that purpose. [17]The principle is the same as that of the soapbox. [18]The advantage is that the speaker does not have to worry about rotten tomatoes.

_____

_____

_____

_____

_____

_____

_____

_____

_____

_____

_____

_____

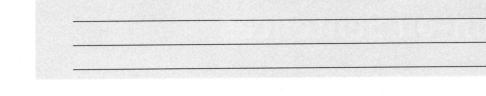

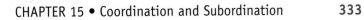 For support and practice meeting this chapter's goal, log in to www.mywritinglab.com and select **Combining Sentences.**

CHAPTER 16

Run-on Sentences

🎶 Chapter Goal: Identify and correct run-on sentences.

Two cars spin in a crazy dance
And spiral to a stop,
Locked in a less-than-fond embrace
Both destined for the shop.

And so it is with sentences
When they're too closely linked.
It's up to you to put them right
And make them each distinct.

A fender-bender is an unfortunate incident. Aside from the damage to the cars, there's the red tape of insurance claims and maybe even a costly traffic ticket. Run-on sentences are similarly unfortunate. Aside from the damage to sentence structure, there's red ink on your essay, and maybe even a grade penalty. Run-on sentences can be corrected or avoided. This chapter will show you how.

🎶 What Is a Run-on Sentence?

mywritinglab

Visit My Writing Lab for additional practice identifying run-on sentences.

A **run-on sentence** is not one sentence, but two or more, run together without proper punctuation. The following sentence is a type of run-on that is often called a **fused sentence** because two thoughts are fused together with no punctuation to separate them. In this text, the fused sentence type of run-on is simply referred to as a *run-on*.

X Two pieces of paper slipped out of Josh's notebook he stopped to pick them up.

By examining the sentence, you can probably decide where the first thought ends and the second begins—between *notebook* and *he*. Grammatically, too, you

334

can figure out why the thoughts should be separate. Each has a subject and a verb and is an **independent clause**, a clause that can stand alone as a sentence or that can be combined with other clauses in specific patterns.

Another type of run-on is called a **comma splice** because two independent clauses are spliced, or joined, with a comma.

✗   Two pieces of paper slipped out of Josh's notebook, he stopped to pick them up.

The first step toward writing paragraphs and essays that are free of run-on sentences is to learn to recognize run-ons and comma splices. When you see a sentence that you believe is a run-on, test it. Read the first part. Is it a sentence that could stand alone? If your answer is yes, read the second part, asking the same question. If your answer is again yes, the sentence is probably a run-on.

PRACTICE 1   RECOGNIZING RUN-ONS AND COMMA SPLICES

In each sentence, underline the spot where the run-on occurs. Mark *RO* in the blank to the left of the sentence if the sentence is a run-on (fused sentence) and *CS* if it is a comma splice.

_____ **1.** An old, bent woman trudged alongside the busy highway she wore several layers of clothing and pushed a shopping cart laden with her belongings.

_____ **2.** The computer screen was hard to read, light from the window created a reflection on the screen's surface.

_____ **3.** Fitness is important to Alexis, she jogs every morning.

_____ **4.** "What does it take to be successful?" Anthony asked his boss Ms. Gray told him, "You have to be willing to make a lot of mistakes."

_____ **5.** Vanessa's brother goes to the university her sister attends a technical school.

_____ **6.** The store will open in the morning, it is closed for inventory today.

_____ **7.** Yesterday's meeting was supposed to last for an hour one hour and forty-five minutes later, it was still in progress.

_____ **8.** Saffron had a part-time job, an active social life, and a full load of courses after she received her first test grade, she decided she needed to spend more time on her coursework.

_____ **9.** No matter how many times Antwan went by his instructor's office, she wasn't there after a while, he decided he needed to make an appointment.

_____ **10.** The microwave's buzzer sounded dinner was ready.

Correcting Run-ons

mywritinglab

Visit MyWriting Lab for additional practice correcting run-on sentences.

Five methods of correcting run-ons are presented in the following sections. The first three methods are simple; the remaining two are more complex. Learning all five methods will give you more than just ways to correct run-ons; it will give you a variety of sentence patterns and transitional words to use in your writing.

Method 1: Period and Capital Letter

Correcting a run-on with a period and capital letter is the easiest method to use. The hard part is knowing when and how often to use it. Short, single-clause sentences can emphasize ideas by setting them apart. Too many short sentences can make your writing seem choppy and disconnected.

> **Pattern**: <u>Independent clause</u>. <u>Independent clause</u>.

Put a period between the two sentences. Use a capital letter to begin the new sentence.

Example of a Run-on Corrected with a Period and Capital Letter

✗   The technician flipped a switch red and green lights blinked on the control panel.

✓   The technician flipped a switch. Red and green lights blinked on the control panel.

PRACTICE 2   CORRECTING RUN-ONS WITH A PERIOD AND A CAPITAL LETTER

In each sentence, underline the spot where the run-on (fused sentence) or comma splice occurs. Write *RO* in the blank to the left of the sentence if it is a run-on, *CS* if it is a comma splice. Then correct each sentence using a period and a capital letter.

_____   1.   Nonessential water usage has been banned, people are asked not to wash their cars or water their lawns until the drought ends.

_____

_____   2.   Evan walked over to a display of books she picked up a novel by Stephen King.

_____

_____   3.   In the checkout line, Olivia dropped a quarter it rolled across the floor until an elderly man placed his foot on it to stop its progress.

_____

_____ 4. Wearing his bathrobe, Lou sleepily walked to the end of the driveway, he picked up the newspaper and headed back toward the house.

_____

_____ 5. Americans are becoming more aware of the need to exercise the sale of treadmills, stationary bikes, and weight training equipment has increased over the last decade.

_____

Method 2: Comma and FANBOYS Conjunction

Coordinating conjunctions, or FANBOYS conjunctions, are among the most useful and powerful connecting words in the English language. If you can remember the nonsense word FANBOYS, you can remember the seven coordinating conjunctions: **f**or, **a**nd, **n**or, **b**ut, **o**r, **y**et, **s**o.

Pattern: <u>Independent clause</u>, and <u>independent clause</u>.

When a FANBOYS conjunction is used with a comma to separate two clauses, the comma goes before the FANBOYS conjunction.

Example of a Run-on Corrected with a Comma and FANBOYS

✗ Andrea had the day off, she went shopping.

✓ Andrea had the day off, so she went shopping.

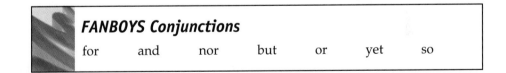

FANBOYS Conjunctions						
for	and	nor	but	or	yet	so

PRACTICE 3   Correcting Run-ons with a FANBOYS Conjunction

In each sentence, underline the spot where the run-on (fused sentence) or comma splice occurs. Write *RO* in the blank to the left of the sentence if it is a run-on, *CS* if it is a comma splice. Correct each run-on or comma splice by using a comma and a FANBOYS conjunction.

_____ 1. The house was painted brown the shutters and trim were red.

_____

_____ **2.** The letter carrier had never seen the two dogs before, she approached them cautiously.

_____

_____ **3.** The park was overgrown with weeds the city workers were on strike.

_____

_____ **4.** Eating raw eggs used to be considered healthy now people worry about the dangers of salmonella.

_____

_____ **5.** Karen is a grouch when she first wakes up, after her first cup of coffee, she feels human again.

_____

Method 3: Semicolon

Using a semicolon to join clauses works best with ideas that are closely connected and need no transitional word to explain the connection between them. The semicolon is the grammatical equivalent of a period, but the first letter of the clause after the semicolon is *not* capitalized.

   Pattern: Independent clause; independent clause.

The semicolon goes between the two clauses.

Example of a Run-on Corrected with a Semicolon

✗   The book section is to the right as patrons enter the library, journals and periodicals are to the left.

✓   The book section is to the right as patrons enter the library; journals and periodicals are to the left.

PRACTICE 4   CORRECTING RUN-ONS WITH A SEMICOLON

In each sentence, underline the spot where the run-on occurs. Write *RO* in the blank to the left of the sentence if it is a run-on (fused sentence), *CS* if it is a comma splice. Then correct the sentences using a semicolon alone.

_____ **1.** Registration for classes will be held until Thursday the late registration period runs through Monday.

_____

_____ **2.** Stephanie bought a five-year-old Toyota, newer cars were too expensive.

_____

_____ **3.** Diego fell from a swing and broke her arm at recess, the school could not immediately reach either of his parents.

_____

_____ **4.** Jason buys a lottery ticket every week, he calls it his retirement plan.

_____

_____ **5.** Books lined the shelves in the small classroom, maps were displayed on the walls.

_____

Method 4: Semicolon and Transitional Expression

A run-on sentence may also be corrected with a connecting word or phrase that functions as a transitional expression, underscoring the relationship between the two clauses.

    Pattern: <u>Independent clause</u>; therefore, <u>independent clause</u>.

A semicolon precedes the transitional expression and a comma follows it. With the words *thus* and *then,* the comma is often omitted.

Example of a Run-on Corrected with a Semicolon and Transitional Word

✗ Traffic was heavy the rain made it almost impossible to see the road.

✓ Traffic was heavy; furthermore, the rain made it almost impossible to see the road.

Transitional Words and Expressions Used with a Semicolon

accordingly	furthermore	nevertheless
after	how	what
also	however	of course
as a result	in addition	on the other hand
besides	in fact	then
finally	instead	therefore

for example   meanwhile   thus
for instance   namely

<u>PRACTICE 5</u>   **CORRECTING RUN-ONS WITH A SEMICOLON AND A TRANSITIONAL EXPRESSION**

In each sentence, underline the spot where the run-on occurs. Write *RO* in the blank to the left of the sentence if it is a run-on (fused sentence), *CS* if it is a comma splice. Then correct the sentence using a semicolon and an appropriate transitional expression.

_____ 1. Tia thought she could get by without studying, her grades suffered.

_____

_____ 2. The lake was beautiful and clear, cans, bottles, and fast-food wrappers littered the beach alongside it.

_____

_____ 3. Felipe looked at expensive home theater equipment for hours, he decided that what he had was good enough.

_____

_____ 4. Dogs have lost their position as the most popular pet, Americans now own more cats than dogs.

_____

_____ 5. In relatively wealthy countries, people can afford to have pets in some countries, dogs and cats are used as food.

_____

Method 5: Dependent Word

Placing a dependent word in front of an independent clause makes it a dependent clause, a clause that can no longer stand on its own as a sentence. It now *depends on* the sentence it is attached to and can no longer be separated from it.

Example of a Run-on Corrected with a Dependent Word

Each of the independent clauses shown below stands on its own as a sentence.

            independent clause   independent clause

✓   The orchestra began to play. Fireworks appeared in the night sky.

When the word *as* is added to the first clause, it becomes a *dependent clause*. Now, it cannot stand on its own but must depend on—or remain attached to—the independent clause.

dependent clause   independent clause
✓ <u>As the orchestra began to play,</u> fireworks appeared in the night sky.

Two Patterns Using the Dependent Clause

Sentences containing dependent clauses take on various patterns. Two of those patterns are shown below. In the first pattern, the dependent clause introduces the sentence and is followed by a comma. In the second pattern, the dependent clause ends the sentence.

Pattern 1: Dependent clause as an introductory clause
As <u>dependent clause, independent clause.</u>

When the dependent clause acts as an introductory clause, a comma follows it.

Example of a Run-on Corrected in Two Ways

✗ Margaret walked into her office, the phone began to ring.
✓ As Margaret walked into her office, the phone began to ring.

Pattern 2: Dependent clause last
<u>Independent clause</u> as <u>dependent clause.</u>

When the dependent clause comes last in the sentence, no comma is used.

✓ Margaret walked into her office as the phone began to ring.

Commonly Used Dependent Words

after	because	that	whenever
although	before	though	where
as	even though	unless	wherever
as if	if	until	which
as long	once	what	while
as soon as	since	whatever	who
as though	so that	when	

PRACTICE 6 CORRECTING RUN-ONS WITH A DEPENDENT WORD

In each sentence, underline the spot where the run-on occurs. Write *RO* in the blank to the left of the sentence if it is a run-on (fused sentence), *CS* if it is a comma splice. Correct the following sentences, using a different dependent word with each.

_____ 1. The throbbing in Ryan's jaw became worse he picked up the phone to call the dentist.

_____

_____ 2. The setting sun painted the lake red-gold, the breeze ruffled its mirrored surface.

_____

_____ 3. A water shortage developed the city imposed a ban on outdoor watering.

_____

_____ 4. The women's softball team has won every game this season, the men's team has turned in its worst performance ever.

_____

_____ 5. Helen won tickets to the concert she is looking for someone to go with her.

_____

A Special Case: The Word *That*

Occasionally, the dependent word *that* is implied rather than stated in a sentence. The sentence may look like a run-on, but it is not.

Example of a Sentence with Implied *That*

✓   The mechanic didn't think he could fix the car.

Five Ways to Correct Run-on Sentences

Method 1: Period and Capital Letter

Pattern: <u>Independent clause</u>. <u>Independent clause</u>.

Method 2: Comma and FANBOYS Conjunction

Pattern: <u>Independent clause</u>, and <u>independent clause</u>.

A comma goes before the FANBOYS conjunction in this pattern.

FANBOYS Conjunctions

| for | and | nor | but | or | yet | so |

Method 3: Semicolon

Pattern: <u>Independent clause</u>; <u>independent clause</u>.

Method 4: Semicolon and Joining Word

Pattern: <u>Independent clause</u>; therefore, <u>independent clause</u>.

A semicolon goes before the joining word, and a comma follows it.
    Exceptions: With the words *thus* and *then*, the comma is often omitted.

Joining Words Used with a Semicolon

also	however	of course
as a result	in addition	on the other hand
besides	in fact	then
finally	instead	therefore
for example	meanwhile	thus

Method 5: Dependent Word

Pattern: Although <u>dependent clause</u>, <u>independent clause</u>.

When a dependent word begins the sentence, a comma is used between the dependent and independent clause.

Pattern: <u>Independent clause</u> when <u>dependent clause</u>.

When the dependent clause ends the sentence, a dependent word separates the clauses.

Dependent Words

although	because	that	whenever
as	before	though	where
as if	if	unless	wherever
as long	once	until	which
as soon as	since	whatever	while
as though	so that	when	who

This sentence could be mistaken for a run-on. "The mechanic didn't think" has a subject, *mechanic,* and a verb, *did think,* and is not preceded by a dependent word. It could stand alone as a sentence. "He could fix the car" also has a subject, *he,* and a verb, *could fix.* It, too, could stand alone as a sentence. But is the sentence a run-on? No. The two thoughts are connected by the implied dependent word *that.* The meaning of the sentence is "The mechanic did not think *that* he could fix the car." Sentences in which the dependent word *that* is implied do not need correction—it is not always necessary to insert the word *that.*

PRACTICE 7   RECOGNIZING AN IMPLIED *THAT*

Write *OK* by the sentences that contain the implied word *that.* Write *RO* by the run-ons.

_____ 1.   The lawyer had a feeling her client was withholding information.

_____ 2.   On the desk sat a mystery novel Sachiko had not read.

_____ 3.   On the desk sat a mystery novel Sachiko had not read it.

_____ 4.   Last night Andrew dreamed he had forgotten to take his final exams.

_____ 5.   Jason was afraid his instructor would find out he had cheated on the exam.

_____ 6.   In the parking lot, Lauren ran over a nail it went through her tire and out the sidewall.

_____ 7.   The technician at the tire store told her it would be too dangerous to patch the sidewall.

_____ 8.   Lauren had planned to buy a new pair of shoes she bought a tire instead.

_____ 9.   As the police officer wrote the ticket, she reminded Bryan his driver's license would need to be renewed in a month.

_____10.   The ceiling fan cooled the room an air conditioner would have done a better job.

Review Exercises

Complete the Review Exercises to see how well you have learned the skills addressed in this chapter. As you work through the exercises, go back through the chapter to review any of the rules you do not understand completely.

| REVIEW EXERCISE 1 | CORRECTING RUN-ONS USING VARIOUS METHODS |

Correct the ten run-on sentences below, using each of the five methods at least once. Rewrite the corrected portion of each sentence on the line provided.

1. The bus was late this morning the driver was delayed by a wreck on Miller's Hill Road.

   _____

2. Zandra likes her unusual name she wonders how some parents can saddle their children with names like "Bob" or "Ann."

   _____

3. We met our new neighbors today, their names are Gary and Vicki.

   _____

4. Vijay worked for two hours on his research paper then he went out for pizza with his friends.

   _____

5. The shallow lake near the college is a popular gathering place everyone calls it Lake Knee Deep.

   _____

6. In the clear night sky, the Belt of Orion shone brightly Tasha could not find the Big Dipper.

   _____

7. The Andersens didn't have time for a camping trip, they pitched their tent in the back yard for a weekend mini-vacation.

   _____

8. Sonya's job in the Gaslight Grill pays less than minimum wage her tips, however, more than compensate for her low wages.

   _____

9. The gym was crowded at 6:00 p.m., Bert had to wait fifteen minutes for a treadmill.

   _____

10. Seven fragile cups sat in a row on the cupboard shelf, the eighth lay in pieces on the tile floor.

   _____

REVIEW EXERCISE 2   CORRECTING RUN-ON SENTENCES USING VARIOUS METHODS

Correct the ten run-on sentences below, using each of the five methods at least once. Rewrite the corrected portion of each sentence on the line provided.

1. Chandra is a vegetarian her husband complains he has not seen a hamburger for months.

    _____

2. Alex answered the telephone only silence greeted him on the other end.

    _____

3. Jan likes blues and rock, her husband prefers Beethoven and Bach.

    _____

4. Highlighters are useful for marking textbooks experts say only 10 to 20 percent of the material should be highlighted.

    _____

5. Orientation and study skills courses are a good way to learn to adjust to the demands of college many students say they benefit from such courses.

    _____

6. A roll of pennies contains fifty pennies a roll of nickels contains only forty nickels.

    _____

7. Bank tellers count money rapidly they always count it twice to make sure the amount is correct.

    _____

8. Smoke billowed from the forest fire the sky turned a muddy brown.

    _____

9. Annette always forgot to water the plants on her porch they eventually died.

    _____

10. Tyler is an optimist he always looks at the positive side of any situation.

    _____

| REVIEW EXERCISE 3 | CORRECTING RUN-ONS IN SENTENCE GROUPS |

Correct the two run-ons in each of the following sentence groups, writing your corrections on the lines provided.

1. Isabel sat down at her computer to do homework fifteen minutes later she was posting on a social network. College students are not alone in being distracted by the Internet, office workers also spend a significant amount of work time surfing the Net.

   _____

   _____

2. Alfreda gets her oil changed at Lube'n'Go, her husband goes to Slick City and pays twice as much. Alfreda does not understand why he continues to pay exorbitant prices, he claims, however, that Slick City does a better job.

   _____

   _____

3. Society's expectations about education have changed, a high school diploma is no longer adequate preparation for most jobs. Employers are demanding a more educated workforce a college or technical school diploma is required for many jobs.

   _____

   _____

4. Adults return to school for various reasons, some want new careers or job promotions. Others regret not having attended college when they were younger, often these students find new confidence and a new zeal for learning.

   _____

   _____

5. News is readily available from a variety of media, including radio and TV it is even available through a computer. Many people prefer to read a newspaper it is portable and offers more depth than many other sources of information.

   _____

   _____

| REVIEW EXERCISE 4 | CORRECTING RUN-ONS IN SENTENCE GROUPS |

Correct the two run-ons in each of the following sentence groups, writing your corrections on the lines provided.

1. Marian is trying to save money on her grocery bill she cuts coupons, watches the sales, and shops carefully. Her husband Pete is not as frugal with one trip to the grocery store, he can destroy Marian's entire budget.

    _____

    _____

2. Pirby, Nick's Persian cat, loves to sleep in the sun it warms his old bones. As the day progresses, the sunlight inches across the floor Pirby moves with it.

    _____

    _____

3. After work each day, Henry works in his garden he raises daffodils and enters them in a flower show every year. Henry's nephew Billy visited last weekend he trampled most of Henry's delicate split-cup daffodils into the ground.

    _____

    _____

4. The snowstorm moved in overnight by morning a glistening blanket of white covered city streets. Soon cars and trucks would turn the snow to dirty slush the pristine white beauty would not last long.

    _____

    _____

5. Art, the assistant salad chef at Fisher House, likes to play practical jokes he once tossed a plastic cockroach in with the salad. The cockroach was served to a customer Art's boss was not amused.

    _____

    _____

REVIEW EXERCISE 5 | **EDITING A PARAGRAPH TO CORRECT RUN-ONS**

Correct the ten run-on sentences in the following paragraph, writing your corrections on the lines provided.

[1]Roberto has never forgotten his first night on the job at the Stake-Out Steak House it was a disaster. [2]Jan, who had been assigned to train him, asked him to take beverages to a table of four then she left to take another order. [3]Carefully, Roberto drew coffee from the large urn on the counter in back and then looked around in confusion where was the tea? [4]He saw a large refrigerator in the tray assembly area, he thought he might find tea there. [5]From the refrigerator, he withdrew a large, heavy jug of brown liquid he poured a tall glassful over ice. [6]He felt self-sufficient and proud, he garnished the glass with a lemon slice and took the beverages to the table. [7]He walked away from the table, the customer called him back, handed him the glass of tea, and said, "Are you trying to poison me?" [8]Roberto cautiously sniffed the brown liquid, then drew back in horror, it was vinegar. [9]Roberto apologized, explaining that it was his first night on the job, to his relief, the man at the table began to laugh. [10]Roberto thought, "I guess I'll laugh about this someday, it won't be today."

1. _____

2. _____

3. _____

4. _____

5. _____

6. _____

7. _____

8. _____

9. _____

10. _____

mywritinglab For support and practice meeting this chapter's goal, log in to www.mywritinglab.com and select Run-Ons.

CHAPTER 17

Sentence Fragments

♫ Chapter Goal: Identify and correct sentence fragments.

A mirror breaks, and someone screams
In horror and in fright.
Must be your English teacher,
Who thinks fragments are a blight.

The woman in the photograph above seems horrified by the fragments of broken mirror that reflect her image. Perhaps she is superstitious and believes that a broken mirror will bring seven years' bad luck. Of course, she could also be an English professor, suddenly reminded of the horror of sentence fragments.

What Is a Sentence Fragment?

mywritinglab

Visit MyWriting Lab for additional practice identifying sentence fragments.

A **sentence fragment** is an incomplete sentence. It may be a dependent clause that cannot stand on its own, or it may lack a subject, a verb, or both. If you read a fragment by itself, without the other sentences that surround it, you will usually recognize that it does not express a complete thought. It is only a part, or fragment, of a sentence.

Examples of Sentence Fragments

✗ Many animals hibernate in winter. *Including woodchucks, ground squirrels, and frogs.*

✗ On Saturday morning, Alvin spent an hour raking leaves. *And sweeping them from his carport.*

The italicized word groups are sentence fragments—pieces of sentences that cannot stand alone.

Dependent Clause Fragments

✗ Jarrod said he did not finish his term paper. *Because his computer had crashed.*

✗ *When Alice arrived at 10:15.* The exam had already started.

Each of the italicized fragments above is a **dependent clause fragment**. A dependent clause fragment always begins with a dependent word. To fix a dependent clause fragment, attach it to a complete sentence. Removing the dependent word will also fix the fragment, but the dependent word may be necessary to strengthen the logical connection between two ideas.

✔ Jarrod did not finish his term paper because his computer had crashed.

✔ Jarrod did not finish his term paper. His computer had crashed.

✔ When Alice arrived at 10:15, the exam had already started.

✔ Alice arrived at 10:15. The exam had already started.

> ### *Punctuation Pointer*
>
> Use a comma to attach a dependent clause fragment at the beginning of a sentence.

Commonly Used Dependent Words

after	how	what
although	if	when
as	once	whenever
as if	since	where
as long as	so that	wherever
as soon as	that	which
because	though	while
before	unless	who
even though	until	whoever

PRACTICE 1   CORRECTING DEPENDENT CLAUSE FRAGMENTS

Correct the dependent clause fragments in the following exercise by attaching them to an independent clause. Write the corrected portion of each sentence on the line provided.

1. Tamika complained that her car did not run well. Unless she used premium gasoline.

   _____

2. Aaron wondered what was wrong with the game console. That he had bought just two weeks ago.

   _____

3. Since Maddie is cold-natured and her roommate is not. They are always battling over the thermostat.

   _____

4. If Jeff did not set his clock fifteen minutes fast. He might never be on time.

   _____

5. The suspect admitted that she had shot her husband. Because the poison she was giving him had not worked quickly enough.

   _____

Verbal Phrase Fragments (*to*, *-ing*, and *-ed*)

✗ *To relax and to develop her creative abilities.* Ann decided to take an art class.

✗ Anita's dog was a familiar sight in the neighborhood. *Running through yards and tearing up flowerbeds.*

✗ *Bored by his job in a warehouse.* Evan bought a lawn mower and cut grass to earn money.

The examples above are **verbal phrase fragments**. A verbal phrase fragment begins with a verb form that is not used as a main verb. Verbal phrase fragments include *to* fragments, *-ing* fragments, and *-ed/-en* fragments.

Correct verbal phrase fragments by attaching them to a complete sentence.

✔ Anita's dog was a familiar sight in the neighborhood, running through yards and tearing up flowerbeds.

✔ To relax and to develop her creative abilities, Ann decided to take an art class.

✔ Bored by his job in a warehouse, Evan bought a lawn mower and cut grass to earn money.

to Fragments

Correct *to* fragments by connecting them to a sentence or by adding a subject and a verb, as shown in the examples below.

Examples of *to* Fragments and Their Corrections

✗ The auto repair shop has begun to open on weekends. To accommodate customers who work during the week.

✔ The auto repair shop has begun to open on weekends to accommodate customers who work during the week.

✗ To ensure that we would not forget to tip him. The server asked, "Do you want change back?"

✔ To ensure that we would not forget to tip him, the server asked, "Do you want change back?"

✗ James programmed his digital video recorder before he left the house. To make sure he would not miss even one inning of the ball game.

✔ James programmed his digital video recorder before he left the house. He wanted to make sure he would not miss even one inning of the ball game.

Punctuation Pointer

A *to* fragment attached to the beginning of a sentence is followed by a comma because it is an introductory phrase. A *to* fragment connected to the end of the sentence needs no comma.

PRACTICE 2   CORRECTING *TO* FRAGMENTS

Underline and correct the *to* fragments in the following exercise. Write the corrected portion of each sentence on the line provided.

1. To give his students plenty of writing practice. The teacher assigned journals.

    _____

2. To give herself a break from the computer. Nora took her dog for a walk.

    _____

3. Samuel was surprised. To see the package outside his door.

    _____

4. To mark his place in his book. Lorenzo used a dollar bill.

    _____

5. Radio stations often hold contests. To keep listeners tuned in.

    _____

-ing Fragments

To correct an *-ing* fragment, connect it to the rest of the sentence with a comma. You may also correct it by adding a subject and a helping verb.

✗ Peering out the window and checking her watch every five minutes. Charlene waited for her guests to arrive.

✔ Peering out the window and checking her watch every five minutes, Charlene waited for her guests to arrive.

✗ Rachel spent the afternoon at home. Listening to Internet radio and reading magazines.

✔ Rachel spent the afternoon at home, listening to Internet radio and reading magazines.

Sometimes, the *-ing* word may be the second or third word in the fragment.

✗ James hopped into his car and left the restaurant's parking lot. Not realizing that he had left his bucket of chicken on the roof of the car.

✔ James hopped into his car and left the restaurant's parking lot, not realizing that he had left his bucket of chicken on the roof of the car.

Punctuation Pointer

Usually, *-ing* fragments can be connected to the rest of the sentence with a comma. When the *ing* fragment acts as an introductory element, place a comma after it. When you add it to the end of a sentence, lead into it with a comma.

PRACTICE 3   **CORRECTING *-ING* FRAGMENTS**

Underline and correct the *-ing* fragments in the following exercise. Write the corrected portion of each sentence on the line provided.

1. Puffing as if she had run a marathon. Bonita completed her first lap on the circular track.

   _____

2. The vines grew thick on the abandoned house. Obscuring the windows and part of the front door

   _____

3. Riding in the back of the pickup truck. The dog wobbled unsteadily as his owner rounded a curve.

   _____

4. Sneaking cigarettes, playing her music too loud, and visiting a male resident after curfew. Aunt Matilda has broken most of the nursing home's rules.

   _____

5. Leslie complains that her neighbor's children are allowed to run wild. Playing loudly in the street until past midnight.

   _____

-ed and *-en* Fragments

Another kind of fragment begins with an *-ed* or *-en* verb form, or past participle. If the verb is a regular verb, the verb form will end in *-ed*, like the verbs *walked*, *called*, and *plotted*. If the verb is an irregular verb, then the verb form will end in *-en* or in another irregular ending. *Broken, grown, found, bought,* and *written* are some of these forms. (For other examples, see the list of irregular verbs in Chapter 13.) This type of fragment is usually corrected by connecting it to a complete sentence.

✗   Spaced evenly and set in rows. The desks seemed ready for the fall term.

✔   Spaced evenly and set in rows, the desks seemed ready for the fall term.

✗   Everyone looked at the white rabbit. Held by the top-hatted magician.

✔   Everyone looked at the white rabbit held by the top-hatted magician.

✗   Caught with his car full of stolen property. The thief could only confess.

✔   Caught with his car full of stolen property, the thief could only confess.

PRACTICE 4   CORRECTING *-ED* AND *-EN* FRAGMENTS

Underline and correct the *-ed* and *-en* fragments in the following exercise. Write the corrected portion of each sentence on the line provided.

1.   Next week, students are invited to a career fair and résumé workshop. Presented by the college's career counseling office.

_____

2.   Cleaned and pressed at the local cleaners. Eldon's old sport coat looked like new.

_____

3.   Drawn by the smell of food. The dog decided to join our picnic.

_____

4.   Kevin has kept his old model trains. Stored on a shelf in a closet in his parents' house.

_____

5.   Encouraged by her parents. Dawn decided to apply for the scholarship.

_____

Missing-Subject Fragments

Fragments beginning with a joining word such as *and, or, but,* or *then* followed by a verb are **missing-subject fragments**. The subject of the verb is usually in a previous sentence. Connect the fragment to the sentence or add a subject to begin a new sentence.

✗   The hurricane changed course and seemed to falter. But gathered strength again before it hit the coast.

✔   The hurricane changed course and seemed to falter but gathered strength again before it hit the coast.

✔   The hurricane changed course and seemed to falter. But it gathered strength again before it hit the coast.

✗   Woodrow held up his prize fish and posed for the camera. Then fell off the end of the fishing pier.

✔   Woodrow held up his prize fish and posed for the camera, then fell off the end of the fishing pier.

PRACTICE 5   CORRECTING MISSING-SUBJECT FRAGMENTS

Underline and correct the missing-subject fragments in the following exercise. Write the corrected portion of each sentence on the line provided.

1. The cat ate the hamburger. But refused the bun.

    _____

2. The baseball player emerged from the dugout. And waved his cap to acknowledge the cheering fans.

    _____

3. At the side of the road, the collie looked both ways. Then crossed the street

    _____

4. On her days off, Ebony reads a book. Or surfs the Internet on her laptop.

    _____

5. Every morning, a wily squirrel bounds into Maurice's backyard and heads for the bird feeder. Then eats the food Maurice has put out for the birds.

    _____

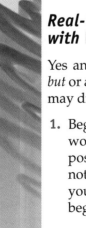

Real-World Writing: Is It Okay to Start a Sentence with But?

Yes and no. Grammatically, it is correct to start a sentence with *but* or any other FANBOYS conjunction. However, your instructors may discourage the practice for two good reasons.

1. Beginning a sentence with *but* is an informal technique. It may work in personal essays but should not be used in formal compositions such as research papers. (This text, you may have noticed, takes an informal, conversational approach, addressing you directly and occasionally using a FANBOYS conjunction to begin a sentence.)

2. Using *but* to begin a sentence can be addictive. *But* is the strongest contrast signal in our language, and it's easy to overuse.

The bottom line: Use conjunctions to begin sentences only if your instructor gives the green light, and then use them sparingly.

Example and Exception Fragments

Fragments often occur when a writer decides to add an example or note an exception. Example fragments often begin with *such as, including, like, for example,* or *for instance.* Exception fragments often begin with *not, except, unless, without,* or *in spite of.* To fix the fragment, connect it to the sentence with which it logically belongs. If the fragment begins with *for example* or *for instance,* it is often best to make the fragment into an independent sentence.

✗   Hollis becomes nervous in high-pressure situations. Such as exams and interviews.

✔   Hollis becomes nervous in high-pressure situations, such as exams and interviews.

✗   Lindsay is trying to put herself through college. Without any help from her parents.

✔   Lindsay is trying to put herself through college without any help from her parents.

✗   Classes with labs require more time than other classes. For example, biology and French.

Punctuation Pointer

Usually, you can connect fragments beginning with *such as, including, not, especially,* and *in spite of* with a comma. Fragments beginning with *except, unless, without,* and *like* are ordinarily connected without punctuation.

A fragment beginning with *for example* or *for instance* may be attached with a comma if it immediately follows the idea it illustrates: **The chef enjoyed cooking with beans, for example, lima beans, garbanzo beans, and kidney beans.** If the idea that the example illustrates is expressed earlier in the sentence, place the example in a new sentence: **Beans are the specialty of the house at Rizzoli's Restaurant. For example, the chef makes delicious dishes from lima beans, garbanzo beans, and kidney beans.**

✔ Classes with labs require more time than other classes. For example, biology and French take more of my study time than history or math.

PRACTICE 6   **CORRECTING EXAMPLE AND EXCEPTION FRAGMENTS**

Underline and correct the example and exception fragments in the following exercise. Write the correction on the line provided.

1. Natalie sets aside specific times to study and lets nothing interfere with her plans. Unless something more interesting comes along.

   _____

2. Leonard complained that nothing grew in his garden. Except weeds.

   _____

3. Thirty years ago, office workers had to get along without modern equipment. Such as computers, copiers, and fax machines.

   _____

4. On New Year's Eve, Alexandra vowed to give up all sweets. Especially chocolate.

   _____

5. If everyone would cooperate, it would be easy to solve some of the community's problems. For example, litter on public streets.

   _____

Prepositional Phrase Fragments

A prepositional phrase, alone or within a series, cannot function as a sentence. Correct a prepositional phrase fragment by connecting it to a sentence with which it logically belongs.

✗ Hamilton finally found his lost history book. In a large mud puddle on the street beside the student union.

✔ Hamilton finally found his lost history book in a large mud puddle on the street beside the student union.

✗ On her way to a three o'clock job interview at Stanfield Corporation. Melanie became lost.

✔ On her way to a three o'clock job interview at Stanfield Corporation, Melanie became lost.

> ### *Punctuation Pointer*
>
> Use a comma after introductory prepositional phrases. No punctuation is required to connect a prepositional phrase to the end of a sentence.

PRACTICE 7   CORRECTING PREPOSITIONAL PHRASE FRAGMENTS

Underline and correct each of the following prepositional phrase fragments. Write your correction on the line provided.

1. After searching frantically for half an hour, Amanda finally found her lost keys. Under a bunch of bananas on the kitchen counter.

   _____

2. In a hanging philodendron on the front porch. The bird had built her nest.

   _____

3. On a sandy beach with a frosty strawberry slush in her hand. Morgan found contentment.

   _____

4. Because she had stayed up all night to study, Deb fell asleep. During the exam.

   _____

5. In a pond beyond the city limits. James and his father fish on the weekends.

   _____

Review Exercises

Complete the Review Exercises to see how well you have learned the skills addressed in this chapter. As you work through the exercises, go back through the chapter to review any of the rules you do not understand completely.

REVIEW EXERCISE 1   IDENTIFYING AND CORRECTING SENTENCE FRAGMENTS

Underline and correct each fragment in the following exercise. Write your correction on the line provided.

1. From the apartment next door. Sharon and her roomate Jill heard a loud thud.

   _____

2. Because of the pouring rain. Duncan couldn't read the exit signs on the highway.

   _____

3. Carlos enjoys being a boxer. Except for the occasional injuries.

   _____

4. Tony took his job at the supermarket seriously. Arriving on time and working hard for his entire shift.

   _____

5. It took three days to complete the walkathon. Which covered 60 miles and benefited breast cancer research.

   _____

6. The coach joked that his team had a perfect record. Because they had never won a game.

   _____

7. Found next to the cash register at the market. Tabloids, gum, and trial size products are placed strategically to persuade customers into impulse purchases.

   _____

8. Amanda went over to the candy dish. And picked out all the green jelly beans.

   _____

9. After cramming all night for a midterm. Mike was too tired to do his best on the exam.

   _____

10. We left the house forty-five minutes early. To catch the first bus.

   _____

REVIEW EXERCISE 2   IDENTIFYING AND CORRECTING SENTENCE FRAGMENTS

Underline and correct each fragment in the following exercise. Write your correction on the line provided.

1. Except for the shower, which produced just a small dribble of water. The hotel room was comfortable and inviting.

   _____

2. Although Mu Lan is happy to be attending college in the United States. She misses her family in Beijing.

   _____

3. When they went on vacation, the Colesons packed everything they thought they would need. But did not consider the possibility of snow.

   _____

4. The young man wore a green shirt. That said, "My parents were kidnapped by aliens and all I got was this lousy T-shirt."

   _____

5. Worn through at the toe and battered from use. Jennifer's sneakers need to be replaced.

   _____

6. With the top down and the music turned up loud. Anita sailed down the moonlit highway.

   _____

7. Cheering loudly and clapping rhythmically. The audience demanded an encore.

   _____

8. Interrupted by dozens of long commercials. The TV show ground slowly toward its conclusion.

   _____

9. Ayesha went to the library to return a book. That was three weeks overdue.

   _____

10. At the garage sale, Mark looked at the worn wooden desk. And wondered if it would fit into the back of his vehicle.

   _____

REVIEW EXERCISE 3   IDENTIFYING AND CORRECTING MULTIPLE SENTENCE FRAGMENTS

Underline and correct the two fragments in each numbered item that follows. Write your corrections on the lines provided.

1. Because grass grows quickly in the South and weeds abound. Many residents plant thick, slow-growing grasses. Such as centipede.

   _____

   _____

2. After he had gone through registration. Edward stood in line at the bookstore. He glanced through his textbooks. And remarked to the student behind him that it was going to be a long semester.

   _____

   _____

3. Though it is common to hear of people hiring gardeners or housekeepers. It is possible to hire someone to do almost any kind of chore. Including shopping or standing in line.

   _____

   _____

4. The teacher said that she could always tell. When students in her class were texting They were the ones with downturned eyes. And furiously moving fingers.

   _____

   _____

5. Before the annual Easter egg hunt, volunteers hid Easter eggs. In bushes, behind benches, and in clumps of grass. They worked for hours hiding eggs. That the children would find in minutes.

   _____

   _____

REVIEW EXERCISE 4   IDENTIFYING AND CORRECTING MULTIPLE SENTENCE FRAGMENTS

Underline and correct the two fragments in each of the following. Write your corrections on the lines provided.

1. High-fashion models wear extreme styles. That most women would not find practical. For example, they wear impossibly high heels. And extremely short skirts and dresses

   _____

   _____

2. One town in Spain holds a tomato festival. In its town square every year. Residents gather in the square. And throw tomatoes at one another until the pavement is inches deep in goo.

   _____

   _____

3. As the hunter traipsed through the snowy woods. His boots crunched loudly in the snow. The noise carried through the forest. Warning every animal within half a mile.

   _____

   _____

4. Though the old rotary phone is battered and cracked. It still works as well as it did forty years ago. However, it does not have programmable speed dial. Or even touch-tone capability.

   _____

   _____

5. Inside the top drawer of the desk, Nick found a stapler, two rolls of pennies, a lime-green note pad, a yellow highlighter, and five catnip mice. That belonged to his five cats. The drawer seemed to hold everything. Except the flash drive he was looking for.

   _____

   _____

REVIEW EXERCISE 5 | EDITING A PARAGRAPH FOR SENTENCE FRAGMENTS

Underline and correct the ten fragments in this exercise. Write your corrections on the lines provided.

[1]The kitchen workers at Arturo's Pizza have invented several games. [2] To relieve boredom when business is slow and Arturo, the owner, is not around. [3] One of their favorite games is "dough ball." [4] Which is a game of catch played with a baseball-sized ball of pizza dough. [5] When they tire of dough ball. [6] They play "doughboy."

[7] This game involves mixing a batch of extremely wet, sticky dough. [8] Then throwing it at each other. [9] At the end of the game, the person with the most dough stuck to him loses. [10] And has to clean up the mess. [11] The kitchen workers have recently invented another game. [12] That they call "beef darts. [13] The object of the game is to earn points. [14] By throwing small balls of raw hamburger at a pizza-sauce target painted on the wall. [15] As their games become more elaborate and messy. [16] The likelihood that they will be caught increases. [17] But they have been lucky. [18] So far. [19] Whenever Arturo returns to the restaurant. [20]The kitchen is spotless and the employees are hard at work.

_____

_____

_____

_____

_____

_____

_____

_____

_____

_____

_____

_____

_____

mywritinglab   For support and practice meeting this chapter's goal, log in to www.mywritinglab.com and select Fragments.

CHAPTER **18**

Pronoun Case

> 🖎 **Chapter Goal:** Recognize subjective, objective, intensive, and reflexive pronouns and use them correctly.

I travel with a pronoun case;
I bring myself and I.
As you and he hop in my case,
Whoever waves goodbye.

We, them, himself, herself, and who
Pile in with she and him.
Someday I'd like to travel light;
The chances seem quite slim.

But when we reach the station,
All getting on the bus,
I look for fellow travelers,
And no one's here but us.

Pronouns are words that stand in for nouns or for other pronouns. They are useful words that keep writers and speakers from tedious repetition of words.

However, the rules that govern pronoun use are complex, and confusion over pronoun use is common. If you have ever hesitated between "Stacy and me" or "Stacy and I," or wondered whether to say "between you and I" or "between you and me," this chapter will help you find the answers.

🖎 Subject and Object Pronouns

mywritinglab

Visit My Writing Lab for additional practice with subject and object pronouns.

Personal pronouns (*I, we, you, he, she it, they*) refer to specific people or things. These pronouns take different forms, called **cases**, as they perform different jobs in a sentence. Look at the example that follows to see how the first person pronoun *I* changes form as its role in a sentence changes.

✔ *I* borrowed a book from the library and forgot about it. Early this week, the library sent *me* a notice saying the book was overdue.

Subject pronouns (*the subjective case*) are used as subjects or subject complements. Some commonly used subject pronouns are *I, we, you, he, she, it,* and *they.*

✔ *I* know James well; *we* have been friends for years.
✔ If *you* are looking for paper clips, *they* are in the desk drawer.
✔ Allison was told that the finalists were John and *she.*

Object pronouns (*the objective case*) are used as objects of verbs or prepositions. Some commonly used object pronouns are *me, us, you, him, her, it,* and *them.*

✔ Rachel spoke to her parents and promised to visit *them* on the weekend.
✔ The police officer was happy to give directions to Raul and *me.*

Subject Pronouns

In most instances, you probably use the subject form of the pronoun correctly without thinking about it. You probably haven't said, "Me went to the park" since you were three years old. However, using the subject form becomes trickier when a *compound subject* is used. Is it "Tiffany and her went to the concert" or "Tiffany and she went to the concert"? Usually, trying the sentence with the pronoun alone will help you hear the correct answer. Without *Tiffany and*, the sentence becomes clear. "*She* went to the concert" is correct, not "*Her* went to the concert."

Checking for Correct Pronoun Use in Compound Subjects

? *Him and his brother* went hunting this morning.

Step 1: To determine if the sentence is correct, try the pronoun alone.
✗ *Him* ~~and his brother~~ went hunting this morning.
✗ *Him* went hunting this morning.

Step 2: If the pronoun sounds incorrect, try changing the form.
✔ *He* went hunting this morning.
✔ *He and his brother* went hunting this morning. (corrected sentence)

PRACTICE 1   USING SUBJECT PRONOUNS

Underline the correct pronoun in each of the following sentences. To determine the correct pronoun form, try the pronoun alone without the compound element.

1.   Cynthia and (I, me) played two games of tennis yesterday afternoon.
2.   Cecil and (they, them) are meeting us over at the new ice-skating rink.
3.   I heard that Wally and (she, her) had made the highest grades in class.
4.   (He and I, Him and me) have been friends since grade school.
5.   Do you think that you and (I, me) could study our grammar together tomorrow?

Subject Pronouns with Linking Verbs

"Hello?"

"May I speak to Tanisha Jones, please?"

"This is she."

"Hello, Tanisha, this is Randall Groover from your biology class. I was wondering . . ."

This polite exchange is typical of the way many telephone conversations begin, and it illustrates a rule that many people use in telephone conversations but ignore otherwise: When a pronoun renames the subject (that is, when it is a *subject complement*) and follows the verb *to be* or any *linking verb*, that pronoun takes the subject form.

Examples of Subject Complements

	subject	linking verb	subject complement
✔ The keynote	speaker	will be	she. (not *her*)

✔ It is *I*. (not *me*)

✔ If you are looking for Mr. Smith, that is *he* in the blue jacket. (not *him*)

✔ Ms. Smith, you say it was the defendant who robbed you. Look at him carefully. Can you be absolutely sure it was *he?* (not *him*)

PRACTICE 2   USING SUBJECT PRONOUNS AFTER LINKING VERBS

In each sentence, underline the correct pronoun.

1.   I would have spoken to Randy, but I wasn't sure that it was (he, him).
2.   If you need to speak with the manager, that is (she, her) at the desk by the window.

3. You said you were looking for your gloves. Are these (they, them)?

4. "Who is it?" said Sandra. "It is (I, me)," said Ken.

5. I have talked to Professor Smalls before, but I did not know at the time that it was (she, her).

Object Pronouns

Object pronouns are used as objects of verbs and prepositions. Again, problems with object pronouns commonly occur in compound constructions. These problems can usually be resolved by isolating the pronoun.

Checking for Correct Pronoun Use in Compound Objects

?   The supervisor asked *Lou and I* to work overtime.

✗   The supervisor asked ~~Lou and~~ *I* to work overtime.

✗   The supervisor asked *I* to work overtime.

✔   The supervisor asked *Lou and me* to work overtime.

Object Pronouns with *between*

Object pronouns always follow the preposition *between.* Thus, it is always *between you and me, between us and them, between him and her, between Larry and him.*

✗   Just between you and *I,* I heard that Alan has found a new job in Phoenix.

✔   Just between you and *me,* I heard that Alan has found a new job in Phoenix.

✗   The argument was between Leo and *she;* I tried to stay out of it.

✔   The argument was between Leo and *her;* I tried to stay out of it.

> ### *Grammar Alert!*
>
> Pronouns are often misused with *between.* Remember to use the object form: between you and *me, him, her,* or *them.*

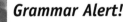

PRACTICE 3   **USING OBJECT PRONOUNS**

Underline the correct pronoun in each of the following sentences.

1. Renata told Sandra and (I, me) where to recycle our glass bottles and aluminum cans.

2. When we went to see the performance at the Grand Opera House, Fran sat between Gerard and (I, me).

3. Anna gave Clay and (she, her) an extra pair of tickets to Tuesday's performance of *Big River*.

4. Someone told Catherine and (I, me) that the wildlife park was worth visiting.

5. It is a small apartment, but it is perfect for Connie and (he, him).

Using *Who* and *Whom*

The use of *who* and *whom* poses difficulties for most people, partly because *whom* seems to be slowly disappearing from everyday speech. However, in academic writing, the distinction is still important.

Although *who* and *whom* may seem intimidating, there is a shortcut to learning how to use these pronouns. Once you have mastered this method, you will feel like an expert in the use of *who* and *whom*.

The Substitution Method for *Who* and *Whom*

The first step in the shortcut is a substitution. You have already seen in this chapter how natural it is—in most cases, anyway—to use the subject pronoun *he* and the object pronoun *him*. You rarely make mistakes with them because you use them all the time. Wouldn't it be nice if *who* and *whom* were as easy as *he* and *him*?

The good news is that they are—almost. *Who* is a subject pronoun, just like *he*, so we can temporarily equate the two, like this:

who (or whoever) = he

Whom is an object pronoun, so we can temporarily equate *whom* with *him*.

whom (or whomever) = him

Now, look at a sentence to see how the system works.

?   No one cared (who, whom) cleaned up the mess.

Step 1: Ignore everything that comes before *who* or *whom*.

?   ~~No one cared~~ (who, whom) cleaned up the mess.

Step 2: Substitute *he* for *who* and *him* for *whom*, and see which one makes sense.

✔ ~~Who~~ He cleaned up the mess.

✗ ~~Whom~~ Him cleaned up the mess.

Because "He cleaned up the mess" makes sense, you can now rewrite the sentence with confidence, using *who* in place of *he*.

✔ No one cared who cleaned up the mess.

PRACTICE 4   USING *WHO* AND *WHOM*

Use the substitution method to decide whether to use *who* or *whom* in the following sentences.

1. Mark was not sure (who, whom) had suggested the idea.
2. Candace could not be sure (who, whom) to trust.
3. The flowers radiated sun-speckled colors as Tomas walked through the park and wondered (who, whom) took care of the exotic blooms.
4. The man (who, whom) we all believed was a poor hermit left two million dollars to the local youth center.
5. Those of us (who, whom) are going to the party should bring a dish to share with the other guests.

Who and *Whom* in Questions

Try another sentence, this time a question.

? John needed help, but (who, whom) could he rely on?

Step 1: Ignore everything that comes before *who* or *whom*.

? ~~John needed help, but~~ (who, whom) could he rely on?

Step 2: Substitute *he* for *who* and *him* for *whom*, and see which one makes sense.

✔ ~~Who~~ He could he rely on.

✗ ~~Whom~~ Him could he rely on.

Neither of these sounds natural, so the thing to do is shuffle them a bit.

✗   He could rely on he.

✔   He could rely on him.

Because "He could rely on him" makes sense, you can now rewrite the sentence with confidence, using *whom.*

John needed help, but whom could he rely on?

PRACTICE 5   *WHO* AND *WHOM* IN QUESTIONS

Use the substitution method to decide whether to use *who* or *whom* in the following sentences.

1. (Who, Whom) planted that tree so close to the house?
2. "The package is for (who, whom)?" asked the bleary-eyed man at the door.
3. (Who, Whom) is responsible for the peanut butter and jelly hand prints on the window?
4. (Who, whom) is that odd-looking person in the trench coat and sandals?
5. Do you know (who, whom) the police plan to charge with the crime?

Who and *Whom* Following a Preposition

Sometimes, a preposition that comes before *who* or *whom* will need to be included in your sentence for it to make sense.

?   I was not sure to (who, whom) I should speak.

Step 1: Ignore everything that comes before *who* or *whom.*

✔   ~~I was not sure~~ to (who, whom) I should speak.

Step 2: Substitute *he* for *who* and *him* for *whom,* and see which one makes sense.

✗   I should speak to he.

✔   I should speak to him.

Since "I should speak to him" makes sense, you can now rewrite the sentence with confidence, using *whom* in place of *him.*

✔   I was not sure to whom I should speak.

PRACTICE 6   *WHO* AND *WHOM* FOLLOWING A PREPOSITION

Use the substitution method to decide whether to use *who* or *whom* in the following sentences.

1. The suitcase had no tag, so the hotel staff were unsure to (who, whom) it belonged.

2. The delivery person returned and said he had not been able to find the person to (who, whom) the flowers had been addressed.

3. To (who, whom) does this set of keys belong?

4. The person for (who, whom) the house was built backed out of the deal at the last minute.

5. Most parents want to know where their children are and with (who, whom) they are associating.

PRACTICE 7   USING *WHO* AND *WHOM*

Use the substitution method to decide whether to use *who* or *whom* in the following sentences.

1. Everyone wondered (who, whom) the new president would be.

2. The sign on the large box read "To (who, whom) it may concern: The contents do not concern you!"

3. Andrea had not decided (who, whom) to invite to her party.

4. The angry district attorney vowed to prosecute (whoever, whomever) had set the fire.

5. Brandy told Eric that she would never date a man (who, whom) gambled, so Eric kept his weekly poker games a secret.

Intensive and Reflexive Pronouns

Personal pronouns also take on forms known as *intensive* and *reflexive forms.* These pronouns are the *-self* pronouns: *myself, ourselves, yourself, himself, herself, itself,* and *themselves.*

Intensive Pronouns

Intensive pronouns are used for emphasis. They let a reader know that an action was performed by or directed toward *only* the person or thing that the pronoun refers to. It is easy to identify intensive pronouns. Because they are used strictly for emphasis, a sentence would make perfect sense and have the same meaning if the intensive pronoun were left out.

✔ The dean *herself* approved Joseph's schedule.
✔ The fire damage was confined to the building *itself* and did not extend to the grounds.
✔ To save money on his home renovation, John did all the painting and tile work *himself*.

Reflexive Pronouns

Reflexive pronouns show that an action was performed by someone on himself or herself (or by something on itself).

✔ Mac accidentally cut *himself* with a knife.
✔ The oven cleans *itself* with no need for chemicals or elbow grease.
✔ The executive blamed *herself* for the company's problems.

PRACTICE 8   **RECOGNIZING INTENSIVE AND REFLEXIVE PRONOUNS**

Underline the *-self* pronoun in each sentence below. Then, in the blank provided, write I if the pronoun is an intensive pronoun and R if it is a reflexive pronoun.

_____ 1. Eric talked himself into taking a job that he really did not want.

_____ 2. Isabella decided to do the job herself.

_____ 3. The mayor himself took the children on a tour of City Hall.

_____ 4. Donald decided to buy himself a birthday present—a new computer.

_____ 5. I know that the store is closing because the owner himself told me.

Problems with Intensive and Reflexive Pronouns

Intensive and reflexive pronouns are often used incorrectly in compound subjects or objects. Look at the following examples.

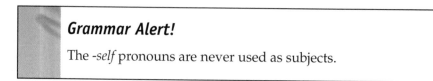

Grammar Alert!

The *-self* pronouns are never used as subjects.

Checking for Correct Use of Intensive and Reflexive Pronouns

✗   Esteban and myself fixed the leaky pipe with duct tape.

When you leave out the compound element, the problem is easier to spot:

✗   Myself fixed the leaky pipe with duct tape.

A subject pronoun is needed to correct the sentence:

✔   I fixed the leaky pipe with duct tape.

✔   Esteban and I fixed the leaky pipe with duct tape.

Checking for Correct Use of Intensive and Reflexive Pronouns

✗   "Molly makes her mother and myself very proud," said Mr. Roberts.

When you leave out the compound element, the problem is easier to spot:

✗   "Molly makes myself very proud," said Mr. Roberts.

An object pronoun is needed to correct the sentence:

✔   "Molly makes her mother and me very proud," said Mr. Roberts.

Grammar Alert!

Never use *hisself, theirself,* or *theirselves.* They are not words. *Himself* and *themselves* are the proper forms.

PRACTICE 9   AVOIDING ERRORS WITH - *SELF* PRONOUNS

Underline the correct pronoun in each sentence.

1.   Andrea looked at (her, herself) in the mirror and decided that she needed a haircut.
2.   Gavin saved his money so that his wife and (he, himself) could go to Hawaii for their vacation.
3.   The argument eventually divided the entire office, but it started between Mike and (me, myself).
4.   Nuri was proud because she had tiled the entire bathroom wall (she, herself), and it looked like a professional job.

5. Vanessa could not wait until summer when (she, herself) and her friends could go to the lake every day.

6. "My sister and (I, me, myself) are always competing against one another," Yolanda said. "In sports and academics, we always try to outdo one another."

7. The store manager (him, himself) interviewed Quinton for the job.

8. Gary wanted to make breakfast for (him, himself), but he had no bread, eggs, or milk.

9. "The boat belongs to my brother and (me, myself)," said Miguel.

10. The governor gave (he, himself) good marks for improving the state's economy.

✍ Review Exercises

Complete the Review Exercises to see how well you have learned the skills addressed in this chapter. As you work through the exercises, go back through the chapter to review any of the rules you do not understand completely.

REVIEW EXERCISE 1   CHOOSING THE CORRECT PRONOUN CASE

Underline the correct pronoun in each sentence.

1. The prize money was divided between Sarah and (he, him, himself).

2. Ms. Carlson (her, herself) will meet with you before next month.

3. If you are going out for lunch, come along with Darren and (I, me, myself).

4. The full moon looked huge to Roger, (who, whom) was staring at it through his bedroom window.

5. That is the woman that Sammy introduced me to last week—at least I think it is (she, her).

6. Since none of the hotels took pets, Brianna wondered where Bongo and (she, her) would stay that night.

7. Laurel reminded (she, herself) that she had promised to call her mother in the morning.

8. The senator complained that the media's attitude toward (he, him) and his fellow members of Congress had changed over the years.

9. Sabrina, a college sophomore, said that (she, her) and her friends were not as likely to be drug users as people of her parents' generation.

10. Aunt Harriet said that if I needed a place to stay, Uncle Edgar and (she, her) would be glad to put me up for a few days.

REVIEW EXERCISE 2   **CHOOSING THE CORRECT PRONOUN CASE**

Underline the correct pronoun in each sentence.

1. When she was offered a transfer, Tamira said that (she, her) and her family would need to discuss it first.

2. Frank admitted that he couldn't remember (who, whom) he had given the money to.

3. "Even though we live far apart now, my brother and (I, myself) always try to get together at least once a year," Jake said.

4. The basketball player tried to resolve the problems between (her, herself) and her coach.

5. When Ron went to the ATM to withdraw cash, the machine said that (he, him) and his wife had no money in their account.

6. "When I graduate," said Angela, "the first thing I will do is buy (me, myself) a new car."

7. The best candidates for the plant manager's job are John and (she, her).

8. Quinton told his mother that he did not know how he could ever repay (she, her) and his father for all they had done for him.

9. "If you don't want that old bicycle," Eric said, "my brother and (I, me) can repair it and use it."

10. Can you keep a secret, just between you and (I, me)?

REVIEW EXERCISE 3   **CHOOSING THE CORRECT PRONOUN CASE**

Underline the correct pronoun in each sentence.

1. The two-year-old insisted that she could tie her shoes (her, herself).

2. Will said that Kelly and (he, him) were meeting at the library to study.

3. Ellen stopped at her favorite store, buying (her, herself) a reward for her hard work.

4. Shamika asked me to give the book to Tim and (she, her) when I was finished with it.

5. "Brian and (I, me) are going to the football game, rain or shine," said Eric.

6. Rob wondered whether (he, his) and ex-girlfriend would ever be on friendly terms again.

7. I think it was Matt (who, whom) gave Emily the good advice about using her student ID to get a discount at some movie theaters.

8. The receptionist said that (she, herself) and other members of the staff wanted to meet with representatives of the department.

9. If there are any problems with the new computer program, please call Pakhi or (I, me, myself).

10. If you need a ride, Liam and (I, me) can take you.

REVIEW EXERCISE 4   IDENTIFYING AND CORRECTING PRONOUN CASE ERRORS

Underline the two errors in each of the following sentences. Then write the corrected sentence on the lines below.

1. The last time that James and myself ate at Galileo's, the server was rude to he and I.

_____

_____

2. Cassandra told Eric and I that her parents, who she has not seen in ten years, will visit in March.

_____

_____

3. Mr. Smith testified that the agreement between the defendant and himself had never included murder. "He may have made an agreement of that sort with someone," Smith said. "But it was not me."

_____

_____

_____

4. "This merger will not only benefit my employees and myself today," said the company's chief executive officer, "but it will also carry we and our stockholders toward a more prosperous future."

_____

_____

_____

5. Brenda and him are scheduled to take their graduate school entrance exams on Saturday. I told her that you and me would have our fingers crossed for them.

_____

_____

mywritinglab   For support and practice meeting this chapter's goal, log in to www.mywritinglab.com and select Pronoun Case.

CHAPTER 19

Pronoun Agreement, Reference, and Point of View

✎ **Chapter Goal:** Identify and correct problems in pronoun agreement, reference, and point of view.

Abbott: *I'm telling you Who is on first.*
Costello: *Well, I'm asking YOU who's on first!*
Abbott: *That's the man's name.*
Costello: *That's who's name?*
Abbott: *Yes.*
Costello: *Well, go ahead and tell me.*
Abbott: *Who.*
Costello: *The guy on first.*
Abbott: *Who!*

From Abbott and Costello's
"Who's on First"

Abbott and Costello's classic comedy routine deliberately causes confusion through the use of pronouns. Sometimes, writers unintentionally cause confusion through errors in pronoun reference, agreement, and point of view. Each sentence following contains a pronoun error. Can you figure out why the pronouns in bold type are incorrect?

✘   The coffee shop usually closes at midnight, but on Sundays, **they** close at 6:00 P.M.

✘   Josh told Marquez that **he** needed to work on his social skills.

✗   Clara did not get the job she wanted, but what can **you** expect if you go to an interview in jeans and a ripped T-shirt?

Each of the sentences above contains a pronoun error that could cause confusion for the reader. The first sentence contains an error in pronoun agreement. The pronoun *they* is plural, but the word it refers to is singular. Here is the corrected sentence:

✔   The coffee shop usually closes at midnight, but on Sundays, it closes at 6:00 P.M.

The second sentence contains an error in pronoun reference. The reader cannot be sure whether *he* refers to Josh or Marquez. The corrected sentence clears up the confusion:

✔   Josh told Marquez, "I need to work on my social skills."

The third sentence contains an error in pronoun point of view. The writer switches from the third person (the job *she* wanted) to the second person (what can *you* expect).

✔   Clara did not get the job she wanted, but what can she expect if she goes to an interview in jeans and a ripped T-shirt?

Keeping your writing free of errors in pronoun agreement, reference, and point of view ensures that your reader will move through your work smoothly and without confusion.

〰 Pronoun Agreement

mywritinglab
Visit MyWriting Lab for additional practice with pronoun agreement.
Pronoun agreement means that a pronoun must agree in number with the word it refers to. In other words, a singular pronoun can refer only to a singular noun or pronoun, and a plural pronoun can refer only to a plural noun or pronoun.

The word that a pronoun refers to is called its **antecedent**. An antecedent may be a noun, a pronoun, or even a compound construction, such as *pens and pencils* or *Sam or Lilah*.

Examples of Correct Pronoun-Antecedent Agreement

antecedent   pronoun
✔   Julian picked up the <u>hammer</u> and put <u>it</u> in the toolbox.

In the sentence above, the singular pronoun *it* refers to one word in the sentence, the singular word *hammer*.

antecedent   pronoun

✔ Julian picked up the <u>upholstery tacks</u> and put <u>them</u> in the toolbox.

In the above sentence, the plural pronoun *them* refers to the plural antecedent *tacks*.

antecedent   pronoun

✔ Julian picked up <u>the measuring tape and the staple gun</u> and put <u>them</u> in the toolbox.

Above, the plural pronoun *them* refers to the compound antecedent *measuring tape and staple gun*.

Problems in Pronoun Agreement

Errors in pronoun agreement occur when a singular pronoun is used to refer to a plural word or when a plural pronoun is used to refer to a singular word.

Examples of Errors in Pronoun-Antecedent Agreement

Error in Pronoun Agreement:

singular   plural

✗ Sarita went to the <u>post office</u>, but <u>they</u> were already closed.

Corrected:

singular   singular

✔ Sarita went to the <u>post office</u>, but <u>it</u> was already closed.

Error in Pronoun Agreement:

plural   singular

✗ Rick ate the <u>cookies</u> even though he knew <u>it wasn't</u> good for him.

Corrected:

plural   plural

✔ Rick ate the <u>cookies</u> even though he knew <u>they weren't</u> good for him.

plural   reworded to eliminate pronoun

✔ Rick ate the <u>cookies</u> even though he knew <u>eating sweets</u> wasn't good for him.

PRACTICE 1   **MAKING PRONOUNS AGREE**

Underline the correct pronoun in each sentence below.

1. The tenor had a rich, strong voice. (It, They) filled the small auditorium without the aid of a microphone.

2. Sharon is prone to migraines, but she has found that avoiding caffeine and chocolate keeps (it, them) to a minimum.

3. My mother likes to shop at Barton's because (it is, they are) locally owned.

4. Sanjay lost his driver's license last week; today he is going to the Division of Motor Vehicles to have (it, them) replaced.

5. The leaves on the peace lily have lost (its, their) shine.

Pronoun Agreement with Indefinite Pronouns

The following indefinite pronouns are always plural.

both   few   many   several

Examples of Pronoun Agreement with Plural Indefinite Pronouns

plural   plural
✔ Both of the children had chocolate on their faces.

plural   plural
✔ Many of the courses in the catalog should be removed because they are seldom offered.

The following indefinite pronouns are singular or plural, depending on their antecedents.

all   any   most   none   some

Examples of Agreement with Singular/Plural Indefinite Pronouns

plural   plural   plural
✔ All of the pines were cut down because they were diseased.

singular   singular   singular
✔ We ate all of the noodle soup in one sitting. It was delicious.

plural   plural   plural
✔ None of the children seemed afraid as they came forward to pet the boa constrictor.

singular   singular   singular
✔ None of the coffee had been drunk, but Karen threw it away because

singular
it was starting to look like sludge.

Memory Jogger

Remember the singular indefinite pronouns more easily by grouping them:

each	all the *bodies*
either	all the *ones*
neither	all the *things*

The following indefinite pronouns are always singular.

anybody	either	neither	one
anyone	everybody	nobody	somebody
anything	everyone	no one	someone
each	everything	nothing	something

Examples of Pronoun Agreement with Singular Indefinite Pronouns

     singular   plural

✗ <u>Somebody</u> called you, but <u>they</u> didn't leave a message.

     singular   singular

✔ <u>Somebody</u> called you, but <u>he</u> didn't leave a message.

   singular   plural

✗ <u>Each</u> of the team members has <u>their</u> own particular strength.

   singular   singular

✔ <u>Each</u> of the team members has <u>her</u> own particular strength.

Pronouns and Gender Fairness

Gender fairness means using gender-neutral terms such as *server, police officer,* and *firefighter.* It means not stereotyping professions: Gary Kubach is a *nurse,* not a *male nurse;* Sarita Gray is a *doctor,* not a *woman doctor.* Naturally, gender fairness also includes avoiding descriptions of women solely in terms of their looks or of men solely in terms of their bank accounts. Those things are fairly simple. The area of gender fairness and pronouns, however, requires more thought. Using *he or she* or *his or her* is often awkward, and constructions such as *he/ she* or *(s)he* are downright ungraceful. How, then, can a writer's language be unbiased, graceful, and grammatically correct, all at the same time? There are several possible solutions.

Example of Incorrect Pronoun-Antecedent Agreement

        singular   plural
✘   <u>Nobody</u> has received <u>their</u> grades from the last term yet.

This sentence contains an error in pronoun agreement. The singular indefinite pronoun *nobody* does not agree with the plural pronoun *their*. The following section shows several ways to correct pronoun agreement errors such as this one while remaining gender-fair.

     Solution 1: Choose a gender and stay with it throughout a single example or paragraph. Then, in your next example or paragraph, switch to the other gender.

        singular   plural
✘   <u>Nobody</u> has received <u>their</u> grades from the last term yet.

        singular   singular
✔   <u>Nobody</u> has received <u>his</u> grades from the last term yet.

        singular   singular
✔   <u>Nobody</u> has received <u>her</u> grades from the last term yet.

     Solution 2: Use a "his or her" construction. Because this solution is grammatically correct but stylistically awkward, use it in situations where you will not have to repeat the construction.

        singular   plural
✘   <u>Nobody</u> has received <u>their</u> grades from the last term yet.

        singular   singular
✔   <u>Nobody</u> has received <u>his or her</u> grades from the last term yet.

     Solution 3: Use plural rather than singular constructions.

        singular   plural
✘   <u>Nobody</u> has received <u>their</u> grades from the last term yet.

          plural   plural
✔   The <u>students</u> have not received <u>their</u> grades from the last term yet.

     Solution 4: Remove the pronoun agreement problem by removing the pronoun.

        singular   plural
✘   <u>Nobody</u> has received <u>their</u> grades from the last term yet.

✔   Nobody has received grades from the last term yet.

singular   singular   plural

✗   <u>Each</u> manager has the same job description, yet <u>each</u> has developed <u>their</u> own style.

✔   Each manager has the same job description, yet each has developed an individual style.

PRACTICE 2   MAKING PRONOUNS AGREE

Correct the pronoun agreement errors in each sentence below. Use all four of the solutions previously listed.

1. Both of the restaurant patrons had finished his coffee.

    _____

2. I do not agree with you, but everybody is entitled to their own opinion.

    _____

3. Does everybody know what their schedule will be for next month?

    _____

4. Nobody on the *Titanic* realized that the trip might be their last.

    _____

5. Neither of the prisoners had seen their children for months.

    _____

6. Each member of the audience took away their own special memory of the singer's performance.

    _____

7. If one of the librarians is not busy, maybe they can help you.

    _____

8. Everyone ate as if they were starving.

    _____

9. If someone finds my wallet, maybe they will turn it in.

    _____

10. Few of the students finished his or her test.

    _____

Pronoun Reference

mywritinglab

Visit MyWriting Lab for additional practice with pronoun reference.
If a sentence has problems with **pronoun reference**, then either a pronoun has no antecedent or it has more than one possible antecedent.

Pronoun Reference Problem: No Antecedent

A pronoun that does not logically refer to any noun or pronoun has no antecedent.

Examples of Pronouns with No Antecedents

✗   When I went to the bank to cash my check, *she* asked for two forms of identification.

✗   Mary applied for a scholarship, but *they* said she didn't meet the requirements.

To correct the problem, replace the pronoun with a more specific word.

✔   When I went to the bank to cash my check, *the teller* asked for two forms of identification.

✔   Mary applied for a scholarship, but the committee said she didn't meet the requirements.

PRACTICE 3   CORRECTING PROBLEMS IN PRONOUN REFERENCE

Correct the pronoun reference problems in each of the following sentences.

1.   Carrie tried to avoid taking college algebra, but they said she had to have it.

     _____

2.   We had looked forward to the concert, but they were so loud we could not enjoy the music.

     _____

3.   When Tomás went to the FotoMart to pick up his vacation photographs, they gave him pictures of a baby's christening by mistake.

     _____

4. April stopped by the dry cleaners on her way home from work, but her husband had already picked it up.

    _____

5. James called the computer repair shop after he turned it on and could not get his mouse or his keyboard to work.

    _____

Pronoun Reference Problem: Two Possible Antecedents

When a pronoun could logically refer to either of two words, it has two possible antecedents.

Examples of Pronouns with Two Possible Antecedents

✔   The <u>supervisor</u> told <u>Mary</u> that <u>she</u> had been nominated for an award.

It is unclear whether Mary or her supervisor has been nominated. To clarify, show the supervisor's exact words.

✔   The supervisor said, "<u>Mary, you</u> have been nominated for an award."

✔   The <u>supervisor</u> said, "Mary, <u>I</u> have been nominated for an award."

✘   The doctor told Clara she needed to exercise daily.

The pronoun *she* could refer to Clara or to the doctor. To clarify, use a direct quotation or reconstruct the sentence.

✔   The doctor told Clara, "You need to exercise daily."

✔   The doctor advised Clara to exercise daily.

PRACTICE 4   USING QUOTATIONS TO CORRECT PRONOUN REFERENCE PROBLEMS

Correct each of the pronoun reference problems by using a direct quotation.

1. The veterinarian told Mrs. Hughes that she had given Lucky the wrong medication.

    _____

2. Joel told his son that he would have to turn down the television.

    _____

3. Marinda told the driver of the BMW that the accident had been her fault.

    _____

4. J. J. told his brother that he had drunk too much to drive.

    _____

5. Annie reminded her neighbor that she had something that belonged to her.

    _____

Special Pronoun Reference Problem: *This* and *Which*

The pronouns *this* and *which* are so often used incorrectly that you should check them every time you see them in your writing.

When you see the pronoun *this* in a sentence, particularly if it begins the sentence, ask the question, "This what?" If you cannot put your finger on a noun that answers that question, then *this* probably has no antecedent.

Examples of Vague Uses of *This*

✗ Many people in the world go to sleep hungry every night. With better management of the world's resources, we could do something about *this*.

✗ It has come to our attention that many residents are keeping pets in violation of the no-pet rule. This will no longer be tolerated.

There are two quick ways to fix the problem. The first is to place a noun that answers the question "This what?" immediately after the word *this*.

✔ Many people in the world go to sleep hungry every night. With better management of the world's resources, we could do something about *this problem*.

✔ It has come to our attention that many residents are keeping pets in violation of the no-pet rule. *This situation* will no longer be tolerated.

The second solution is to take out the pronoun and replace it with an appropriate word or phrase.

✔ Many people in the world go to sleep hungry every night. With better management of the world's resources, we could do something about *hunger*.

✔ It has come to our attention that many residents are keeping pets in violation of the no-pet rule. *Pets* will no longer be tolerated.

Problems with *which* often require you to reconstruct the sentence.

Examples of Vague Uses of *Which*

✘ People throw litter on the highway, which is a problem.

In the sentence above, the pronoun *which* does not have an antecedent—that is, there is no single noun or pronoun that it refers to. *Which* could refer to litter or to the highway, but more likely it refers to the whole idea of "people throwing litter."

✔ Littering is a problem on the highway.

To fix problems with *which*, reconstruct the sentence to eliminate the pronoun.

✘ The summer term is shorter, which means that classes move at a faster pace.

✔ The summer term is shorter, so classes move at a faster pace.

PRACTICE 5   CORRECTING VAGUE USES OF *THIS* AND *WHICH*

Find and correct the vague uses of *this* and *which*.

1. When I drive in for my ten o'clock class, the parking lot is always full. School officials should do something about this.

   _____

2. The landlord of that building has evicted several elderly citizens, which has outraged many people.

   _____

3. Kendra will be the first in her family to earn a college degree. This makes her whole family very proud.

   _____

4. The card on Ann's door said, "Sorry we missed you! A representative of Double Jeopardy Insurance will be back to see you later this week. If this is not convenient, please call to let us know."

   _____

5. Rita tried to work thirty hours a week and attend school full time, but this turned out to be more difficult than she had imagined.

   _____

   _____

6. Sandra's class was canceled, which will cause her graduation to be delayed.

   _____

7. Demetria is having problems in school because her parents are going through a divorce. This is always hard on children.

   _____

8. Ernest decided to get revenge on his bank by leaving a dead fish in his safety deposit box, which might have worked if the box had not been rented in Ernest's name.

   _____

   _____

9. Some people believe that lightning never strikes the same place twice, but this is incorrect.

   _____

10. The police chief's daughter was arrested for stealing, which must have been embarrassing to the chief.

    _____

Pronoun Point of View

mywritinglab

Visit MyWriting Lab for additional practice with pronoun point of view.

It is important to avoid unnecessary shifts in **point of view**, that is, shifts from one person to another. The following chart shows common first-, second-, and third-person pronouns in their singular and plural forms.

Point of View	Singular	Plural
First person (the person speaking)	I	we
Second person (the person spoken to)	you	you
Third person (the person spoken about)	he, she, it singular indefinite pronouns (each, either, neither . . .)	they

Examples of Shifts in Pronoun Point of View

     3rd person   2nd person

✘ Leon does not like to check books out of the city library because you have to return the books after just two weeks.

The sentence contains an unnecessary shift in point of view. *You* do not have to return books; *Leon* has to return them. Note, below, that the verb must also be changed.

     3rd person   3rd person

✔ Leon does not like to check books out of the city library because he has to return the books after just two weeks.

       3rd person   1st person

✘ The members of the class need to get together to study our notes.

       3rd person   3rd person

✔ The members of the class need to get together to study their notes.

     1st person   1st person

✔ We need to get together to study our class notes..

PRACTICE 6 CORRECTING PROBLEMS IN PRONOUN POINT OF VIEW

Correct the point of view problems in the following sentences.

1. Max was disappointed in his poor test grade, but you can't expect good grades without studying.

    _____

2. I don't plan to take a physical education class during the summer term; July is too hot for them to exercise outside.

    _____

3. I will never eat in that restaurant again. You spend half an hour waiting for a server and another forty-five minutes waiting for food.

    _____

4. Raj is looking for a used guitar, and he thinks you can find one at a shop called Play It Again.

    _____

5. Maggie drinks orange juice every morning because it is good for you.

    _____

Review Exercises

Complete the Review Exercises to see how well you have learned the skills addressed in this chapter. As you work through the exercises, go back through the chapter to review any of the rules you do not understand completely.

| REVIEW EXERCISE 1 | IDENTIFYING AND CORRECTING PROBLEMS WITH PRONOUNS |

Choose the correct alternative in each of the following sentences. Then, in the blank to the left of the sentence, indicate whether the problem is one of agreement (singular with singular, plural with plural), reference (making sure the pronoun has a clear antecedent), or point of view (making sure there are no shifts in person).

_____ 1. Someone left (her, their) shower gel in the locker room.

_____ 2. When Kevin asked if he could have an extra day to write his paper, (she, the professor) told him that a letter grade would be deducted for every day the paper was late.

_____ 3. Dennis likes to sit near the door because (you are, he is) the first one to leave.

_____ 4. The woman tried to put a coin in the expired parking meter as a ticket was being written, but (he, the police officer) told her it was too late.

_____ 5. Everyone on the team has (his, their) own opinion about the new coach.

_____ 6. Westside High School will name (its, their) new football coach by the end of February.

_____ 7. Sam told Mr. Perkins (that his dog had been digging up his flowerbed again, "Your dog has been digging up my flowerbed again.")

_____ 8. Francine bought a security system for her home. She is a pilot and (she has, they have) to be away for days at a time.

_____ **9.** Some hockey fans have suggested that a section of the arena be set aside for nondrinkers, and (this, the idea) is under consideration.

_____ **10.** Kim sat at the computer and navigated the Internet as her daughter gave her instructions. (This, The situation) amused Kim's husband.

REVIEW EXERCISE 2   **IDENTIFYING AND CORRECTING PROBLEMS WITH PRONOUNS**

Find and correct the pronoun reference, agreement, or point of view error in each of the following sentences.

1. Carlos bought a new GPS and camera because he would need it on his road trip.

   _____

2. "I don't care if everybody else disobeys their curfew," said Li's mother. "You will be home by midnight."

   _____

3. "I need a better job," said Shaunessy. "This economy is so bad that you can't make ends meet."

   _____

4. Ed watched the children in fascination. You could sense their excitement as they waited for the show to begin.

   _____

5. Without fear, the skateboarder pushed forward from the top of the steepest ramp, which terrified some of their audience.

   _____

6. Neither of the men was sure that they could fill in for Emanuel on Saturday night.

   _____

7. Ellen's new boyfriend advised, "Don't turn your back on your old friends now that you have made some new ones." Ellen said she would never turn her back on it.

   _____

8. Unlike most of the other lionesses at the zoo, it hadn't been born in captivity.

_____

9. "The company has traded hands three times in the last five years," complained Grandpa. "If a person doesn't like the corporate policy, you can just wait a few months, and it will change."

_____

10. Each of the seniors said they were looking forward to graduation.

_____

REVIEW EXERCISE 3 **FINDING AND CORRECTING PRONOUN ERRORS**

Find and correct the two errors in pronoun agreement, reference, or point of view in each numbered item.

1. The local car wash gives anyone a free car wash on their birthday. This generates good will and brings people back to the car wash on other days during the year.

_____

_____

2. Someone left their sunglasses and car keys sitting on the lunch counter. Chances are that the person will return to pick it up.

_____

_____

3. Irvin told Tom he needed to lose some weight. Irvin added, "I think you can lose more weight by exercising than by restricting food."

_____

_____

4. Bill did not buy a cell phone because he thought someone might eavesdrop on your conversations. He had also heard they caused cancer.

_____

_____

5. Sean saw that someone had left their headlights on. He was afraid to try to open the door to turn it off because people might think he was trying to steal the car.

_____

_____

REVIEW EXERCISE 4   **EDITING A PARAGRAPH FOR PRONOUN ERRORS**

Find and correct the error in pronoun agreement, reference, or point of view in the paragraph following.

¹Nell, my roommate, has a King Tut glitter pyramid on her desk, and when anyone sees it, they can't resist picking it up and shaking it. ²It is modeled along the lines of those plastic snow globes that you see in stores around Christmas. ³The difference is that they put a golden replica of Tutankhamen, the boy king, inside a plastic pyramid. ⁴It is filled with glittery flakes, and like golden sand, it spreads out to the four corners of the pyramid. ⁵Nell turns the pyramid upside down and lets all of the glitter collect at the top of the pyramid; then you flip it quickly. ⁶This sends a golden stream of glitter onto the boy king's head. ⁷When the pyramid is shaken, flakes of gold rise and swirl, and it hides Tut's face. ⁸Nell says her little pyramid is practical as well as entertaining because they make good paperweights.

1. _____

2. _____

3. _____

4. _____

5. _____

6. _____

7. _____

8. _____

mywritinglab   For support and practice meeting this chapter's goal, log in to **www.mywritinglab.com** and select **Pronoun Reference and Point of View** and **Pronoun-Antecedent Agreement**.

Editing Exercises: Basic Grammar

The following exercises allow you to test the grammar skills you have learned in Chapters 13 through 19. The exercises focus on verbs, pronouns, run-on sentences, and sentence fragments.

Basic Grammar: Five Editing Exercises

EDITING EXERCISE 1   **SUBJECT-VERB AGREEMENT AND RUN-ONS**

In the following paragraph, correct the subject-verb agreement errors and run-ons.

6 subject-verb agreement errors
2 run-on sentences
2 comma splices

[1]Why does men find the entire question of clothing so much simpler than women do? [2]The answer lie in the differing approach of each sex toward clothing. [3]Most women uses the "outfit" concept of dressing. [4]In this system, each of a woman's dresses, sweaters, and skirts have to be accessorized with the proper shoes, belt, undergarments, jewelry, and hosiery. [5]A woman may own a mid-calf black skirt, a knee-length blue dress, and tan slacks, however, only her long slip, silver-buckled belt, and black shoes go with the mid-calf black skirt. [6]If she chooses to wear the blue dress or tan slacks, she must choose a different slip, belt, and shoes the system is complicated, so women spend a lot of time choosing their clothing. [7]Men, on the other hand, follows the "uniform" concept of dressing. [8]If the dress code in his office require a man to wear a shirt and tie, he will wear a shirt, a tie, and a pair of pants every day. [9]His underwear will go with any shirt or pair of pants he has in his wardrobe except for coordinating the color of his tie with the color of his shirt, he has little to worry about. [10]Men spend less time thinking about what they wear, their system of choosing clothes is a simpler one.

1. _____   6. _____

2. _____   7. _____

3. _____   8. _____

4. _____   9. _____

5. _____   10. _____

EDITING EXERCISE 2   RUN-ONS AND FRAGMENTS

In the following paragraph, correct the fragments, run-ons, and comma splices.

5 fragments
2 run-ons
3 comma splices

[1]Last spring, when I decided to plant a vegetable garden. [2]I discovered that gardening has its unpleasant aspects. [3]Two hours in the garden convinced me of one fact gardening is a dirty job. [4]Even though I wore gardening gloves, dirt found its way under my fingernails, my shoes and jeans were caked with mud. [5]After half an hour of gardening. [6]I discovered a second unpleasant aspect of gardening—heat. [7]The sun beat down on me as I worked. [8]Causing beads of sweat to pop out on my forehead and run into my eyes. [9]Sweat stung my eyes and soaked my T-shirt I was extremely uncomfortable. [10]The dirt and the heat were bad enough, pesky bugs and slimy worms were even worse. [11]The sweat attracted flies, they hovered and buzzed around my head. [12]When I turned over the soil with my trowel, I unearthed slimy worms and grubs that squirmed palely in the sunlight. [13]Then burrowed back into the dark earth. [14]A ripe tomato from the garden may taste better than one from the grocery store. [15]But is not worth the trouble it takes to grow it.

_____

_____

_____

_____

_____

_____

_____

_____

| EDITING EXERCISE 3 | VERBS, RUN-ONS, AND FRAGMENTS |

In the following paragraph, correct the verb errors, run-ons, and fragments.

3 subject-verb agreement errors
2 comma splices
2 fragments
2 irregular verb errors
1 run-on

[1]I can't recall the exact moment when my cat Molly become the true head of the household. [2]Molly came to me as a tiny, defenseless kitten, the neighbor who convinced me to take Molly said that she was the runt of the litter, the kitten that no one wanted. [3]She stood trembling in a cardboard box. [4]Looking up through moist, blue-green eyes and mouthing the first of many silent meows that soon reduced me to a lowly member of her entourage. [5]Over the past few months, the trembling kitten has growed strong and sure, quickly gaining control of the family. [6]She meow loudly if left alone for long without attention. [7]Molly will not be ignored; she hops into my lap and looks offended. [8]If I don't drop everything and pay attention to her. [9]In the morning, she slides a paw under the bedroom door and rattle it loudly to awaken her human servants if breakfast is late. [10]She refuses to eat inexpensive store-brand cat food; instead, she insist on small, expensive cans of name-brand food. [11]If she wants to come in or go out, her meow takes on a demanding tone it almost sounds as if she is saying, "Now!" [12]Molly commands naturally and without a second thought, the timid, trembling kitten is gone forever.

_____   _____

_____   _____

_____   _____

_____   _____

EDITING EXERCISE 4 **FRAGMENTS AND PRONOUNS**

In the following paragraph, correct the sentence fragments and pronoun errors.

6 fragments
4 pronoun errors

¹Smoking may be a vile and harmful habit, but workplaces can go too far. ²In penalizing employees who smoke. ³While few would want to work in an office thick with smoke. ⁴Employers could provide heated smoking areas for employees who smoke. ⁵Instead, sending workers outside in twenty-degree weather to shiver and smoke. ⁶Some workplaces won't allow you to smoke anywhere on company property. ⁷Smokers must wait a jittery eight hours before lighting up. ⁸Or use their lunch hour to drive off company property to smoke. ⁹To keep insurance costs down. ¹⁰Other companies forbid smoking entirely. ¹¹An employee who is caught smoking, even at home, faces dismissal from their job. ¹²Employees who smoke may be more likely to become ill and to use his or her insurance benefits, but the same can be said of people who eat cholesterol-rich diets and even those who are depressed. ¹³What's next, a company representative knocking on your door for a refrigerator inspection or a mood check? ¹⁴Companies should back off and show a little more tolerance. ¹⁵Toward employees who smoke.

_____   _____

_____   _____

_____   _____

_____   _____

_____

EDITING EXERCISE 5 **SUBJECT-VERB AGREEMENT, FRAGMENTS, RUN-ONS, AND PRONOUNS**

In the following paragraph, correct the fragments, run-ons, and errors in pronoun use and subject-verb agreement.

3 subject-verb agreement errors
3 fragments

2 comma splices
2 pronoun errors

[1]Having an account on a social networking site have both advantages and disadvantages. [2]Because so many people have accounts today. [3]You can use it to catch up with old friends or meet new people. [4]Setting up a profile can be fun. [5]Challenging too. [6]You have to be careful not to include any personal information that you don't want to be public knowledge. [7]You should also be cautious when setting security preferences, otherwise they will be able to access your profile. [8]Since many companies search profiles of potential employees on social networking sites. [9]You can hurt your chances of getting a job if your profile reveal anything questionable. [10]Nevertheless, social networking sites is a fun way to stay in touch. [11]Most sites are now available on your mobile phone, you can stay in touch wherever you go. [12]The advantages of social networking outweigh the disadvantages as long as you remember to use caution when posting information online.

_____   _____

_____   _____

_____   _____

_____   _____

CHAPTER 20

Misplaced and Dangling Modifiers

❧ Chapter Goal: Identify and correct misplaced and dangling modifiers.

The Brush-off

The English major caught his eye,
He smelled her sweet perfume.
He said, "While dancing cheek to cheek,
Romance is sure to bloom."

She said, "To say romance can dance
Is silly from all angles,
And I could never love a man
Whose modifier dangles."

While dangling and misplaced modifiers probably won't ruin your next romance, they may confuse your readers. That's reason enough to learn what they are and how to avoid them.

Look at the two versions of the sentence below:

✗ *Perched at the top of the flagpole,* Orville saw a red-tailed hawk.

✔ Orville saw a red-tailed hawk *perched at the top of the flagpole.*

The words in italic type are modifiers. A **modifier** is a word, phrase, or clause that gives information about another word. In the preceding sentences, the placement of the words "perched at the top of the flagpole" makes a great deal of difference. It is easy to imagine a bird sitting on top of the flagpole, but the idea of Orville perched there does not seem logical.

Although they are not always as obvious as the problem in the example, problems with modifiers are always problems in logic. If you approach this chapter—and your writing, in general—with the idea that good writing should above all make sense, you will have an easier time spotting and correcting misplaced and dangling modifiers.

Misplaced Modifiers

mywritinglab

Visit MyWriting Lab for additional practice with misplaced modifiers.

✗ Hot off the griddle, the family enjoyed pancakes.

Do you see what is not logical about the sentence above? Of course. The family is not hot off the griddle, the pancakes are. This type of modifier problem is called a **misplaced modifier**. The modifier *hot off the griddle* is misplaced to modify *family* instead of *pancakes*. To fix a misplaced modifier, remember this principle: **A modifier should be placed as close as possible to the word it modifies.**

✔ The family enjoyed pancakes hot off the griddle.

Examples of Misplaced Modifiers

✗ The dog was examined by a veterinarian that had just had a litter of puppies.

The sentence seems to suggest that the veterinarian had given birth to puppies. Putting the modifier "that had just had a litter of puppies" closer to the word it modifies makes the meaning clear.

✔ The dog that had just had a litter of puppies was examined by the veterinarian.

Reconstructing the sentence is also a possibility.

✔ The veterinarian examined the dog that had just had a litter of puppies.

✗ Hisako watched the movie eating popcorn.

The sentence is worded as though the movie ate the popcorn.

✔ Eating popcorn, Hisako watched the movie.

✗ Pregnant and tired-looking, the old man gave his seat to the young woman.

It sounds as though the old man has defied the laws of nature.

✔ The old man gave his seat to the pregnant and tired-looking young woman.

PRACTICE 1 CORRECTING MISPLACED MODIFIERS

Correct the misplaced modifiers in the following sentences.

1. Antoinette walked the dog wearing high heels.

   _____

2. Dangling from the ceiling fan, Erin saw a spider on a narrow silken thread.

   _____

3. The man kept a close eye on the toddler sitting on a bench and smoking a cigar.

   _____

4. Snapping and growling, the letter carrier was afraid to approach the dog.

   _____

5. The student visited the office of the English professor who needed tutoring in grammar.

   _____

Single-Word Modifiers

A misplaced modifier that is a single word may be more difficult to spot, but the idea is still the same: An error in logic needs to be corrected.

The words *almost, just, nearly,* and *only* are often carelessly misplaced in sentences. Look at the following example to see the difference that word placement can make:

✔ Only James tasted the melon. *(no one but James)*

✔ James only tasted the melon. *(only sampled the melon, or possibly, no one but James)*

✔ James tasted only the melon. *(nothing but the melon)*

✔ James tasted the only melon. (*the only melon available*)

✔ James tasted the melon only. (*nothing but the melon*)

Next, look at the following examples of illogical modifier placements and corrections:

✗ While watching the football game, Kyle *almost* ate a whole pizza.

If he *almost* ate it, he thought about eating it but never actually took a bite. The writer more likely means something like "Kyle ate eight of the ten pieces."

✔ While watching the football game, Kyle ate *almost* a whole pizza.

✗ Cara *nearly* spent a hundred dollars at the mall.

If she *nearly* spent a hundred dollars, she thought about it but decided to keep her money. A more probable meaning is shown below.

✔ Cara spent *nearly* a hundred dollars at the mall.

✗ Because she felt ill, Miriam *just* ate a few bites of chili.

Because *just* can mean "just now" or "only," placement is important. *Just ate* suggests the meaning *just now ate,* but the writer more likely means *ate only a few bites.*

✔ Because she felt ill, Miriam ate *just* a few bites of chili.

✗ Though she received many toys for Christmas, Amber *only* played with her teddy bear.

If she played with the bear and nothing else, then she played with *only* her teddy bear. "Amber only" can mean "no one but Amber."

✔ Though she received many toys for Christmas, Amber played with *only* her teddy bear.

PRACTICE 2   USING SINGLE-WORD MODIFIERS

Place the listed modifier in the sentence to make each sentence match its intended meaning. The first one is done for you.

1. The distraught mother believed her child was gravely ill.

   Modifier to insert: *only*

   Intended meaning: *No one but the mother believed it.*

   New sentence: Only the distraught mother believed her child was gravely ill.

2. Kim ate a whole bucket of popcorn at the movies.
   Modifier to insert: *nearly*
   Intended meaning: *She ate all but a handful or two.*

   New sentence: _____

   _____

3. Simon's reading speed test shows that he reads 400 words per minute.
   Modifier to insert: *almost*
   Intended meaning: *He reads 394 words per minute.*

   New sentence: _____

   _____

4. Deborah took a job in Seattle for $30,000 per year.
   Modifier to insert: *almost*
   Intended meaning: *She thought about it but did not take the job*

   New sentence: _____

   _____

5. Marisa says her math professor is grumpy on days that end in *y*.
   Modifier to insert: *only*
   Intended meaning: *The professor is grumpy just on the days mentioned.*

   New sentence: _____

   _____

PRACTICE 3   CORRECTING MISPLACED MODIFIERS

Correct the misplaced one-word modifiers in the following sentences.

1. Chad nearly got two weeks' vacation last month.

   _____

2. Alice only waited on four tables of customers all evening.

   _____

3. Giorgio nearly wrote a paper of five hundred words.

   _____

4. The list of people Ben wanted to invite amost included all his friends.

   _____

5. Grover only gave his love to one woman.

   _____

Dangling Modifiers

mywritinglab

Visit MyWriting Lab for additional practice with dangling modifiers.

Unlike a misplaced modifier, which needs to be moved closer to the word it modifies, a dangling modifier has no word to modify.

✗ With a wave of his wand, the rabbit was pulled from the magician's hat.

The phrase "with a wave of his wand" has no word in the sentence to modify. The only two possibilities are *rabbit* and *magician's hat,* neither of which is likely to wave a wand. To fix the misplaced modifier, you have to put a magician in the sentence. The easiest way to fix a dangling modifier is to give it a word to modify. Place the word immediately after the dangling modifier.

✔ With a wave of his wand, **the magician** pulled a rabbit from his hat.

The sentence may also be reconstructed.

✔ As the magician waved his wand, he pulled a rabbit from his hat.

✗ Waking from a nightmare, Makeisha's alarm buzzed loudly.

Obviously, it is Makeisha who has had a nightmare, not her alarm. The easiest way to fix the sentence is to put the word *Makeisha* (not the possessive form Makeisha's) immediately after the modifier.

✔ Waking from a nightmare, **Makeisha** heard her alarm buzz loudly.

But it is also permissible to reconstruct the sentence entirely.

✔ The alarm buzzed loudly as Makeisha awoke from a nightmare.
✔ Makeisha's alarm buzzed loudly as she awoke from a nightmare.

✗ By carefully constructing a résumé, the potential employer is impressed.

It is not the employer who constructs the résumé, but the applicant. The sentence can be fixed by indicating, immediately after the modifier, who constructed the résumé.

✔ By carefully constructing a résumé, an applicant can impress a potential employer.

The sentence can also be reworked entirely.

✔ A carefully constructed résumé can impress a potential employer.

✗ Bored and restless, the minutes seemed to crawl.

Who was bored and restless? (If the sentence does not say, the decision is yours.)

✔ Bored and restless, **I** felt the minutes crawl.

✔ Because **Sherman** was bored and restless, the minutes seemed to crawl.

✗ Listless and feverish, the pediatrician suspected the flu.

Sometimes, the only solution is to reconstruct the sentence. If you try putting "the child" after *listless* and *feverish,* you will probably change the meaning of the sentence.

✔ The pediatrician suspected that the listless and feverish child had the flu.

✔ Because the child was *listless* and *feverish,* the pediatrician suspected the flu.

PRACTICE 4 CORRECTING DANGLING MODIFIERS

Correct the dangling modifiers in the following sentences.

1. Walking across the tile floor, the coffee cup slipped from my hand.

    _____

2. Unhappy with his current job, Malcolm's résumé was updated and employment ads scanned.

    _____

    _____

3. Blinded by the setting sun, Janna's car nearly ran off the road.

    _____

4. By spending hours in the library, careful research for a term paper can be done.

_____

5. Whistling cheerfully, the luggage was loaded into Quinton's trunk.

_____

Review Exercises

Complete the Review Exercises to see how well you have learned the skills addressed in this chapter. As you work through the exercises, go back through the chapter to review any of the rules you do not understand completely.

REVIEW EXERCISE 1	CORRECTING DANGLING AND MISPLACED MODIFIERS

Rewrite the sentences to correct the italicized misplaced or dangling modifiers.

1. *After sitting in a jar of brandy for a month,* Mrs. Smith decided that her "drunken peaches" were ready to serve.

_____

2. *Speaking in a stern voice,* the children soon became quiet.

_____

3. The bride walked down the aisle with her father *dressed in a white satin gown.*

_____

4. *Working with full concentration,* the hours passed quickly.

_____

5. *Hanging on a chain,* Melinda wears her child's picture around her neck.

_____

6. *Sitting on the deck,* the light became too dim for reading.

_____

7. *By shopping early for Christmas,* a last-minute rush will be avoided.

   _____

8. Jared *almost* saved 15 percent of his income last year.

   _____

9. *With a huge yawn,* Al's TV was turned off and the door was locked.

   _____

10. *Paying for my groceries,* the clerk said that the store was going out of business.

    _____

    _____

REVIEW EXERCISE 2   **IDENTIFYING AND CORRECTING DANGLING AND MISPLACED MODIFIERS**

Correct the dangling and misplaced modifiers in the following sentences.

1. Ringing loudly through the silent house, the terrified father leaped out of bed to answer the doorbell.

   _____

   _____

2. Dressed in a stunning white gown, the groom glowed with happiness as he gazed down the aisle at his future wife.

   _____

   _____

3. Diligently cared for and well maintained, Terry was sure that the car would survive another winter.

   _____

   _____

4. By setting aside time to study everyday, a grade point average is sure to improve.

   _____

   _____

5. Anne picked up the groceries on the floor that had fallen when the bag ripped.

_____

| REVIEW EXERCISE 3 | **USING ONE-WORD MODIFIERS** |

Place the listed modifier in the sentence to make each sentence match its intended meaning.

1. The applicant for the job was offered half the salary she expected.

Modifier to insert: _only_

Intended meaning: _She was offered $20,000 per year; she expected $40,000._

New sentence:

_____

2. Carol has been interested in science since she was twelve years old.

Modifier to insert: _nearly_

Intended meaning: _She was eleven years, ten months, and two days old when she first discovered an interest in science._

New sentence:

_____

3. Perry told the officer, "I was going under fifty miles per hour."

Modifier to insert: _just_

Intended meaning: _He was going 49.5 miles per hour._

New sentence:

_____

4. The officer replied, "Sir, you were going sixty-five."

Modifier to insert: _almost_

Intended meaning: _He was going 64.5 miles per hour._

New sentence:

_____

5. I gave Mary twenty dollars.

Modifier to insert: _almost_

Intended meaning: *I thought about it but did not give it to her.*

New sentence

_____

| REVIEW EXERCISE 4 | **IDENTIFYING AND CORRECTING DANGLING AND MISPLACED MODIFIERS** |

Underline and correct the two misplaced or dangling modifiers in each sentence group.

1. My mother did the best she could for my brothers and me. As a single mother with three children, few luxuries were available. By working long hours for little pay, the basic needs of life were met.

    _____

    _____

2. Sharon saw a polar bear visiting the zoo on Sunday. Sitting on a block of ice, she noticed that although his fur was white, his nose and paw pads were coal black.

    _____

    _____

3. Shakira almost had to wait three hours to see the doctor. Waiting for hours with no magazines to read, the doctor must not have cared how the patients felt.

    _____

    _____

4. Last week, my six-year-old and I visited the Humane Society to pick out a puppy. Furry and cute, my daughter was captivated by a white terrier that she named Roscoe. Though not yet paper trained, my daughter loves Roscoe so much that I don't mind cleaning up his messes.

    _____

    _____

    _____

5. Leah nearly took piano lessons for two years, but she can't play a note. Her brother, on the other hand, plays beautifully. Interested in music even as a child, a career in music seems right for Daniel.

    _____

    _____

    _____

REVIEW EXERCISE 5   EDITING FOR DANGLING AND MISPLACED MODIFIERS

Find and correct the misplaced and dangling modifiers in the following paragraph.

[1]Creamy, sweet, and irresistible, Betty does crazy things to feed her addiction to chocolate. [2] Last Monday, desperate for chocolate, a thunderstorm did not deter her from going out for candy. [3] Squinting past the windshield wipers, sheeting rain poured as she splashed into the parking lot of Food Town. [4] Minutes later, wet but triumphant, her purchase was made. [5] The store nearly charged five dollars for the candy, but she did not mind. [6]She munched on it straight from the bag as she drove on the seat beside her. [7]Eating and driving at the same time, an accident was barely avoided when she swerved to keep from hitting a pedestrian. [8]She only saw him at the last minute. [9]Then, struck by a bolt of lightning, she saw a huge tree that had split down the middle. [10]She realized that she had taken an unnecessary risk in going out for candy in a thunderstorm that she did not really need at all.

1. _____

_____

2. _____

_____

3. _____

_____

4. _____

5. _____

6. _____

7. _____

_____

8. _____

9. _____

_____

10. _____

_____

mywritinglab For support and practice meeting this chapter's goal, log in to www.mywritinglab.com and select Misplaced or Dangling Modifiers.

CHAPTER 21

Parallel Structure

> ✎ **Chapter Goal:** Identify and revise constructions that are not parallel.

Choose the best answer to complete each sequence.

1. **a, b, c,** _____   a. **t**   b. **z**   c. **d**
2. ↘, ↗↗, ↘, ↗↗, _____   a. ↗   b. ↗↗   c. ↘
3. 20, 40, 60, _____   a. 10 b. 120 c. 80
4. ▶, ■, _____   a. •   b. □   c. ◉

If you chose *c* each time, you are correct. Your mind was responding to the patterns you saw developing in each sequence. Patterns are pleasing to the human mind, and that is why parallel structure works.

In any famous speech, such as Abraham Lincoln's Gettysburg Address or Martin Luther King, Jr.'s "I Have a Dream," you hear the regular, memorable rhythm of **parallel structure**—parallel words, parallel phrases, and parallel clauses. You see it in good writing, too, lending elegance to ordinary sentences. Once you are used to seeing parallel structure, anything else seems awkward. Look at the following lists to see examples of nonparallel and parallel structure.

mywritinglab

Visit MyWriting Lab for additional practice with parallel structure.

Examples of Nonparallel and Parallel Structure

✗   **Nonparallel:**

eating at fast-food places

to snack on sweets and chips

avoiding exercise

The phrase *to snack on sweets and chips* is not parallel with the *-ing* constructions of the other two phrases.

✓   **Parallel:**

eating at fast-food places

snacking on sweets and chips

avoiding exercise

All phrases in the revised list above have the same structure; that is, they are parallel.

✗   **Nonparallel:**

medium blue

light gray

with a bright orange hue

✓   **Parallel:**

medium blue

light gray

bright orange

✗   **Nonparallel:**

studied for her midterm exam

worked on her term paper

researching at the library was also done

✓   **Parallel:**

studied for her midterm exam

worked on her term paper

researched at the library

PRACTICE 1   USING PARALLEL STRUCTURE

Each of the following lists contains one item that is not parallel. Cross out the nonparallel item, and reword it to make it parallel with the other items. Then write the reworded version on the line provided.

1. sitting on the deck
    reading a book
    to swat at mosquitoes

    _____

2. calm
    had an easygoing personality
    friendly

    _____

3. frustrated by deadlines
    under pressure from her boss
    hassled by customers

    _____

4. a beautiful campus
    excellent food service
    dorm rooms that are large

    _____

5. the fact that it was unheated
    it had no television
    it had no lights

    _____

In sentences, items given equal emphasis should be parallel in structure whenever possible. These items include words, phrases, and clauses in pairs or lists. Look at the following examples of nonparallel and parallel structure within sentences.

Examples of Nonparallel and Parallel Structure

✗   The chef *chopped* the garlic and then *was sprinkling* it on the pizza.

✓   The chef *chopped* the garlic and then *sprinkled* it on the pizza.

✗   Alberto is sometimes late for class because he has to *wait* for elevators, *looking* for access ramps, and *navigate* his wheelchair through crowded hallways.

✓   Alberto is sometimes late for class because he has to *wait* for elevators, *look* for access ramps, and *navigate* his wheelchair through crowded hallways.

✗   Kristi hoped for a roommate who was *quiet, studious,* and *who was also friendly.*

✓   Kristi hoped for a roommate who was *quiet, studious,* and *friendly.*

✗   James feared *he would fail* but knew *quitting was not an option.*

✓   James feared he would fail but knew he could not quit.

PRACTICE 2   USING PARALLEL STRUCTURE

Each of the following sentences contains one item that is not parallel. Cross out the nonparallel item and reword it to make it parallel with the other items. Then write the reworded version on the line provided.

1. Swimming, jogging, and to waterski are my athletic sister's favorite pastimes.

   _____

2. The squirrel leaped from the roof, had scampered up a tree, and watched us from the safety of a high branch.

   _____

3. For dinner, Lisa had iced tea, a tomato sandwich, and she also ate a salad.

   _____

4. Mandy could not concentrate because the dogs were barking, the children were whining, and because the television also blared.

   _____

5. Ed's yard sale table looked good once he stripped the old paint, the rough spots had been sanded, and painted the table white.

   _____

〰 Review Exercises

Complete the Review Exercises to see how well you have learned the skills addressed in this chapter. As you work through the exercises, go back through the chapter to review any of the rules you do not understand completely.

REVIEW EXERCISE 1   MAKING LISTS PARALLEL

Each of the following lists contains one item that is not parallel. Cross out the nonparallel item, and reword it to make it parallel with the other items. Then write the reworded version on the line provided.

1. to visit Europe   2. smart
   singing at a local coffeeshop   capable
   to climb a mountain   having many friends

   _____   _____

3. getting a scholarship
working part time
loans

_____

4. soft fabrics
attractive colors
styles that were cutting-edge

_____

5. graduating
getting a great job
move into a new apartment

_____

6. gain speed
jump high
moving gracefully

_____

7. new outfit
fresh haircut
applying discreet makeup

_____

8. in classrooms
hanging out in the cafeteria
at the dorms

_____

9. experiencing some confusion
irritated
lost

_____

10. finish my homework
eat dinner
early bedtime

_____

REVIEW EXERCISE 2   MAKING SENTENCES PARALLEL

In each of the following sentences, one italicized item is not parallel. Cross out the nonparallel item and reword it to make it parallel with the other items. Then write the reworded version on the line provided.

1. When it's time to study, Carl always remembers that he has to _do his laundry, shop for groceries,_ or _his car needs washing._

_____

2. Today the children want _to go to the movies_ and _visiting the museum._

_____

3. Kevin's project failed because he ran _out of time, out of money,_ and _he also had bad luck._

_____

4. The tail of a comet always _points_ toward the sun, while the nose _is pointed_ away from the sun.

_____

5. Grandma says she remembers when gas stations *filled the tank, they would check the oil,* and *washed the windshield.*

   _____

6. Before going to bed, Kay checked to make sure *her children were in bed* and *that she had locked the door.*

   _____

7. Real estate agents say that there are three important considerations when buying property: *location, where it is located,* and *location.*

   _____

8. The lion's *scratched nose* and *ear that was torn* bore testimony to the many battles he had fought.

   _____

9. Sam said he was having *problems at work, problems with his math class,* and *health problems.*

   _____

10. "My neighbors are a pain," said Michelle. "*Their music is loud, their yard is messy,* and *they have children who are rude.*"

    _____

REVIEW EXERCISE 3   IDENTIFYING AND CORRECTING ERRORS IN PARALLEL STRUCTURE

Each of the following sentences contains one item that is not parallel. Cross out the nonparallel item, and reword it to make it parallel with the other items. Then write the reworded version on the line provided.

1. Magazines devoted to news, science magazines, and science fiction novels are Sierra's favorite reading material.

   _____

2. Next fall, Gus plans to take English, biology, and a course in sociology.

   _____

3. The eerie old house was filled with musty corridors, stairs that creaked, and dark, curtained rooms.

   _____

4. "If I have my family, my home, and I suppose a job could be added to the list, then I have everything I need," said Clarice.

   _____

5. Ants zigzagged along the flagstone path; some traveled toward the anthill, and others were traveling away.

   _____

6. When baby animals play, they are really learning how to behave socially and how hunting is done.

   _____

7. After the flood, Don's basement was filled with water, mud covered his floor, and his lawn was carpeted with debris.

   _____

8. Because of good weather and the traffic was light, Alex made the trip in less than two hours.

   _____

9. Sarita says she barely has time for work between attending night school and because she has to chauffeur her kids to their softball games.

   _____

10. On weekends, Daniel likes to spend time with his kids, working in his garden, and restoring his old Chevrolet.

    _____

mywritinglab   For support and practice meeting this chapter's goal, log in to www.mywritinglab.com and select Parallelism.

CHAPTER 22

Verb Shifts

✍ **Chapter Goal:** Use shifts in verb tense and voice correctly; recognize active and passive voice.

Shifts happen.
You can fix them.

Look at the sentences below:

✗ The balloon floated lazily upward and becomes a small dot against the blue sky.

✗ At the clothing store, Eric tried on several jackets, but none were purchased.

The previous sentences contain two common types of **verb shifts**. The first sentence contains an unnecessary shift from past tense to present tense, and the second contains an unnecessary shift from active voice to passive voice. Following are the corrected versions of the sentences.

- ✔ The balloon floated lazily upward and *became* a small dot against the blue sky.
- ✔ At the clothing store, Eric tried on several jackets, but he purchased none.

In this chapter, you will learn to correct unnecessary shifts from past to present tense and to make necessary shifts into the past perfect tense. You will also learn to recognize active voice and passive voice and to correct unnecessary shifts between the two.

Shifts in Tense

mywritinglab

Visit MyWriting Lab for additional practice avoiding shifts in tense.

Verb tenses give the English language its sense of time, its sense of *when* events occur. The following timeline shows six verb tenses, and the chart below the timeline briefly explains how each tense is used.

Verb Tense Timeline

	past	present	future
	I walked	I walk	I will walk

past ◊← - - - - - * - - - - - * - - - - - - - - - * - - - - - * - - - - - - - * - - - - - - - →◊ future

I had walked	I have walked		I will have walked
past	present		future
perfect	perfect		perfect

Verb Tense Chart

◊◊◊	Furthest in the past; happened before another past action	past perfect *had+ -ed* verb form	I *had walked* up the stairs, and I was out of breath.
◊◊	In the past; happened before now.	past *-ed* verb form	I *walked* all the way around the nature trail.
◊ •	In the past but extending to the present	present perfect *have* or *has* + *-ed* verb form	I *have walked* every day for the last month. He *has walked* a mile already.

- Happens regularly or often, or is happening now

present
base verb
form or base
verb+ -s

I *walk* at least five miles a week.
She *walks* quickly.

◊ Happens in the future but before another future event

future perfect
will have
+ - *ed* verb form

By the time you join me on the track, I *will have walked* at least two miles.

◊◊ Happens at some time in the future

future
will + base
verb

I *will walk* with you tomorrow if we both have time.

Avoiding Unnecessary Tense Shifts

With so many ways of designating time, it is easy to make mistakes. The most common error in verb tense is an unnecessary shift from past tense to present tense. A writer may become so caught up in describing a past event that it becomes, at least temporarily, a part of "the now." Look at the following examples to see the difference between a necessary shift and an unnecessary shift in verb tense.

Examples of Necessary and Unnecessary Tense Shifts

Necessary Shift:

  past   present

✓ Coral <u>was</u> a poor student in high school, but she <u>is doing</u> well in college.

Because the sentence above refers to both the *past* (high school) and the *present* (college), the verb tense shift is necessary.

Unnecessary Shift:

   past   present   present

✗ When Joe <u>came</u> into the room, he <u>breaks</u> into a big smile and <u>says,</u> "Guess what?"

Since the action in this sentence is a single, continuous event, there is no need for a shift to present tense. To correct an unnecessary tense shift, decide which tense is appropriate, and use that tense for all verbs in the sentence.

Corrected:

   past   past   past

✓ When Joe <u>came</u> into the room, he <u>broke</u> into a big smile and <u>said,</u> "Guess what?"

Unnecessary Shift:

past   present

✗ Annie <u>boarded</u> the bus, and she <u>sees</u> her friend Chloe sitting in a window seat.

Corrected:

past   past

✓ Annie <u>boarded</u> the bus, and she <u>saw</u> her friend Chloe sitting in a window seat.

PRACTICE 1   MAINTAINING CONSISTENT TENSE

Underline the correct verb in each sentence.

1. When Amanda finally arrived at the restaurant, her friends (have, had) already ordered.
2. The plumber knocked on the door, checking his watch impatiently, but no one (is, was) home.
3. The car rounded the corner too quickly, skidded on the wet pavement, and (slams, slammed) into a telephone pole.
4. Every day, Horace works in his garden until the sun (falls, fell) below the horizon.
5. The trees in the front yard look beautiful all year long; however, they (bloom, bloomed) only in spring.

PRACTICE 2   CORRECTING UNNECESSARY TENSE SHIFTS

In each of the following sentences, correct the unnecessary shift from past to present.

1. Yoshi had just settled down to watch the ball game when suddenly his cable goes out.

   _____

   _____

2. The plane gained speed as it moved down the runway, and then it is airborne.

   _____

3. Edward accidentally left his headlights on, so his car battery dies before he gets out of class.

    _____

    _____

4. After I had put my heart and soul into studying the first six chapters, the professor moves the test to next Friday.

    _____

    _____

5. The troops moved quietly, knowing enemy soldiers are nearby.

    _____

Providing Necessary Tense Shifts

Another common type of verb tense error is likely to occur when a writer needs to shift from the past tense into the more distant past, using the past perfect tense. Often, writers omit this needed shift and stay in the simple past tense, thus taking the risk of confusing the reader.

Examples of Necessary Tense Shifts

             past   past

✗ By the time Jill <u>woke</u> up, her husband <u>made</u> coffee.

Made coffee should be further in the past than *woke up. Had* needs to be used to push *made* to a time before that indicated by the simple past tense verb *woke*.

✗ The minister said a prayer at the grave of Florence Jones, who attended his church.

Without *had*, the two verbs in the sentence are, as far as the reader can tell, occupying the same space in the past. Look at the corrected versions of the sentences:

             past   past perfect

✓ By the time Jill <u>woke</u> up, her husband <u>had made</u> the coffee.

                  past

✓ The minister <u>said</u> a prayer at the grave of Florence Jones, who <u>had</u>
  past perfect
<u>attended</u> his church.

Notice in the following example that if the sequence of events is clearly shown in other ways, the past perfect tense is not needed:

✓ Carl made coffee *before* Jill woke up.

PRACTICE 3   MAKING NECESSARY TENSE SHIFTS

In the following sentences, provide the necessary shift to the past perfect tense by using *had* + the past participle (the *-ed* or *-en* form of the verb). Some of the verbs in the sentences below are irregular and do not form their past participle by adding *-ed*. (If you are uncertain of the past participle of irregular verbs, consult the list in Chapter 13.)

1. I was stranded on a lonely road, and I left my cell phone at home.

   _____

2. When the landlady called about the rent, I told her I mailed it.

   _____

3. When Vijay asked his daughter if she had homework, she told him she finished it.

   _____

4. When someone asked Michael for a cigarette, he said he quit smoking.

   _____

5. The dog ate as if no one fed him for days.

   _____

Active Voice and Passive Voice

mywritinglab

Visit MyWriting Lab for additional practice with active and passive voice.

Active voice means that the subject of a verb performs the action described by the verb, as in the following sentence:

✓ Tom <u>ate</u> the hamburger.

In this sentence, *Tom,* the subject, performs the action described by the verb *ate.* Rewritten in **passive voice**, the sentence looks like this:

✓ The hamburger <u>was eaten</u> by Tom.

What has changed? Simply put, the subject of the verb is not *acting*, but is *acted upon*. The subject *hamburger* performs no action, but instead is acted upon by the person who eats it. Notice, too, another hallmark of the passive voice: The verb contains a helping verb that is a form of the verb *to be*. Though an active voice verb also may have a helping verb such as *is, was, were, have been, will be*, or another form of *to be*, a passive voice verb *always* has a helping verb. Another hallmark of the passive voice is the *by* construction that sometimes tells who or what acted upon the subject.

Memory Jogger

In *active voice*, an action is done *by* the grammatical subject.
In *passive voice*, an action is done *to* the grammatical subject.

PRACTICE 4   EXAMINING ACTIVE VOICE AND PASSIVE VOICE VERBS

Look at the following sets of sentences and answer the questions about them. The first one is done for you.

Set 1

Active: The National Weather Service predicts rain for tomorrow.

The subject of the verb is National Weather Service.

The verb that shows the action done *by* the subject is predicts.

Passive: Rain is being predicted for tomorrow by the National Weather Service.

The subject of the verb is rain.

The verb that shows the action done *to* the subject is is being predicted.

Set 2

Active: Andrea read the book over the weekend.

The subject of the verb is _____.

The verb that shows the action done *by* the subject is ____.

Passive: The book was read by Andrea over the weekend.

The subject of the verb is ____.

The verb that shows the action done *to* the subject is _____.

Set 3

Active: Terrell completely reorganized the company's delivery system.

The subject of the verb is _____.

The verb that shows the action done *by* the subject is _____.

Passive: The company's delivery system was completely reorganized by Terrell.

The subject of the verb is _____.

The verb that shows the action done *to* the subject is _____.

Set 4

Active: In the bottom of the ninth inning, the Expos won the game.

The subject of the verb is _____.

The verb that shows the action done *by* the subject is ____.

Passive: In the bottom of the ninth inning, the game was won by the Expos.

The subject of the verb is _____.

The verb that shows the action done *to* the subject is _____.

Set 5

Active: After the park closes, work crews rake leaves, sweep sidewalks, and clean restrooms in preparation for the next day.

The subject of the verb is _____.

The verbs that show the action done *by* the subject are _____.

Passive: After the park closes, leaves are raked, sidewalks are swept, and restrooms are cleaned in preparation for the next day.

The subjects of the verbs are _____.

The actions done *to* the subjects are _____.

Uses of Active Voice and Passive Voice

Active voice, with its directness and vitality, is stronger than passive voice and is preferred in most situations. There are times, however, when you may want to emphasize the recipient of the action rather than the actor. At those times, use passive voice. If you were composing a paragraph about an old mansion, you would probably say "The Wetherby mansion was built in 1897 by Augustus L. Wetherby," not "Augustus L. Wetherby built the Wetherby mansion in 1897." If your paragraph were about Augustus Wetherby, however, the second sentence would be a better choice. While active voice is ordinarily preferred, decisions about active and passive voice depend on the focus and purpose of each sentence.

Shifts between active and passive voice are avoided unless they are necessary, as in the following sentence:

active
✓ The entire nation <u>mourned</u> when President John F. Kennedy
   passive
<u>was assassinated.</u>

The shift is necessary because to stay in active voice the writer of the sentence would have to take the focus away from Kennedy by writing a sentence like this one: "The entire nation mourned when Lee Harvey Oswald assassinated President John F. Kennedy."

Writing Sentences in Active Voice and Passive Voice

To avoid unnecessary shifts between active voice and passive voice, you need to be able to recognize and write sentences in both voices. The next section of the chapter will give you practice in switching from passive to active voice and from active to passive voice.

Switching from Passive Voice to Active Voice

To switch from passive voice to active voice, first determine who or what acts upon the subject of the sentence. Then rewrite the sentence to make that actor the subject.

Examples of Sentences Rewritten in Active Voice

✓ **Passive:** The contract <u>was drawn</u> up by the company's lawyers.

Because the sentence is in passive voice, you know that the subject, *contract*, is acted upon. To switch this sentence to active voice, first look for the word or phrase that tells who or what acted upon the subject. In a passive voice sentence, the information will come after the verb. In this sentence, *the company's lawyers* drew up the contract. Next, make that word or phrase the subject of the sentence. Finally, change the verb to active voice—in this case, by removing the helping verb and converting it to simple past tense.

✓ **Active:** The company's lawyers <u>drew up</u> the contract.

Sometimes, the *by* construction will be omitted, and you will need to mentally fill in the blank to put an actor into the sentence:

✓ **Passive:** The prisoner <u>was sentenced</u> to life without parole.

The sentence does not say who sentenced the prisoner, but logic tells you that it must have been a judge. To rewrite the sentence in active voice, supply the missing judge as the subject of the sentence:

✓ **Active:** The judge <u>sentenced</u> the prisoner to life without parole.

PRACTICE 5   CHANGING PASSIVE VOICE TO ACTIVE VOICE

Each of the following sentences is in passive voice. Rewrite each sentence in active voice.

1. The chairs were ordered by Herman on May 12.

    _____

2. The wedding was attended by one hundred people.

    _____

3. At the scene of the crime, an address book containing names of suspected drug dealers was found by police.

    _____

    _____

4. In English class today, our graded essays were returned.

    _____

5. The clock was sent to us by Aunt Matilda and Uncle Norris.

    _____

Switching from Active Voice to Passive Voice

To switch from active voice to passive voice, reverse the position of the actor (the subject of the verb) and the recipient of the action (the object of the verb).

Examples of Sentences Rewritten in Passive Voice

✓ **Active:** The cheering fans <u>watched</u> the game.

The actor (the subject of the verb) is *cheering fans*. The recipient of the action (the object of the verb) is *the game*. To convert the sentence to passive voice, switch the positions of the two. Then change the verb to passive voice by adding a helping verb:

✓ **Passive:** The game <u>was watched</u> by hundreds of cheering fans.

Here is a second example:

✓ **Active:** The Committee for Park Beautification and the Citizens' Council <u>planted</u> fifty new trees in Gregory Frasier Park.

✓ **Passive:** Fifty new trees <u>were planted</u> in Gregory Frasier Park by the Committee for Park Beautification and the Citizens' Council.

PRACTICE 6   CHANGING ACTIVE VOICE TO PASSIVE VOICE

Each of the following sentences is in active voice. Rewrite each sentence in passive voice.

1. Children's drawings and magnets of various types covered the refrigerator door.

    _____

    _____

2. The technician expertly cleaned and repaired the old lawnmower.

    _____

3. The head chef supervised the cooking and menu planning in the restaurant.

    _____

4. Women of ancient times washed clothes in streams and rivers.

    _____

5. The ringing of the telephone broke Bonnie's concentration.

    _____

Correcting Shifts in Voice

When an unnecessary shift in voice occurs within a sentence, rewrite the sentence so that it is in one voice. (Active voice is usually preferred.)

Examples of Unnecessary Shifts in Voice Corrected

Unnecessary Shift:

        active   passive

✗ Before I left for the airport, a phone call was made to confirm my reservations.

Corrected:

        active   active

✓ Before I left for the airport, I called to confirm my reservations.

Unnecessary Shift:

           active   passive

✗ George's car needed work, so it was left at the shop.

Corrected:

           active   active

✓ George's car needed work, so he left it at the shop.

PRACTICE 7   CORRECTING SHIFTS IN VOICE

Each of the following sentences contains a shift in voice. Cross out the passive voice portion of each sentence and rewrite it in active voice. The first one is done for you.

1. The dog's former owner had abused it, but ~~it was treated well by Sarah~~.

   The dog's former owner had abused it, but Sarah treated it well.

2. We had plenty of cake left over, but **all of the fruit had been eaten by the guests.**

   _____

3. By the time we came home, **all the food in the dog's bowl had been eaten.**

   _____

4. Fran wrote the letter, but **it was signed by all ten of us.**

   _____

5. Because **the plants were carefully watered and fertilized by Martin,** they were tall and healthy.

   _____

6. Icicles hung from the trees like Christmas decorations, and the street was covered by a glassy sheet of ice.

_____

_____

7. Chelsie was serious about sticking to her budget, so every expenditure was recorded.

_____

8. At the salon, Andrea's hair was expertly cut and styled by the beautician while the manicurist buffed and painted her nails.

_____

_____

9. Firefighters arrived on the scene, and the blaze was soon extinguished.

_____

10. As we sat on the porch, a siren was heard.

_____

Review Exercises

Complete the Review Exercises to see how well you have learned the skills addressed in this chapter. As you work through the exercises, go back through the chapter to review any of the rules you do not understand completely.

| REVIEW EXERCISE 1 | CORRECTING UNNECESSARY SHIFTS IN TENSE AND VOICE |

The italicized portions of the following sentences contain unnecessary shifts in voice or tense, or a verb that needs to be shifted from the past to the past perfect tense. Correct the problem in each sentence.

1. Kendall is graduating in June, and a celebration party _is being given by him._

_____

2. I saw Mark at the grocery store, and _he says,_ "Have you seen Vernon lately?"

_____

3. We offered Jim dinner, but he said _he ate._

_____

4. Sandra and Tom were pronounced husband and wife, and then *they light* a single candle to symbolize their union.

_____

_____

5. When the jury walked into the courtroom, everyone tried to read the jurors' expressions to see what *verdict had been reached.*

_____

_____

6. As they walked through the produce department, Lynn and her mother picked up bananas, pears, and apples, and then *they decide* to get some cherries, too.

_____

_____

7. We discussed the price and the terms of payment, and *the deal was sealed* with a handshake.

_____

_____

8. Karen *already worked* an eight-hour shift and did not appreciate being asked to work overtime at the last minute.

_____

_____

9. Last night, as we sat down to the first family dinner we had had all week, *the phone rings.*

_____

_____

10. Evelyn felt she should have been promoted before Bill because *she worked* at KC Corporation for five years longer than he.

_____

_____

REVIEW EXERCISE 2   **RECOGNIZING AND CORRECTING VARIOUS TYPES OF SHIFTS**

The italicized portions of the following sentences contain unnecessary shifts in voice or tense, or verbs that need to be shifted from the past to the past perfect tense. Circle *a, b,* or *c* to indicate the type of problem in each sentence; then correct the problem.

1. In the morning, we left our beds unmade, and when we came back to the hotel room, the housekeeping staff *cleaned the room and made up the beds.*
    The problem in this sentence is
    a. a shift in voice
    b. a shift between past and present tense
    c. past tense verbs that need to be further in the past (past perfect)

    _____

    _____

2. We walked into the house, and May and Chad were sitting there with smug smiles, as *if they know a secret* that we didn't.
    The problem in this sentence is
    a. a shift in voice
    b. a shift between past and present tense
    c. a past tense verb that needs to be further in the past (past perfect)

    _____

    _____

3. In the stands, hockey fans danced the Hokey-Pokey and the Macarena *while hot dogs, soft drinks, and beer were sold by vendors.*
    The problem in this sentence is
    a. a shift in voice
    b. a shift between past and present tense
    c. a past tense verb that needs to be further in the past (past perfect)

    _____

    _____

4. Out in the yard, the two dogs worried a small rodent *that had been caught by them.*
    The problem in this sentence is
    a. a shift in voice
    b. a shift between past and present tense
    c. a past tense verb that needs to be further in the past (past perfect)

    _____

5. When Jack got to the veterinarian's office with Prince, he realized he *left* the dog's urine sample in the refrigerator at home.
    The problem in this sentence is
    a. a shift in voice
    b. a shift between past and present tense

c. a past tense verb that needs to be further in the past (past perfect)

_____

_____

| REVIEW EXERCISE 3 | CORRECTING PROBLEMS IN TENSE AND VOICE |

Correct the voice or tense problem in each sentence.

1. The waitress asked us if we ate here before.

_____

2. We were almost done sorting the silverware when the drawer falls off its tracks and its contents spill across the floor.

_____

_____

3. The wind was blowing the leaves everywhere, so John decides to rake tomorrow.

_____

4. The quiz was scheduled for Friday by the professor.

_____

5. The alarm rang, and Laney presses snooze right away.

_____

6. While visiting the state college, Emilia tried to visit her friend Jamie, but Jamie transferred to a different college.

_____

_____

7. It was not Paul's day. He was on time for his shift despite fighting heavy traffic, but when he got there, the manager tells him that he isn't on the schedule.

_____

_____

8. When I asked Lin about the painting hanging on her wall, she said she had it for years.

_____

_____

9. The office was a disorderly array of files, papers, and potted plants; boxes of supplies are stacked on the only chair.

_____

_____

10. Dora collects coins. This year five impressive pieces were obtained by her.

_____

REVIEW EXERCISE 4   **EDITING A PARAGRAPH FOR PROBLEMS IN TENSE AND VOICE**

Each sentence in the following paragraph contains a voice or tense problem. Correct the problem by rewriting a verb in past tense or past perfect tense or by changing a passive voice construction to active voice.

[1]Yesterday, as I ran my Saturday errands, some of the people who were seen by me made me think of Robert Burns' poem about seeing ourselves as others see us. [2]At the drugstore, I see a woman in tight jeans, a stained shirt, and huge pink curlers. [3] If she thought of how others might view her before she left the house, she might have taken the time to change clothes and comb out her hair. [4]One young man drove through a downtown street with his stereo at full blast, not caring that others might not like the same music that was liked by him. [5]He may have seen himself as sophisticated; to others on the street that day, he is an annoyance. [6]An attractive middle-aged woman in a business suit did not behave attractively toward the poodle that walks beside her. [7]She jerked its leash and speaks harshly to it, revealing a bad temper under a polished exterior. [8] Finally, disgusting behavior was exhibited by one man as he sat at a traffic light. [9]He casually picks his nose as if his car had rendered him invisible. [10]On that Saturday, some people were seen by me who could not see themselves as others saw them.

1. _____

2. _____

3. _____

4. _____

5. _____

6. _____

7. _____

8. _____

9. _____

10. _____

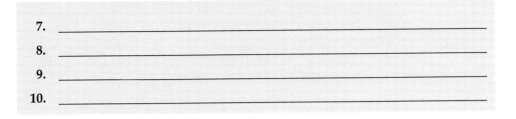

mywritinglab   For support and practice meeting this chapter's goal, log in to www.mywritinglab.com and select Consistent Verb Tense and Active Voice.

Editing Exercises: Advanced Grammar

Advanced Grammar: Three Editing Exercises

EDITING EXERCISE 1   **MISPLACED MODIFIERS, DANGLING MODIFIERS, AND PARALLEL STRUCTURE**

Correct the following misplaced and dangling modifiers and parallel structure errors.

6 parallel structure errors   4 dangling and misplaced modifiers

[1]Stress is a normal response to change, good and bad, in people's lives, and everyone nearly experiences stress. [2]*Eustress* (from the Greek root *eu,* meaning *good or well*) is stress in response to a positive event such as going on vacation, to win the lottery, or receiving a job promotion. [3]Deciding whether to buy a Mercedes or a BMW with lottery winnings, the pressure may seem overwhelming. [4]Eustress, however, is temporary; families remember the beauty of a wedding and forget that they almost spent all the time prior to the wedding squabbling over trivial things. [5]*Distress,* stress in response to negative events, presents more serious problems and causing more harm. [6]This type of stress is often a response to traumatic events such as loss of a job or a family member dies. [7]Having lost the status and income that a job provides, anger and despair can overwhelm a person who has been fired or downsized. [8]Anger, nightmares, or to lose

weight are often the results of distress. [9]Chronic stress is also said to contribute to illnesses such as heart disease, depression, and having some form of cancer. [10]The good news is that for most people, stress and its symptoms fading and disappear after a period of adjustment.

1. _____

2. _____

3. _____

4. _____

5. _____

6. _____

7. _____

_____

8. _____

9. _____

10. _____

EDITING EXERCISE 2 | **MISPLACED AND DANGLING MODIFIERS, PARALLEL STRUCTURE, AND VERB SHIFTS**

Correct the following misplaced and dangling modifiers, parallel structure errors, and shifts in verb tense and voice in the following paragraph.

1 parallel structure error   5 shifts in verb tense
2 misplaced and dangling modifiers   1 shifts in voice

[1]I enjoy watching the previews when I went to the movie theater every weekend. [2]Unfortunately, many people speak loudly to their friends, unaware that other moviegoers are annoyed by their whispers. [3]This week there were previews for a romantic comedy, a horror movie, and a movie with lots of action. [4]Because so many people were talking, I miss the three previews. [5]Interested in romantic comedies, *One Plus One* might have interested me. [6]I believe that many moviegoers are annoyed by this rude behavior because I often saw patrons shoot accusatory looks at offenders or hiss a "Shhhh" in the general direction of the noise. [7]On rare occasions, when patrons are exceptionally disruptive, ushers intervened. [8]If ushers are not around, popcorn may be thrown at noisy audience

members by irritated moviegoers. [9]When I go to the movies, I tried to be respectful of other members of the audience. [10]It's important to me that I can watch the movie uninterrupted by annoying whispers, as an avid film fan.

1. _____

2. _____

   _____

3. _____

4. _____

5. _____

6. _____

7. _____

8. _____

9. _____

10. _____

EDITING EXERCISE 3   VERB SHIFTS, PARALLEL STRUCTURE, AND DANGLING OR MISPLACED MODIFIERS

In the following editing exercise, correct the following verb shifts, parallel structure errors, and dangling or misplaced modifiers.

3 shifts in tense   1 misplaced modifier
1 shift in voice   3 parallel structure errors
2 dangling modifiers

   [1]The city sprawls out for miles, but no matter where I drive, I see the fragile-looking woman I called "the walking lady." [2]Crowded with speeding cars, I see her in the summer, walking along a dangerous four-lane highway. [3]Her fair skin is sheltered from the sun by a flowered umbrella, but her wavy blonde hair was straggly and damp in the humid summer air. [4]Her shoes are not the sturdy athletic shoes that people wear for exercise, but flats that are worn, flimsy, and looking much too loose for her feet. [5]In winter, I see her walking the narrow downtown streets in the pouring rain, the biting wind, and the snow that falls. [6]Wearing a thin coat, the same

fragile shoes enclose her wide, flat feet. [7]One spring day, sitting on a bench in the park, she walked right past me. [8]Up close, her blonde hair looked thin, her bare legs were mapped with blue veins, and swollen ankles also were a problem. [9]She looked straight ahead as she walks, and a quiet dignity surrounded her like an eggshell enclosing a yolk. [10] She is still seen by me as she walks the city's streets and highways, and I always wonder how she lives, where she eats, and most of all, why she endlessly walks.

1. _____

2. _____

_____

3. _____

4. _____

5. _____

6. _____

7. _____

8. _____

9. _____

10. _____

CHAPTER 23

Sentences with Style

> 🖋 **Chapter Goal:** Write sentences that use vivid verbs and avoid overreliance on *to be* verbs or *there is/are* constructions; write sentences that use varied openings, structures, and lengths.

Style. Everyone wants it. Few have it.

Even sentences need style. This chapter will give you all the tips and tricks you need to make your sentences strut, sashay, and stride through your essays.

What is that indefinable thing called *style?* Perhaps you recognize it in the way someone dresses, performs a job, or interacts with others. Style is not always easy to pin down, but most people know it when they see it. Writing can have style, too. It can be a certain smoothness that makes reading seem effortless. It can be the surprise of a sudden change of pace. It can be the use of exactly the right word or the selection of verbs so lively that they practically jump off the page. Whatever it is, style is a quality to be desired.

Of course, you want to be clear and grammatically correct when you write. But that's just the beginning. If you want to be a writer who catches and holds a reader's attention, then you also want to write with style.

What adds style to your writing depends on many factors. Among them are your personality, your vocabulary, and your natural way of expressing yourself. Unless you are writing a police report, a description of a scientific experiment, or something else for which you deliberately conceal your natural mode of expression, the "you factor" should always come through in your writing.

Although style is partly an expression of who you are, it is also an expression of what you know: how large your vocabulary is, how well you know grammar, and how agile you are with sentence structure. This brief chapter presents a few tips and tricks of the trade that will start you on your way to writing sentences with style.

Style Tip 1: Limit Your Use of the Verb "To Be"

The verb *to be* in all its many forms (*is, are, was, were, has been, will be,* and so on) is a cornerstone of the English language, always there, always reliable. But writers can rely on it too much and too often.

Look at the following sentence. Notice the improvement when the verb *to be* is replaced by a more energetic verb.

✘ Anita *is* a server at the Blue Moon Café.

✔ Anita *waits tables* at the Blue Moon Café.

In some sentences, changing the verb *to be* can help eliminate words and make sentences more concise.

✘ Math *is* a subject that many students find intimidating.

✔ Math *intimidates* many students.

✘ Two puppies *were playing and tumbling* in the front yard.

✔ Two puppies *played and tumbled* in the front yard.

In other cases, eliminating the verb *to be* makes room for further detail. You can have fun with sentences like these.

✘ The diamond was huge.

✔ A huge diamond sparkled on her left hand.

✘ The truck was newly washed.

✔ The newly washed truck shone like glass in Jason's driveway.

Some sentences do not lend themselves to revision through removal of the verb *to be*. If that is the case, don't force it.

✗   Anne told us that her brother *was* a police detective.

✗   Anne told us that her brother detected . . . *no.*

✗   Anne told us that her brother fought crime . . . *no.*

✔   Anne told us that her brother *worked as* a police detective.

This change is acceptable, but not appreciably better than the sentence with *was*.

PRACTICE 1   REPLACING THE VERB *TO BE*

Rewrite the following sentences, replacing a form of the verb *to be* with a lively, well-chosen verb.

1.   The sun is a symbol of life and strength.

2.   The toddler was in his mother's arms.

3.   Jacob was struggling with his English homework.

4.   Art is a topic that many people find fascinating.

5.   Hannah is a teacher at Skyview Elementary School.

Rewrite the following sentences to replace the verb *to be* and to add detail.

6.   The clouds were fluffy.

7.   The prisoner's sentence was long.

8.   The bills were crisp and new.

9. The fireworks were loud.

   _____

10. The hamburger was juicy.

    _____

✎ Style Tip 2: Replace Ordinary Verbs with Vivid, Descriptive Verbs

The kite *flew* through the air, then *fell* into the trees below.

✔ The kite *soared* through the air, then *crashed* into the trees below.

Paul *put* money in his savings account every payday, hoping to accumulate enough for a used car.

✔ Paul *stashed* money in his savings account every payday, hoping to accumulate enough for a used car.

The gymnast did a series of cartwheels across the mat.

✔ The gymnast cartwheeled across the mat.

PRACTICE 2   USING VIVID VERBS

Replace ordinary verbs with vivid, descriptive verbs.

1. Clean laundry *hung* on a clothesline stretched between two buildings.

   _____

2. The hungry dog *ate* the piece of hamburger.

   _____

3. Glamorous models *proceeded* down the runway, showing off the designer's latest collection.

   _____

4. Rachel *put* on a coat before leaving her house.

   _____

5. As the child darted in front of the car, the driver *came* to a stop.

   _____

6. The leftover macaroni and cheese *heated* in the microwave.

   _____

7. The poodle, clipped and bathed by the groomer, *walked* happily at the end of his leash.

   _____

8. In the background, annoyingly loud rock music *played*.

   _____

9. Anita *held* a baseball bat in her right hand as she cautiously *walked* outside to investigate a noise in her back yard.

   _____

10. Roberto *lay* in a hammock stretched between two trees.

   _____

Style Tip 3: Revise Sentences That Begin with *There is* or *It is*

Sentences that begin with "There is" or "It is" (or "There are," "It was," and so on) often sound stiff and awkward. Revising them usually results in stronger sentences.

Sentences Beginning with *There is*

✗ There were three men standing at the door.

✔ Three men were standing (or better yet, *stood*) at the door.

✗ There is a bee crawling on Angela's shirt.

✔ A bee is crawling on Angela's shirt.

PRACTICE 3   REVISING SENTENCES THAT BEGIN WITH *THERE IS*

Revise the following sentences to eliminate *There is, There are, There was,* or *There were.*

1. There are flowers in window boxes at the front of the house.

   _____

2. In the morning, there was snow on the ground.

    _____

3. There is a lone goldfish in a bowl on a table by the wall.

    _____

4. There were fudgy fingerprints on the front of the white refrigerator.

    _____

5. There was a wreath of fall leaves on the front door.

    _____

Sentences Beginning with "It is"

Sentences that begin with *It is* are, too often, stiff, passive-voice nightmares. In some cases, fixing a sentence that begins with *It is* requires only chopping off the beginning of the sentence. In other cases, you may need to rewrite the entire sentence. Don't be afraid to scrap a bad sentence and substitute a good one.

✗   It is a fact that many people are depressed during the holidays.

    This sentence is easily fixed by removing the words "it is a fact that."

✔   Many people are depressed during the holidays.

✗   It is regrettable that John has chosen to leave the company.

    The solution to this sentence is a complete rewrite:

✔   John's decision to leave the company is regrettable.

✔   Everyone is sorry to see John leave the company.

PRACTICE 4   REVISING SENTENCES THAT BEGIN WITH *IT IS*

Revise the following sentences to eliminate *It is* constructions.

1. It is clear that I need better study habits.

    _____

2. It is understandable that you do not wish to incur any additional expense.

    _____

3. It is expected that all employees will conform to the dress code.

    _____

4. It is my opinion that trying to solve a problem works better than letting it solve itself.

_____

5. It is recommended that you make reservations in advance.

_____

Style Tip 4: Vary Sentence Openings

mywritinglab

Visit MyWriting Lab for additional practice varying sentence openings.

The most common sentence pattern in English is one that opens with a subject followed by a verb, as in the following sentences:

✔ The two horses ran across the finish line together in a photo finish.
✔ Dappled cows grazed peacefully in a field of bright green.

This pattern is common because it is strong and dynamic and gets the job done quickly. While you never want to give up this pattern, varying it can energize your writing. One of the easiest ways to vary the pattern is to open with a prepositional phrase.

Often, prepositional phrases appear at the end of a sentence:

✔ A yellow light shone from the window.
✔ Bob went to the deli during his lunch hour.

Occasionally, try beginning a sentence with a prepositional phrase:

✔ From the window, a yellow light shone.
✔ During his lunch hour, Bob went to the deli.

PRACTICE 5   BEGINNING SENTENCES WITH PREPOSITIONAL PHRASES

Rearrange each sentence to begin with a prepositional phrase.

1. Anna made a quick note of the appointment on a page of the calendar.

_____

2. Michael picked up the rain-soaked newspaper from the driveway.

_____

3. Perry heard wild laughter and loud music from the next room.

_____

4. The children played hopscotch on a chalk diagram.

_____

5. Bryan seemed quiet and shy at first.

_____

✍ Style Tip 5: Vary Sentence Structure and Length

One sure-fire way to keep a reader's interest is to vary sentence structure and length. If you fall into the habit of writing one-clause sentences that all have the subject first, followed immediately by the verb, your writing may fall into an unfortunate sing-song pattern. By the same token, if your sentences are all approximately the same length, inject some variety. Surprise the reader with a short, pithy sentence. Throw in a question. Begin a sentence with a prepositional phrase.

Varying your sentences is a skill that you will develop as you practice writing. It will come naturally as you become a better writer. For now, if you are not satisfied with the sentence variety in your essays, try editing your papers for sentence variety after you have written them.

In the following paragraph, all sentences have similar structure and length:

> A hummingbird feeder can provide hours of entertainment. Hummingbird feeders are readily available at discount and hardware stores. The feeders can be hung by a chain or attached to the window with a suction cup. They hold sugar water that is colored red to attract the hummingbirds. The hummingbirds spot the red liquid and come to feed. Their wings seem almost invisible because they move so rapidly. The birds are quite territorial and try to chase other hummingbirds away from the feeder. Hummingbirds are beautiful, jewel-toned birds. They are funny and fascinating and delightful to watch.

Look at the same paragraph, revised to vary sentence structure and length.

> A hummingbird feeder can provide hours of entertainment. Readily available at discount and hardware stores, the feeders can be hung by a chain or attached to the window with a suction cup. The feeders hold sugar water that is colored red to attract the hummingbirds. When the hummingbirds spot the red liquid, they come to feed, their wings moving so rapidly that they are almost invisible The beautiful, jewel-toned birds are quite territorial and try to chase other hummingbirds away from the feeder. They are funny and fascinating and delightful to watch.

PRACTICE 6   EDITING FOR SENTENCE VARIETY

The following paragraph has little sentence variety. Edit it to vary sentence length and structure.

The hallway was crowded. I had just ten minutes between classes. I needed to feed my soft drink addiction. I entered the little room off the main hallway. Brightly lit vending machines stood in a row. They invited onlookers to pop in a bill, a charge card, or several coins. Students crowded around the machines. I heard a muffled curse from the front of the crowd. Someone began to shake one of the machines. I heard someone else call, "Look out!" The large machine began to tip forward. People screamed and scattered out of the way. The heavy machine landed against the opposite wall with a crash. Everyone suddenly seemed in a hurry to get to class. I left, too. I headed for the stairs. I never did get my soft drink.

_____

_____

_____

_____

_____

_____

_____

_____

_____

mywritinglab   For support and practice meeting this chapter's goal, log in to www.mywritinglab.com and select **Varying Sentence Structure.**

CHAPTER 24

Commas

> **Chapter Goal:** Use commas correctly.

Unreliable Rules

"When in doubt, leave it out."

"Put a comma where there is a natural pause."

"Sprinkle them sparingly, like salt."

Comma rules exist in such abundance that, in desperation, people often resort to makeshift rules like the ones above. Unfortunately, these blanket statements don't always work. When it comes to commas, rules—and exceptions—abound. The rules presented in this chapter will give you a head start in coping with the complexities of comma usage.

Commas to Set Off Introductory Words, Phrases, and Clauses

mywritinglab

Visit MyWriting Lab for additional practice using commas.

Use commas after an introductory word, phrase, or clause.

Examples of Commas Used with Introductory Elements

✔ Instead, Van decided to take the summer off.

✔ The next morning, the newspaper reported the election results.

✔ Since the class did not meet yesterday, Mitzi spent the day in the library.

PRACTICE 1   USING COMMAS WITH INTRODUCTORY ELEMENTS

Insert commas after introductory words, phrases, and clauses.

1. Reluctantly the instructor agreed to postpone the test.

   _____

2. When Kim plays video games she shuts out the world.

   _____

3. During the seventh-inning stretch Harry Caray used to lead the fans in "Take Me Out to the Ball Game."

   _____

   _____

4. In fact the car has had very few problems.

   _____

5. Yawning loudly Eric said, "Is it morning already?"

   _____

Commas to Join Items in a Series

mywritinglab

Visit MyWriting Lab for additional practice using commas.

When a series of three or more words, phrases, or clauses is connected with *and* or *or*, place a comma after each item except the last one. The final comma goes before *and* or *or*.

Real-World Writing

In journalism, it is becoming customary to omit the comma before *and, or,* or *nor* when items are joined in a series. Academic usage is more traditional and favors keeping the final comma.

Examples of Commas Used to Join Items in a Series

✔ Iguanas, chameleons, and salamanders were Ted's passion when he was seven.

✔ Motorcycles, off-road vehicles, and cars are his passion at seventeen.

✔ The dog had tracked mud across the porch, into the kitchen, and up the stairs.

✔ The doctor asked Neville if the pain occurred before he ate, after he ate, or while he ate.

If only two items appear in the series, no comma is used.

✔ Stacy said her two worst vices were soap operas and talk shows.

✔ Arnold was slowed by a traffic tie-up in the tunnel and a wreck near the downtown connector.

✔ Jason takes care of his parents because they are old and because they once took care of him.

PRACTICE 2   USING COMMAS TO JOIN ITEMS IN A SERIES

Insert commas to join words, phrases, and clauses in a series of three or more. Write *correct* below the sentence that does not need a comma.

1. Mycology is the study of yeasts molds mushrooms and other fungi.

   _____

2. The ancient Maya restricted the consumption of cocoa to the aristocracy because of the cost of growing the beans and the labor involved in processing them.

   _____

3. The dog looked as if he had been dipped in water coated with dirt and set out to dry.

   _____

4. The children watched in fascination as the magician reached into his hat pulled out a dove and released it into the air.

   _____

5. Students screamed as the lights flickered the alarm sounded and the elevator jerked to a halt.

   _____

Commas to Join Independent Clauses

mywritinglab

Visit MyWriting Lab for additional practice using commas.

Use a comma with a FANBOYS conjunction (*for, and, nor, but, or, yet, so*) to join independent clauses.

Examples of Commas Used to Join Independent Clauses

✔ Harrison thought that researching would be the easy part of his project, but it turned out to be the hardest.

✔ I feel exhausted already, and tomorrow is just Tuesday.

✔ Karen's sinus medication makes her sleepy, so she avoids taking it during the day.

Do not use a comma if the FANBOYS connects verb to verb rather than clause to clause. In other words, do not use a comma unless there is a complete sentence on both sides of the FANBOYS.

✔ Ernestine lay in a hammock and read a book.

✔ Nick looked for his glasses but couldn't find them.

✔ Alberto couldn't decide whether to sign up for biology in the fall or wait until spring.

PRACTICE 3   Using Commas to Join Independent Clauses

Place commas before FANBOYS conjunctions that join two independent clauses. One of the sentences does not need a comma.

1. The weeds were tall and the mower died whenever Helen tried to cut through them.

   _____

2. The upholstery was worn and faded but the couch was still comfortable.

   _____

3. Leo received a credit card in the mail but did not remember requesting it.

   _____

4. Lorenzo was studying so he let the answering machine pick up his calls.

   _____

5. "You can pay now or you can take up to ninety days to pay on our easy credit plan," said the salesclerk.

   _____

✎ Commas Around Interrupters

mywritinglab

Visit MyWriting Lab for additional practice using commas.

An **interrupter** is a word, phrase, or clause inserted into a sentence to give more information about some element within the sentence. An interrupter is never essential to the structure of the sentence. If you took it out, the sentence would still make perfect sense.

Examples of Commas Used Around Interrupters

✔ The dog, his tail wagging, bounded toward his owner.
✔ The student, disappointed by her grades, withdrew from the course at midterm.

PRACTICE 4   USING COMMAS AROUND INTERRUPTERS

Insert commas around interrupters in the following sentences.

1. The interruption brief as it was distracted Heather and made it hard for her to focus on her work again.

   _____

2. Mr. Angelo a friend of my family runs the delicatessen on Third Street.

   _____

3. Breanna sighing heavily opened her book to study.

   _____

4. The banana apparently left by one of the children lay forgotten in the back seat until it shriveled and turned brown.

   _____

5. The peace symbol which appeared in 1958 is popular again in the twenty-first century.

   _____

✎ Commas with Direct Quotations

mywritinglab

Visit MyWriting Lab for additional practice using commas.

A **direct quotation** is an exact repetition of the words that someone speaks or thinks. The rules governing the punctuation of direct quotations are outlined on the next page.

1. When a direct quotation is followed by a tag (such as *he said*), a comma goes after the quoted words and *in front of the quotation mark*:

    ✔ "I think I can find the information I need on the Internet," Javier said.

2. When a tag leads into a direct quotation, a comma goes after the tag and *in front of the quotation mark*:

    ✔ Sophie said, "If I had the time, I would audit a world history class."

3. When a sentence is written as a split quotation, commas are placed *in front of the quotation marks*:

    ✔ "If it had not been for Hal," said the supervisor, "I don't know what we would have done."

PRACTICE 5   USING COMMAS WITH DIRECT QUOTATIONS

Insert commas to set off direct quotations in the following sentences.

1. Karin asked "Would you mind helping me move this ladder?"

    _____

2. "If you are not going to watch television" said Patrick "let me have the remote control."

    _____

3. "I can never remember where I put my keys" said Mike.

    _____

4. "You may like that herbal tea" said Gerry "but it tastes like dishwater to me."

    _____

5. Ben Franklin said "Lost time is never found again."

    _____

Commas in Names and Dates

mywritinglab
Visit MyWriting Lab for additional practice using commas.

When a professional title or family designation follows a name, it is set off with commas.

✔ The woman's name tag read, "Judy Smith, L.P.N."
✔ Raymond J. Johnson, C.P.A., rented an office on Second Street.

When you write the month, day, and year, a comma goes between the day and year.

✔ The Declaration of Independence was signed on July 4, 1776.

When you write just the month and year, no comma is used.

✔ The Declaration of Independence was signed in July 1776.

PRACTICE 6   USING COMMAS IN NAMES AND DATES

Insert commas as needed in the following sentences. One sentence needs no comma.

1. Dave says he quit smoking on January 1 2011.

2. The letter was addressed to Jeana S. Reynolds D.D.S., but there was no return address.

3. Avery says he will graduate in June 2014.

4. Carla Anderson C.P.A. will hold a seminar on the new tax laws.

5. Jonathan Burns M.D. has been our family doctor for five years.

✎ Review Exercises

Complete the Review Exercises to see how well you have learned the skills addressed in this chapter. As you work through the exercises, go back through the chapter to review any of the rules you do not understand completely.

REVIEW EXERCISE 1   USING COMMAS IN SENTENCES

Insert commas where they are needed in the following sentences.

1. Infotainment is a store that sells books video games and movies.

2. In fact only 12 percent of the students surveyed said they had seriously considered dropping out during their year of college.

_____

3. Kudzu a vine native to Japan now flourishes throughout the South.

_____

4. At the end of June 2012 Felicia graduated from the university.

_____

5. As the plane disappeared into the clouds Andrea turned away from the window and walked slowly toward the parking lot.

_____

6. Broken shells dead jellyfish and tangled seaweed were left behind by the receding tide.

_____

7. Darlene knew she was too ill to work but she still felt guilty about calling in sick.

_____

8. The DVD had a gummy substance on it and Raoul was afraid to put it into the player.

_____

9. A graduation tassel a pair of fuzzy dice and a pine air freshener hung from the car's rearview mirror.

_____

10. Renaldo the dispatcher on duty said that it had been a quiet night.

_____

| REVIEW EXERCISE 2 | USING COMMAS IN SENTENCES |

Insert commas where they are needed in the following sentences.

1. Kelly studied for her exam ate dinner and went to bed early.

_____

2. Dr. Chitra Banerjee D.D.S. was highlighted in a local newspaper as the area's best dentist.

_____

_____

3. Because the forecast predicted heavy snowfall school was cancelled.

   _____

4. James hoping for a parking space close to the stadium was disappointed to see a small car tucked into what he had thought was an empty parking space.

   _____

   _____

5. Eager to soak up the sun students swarmed the local beaches.

   _____

6. Jessica desperate for a day off from work lied to her manager.

   _____

7. The coffeeshop was filled with students studying chatting and drinking caffienated beverages.

   _____

   _____

8. The website listed the lawyer as Mark Ortega J.D.

   _____

9. When she came home for the weekend Sandra visited her favorite restaurant.

   _____

10. Paul went to the grocery store to pick up milk oranges and bread.

    _____

REVIEW EXERCISE 3   USING COMMAS CORRECTLY

Insert commas where they are needed in the following sentences. Each question contains two types of problems that require the addition of a comma or commas.

1. "I can be a full-time student" said Kasey "or I can be a full-time worker. However I can't do both."

   _____

   _____

2. Because Ashley won the coin toss she was the one who chose the toppings for the pizza. She ordered mushrooms black olives onions and pepperoni.

   _____

   _____

3. Putting toe tags on the preserved frogs planting clues to point to the "murderer" and letting the students serve as coroners were ways to get students interested in dissection. "Science can be fun as well as educational" said the teacher.

    _____

    _____

    _____

4. The apartment was small cramped and dark. "I can't believe the landlord wants $500 a month for this place" said Felice.

    _____

    _____

5. "The label on this freezer bag says June 6 2010," Harold told his wife. "Should I throw the bag away or should we keep it as a souvenir?

    _____

    _____

REVIEW EXERCISE 4   USING COMMAS CORRECTLY

Insert commas where they are needed in the following sentences.

1. Even as an adult Jamie remembers a particular Christmas from his childhood. On the evening of December 24 1999, Santa Claus did not visit the Thaxton household.

    _____

    _____

2. Sounding cranky Melissa sleepily answered the phone. "This had better be important" she told the caller.

    _____

    _____

3. As he came in from his morning run Andre kissed his daughter. "You smell like an old, sweaty shoe" she told him.

    _____

    _____

4. Clouds slid in from the west and the wind began to pick up. "At least the rain will cool things off" said Calvin.

    _____

    _____

5. A golf ball had smashed through the window striking a mirror. Glass lay on the windowsill on the floor and on the arm of the sofa.

    _____

    _____

REVIEW EXERCISE 5   EDITING A PARAGRAPH FOR COMMA USE

Insert commas where they are needed in the paragraph below. Each sentence contains one type of comma problem, which may require more than one comma to correct.

[1]For many people waiting is a fact of life. [2]People wait in train stations doctor's offices and employment offices. [3]However people's attitudes about waiting are even more interesting and varied than the places where they wait. [4]My dentist Jack Davis values his time and his patients' time. [5]"I hate to wait" he says "so I don't keep my patients waiting, either." [6]Some people become angry and they make sure that those who keep them waiting get the message. [7]One of my neighbors once told me "If I'm kept waiting more than an hour, I send a bill for my time." [8]Other people endowed with more philosophical natures try to make waiting productive. [9]These are the people who are seen in airport terminals and doctors' offices reading books knitting or catching up on their correspondence. [10]Though some endure it more patiently than others waiting is a fact of life for everyone.

1. _____

2. _____

3. _____

4. _____

5. _____

6. _____

7. _____

8. _____

9. _____

10. _____

mywritinglab   For support and practice meeting this chapter's goal, log in to www.mywritinglab.com and select Commas.

CHAPTER 25

Other Punctuation

Chapter Goal: Use periods, exclamation points, quotation marks, semicolons, colons, dashes, and parentheses correctly.

When Punctuation Attacks

Punctuation marks other than the comma are the focus of this chapter. Some of these punctuation marks, such as the period and the question mark, are quite familiar to you. Others, such as the dash and the colon, are more exotic and less often used. This chapter reinforces the familiar and introduces the less familiar marks of punctuation.

End Punctuation: Period, Question Mark, and Exclamation Point

mywritinglab

Visit MyWriting Lab for additional practice with end punctuation.

The period, the question mark, and the exclamation point are all forms of **end punctuation**; that is, they signal the end of a sentence.

The Period

The **period** is used to mark the end of a sentence that makes a statement.

Examples of Periods to End Sentences

✔ The GPS units advertised at Electronix Unlimited were gone by the time Frank got there.

✔ The elephant's trunk was ringed with deep wrinkles.

Periods are also used to signal an appropriate abbreviation. Except for abbreviations in courtesy titles, such as *Mr., Ms., Dr.,* and *Rev.,* used before proper names, do not abbreviate words in your paragraphs and essays.

Examples of Periods to Denote Abbreviations

✘ Jas. has an appt. with the dr. on Wed. afternoon.

✔ James has an appointment with the doctor on Wednesday afternoon.

✔ James has an appointment with Dr. Davis on Wednesday afternoon.

The Question Mark

A **question mark** is used at the end of a direct question.

✔ What time are we leaving?

✔ Did you know that the bar code system used in retailing was invented in 1970?

No question mark is used with an indirect question.

✔ I wonder why Ursula always wears black.

✔ Mr. Smith asked why the meeting was being held on Friday.

The Exclamation Point

Exclamation points are used to show extreme excitement or surprise. They are seldom needed in a college essay. Unless you are quoting someone who has just discovered that the building is on fire (or has another reason for extreme excitement), there will be few opportunities to use an exclamation point. Interjections such as "Ouch!" and "Yikes!" are followed by exclamation points but are seldom needed for college writing. So use exclamation points when you quote someone who is shouting or speaking excitedly. Otherwise, let your words, not your punctuation, convey the excitement of your essay.

Examples of Clumsy versus Effective Use of Exclamation Points

✗   I noticed an orange glow under the door, and I realized that my house was on fire!

✔   I noticed an orange glow under the door, and I realized that my house was on fire.

✗   I reached for the doorknob! It was hot!

✔   I panicked and reached for the doorknob. It was as hot as a live coal.

✔   "Fire!" I yelled.

PRACTICE 1   USING END PUNCTUATION AND APPROPRIATE ABBREVIATIONS

In each sentence, correct an inappropriate abbreviation or place a period after an appropriate abbreviation. Then place end punctuation (period, question mark, or exclamation point) where needed.

1. Did Rev Madison really order fourteen boxes of your daughter's Girl Scout cookies

_____

2. I asked the prof if I could make up the test, but she said it was too late

_____

3. "Look out" Ms Muller yelled as the child stepped into the path of the oncoming truck.

_____

_____

4. Aunt Daisy wants to know if we can take our vacation in Oct to come to the family reunion

_____

_____

5. After I graduate, I hope to work for a big automobile corp like Ford

_____

_____

The Semicolon

Semicolon to Join Independent Clauses

mywritinglab

Visit MyWriting Lab for additional practice with the semicolon.

A **semicolon** may be used with a transitional expression between independent clauses or may be used alone between independent clauses that are closely related. (For a more detailed discussion of this use of the semicolon, see Chapter 16, "Run-on Sentences.")

Examples of Semicolons to Join Independent Clauses

✔ The office's trash can was much too small; it had to be emptied twice a day.

✔ Elise was half an hour late; furthermore, she took an extra fifteen minutes for lunch.

Semicolon to Join Items in a List

Ordinarily, items in a list are joined by commas. However, if the items themselves contain commas, avoid confusion by using semicolons to join the items.

Examples of Semicolons to Join Items in a List

✔ The plane made stops in Richmond, Virginia; Atlanta, Georgia; and Houston, Texas.

✔ The journal article was written by Samuel Ellis; Jametta Holly, Ph.D.; and Laramie Spicer, M.D.

PRACTICE 2   USING SEMICOLONS

Use semicolons in the following sentences to join independent clauses or items in a series.

1. The crowd fell silent not even a cough could be heard.

   _____

2. Mike's performance on the tennis court was better than usual however, he still lost the match.

   _____

   _____

3. Almost everyone knows what happened on July 4, 1776 December 7, 1941 and September 11, 2001.

   _____

   _____

4. In spite of her poor prognosis, the woman did not die in fact, she outlived her doctor.

   _____

   _____

5. The cathedral gave the impression of immense height its spires seemed to reach the clouds.

   _____

   _____

✐ Colons and Dashes: Formal and Informal Punctuation

The Colon

mywritinglab

Visit MyWriting Lab for additional practice with colons and dashes.

The **colon** is used to introduce a list, a restatement, or a clarification. The single most important thing to remember when you use a colon is that a complete sentence *always* comes before the colon.

A colon is sometimes used to introduce a list. A complete sentence must come before the colon.

Examples of a Colon to Introduce a List

✗   In her purse, Dot carried: a pen, a checkbook, her credit card, and a lipstick.

This sentence is incorrect because a complete sentence does not come before the colon. Below, the sentence is corrected.

✔   In her purse, Dot carried the necessities: a pen, a checkbook, her credit card, and a lipstick.

It is also correct—and sometimes simpler—to integrate a list into a sentence without using a colon.

✔   In her purse, Dot carried a pen, a checkbook, her credit card, and a lipstick.

A colon is used to introduce a restatement or clarification of an idea. A complete sentence must come before the colon.

Examples of a Colon to Introduce a Restatement or Clarification

✔   Brian says his kids have just one method of locomotion: running.

The word *running* restates and clarifies *method of locomotion.* It is introduced with a colon.

✔   The workers were enthusiastic in their praise of Ed's managerial style: He believed in fixing the problem, not in fixing the blame.

The colon introduces a clarification of *Ed's managerial style.*

The Dash

While the colon is a formal mark of punctuation, the **dash** is an informal mark. Like a colon, a dash is used to introduce a list, restatement, or clarification. A dash is also used to set off material that a writer wants to emphasize.

A dash introduces a list or restatement. When used in this way, a dash must be preceded by a complete sentence. A dash is typed as two hyphens, with no spaces before or after.

Example of a Dash to Introduce a List

✔   In her purse, Dot carried the necessities—a pen, a checkbook, her credit card, and a lipstick.

The dash is used here to introduce a list of the items in Dot's purse.

Example of a Dash to Introduce a Restatement

✔ Brian says his kids have just one method of locomotion—running.

The dash is used here to introduce a restatement and clarification of *method of locomotion.*

A dash is used to set off material that the writer wants to emphasize.

Examples of Dashes Used to Emphasize

✔ It was her kindness—not her money or her fame—that made people love her.

A more formal way of punctuating this sentence would be to use commas to set off the interrupter.

✔ It was her kindness, not her money or her fame, that made people love her.

✔ The office was such a mess—books scattered on the floor, papers and unopened mail stacked on the desk—that Natalie was not sure where to start.

One way of expressing the idea in the sentence more formally would be to use two sentences.

✔ The office was such a mess that Natalie was not sure where to start. Books were scattered on the floor; papers and unopened mail were stacked on the desk.

Parentheses: Tools of Understatement

mywritinglab

Visit MyWriting Lab for additional practice with parentheses.

While dashes emphasize, **parentheses** downplay or de-emphasize. Parentheses are used to enclose material that a reader could skip over without missing the more important ideas.

Examples of Parentheses Used to De-emphasize

✔ The Drama Club will meet in the Humanities Conference Room (Room 222, Stetson Hall) at 1:00 P.M. on Tuesday, May 26.

✔ Ann knew the apartment was not for her. She hated the color of the walls (mint green), didn't like the location (Bass Road), and was horrified at the price ($800 per month).

PRACTICE 3   USING COLONS, DASHES, AND PARENTHESES

Rewrite each of the following sentences as indicated, punctuating the italicized portion of the sentence with a colon, a dash (or dashes), or parentheses.

1.   Jeremy brought several items with him to the beach. He brought a radio, a Frisbee, a beach towel, sun block, and a cooler filled with sandwiches and soft drinks.

     Directions: Rewrite as one sentence, with a colon introducing the list. Remove words as needed.

     _____

     _____

2.   Tiana bought her textbook, *Understanding Psychology*, secondhand for only eighteen dollars.

     Directions: De-emphasize the title of the textbook.

     _____

     _____

3.   Professor Jones says that if he were stranded on a desert island, he would need just one thing: *a copy of the complete works of Shakespeare.*

     Directions: Set off the restatement in an informal way rather than a formal way.

     _____

     _____

4.   The tie (*the same one he wore every Friday*) was black with bright yellow happy faces.

     Directions: Emphasize the parenthetical material. Assume that the context is informal.

     _____

     _____

5.   The speaker emphasized the difficulties of entrepreneurship—the long hours, the crushing responsibility, and the uncertainty that the hard work will pay off.

     Directions: Introduce the list in a formal way.

     _____

     _____

✍ Review Exercises

Complete the Review Exercises to see how well you have learned the skills addressed in this chapter. As you work through the exercises, go back through the chapter to review any of the rules you do not understand completely.

REVIEW EXERCISE 1   **EXPLAINING THE RULES USED TO PUNCTUATE SENTENCES**

Look at the punctuation printed in color in each sentence; then briefly explain the rule that justifies its use. The first one is done for you.

1. Maryann said she needed only three simple things: food, shelter, and unlimited money.

   _____

2. The hamburger—the first thing I had eaten all day—was juicy and delicious.

   _____

3. "Wait! You forgot your change!" the cashier called after the customer.

   _____

   _____

4. Hazel's exams are on Friday, May 18; Monday, May 22; and Wednesday, May 23.

   _____

   _____

5. The review exercise was long and tedious; Carol thought she would never finish.

   _____

   _____

REVIEW EXERCISE 2   **CHOOSING CORRECT PUNCTUATION**

Fill the blank(s) in each sentence with a period, question mark, exclamation point, semicolon, colon, dash (or dashes), or parentheses. For some questions, more than one answer may be possible. Be sure you can justify the answer you choose.

1. Sam slowed to 75 when he saw the car ___ the one with the siren and flashing lights ___ pull up behind him.

   _____

2. Though the 1960s were a time of political passion, concern for the environ-ment, and dedication to peace and equality, they are linked to less elevated pursuits by a slogan of sixties_ "Sex, drugs, and rock and roll."

_____

3. "Run for your lives_" the firefighter shouted.

_____

4. The requirement can be fulfilled by taking an American history course _History 2510 or 2520_ or by taking an exam.

_____

5. "Curses_" spat the villain, twirling his black mustache.

_____

6. Holidays will be observed on Thursday, November 27_ Friday, November 28_ Thursday, December 26_ and Friday, December 27.

_____

7. The pushpin had fallen from the bulletin board and lodged in the rug behind the desk_ Marcie hoped Gato would not eat it.

_____

8. "Why was I born_ Why do I exist_" Arturo moaned, banging his head on the desk.

_____

9. Crumpling his test paper into a ball, Martin felt himself seized by quiet determination_ he would not fail again.

_____

_____

10. The change in Brad's pocket ____ two quarters and a nickel ____ was not enough to get a snack from the vending machine.

_____

_____

REVIEW EXERCISE 3	PUNCTUATING SENTENCES

In each sentence, add a period, question mark, exclamation point, semicolon, colon, dash (or dashes), or parentheses.

1. "Stop" Julia screamed as the mugger dashed off with her purse

_____

2. "Do you want to lose ten pounds in ten minutes a day" asked the late night infomercial

_____

_____

3. After listening to today's lecture in her medical ethics class, Janet wondered what her opinion on the issue of stem cells was

_____

_____

4. Most of the time, Ingrid was confident that social work was the right major for her however, she could not help but wonder if she should switch to a field with higher income potential.

_____

_____

_____

5. Have you tried using a high quality olive oil the kind available only in specialty markets in your pasta sauce

_____

_____

6. The article's title took the form of a question "Is Happiness in Our Genes?"

_____

7. The list of interesting majors nursing, education, and history, among others made Alissa shake her head in confusion.

_____

_____

8. The awards were presented to the following students: Sam Wao, Biology Award Jorge Donoghue, Mathematics Award Amy Nguyen, Outstanding Social Sciences Student Award and Dan Jones, Mentor Program Award.

_____

_____

_____

9. The Caribbean cruise was scheduled to make several stops Jamaica, Martinique, Puerto Rico, and Anguilla.

_____

_____

10. Audrey's jeans faded with several holes in the legs were not permitted according to the dress code

_____

_____

| REVIEW EXERCISE 4 | EDITING A PARAGRAPH FOR PUNCTUATION |

Fill in the blanks with the correct punctuation.

^{1}My Aunt Susie has been trying to lose weight ___ she calls it "the battle of the bulge"___ for at least forty years. ^{2}She says that weight control has changed in three ways over the years _ the foods allowed, the role of calorie counting, and the emphasis on exercise. ^{3}When she first began trying to lose weight, her family physician _ who has since retired _ told her to cut out all breads. ^{4}Dr_ Smith told her to eat plenty of protein, including bacon and beef. Now, bread is allowed on diets _ however, meats are limited. ^{5}Aunt Susie also remembers making lists and writing down every calorie she ate: one carrot, 25 calories _ one chocolate chip cookie, 100 calories _ one slice of bread, 60 calories. ^{6}When she went on her latest diet, she asked, "Should I count calories _ ^{7}Her nutritionist told her that today, the emphasis is on watching fat intake and eating nutritiously _ very low calorie diets are strictly discouraged. ^{8}In the past, doctors prescribed one exercise _ pushing away from the table. ^{9}Now, the leader of Aunt Susie's diet group ends each meeting by yelling, "Get out there and move _ ^{10}Methods of weight loss have changed _ unfortunately, losing weight remains as difficult as ever.

mywritinglab   For support and practice meeting this chapter's goal, log in to **www.MyWritingLab.com** and select **Final Punctuation** and **Semicolons, Colons, Dashes, and Parentheses.**

CHAPTER 26

Word Choice

> 📝 **Chapter Goal:** Identify and eliminate slang, clichés, wordiness, and conversational constructions in your writing.

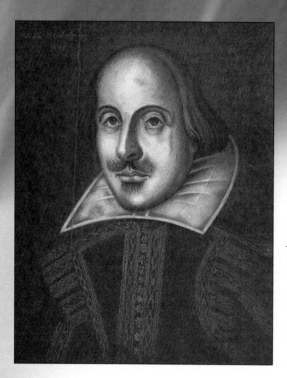

"Here are a few of the most unpleasant'st words that ever blotted paper!"

—The Merchant of Venice, *Act iii, Scene 2*

Would Shakespeare have used the words above to describe slang or textspeak? Probably not. Shakespeare enjoyed language in all its forms. He also knew that different types of language had different uses. If the Bard of Avon were alive and attending college with you today, he might send you a text that said "LOL! Srsly, dude?" but he would never use textspeak in his history research paper.

With so many ways to speak and write, it is no surprise that word choice can be problematic. We all use different levels of language depending on the situation. In a single day, you may shift your way of speaking several times, bringing out your best grammar and vocabulary for a job interview, speaking simply and in short sentences to a child, and using slang or even profanity with good friends. Most people make these shifts automatically, without much thought.

Similarly, it is necessary to make shifts in the way you write. The language you use for texting is not the same language you use in an email to your parents. The language you use to write a paper in your English class is not the same language you use to post messages on a social networking site. Shifting from one form of writing to another is one of the skills that everyone needs. This chapter helps you fine-tune that skill and recognize categories of word choice that are generally not appropriate for college writing: slang, clichés, wordiness, and conversational constructions.

Slang and Textspeak

mywritinglab

Visit MyWriting Lab for additional practice avoiding slang and textspeak.

People enjoy using **slang** because it is informal, up to the minute, and fun. **Textspeak** or *txtspk* is the abbreviated language that people use to send text messages on cell phones or online in chat rooms. Just as a common language is a bond among those who speak it, so is slang or textspeak a bond among the members of the groups that use it. Yet the very things that make slang and textspeak appealing make these types of language unsuitable for writing to a broad audience.

Writing requires a common language and is usually more formal than conversation. Slang expressions are informal and tend to go out of date quickly. No writer wants to use words that may be out of date and even laughable years later. Slang expressions such as *the bee's knees, hunky-dory,* and *daddy-o* may have sounded up to the minute decades ago, but now they are relics of another time.

Textspeak is a relatively new form of abbreviated written language that is mainly used in text messages and sometimes in emails, online posts, and chat rooms. Textspeak uses acronyms, words formed from the first letter of each word in an expression. Thus, *laughing out loud* becomes *LOL.* Single letters can stand in for words: *See* becomes *c,* and *you* becomes *u.* Sometimes, numbers are used as part of a word, and *later* becomes *l8r,* or *anyone* becomes *ne1.* Vowels are also omitted from words to shorten them; the word *vowels,* for instance, might be shortened to *vwls.*

Group Exercise 1 Discussing Slang Terms and Textspeak

Form small groups. Try to include both sexes and as many different ages and ethnic groups as possible. Each group member should write down five slang terms and five textspeak terms and then share the list with other group members.

Are some of the terms different? (The more diverse the group, the more likely that it will generate a variety of slang and texting terms.) Are there any expressions that not all group members are familiar with? What conclusions can the group draw about the use of slang and textspeak? Choose one spokesperson to report the group's findings, along with a few of the most interesting terms, to the class.

PRACTICE 1   AVOIDING SLANG

Underline the two slang expressions in each sentence; then substitute more traditional word choices.

1. I decided that Vincent van Gogh was a few sandwiches short of a picnic, especially after I read that the dude had cut off his own ear.

   _____

   _____

2. Raymond was supposed to take an exam yesterday, but he blew it off so he could catch a few z's.

   _____

   _____

3. Allison bombed her test because she never hit the books.

   _____

4. We were hyper about the exam, but the professor told us to chill.

   _____

5. Sam was all about getting new rims for his car but he did not have enough dead presidents to buy them.

   _____

   _____

PRACTICE 2   AVOIDING TEXTSPEAK

Underline the two textspeak expressions in each sentence; then substitute more traditional word choices.

1. Catherine was LOL at the new comedy, she thought it was gr8.

   _____

2. Romeo and Juliet thought that their <3 would last 4eva, but their lives were tragically cut short.

_____

3. If ur thinking about changing majors, b sure to visit the career counseling center to research employment opportunities in the new field of study.

_____

4. Our professor gave us the 411 on Renaissance art and said we would have a quiz l8r in the week.

_____

5. My BFF called me to tell me the latest on her problems with her boyfriend, but I had to tell her it was TMI.

_____

Clichés

mywritinglab

Visit MyWriting Lab for additional practice avoiding clichés.

While slang is fresh and new, **clichés** are expressions used so often for so long that they have become worn out. The cliché *burn the midnight oil,* for instance, is a relic of a time when working until midnight meant lighting an oil lamp. Because they are easy to remember and widely used, clichés are often the first expressions that come to mind. It takes a deliberate effort to recognize them and eliminate them from your writing. Look at the following list of clichés. Can you think of others?

a heart of gold	cream of the crop	handwriting on the wall
apple of my eye	dead as a doornail	happy as a clam
at the drop of a hat	eat like a bird	on thin ice
burn the midnight oil	fit as a fiddle	sick as a dog

PRACTICE 3   AVOIDING CLICHÉS

Underline the two clichés in each sentence; then rewrite the sentence to eliminate the clichés.

1. Some older people become sick or depressed, but my grandmother is fit as a fiddle and happy as a clam.

_____

_____

2. Sara eats like a horse, but she is still as thin as a rail.

    _____

3. I heard that Mrs. Jones was as sick as a dog and probably not long for this world.

    _____

4. When office gossip landed Kerry in hot water with her boss, she decided to take the bull by the horns.

    _____

    _____

5. Preston has been on thin ice at work for some time now, and if you ask me, the handwriting is on the wall.

    _____

    _____

Wordiness

Wordiness sometimes happens when writers do not take the time to be concise. The shortest and simplest way of expressing an idea is usually the best way.

The following words and phrases contribute to wordiness and can usually be omitted:

actually	~~actually~~ often unnecessary
basically	~~basically~~ performs no function in most sentences
definitely	is ~~definitely~~ a space-waster
in my opinion	usually weakens a sentence ~~in my opinion~~
really	not ~~really~~ necessary
the fact is that	~~The fact is that~~ Facts, like opinions, can usually be stated without preamble
seriously	~~seriously~~ overused
totally	usually ~~totally~~ unnecessary
very	can ~~very~~ often be omitted

The following phrases are wordy and can usually be shortened and strengthened.

Wordy	Concise
at the present time	now, today
due to the fact that	because, since
for the reason that	because, since
in point of fact	in fact
in today's society	today
long in length	long
we as people	we, people

Examples

✗ The course was *definitely* a good introduction to the *basic fundamentals* of algebra.

✔ The course was a good introduction to the fundamentals of algebra.

✗ *Due to the fact that* we are understaffed *at the present time*, Linda has a good chance of being hired.

✔ Since we are understaffed, Linda has a good chance of being hired.

PRACTICE 4   ELIMINATING WORDINESS

Rewrite the sentences to eliminate wordiness.

1. During the solar eclipse of the sun, the light outside seemed blue in color.

   _____

2. In my opinion, we as people often make judgments based on first impressions.

   _____

3. The form basically asked us to write down the annual salary that we receive each year.

   _____

4. In point of fact, the key to success in today's society is a good education.

   _____

5. I found it hard to get up at six A.M. in the morning due to the fact that I had studied until midnight.

   _____

Conversational Constructions

mywritinglab

Visit MyWriting Lab for additional practice avoiding clichés.

Sometimes it's hard to strike just the right tone when you write an informal paper. Even the word "informal" can be somewhat misleading. It is not an invitation to sprinkle a paper with *LOL*s and smiley faces. In college-level writing, an informal paper is one in which contractions and the pronoun *I* are probably permitted, as opposed to a formal research paper, which must be cast in formal, third-person language throughout. When you write an informal paper, you strive for a conversational tone, one that does not distance the reader, one that sounds natural as opposed to stiff and stilted. It's an upgraded, edited version of your own unique voice. One way to achieve that voice is to ruthlessly edit out the filler words and phrases that characterize so many conversations and emails. Many of them are perfectly legitimate words that are used as filler in conversation. When people speak, they often use filler words, phrases, or sounds to give themselves time to think *(well, uh, you know)* or to be funny or trendy *(well DUH)*. Usually, these **conversational constructions** can simply be edited out of your paper. They will never be missed.

Conversational Constructions to Eliminate from Your Writing

- *Gonna*, a conversational shortening of "going to"
- *I mean,* when used without purpose, as in "It must have been 100 degrees yesterday. I mean, you could have fried an egg on the asphalt."
- *man,* when used as an interjection, as in, "Man, I had no idea what was happening."
- *Okay,* when used to open a sentence.
- *plus,* when used to mean "and"
- *so,* when used without purpose, as in, "So what is your major?"
- substandard substitutions for "said" such as *was all, was like, goes, or went*
- *this or these,* when used as adjectives to demonstrate something that is not present for the writer or the reader, as in "My neighbor had this dog" (My neighbor had a dog) or "The restaurant had these shrimp basted in wine" (The restaurant had shrimp basted in wine).
- *well,* when used to open a sentence
- *well,* DUH, under any circumstances
- *you know,* when used to open a sentence or as a sentence filler, as in "Jamie was, you know, not very happy with her instructor."

Examples

✗ The job candidate was overqualified for the job as hotel desk clerk. *I mean,* she had managed a resort hotel in Florida. *Plus* she had a master's degree from a prestigious college.

✔ The job candidate was overqualified for the job as hotel desk clerk. She had managed a resort hotel in Florida and had a master's degree from a prestigious college.

✗ When Baxter asked the professor if he could turn his paper in late, the professor *was all,* "What does the syllabus say?" Baxter was like, "*Well, DUH!* If I knew that, I would not be asking."

✔ When Baxter asked the professor if he could turn his paper in late, the professor said, "What does the syllabus say?" Baxter said, "If I knew that, I would not be asking."

PRACTICE 5   ELIMINATING CONVERSATIONAL CONSTRUCTIONS

Rewrite the sentences to eliminate conversational constructions.

1. Seriously, dude, that was a ruby-throated hummingbird hovering over the trumpet vine.

    _____

2. We study literature because it, like, reflects the age in which it was written, plus it helps us understand ourselves.

    _____

    _____

3. So when Joseph saw the time, he knew he would be late for math class, plus the professor was giving a test.

    _____

4. The veterinarian was all, "If people would routinely spay or neuter their animals, then shelters would not be overflowing with unwanted pets." Well, DUH.

    _____

    _____

5. Udder Delights is an ice cream shop that has these banana splits that are, like, the best I've ever had.

    _____

✐ Review Exercises

Complete the Review Exercises to see how well you have learned the skills addressed in this chapter. As you work through the exercises, go back through the chapter to review any of the rules you do not understand completely.

| REVIEW EXERCISE 1 | IDENTIFYING AND CORRECTING WORD CHOICE PROBLEMS |

In the blanks, indicate whether the italicized expressions are slang, textspeak, clichés, wordiness, or conversational constructions. Then rewrite the sentence to correct the problem in word choice.

_____ 1. Jessica *8 a gr8* meal of microwaved ramen noodles.

_____

_____

_____ 2. Janice said her boss would *go ballistic* if she came
                             in late for work.

                             _____

                             _____

_____ 3. Ahmed *kept his nose to the grindstone* and finally
                             finished his term paper.

                             _____

                             _____

_____ 4. Paulo was sorry he could not come with us, but
                             he had *prearranged plans that he had made at an
                             earlier time.*

                             _____

                             _____

_____ 5. *In conclusion, I would like to sum up by saying that*
                             having a semi-pro baseball team will benefit the
                             city in several ways.

                             _____

                             _____

_____ 6. Professor Smith was *as pleased as punch* with the grades on the exam.

_____

_____

_____ 7. When I left class, there was *this* huge crowd in the hall, but I did not stop to see what was happening.

_____

_____ 8. After the guests *scarfed up* all the food, they went home.

_____

_____ 9. *Well*, I'd rather take a difficult class and learn something than waste my time in an easy one.

_____

_____

_____ 10. Grover Cleveland was born in 1837, served two terms as president, and *croaked* in 1908.

_____

_____

| REVIEW EXERCISE 2 | CORRECTING WORD CHOICE PROBLEMS |

Underline and correct the two word choice problems in each sentence below.

1. We all thought Harold was guilty as sin, but he swore he was innocent as a lamb.

_____

2. I hit the sack early last night, and almost before my head hit the pillow, I was sawing logs.

_____

_____

3. When the sound of a heartbeat persists in continuing, the narrator of "The Tell-Tale Heart" is definitely unnerved.

   _____

   _____

4. A scrawny cat slept on the lid of a garbage can, and my friend was like, "That must be a stray." Well DUH!

   _____

   _____

5. Lorenzo bought a pair of really cool shades at the mall, but he paid big bucks for them.

   _____

   _____

REVIEW EXERCISE 3   EXPLORING ALTERNATE MEANINGS OF SLANG EXPRESSIONS

Some slang expressions have alternate meanings that are not slang. For each of the sentence pairs in the exercise, choose the expression from the following list that fits both sentences in the pair. Then write the slang meaning of the expression and the standard meaning of the expression in the blanks provided.

bag	cool	gross	ticked off
bug	crash	shaft	toast
bust	freak		

1. Sentence pair 1

   a. Sarah was really _____ when she found out she hadn't made the basketball team.

   b. As the students filed into the exam room, the proctor checked his roster and _____ each name.

   Slang meaning: _____

   Standard meaning: _____

2. Sentence pair 2

   a. "I am calling to report an error," said Mr. Sneed. "Not a _____ error, but an error nevertheless. I ordered a _____ of pencils, but I counted them twice, and one is missing. There are only 143 in the box."

    b. "I don't know what that was that the dining hall served for lunch," said Steve, "but it was so _____ I couldn't eat it."

Slang meaning: _____

Standard meaning 1: _____

Standard meaning 2: _____

3. Sentence pair 3

    a. Kim's parents were horrified by her tattoo, but Kim thought it was _____.

    b. At this time of year, days are warm but nights are _____.

Slang meaning: _____

Standard meaning: _____

4. Sentence pair 4

    a. One of these days the campus police are going to _____ me for parking in the faculty lot.

    b. On the piano a folder of sheet music lay next to a _____ of Mozart.

Slang meaning: _____

Standard meaning: _____

5. Sentence pair 5

    a. When Elaine woke up, she realized she had slept through her alarm. "I'm late for work," she moaned. "I'm _____."

    b. When Elaine looked in the cabinet, she saw that she was out of cereal. "I'll have _____," she decided.

Slang meaning: _____

Standard meaning: _____

6. Sentence pair 6

    a. Marina yawned as she got up from the couch. "It's late," she said. "I'm going to _____."

    b. Edgar screamed as the car hurtled toward a stand of trees. "Look out!" he yelled. "We're going to _____!"

Slang meaning: _____

Standard meaning: _____

7. Sentence pair 7

    a. The young woman carried a large canvas tote that said "Art is my

        _____."

    b. The cashier asked Paul if he wanted his groceries in a paper or plastic

        _____.

    Slang meaning: _____

    Standard meaning: _____

8. Sentence pair 8

    a. The children were warned repeatedly not to go near the old mine

        _____.

    b. After his divorce, Earl went down to the honky-tonk, ordered a root beer, and stood by the jukebox playing his favorite country song, "She Got the Gold Mine, I Got the _____."

    Slang meaning: _____

    Standard meaning: _____

9. Sentence pair 9

    a. Unexpectedly in early April, a _____ snowstorm blanketed the area.

    b. "All of a sudden Amy started yelling and throwing things," said Jonathan. "I knew she was angry, but I never expected her to _____."

    Slang meaning: _____

    Standard meaning: _____

10. Sentence pair 10

    a. "I'm trying to watch this program," Elena told her little brother. "Don't _____ me."

    b. Under a picture of a giant cockroach, the caption on the billboard read, "See a _____? Call Rid-a-Pest."

    Slang meaning: _____

    Standard meaning: _____

REVIEW EXERCISE 4   CORRECTING WORD CHOICE PROBLEMS

Rewrite the following sentences to correct word choice problems.

1. It was the unanimous consensus of all the members that the club should not meet the Wednesday before Thanksgiving, so the meeting was postponed until a later time.

    _____

    _____

2. Seriously, dude, "Dialog in the Dark" is an interactive museum exhibit that allows visitors to experience familiar settings in total darkness with a blind person as a guide.

    _____

    _____

3. Brian says he got ripped off by the car dealership when he bought his first car. Now he wishes he hadn't been so clueless.

    _____

    _____

4. Due to the fact that he has not learned his way around campus, Louis is basically late for every class.

    _____

    _____

5. When my little brother rubs me the wrong way, I just tell him to take a hike.

    _____

    _____

REVIEW EXERCISE 5   EDITING A LETTER TO ELIMINATE WORD CHOICE PROBLEMS

Correct the ten sentences in the following letter to eliminate word choice errors.

Dear Mom and Dad,

[1]I was really bummed to hear that Dad sprained his ankle. [2]Dad, I hope by now you are fit as a fiddle. [3]I am battling a cold—I am basically taking cold capsules and getting plenty of rest.

[4]The earthquake we had the other day was just a mild tremor, but everyone was running around like chickens with their heads cut off. [5]I was just LOL @ them, b/c I had been thru quakes in

California. [6]Some people actually slept through the quake, but they were few in number.

[7]Well, I saw an article in the paper about the company where you work, Mom. [8]The article said the company is raking in the dough since it changed its marketing strategy. [9]I think it is totally way cool that you were behind that strategy.

[10] Okay, I'm going to man up and get my term paper started.

Love,
Sam

_____

_____

_____

_____

_____

_____

_____

_____

_____

_____

_____

_____

mywritinglab   For support and practice meeting this chapter's goal, log in to www.mywritinglab.com and select **Standard and Nonstandard English.**

CHAPTER 27

Words Commonly Confused

> 🐾 **Chapter Goal:** Choose the correct word when faced with commonly confused words, such as *there* and *their*, *less* and *fewer*, or *to*, *too*, and *two*.

I think that I shall never see
Someone who looks so much like me,
With the same hair and eyes and teeth,
But not the same deep underneath.

It is the same way when we write:
Some words that look or sound alike
Are different in the way they're used;
These words are commonly confused.

It's hard to tell identical twins apart unless you know them well. Similarly, unless you know them well, words that sound alike when you say them are easy to confuse when you use them in writing. This chapter reviews words that are commonly confused. Take note of the ones that confuse you, and learn them well.

✐ Words Commonly Confused

mywritinglab

Visit MyWriting Lab for additional practice using commonly confused words.

a, an   The article *a* is used before consonant sounds. The article *an* is used before vowel sounds.

> **a** cat, **a** sandy beach, **a** widely held opinion; **an** advanced class, **an** egg, **an** ostrich.

But you must base your choice on the consonant or vowel *sound*. Some words— such as those beginning with a silent *h* or with a *u* that is pronounced like *y*—require careful treatment. If the *h* is silent, *an* is used—**an** honor, but **a** house. If a *u* is pronounced like the consonant *y*, the word is preceded by *a*—*a used car* but **an** *uncle*.

> ✔ In the music store, Bob looked at **a** guitar, **a** used snare drum, **a** ukulele, and **a** harmonica. As he waited for **a** salesclerk, he saw **a** customer— obviously not **an** honest person—steal **a** guitar pick. Bob wondered if he should alert **an** employee, but the thief quickly moved to **an** exit and left the store.

accept, except   To *accept* is to take or believe; the word *except* means *but* or *with the exception of.*

> ✔ I cannot **accept** your excuse; everyone **except** you has finished the project.

advice, advise   *Advice* is a noun; one gives advice or asks for it. *Advise* is the verb form; one person *advises* another.

> ✔ I needed some **advice** about fertilizer, so I asked Tim to **advise** me.

affect, effect   *Affect* is the verb form. It means *to alter* or *influence*. *Effect* is the noun form. It means *result*.

> ✔ Will the weather **affect** the turnout for the concert?
> ✔ The **effect** of the tornado was devastating.

all right, ~~alright~~   *All right* is the only correct spelling of this term. It is never all right to write *alright*.

> ✔ Tina said that the change in the schedule was **all right** with her.

alone, along   To be *alone* is to be by yourself. If someone else is *along*, you aren't alone.

✔ I didn't want to be **alone,** so I took my dog Nina **along.**

a lot, ~~alot~~, allot   *A lot* is always written as two words, never *alot.* When you mean *much* or *many,* it's considered better form to use a word such as *much, many, several,* or a specific amount instead of *a lot.* The word *allot* means to *allow* or *set aside* for a special purpose: *The Student Affairs Committee allotted two thousand dollars to the college's debate team.*

✔ **acceptable:** Isabel's grandmother has several old Barbie dolls that are worth **a lot** of money.
✔ **better:** Isabel's grandmother has several old Barbie dolls that are worth **over a hundred dollars each.**

among, between   *Among* is used with three or more persons or things; *between* is used with two.

✔ Chadrick found it easy to choose **among** the cars on the lot, but he found it difficult to choose **between** a lease option and a purchase agreement.

breath, breathe   *Breath* is the noun form: A person can take a *breath* or be out of *breath. Breathe* is the verb form: Someone may *breathe* heavily after exercising.

✔ "Please don't **breathe** on me," said Amelia. "You have morning **breath.**"

by, buy   *By* means *beside* or *through. Buy* means *to purchase.*

✔ Nick said he was going **by** the store because he needed to **buy** some cat food.

feel, fill   *Feel* means to touch or to experience emotions. Some writers confuse it with *fill: to make full.*

✔ I **feel** there are better ways to **fill** my time than to watch television.

fewer, less   Use *fewer* when writing about something you can count; *less* if you would measure it in some other way. Specifically, if you could put a number in front of a word (five acres), use *fewer.* If you cannot put a number in front of a word (~~five~~ land), use *less.* You would write *fewer* rocks but *less* sand, *fewer* cookies but *less* flour.

✔ Because Raj is working **fewer** hours, he is making **less** money.

good, well   *Good* is an adjective that answers the question "What kind?" *Well* is an adverb that answers the question "How?" or "In what manner?" Therefore, a person writes a *good* essay. (*Good* answers the question, "What kind of essay?") But he writes it *well*. (*Well* answers the question, "How did he write it?")

✔ Jennifer is a **good** student, but she did not do **well** on the last test.

himself, ~~hisself~~   The word is always *himself*, never *hisself*.

✔ Aiden congratulated **himself** for getting a good deal on the used washer.

its, it's   *Its* is the possessive pronoun. *It's* always means *it is* or *it has*.

✔ The old sofa has served **its** purpose, but **it's** time to get a new one.

knew, new   *Knew* is the past tense of *know; new* means *not old*.

✔ Frances **knew** it would be costly to fix her old television, so she decided to do without until she could afford a **new** one.

know, no   *Know* means *to understand; no* means *not any* or the opposite of *yes*.

✔ "Rex does not **know** what '**no**' means," said Rita as her dog chewed the sofa.

loose, lose   *Loose* is the opposite of *tight; lose* is the opposite of *find*.

✔ Anthony's watch was so **loose** that he was afraid he would **lose** it.

obtain, attain   To *obtain* is *to get* or *to acquire*. To *attain* is *to reach*. A person *obtains* an education but *attains* a goal.

✔ **Obtaining** a job in the field of genetic engineering is a goal Mai has always hoped to **attain.**

past, passed   *Past* is a noun meaning *an earlier time* or an adjective meaning *beyond* or *before now*. *Passed* is a verb that means *went by*.

✔ "In the **past,** I might have **passed** that car," said Chelsea, "but now I'm a more cautious driver."

peace, piece   *Peace* means *calm* or *tranquility; piece* means a *part*.

✔ Kendra knew she would get no **peace** until she gave Trinket a **piece** of her hamburger.

plain, plane   *Plain* refers to flat land or means *clear* or *unadorned. Plane* is a form of air transportation, a carpenter's tool, or a geometric surface.

✔ It's **plain** that Kendall is afraid to travel by **plane.**

principal, principle   *Principal* means *chief* (*principal* reason) or *a person in charge of a school* (*principal* of Westmore High). A *principle* is a policy or a rule.

✔ Christopher's **principal** purpose in life is to make money, and he does not mind sacrificing his **principles** to do it.
✔ The school's **principal** tries to set a good example for her students.

quit, quite, quiet   To *quit* is to stop. *Quite* means *very,* and *quiet* means *hushed.*

✔ "Please be **quiet,**" Cliff whispered to his son. "I will be **quite** angry if you don't **quit** making noise in church."

regardless, ~~irregardless~~   Regardless of the number of times you may have seen it, *irregardless* is not a word. The word is *regardless.*

✔ **Regardless** of her doctor's warnings, Lisa plans to fly to Tucson for her granddaughter's graduation.

themselves, ~~themself~~, ~~theirself~~, ~~theirselves~~   The word is always *themselves.*

✔ After they painted the living room, Bettina and Tom decided to give **themselves** a day off.

then, than   *Then* is used to show time or cause and effect; *than* is used to compare.

✔ Call me tomorrow; by **then** I will have an answer.
✔ If rainfall is not sufficient, **then** crops will be poor.
✔ Fat takes up more space **than** muscle because it is less dense.

there, their, they're   *There* is used to mean *in that place* or to start a sentence or clause. *Their* means *belonging to them,* and *they're* means *they are.*

✔ "**They're** here already!" Kim yelled as her aunt and uncle pulled into the driveway.
✔ "**There** are fewer insects in Wisconsin," said Sal, who had lived **there.**
✔ "I need to take Tricky and Treat to the vet; **their** vaccinations are due," said Stacy.

through, threw   *Through* means *within*, *between*, or *finished*. *Threw* is the past tense of the verb *throw*.

✔   After they were **through** with their picnic, they **threw** their paper plates and napkins in a nearby trash can and went on a stroll **through** the park.

two, too, to   *Two* refers to the number two; *too* means *also* or indicates an excessive amount. Any other use requires *to*.

✔   Alfredo said he wanted **to** go **to** the beach **too,** but I told him we had **too** many people unless someone else agreed **to** drive so that we could take **two** cars.

weather, whether, rather   *Weather* includes natural phenomena such as temperature, rainfall, and wind velocity. *Whether* indicates the existence of two possibilities and is often paired with *or not*. *Rather* means *prefer to* and indicates a choice.

✔   The **weather** was too cold for our picnic on the beach.
✔   Tahia is not sure **whether** to take a computer course or a biology course.
✔   Would you **rather** eat barbecue at Pig in a Pit or Satterfield's?

where, were   *Where* rhymes with *air* and refers to *place*. *Were* rhymes with *fur* and is a past tense form of the verb *to be*.

✔   When you did not answer the phone, I wondered **where** you **were.**

Review Exercises

Complete the Review Exercises to see how well you have learned the skills addressed in this chapter. As you work through the exercises, go back through the chapter to review any of the rules you do not understand completely.

REVIEW EXERCISE 1   CHOOSING BETWEEN COMMONLY CONFUSED WORDS

Refer to the explanations in this chapter to choose the correct word from each of the pairs in the following sentences. Underline the correct choice.

1.   There was (a, an) editorial in this morning's paper that I found (quite, quiet) interesting.

2.   Giselle asked Marc (rather, whether) he would prefer to stay home or go (alone, along) with her.

3. Although she went (threw, through) all her desk drawers, Kim could not find the report or remember (were, where) she had put it.

4. "My ex-husband should be ashamed of (himself, hisself) for getting so far behind on child support," said Laurie. "I can't even afford to (buy, by) the children new school clothes."

5. The new homes (were, where) attractively priced but had only (too, to, two) bedrooms.

REVIEW EXERCISE 2   **CHOOSING BETWEEN COMMONLY CONFUSED WORDS**

Refer to the explanations in this chapter to choose the correct word from each of the pairs in the following sentences. Underline the correct choice.

1. I needed (advice, advise) on what classes to take in the fall, so I scheduled a conference with my advisor (to, too, two) learn more about my options.

2. "I'll be (alright, all right) when I (obtain, attain) a passing grade in this class.

3. The sad movie (affected, effected) Carlos deeply, so he tried tell (himself, hisself) funny jokes in his head to keep from crying.

4. Janelle is extremely clumsy, but her family (accepts, excepts) that (its, it's) part of her charm.

5. When Eric was (threw, through) tallying the costs for his dinner party, he decided to invite (fewer, less) guests.

REVIEW EXERCISE 3   **IDENTIFYING AND CORRECTING ERRORS IN WORDS COMMONLY CONFUSED**

Find and correct the two word choice errors in each of the numbered items below.

1. Marie found it hard to choose between the seventeen books on the life of Emily Dickinson. "If there were less books it would be an easier choice," she said.

_____

_____

2. "I don't think computers will ever be smarter then humans," said Jeff. "A computer is just a adding machine with a few extra features."

_____

_____

3. "Ms. Jordan said I did good on the test," said Vernell. "She also said that hard work would help me obtain my goals."

_____

_____

4. After saving all year, Milton and Deloris treated theirselves too a trip to Disney World.

_____

_____

5. "I am trying to get more exercise and consume less calories," said Willie. "I fill a lot more energetic, too."

_____

_____

REVIEW EXERCISE 4   IDENTIFYING AND CORRECTING ERRORS IN WORDS COMMONLY CONFUSED

Find and correct the two word choice errors in each of the numbered items below.

1. Michelle new that a lie would get her out of working late. However, she decided to stick to her principals.

_____

_____

2. Eric's hamster got out of it's cage last night. He wondered weather his mother would be angry that it had gotten loose.

_____

_____

3. Stan said he couldn't except Rachel's resignation while tempers were running high. "Think about it tonight, and then tell me how you fill," he said.

_____

_____

4. Andrew said that their were less people at the concert than he had expected to see.

_____

_____

5. As she turned to look at the clock, Althea saw that ten minutes had past while she had been standing in line. "I new I should not have come to the post office on my lunch hour," she thought.

_____

_____

REVIEW EXERCISE 5   **EDITING A PARAGRAPH FOR ERRORS IN WORDS COMMONLY CONFUSED**

Correct the word choice error in each sentence of the following paragraph.

[1]When I was a child, my parents took my sister and me too the circus. [2]I can remember walking threw the flaps of a large circus tent and sitting on tiered bleachers around a center ring. [3]The circus began with clowns on bicycles circling the ring, waving at the crowd, and tooting their bicycle horns as they past. [4]They were followed by tumblers who flipped and rolled across the ring and a contortionist who twisted herself into pretzel shapes and did everything accept turn herself inside out. [5]Next came a beautiful woman wearing a spangled bodysuit and standing on the back of a elephant. [6]Finally, the ringmaster called for complete quite for the dangerous trapeze act, performed without a net. [7]No one in the audience seemed to breath as the trapeze artists, a man and a woman, began to swing in wider and wider arcs above the heads of the audience. [8]The woman launched herself into the air, were she seemed to hang suspended, arms outstretched for her partner. [9]Then, with a smack that I could hear in the hushed air, they firmly caught one another buy the wrists. [10]As I left the circus that day, I remember telling my parents that I wanted to go their again soon.

_____

_____

_____

_____

_____

_____

_____

_____

_____

_____

_____

_____

_____

_____

mywritinglab   For support and practice meeting this chapter's goal, log in to
www.mywritinglab.com and select Easily Confused Words.

CHAPTER 28

Capitalization

> 🖋 **Chapter Goal:** Use capitalization appropriately.

Letters from a keyboard,
Scattered carelessly.
Usually, capitals
Are treated carefully.

Most of the rules of capitalization are already familiar to you, but a few of them may surprise you. For example, would you write "my *Grandmother*" or "my *grandmother*"? Do you watch the sun set in the *West* or in the *west*? Would you take a *Summer* vacation or a *summer* vacation? Do you take *Algebra* and *English* or *algebra* and *English*? Are you sure? Read on to review the fundamentals and study the fine points of capitalization.

Capitalization of Words That Begin Sentences

mywritinglab

Visit MyWriting Lab for additional practice with capitalization.

Capitalize the first word of a sentence or a direct quotation.

Examples of Capitalization to Begin Sentences and Direct Quotations

✔ The woman told a reporter that she was walking down the street when a cat fell on her head.

✔ In some places, snow tires are a necessity.

✔ Then Martino said, "I hope you remembered to mail the birthday card to Dad."

Capitalization of Words Referring to Individuals

Names and the Pronoun *I*

mywritinglab

Visit MyWriting Lab for additional practice with capitalization.

Capitalize people's names and the pronoun *I*.

Examples of Capitalization of Names and the Pronoun *I*

✔ I heard that James Maldonado made the hockey team.

✔ Mr. Benton, the music professor, told Khadijah that she had a musical-sounding name.

Family Relationships

Family Designations Used in Place of a Name

Capitalize a word that designates a family relationship if it is used in place of a name. To make sure that the word is used as a name, try substituting a name for the word. If it is used as a name, the substitution will sound natural.

Example of Substitution to Check Correctness

✔ I drove Mother to her doctor's appointment.

✔ I drove ~~Mother~~ Ella Satterfield to her doctor's appointment.

"I drove Ella Satterfield to her doctor's appointment" sounds natural, so the capitalization of *Mother* is correct.

Try your own substitution in the next sentence. If substituting a name for *Grandpa* sounds natural, the capitalization is correct.

"I will not retire," Grandpa said, "because I'd rather wear out than rust out."

Family Designations Used with Possessives and Articles

No capital letter is used when family designations such as father, mother, or great-uncle Elmo are preceded by a possessive pronoun (*my, her, his, their*), a possessive noun (*Ted's, Penny's*), or an article (*a, an,* or *the*). For additional proof, try directly substituting a name for the family designation. It will sound awkward.

Examples of Substitution to Check Correctness

✔ My grandmother manages an income tax preparation business.
✔ My ~~grandmother~~ Sally Lewis manages an income tax preparation business.

"My Sally Lewis" does not sound natural, confirming that the word *grandmother* need not be capitalized.

✔ I took my mother to her doctor's appointment.

In this sentence, substituting a name does not work. "I took my Ella Satterfield to her doctor's appointment" sounds awkward.

Professional Titles

Do not capitalize professional titles unless they are used immediately before a name.

Examples of Capitalization of Professional Titles

✔ Harold Smith is my family *doctor*.
✔ I took the children to *Dr.* Harold Smith for their vaccinations.
✔ Antoinette Wheatley is my American history *professor*.
✔ I am taking American history with *Professor* Antoinette Wheatley.

PRACTICE 1   CAPITALIZING WORDS REFERRING TO INDIVIDUALS

Correct the two capitalization mistakes in each sentence.

1. aunt Florence said Timothy was brave when the Doctor gave him his shots.

_____   _____

2. My Grandmother said, "be careful what you wish for; you might get it."

   _____   _____

3. Sam and elaine are going to take professor Edith Cartwright's drama class next fall.

   _____   _____

4. Aunt Phoebe told uncle Bill that my Grandmother was losing her memory.

   _____   _____

5. Mrs. harris called her City Council Representative and said, "Please, Council-woman Jones, can't you do something about the potholes in Broad Street?"

   _____   _____

Capitalization of Words Referring to Groups

Religions, Geographic Locations, Races, and Nationalities

mywritinglab

Visit MyWriting Lab for additional practice with capitalization.

Capitalize words that refer to specific religions, geographic locations, races, and nationalities.

Examples of Capitalization of Religions, Geographic Locations, Races, and Nationalities

✔ People who consider themselves multiracial may have trouble filling out a form that asks if they are Asian, Caucasian, African American, Hispanic, or Native American.

✔ Though Ilsa is originally from Denmark, she considers herself a New Yorker. She collects African art, drinks Irish whiskey, and drives a German car.

✔ Ann was brought up as a Catholic, but she now considers herself a Buddhist.

Organizations, Businesses, and Agencies

Capitalize specific names of organizations, businesses, and government agencies.

Examples of Capitalization of Names of Organizations, Businesses and Agencies

✔ Haley belongs to the Spanish Club, Phi Beta Kappa, and the Association of Engineering Students.

✔ Sam works at the Criterion Corporation, and his wife works at IBM.

✔ After Ami graduates, she wants to work for the Internal Revenue Service.

Do not capitalize nonspecific or generic organization names.

Examples of Lower Case Used with Nonspecific Names of Organizations

✔ Cliff is active in the church and is also a member of the choir.

✔ As a top executive in a large corporation, Ms. Simmons often travels on the company plane.

✔ After Ami graduates, she wants to work for the government.

PRACTICE 2   CAPITALIZING WORDS REFERRING TO GROUPS

Correct the two capitalization mistakes in each sentence.

1. Talisha hopes her Government job at the bureau of alcohol, tobacco, and firearms will not be affected by budget cuts.

   _____

2. The funds raised by shriners go to the scottish rite children's hospital.

   _____

3. When he began working for general motors, Allan joined the Union.

   _____

4. Some of the faculty at the College belong to the american association of university professors.

   _____

5. Our Company buys its paper and office supplies from office depot.

   _____

Capitalization of Words Referring to Time and Place

Dates, Days, Holidays, and Seasons

mywritinglab

Visit MyWriting Lab for additional practice with capitalization.

Capitalize months of the year, days of the week, and names of holidays.

Examples of Capitalization of Dates, Days, Holidays, and Seasons

✔ Memorial Day is officially celebrated on the last Monday in May.

✔ Christmas, Hanukkah, and Kwanzaa all fall in December.

Do not capitalize the names of the four seasons.

✔ Marcy wants to do some spring cleaning before her children get out of school for the summer.

Place Names

Capitalize *specific* place names.

Examples of Capitalization of Specific Place Names

✔ On our trip to Atlanta, we visited Six Flags Over Georgia, the High Museum of Art, and Ebenezer Baptist Church, where Dr. Martin Luther King, Jr., preached.

✔ We also saw a show at the Fox Theater and took in a Braves game at Turner Field.

✔ Starla said that her little sister plans to attend Spelman College after she graduates from Westside High School.

✔ The robber ran out of the First National Bank and tore down State Street.

Do not capitalize *general, nonspecific* place names.

✔ On our trip to Atlanta, we visited an amusement park, an art museum, and the historic church where Dr. Martin Luther King, Jr., preached.

✔ We also saw a show at a theater and took in a Braves game at the stadium.

✔ Starla plans to attend college after she graduates from high school.

✔ The robber ran out of the bank and tore down the street.

Compass Points

Do not capitalize compass points unless they refer to a specific geographical area.

Examples Showing When to Capitalize Compass Points

✔ Head east on Eisenhower Parkway; then take Interstate 75 north until you reach Exit 255.

✔ Having lived on the West Coast all his life, Doug found it hard to adjust to the heat of the South.

PRACTICE 3 **CAPITALIZING WORDS REFERRING TO TIME AND PLACE**

Correct the two capitalization mistakes in each sentence.

1. When we visited Washington, D.C., we visited the Lincoln Memorial, the white house, and other Historic Places.

   _____   _____

2. If a person is at the exact center of the north pole, can he move without going South?

   _____   _____

3. People living in new mexico sometimes have trouble convincing people that they live in the united states.

   _____   _____

4. When he visited his old High School, Ed was shocked to realize that the Principal was younger than he was.

   _____   _____

5. The state of west Virginia is known for its beautiful blue ridge mountains.

   _____   _____

✏ Capitalization of Words Referring to Things and Activities

School Subjects

mywritinglab

Visit MyWriting Lab for additional practice with capitalization.

Do not capitalize subjects studied in school unless they are part of a specific course title.

Examples of Capitalization of Specific Course Titles

✔ Diego is taking history, English, and biology this term.

✔ Diego is taking History 2212, English 1151, and Biology 2202 this term.

✔ Diego is taking World Civilization, Introduction to Poetry, and Principles of Biology this term.

Titles

Capitalize titles of novels, short stories, poems, newspapers, magazines, articles, works of art, television shows, movies, and songs and other musical works. There are exceptions to many rules in English, and this rule has more exceptions than most. Some newspapers and journals capitalize only the first word in the title of an article. Some writers, like e. e. cummings, do not follow the conventional rules of capitalization. In general, when you write about an article, a poem, or any other piece of writing, preserve the title as it was published.

Otherwise, follow these rules: Capitalize the first word of a title. Do not capitalize articles (*a, an, the*) or short prepositions (*to, of, from,* and similar short prepositions) unless they are the first or last word in a title. Capitalize all other words.

Examples of Capitalization of Titles

✔ Hoshiko read an article in *Archaeology* called "Faces from the Past."

✔ The class read *Hamlet* and *Death of a Salesman.*

✔ Andre wrote his paper on "The Weary Blues" by Langston Hughes and "kitchenette building" by Gwendolyn Brooks. (In this example, Gwendolyn Brooks's title has been written just as it was published.)

✔ With at least three more hours to drive, Fay and Lamar regretted having taught their children the words to "It's a Small World."

Consumer Products

For consumer products, capitalize the brand name but not the general product name. Often, the general product name is omitted.

Examples of Capitalization of Brand Names of Consumer Products

✔ My mother always washes her clothes with Tide detergent and Downy fabric softener.

✔ My mother always washes her clothes with Tide and Downy.

✔ Jamal's old Nissan broke down in front of the drive-through at Wendy's.

Abbreviations

Capitalize some common abbreviations. Abbreviations of organizations, corporations, and professional designations are capitalized. Some examples include NBC, AFL-CIO, FBI, NAACP, CIA, UPS, C.P.A., M.D., Ph.D., D.D.S. The disease AIDS is always written in all capitals.

PRACTICE 4   CAPITALIZING WORDS REFERRING TO THINGS AND ACTIVITIES

Correct the two capitalization mistakes in each sentence.

1. At Seaside Snacks, we ordered two diet cokes and two bags of fritos.

   _____   _____

2. Monica opened a can of friskies cat food and a can of bumble bee tuna, but her finicky cat refused them both.

   _____   _____

3. Andy reads the new york times or watches nbc to get the latest news.

   _____   _____

4. Since she was out of Folger's Coffee, Edna decided to have some Lipton Tea.

   _____   _____

5. The article in time was called "cartoons are no laughing matter."

   _____   _____

〰️ Review Exercises

Complete the Review Exercises to see how well you have learned the skills addressed in this chapter. As you work through the exercises, go back through the chapter to review any of the rules you do not understand completely.

REVIEW EXERCISE 1   IDENTIFYING AND CORRECTING CAPITALIZATION ERRORS

Correct the two capitalization mistakes in each sentence.

1. Valerie used to buy her children's clothes at walmart, but now the kids think they need expensive tommy hilfiger clothing.

   _____   _____

2. Samantha told her Mother that she liked only green giant vegetables.

   _____   _____

3. Santa claus sat in the middle of the shopping mall, calling out, "ho, ho, ho!" to passing children.

   _____   _____

4. I went to High School with Andrew, but I did not know he had gone to work for the fbi.

   _____   _____

5. Ms. Chatfield warned the girl scout troop, "never get in a car with anyone you don't know."

   _____   _____

REVIEW EXERCISE 2   IDENTIFYING AND CORRECTING CAPITALIZATION ERRORS

Correct the two capitalization mistakes in each sentence.

1. Justin's favorite television shows are *sportscenter* and *pardon the interruption*.

   _____

2. Having always lived in the south, Liz cried as her train headed to her new home in northampton, MA.

   _____

3. At tuesday's trial, the lawyer interrogated officer David Jenkins for over an hour before the judge called a recess.

   _____

4. As Jules reached into her box of oreos, she realized the clerk at the snack counter had given her cheez-its.

   _____

5. Some mammals, such as the polar bear, are under threat from environmental changes that the north pole is experiencing this Winter.

   _____

REVIEW EXERCISE 3   IDENTIFYING AND CORRECTING CAPITALIZATION ERRORS

Correct the two capitalization mistakes in each sentence.

1. The bainbridge bass club is sponsoring a fishing tournament at lake seminole.

    _____   _____

2. The aids support group met at the unitarian universalist church.

    _____   _____

3. When jimmy tried to buy a pack of camel cigarettes at the convenience store, the clerk asked him for proof of age.

    _____   _____

4. Anthony Small is President of the local chapter of the afl-cio.

    _____   _____

5. On the first sunday in march, the Packards will have their family reunion.

    _____   _____

REVIEW EXERCISE 4   IDENTIFYING AND CORRECTING CAPITALIZATION ERRORS

Correct the twenty capitalization errors (two per sentence) in the paragraph below.

[1]Every morning, my retired neighbor, mrs. grimes, takes a brisk walk down harrison street. [2]In her nikes and her chicago cubs hat, she is a familiar sight to people along her route, which never varies. [3]She walks south toward bob's handi-mart, where she pops in for her morning cup of maxwell house coffee. [4]She chats with hassan, who works the cash register, and buys a copy of the *snellville times*. [5]Then she walks west down pauldo avenue toward st. luke's church. [6]At the church, her route veers north past the ymca and the little row of shops on milk street. [7]At wet pets, the tropical fish store, she stops to look in the window at the colorful fish and the stacked displays of hartz mountain fish food. [8]Then she walks on past emil's cut and style and baskin-robbins. [9]If she continued north, she would pass woodrow wilson high school and the washington memorial library. [10]Instead, sophia grimes, always predictable, turns back onto harrison street and heads home.

1. _____
2. _____
3. _____
4. _____
5. _____
6. _____
7. _____
8. _____
9. _____
10. _____

mywritinglab For support and practice meeting this chapter's goal, log in to www.mywritinglab.com and select Capitalization.

CHAPTER 29

Apostrophes

♫ Chapter Goal: Use apostrophes correctly.

HARRYS
APPLE'S
50¢ EACH

Harry's apples are the best—
Juicy, sweet, and tart.
As for his apostrophes,
He's never learned
the art.

The handmade sign above announces a roadside vendor's stand. Harry's apples may be the best, but his use of the apostrophe leaves a great deal to be desired. Can you pinpoint the problems? If you can't now, you will be able to by the time you finish this chapter, which outlines the two main uses of apostrophes: to form contractions and to show possession.

Apostrophes in Contractions

mywritinglab

Visit MyWriting Lab for additional practice with apostrophes.

Contractions are informal or conversational shortenings of words: *can't* for *cannot, doesn't* for *does not,* and *it's* for *it is* or *it has.* Contractions are used in informal writing but are generally inappropriate for formal or scholarly writing. You will find contractions in some journalistic writing, in some textbooks, in works of fiction, and in informal essays. Contractions are considered inappropriate in reports of academic research and in legal documents. Your instructor will specify the level of formality you should use in your essays and other writings.

To form a contraction, replace omitted letters with a single apostrophe. Close any spaces between words.

Examples of Apostrophe Use in Contractions

✔ isn't = is not

✔ hasn't = has not

✔ couldn't = could not

✔ don't = do not

✔ won't = will not (an irregular contraction: the *i* in *will* changes to an *o*)

✔ wouldn't = would not

PRACTICE 1   USING APOSTROPHES IN CONTRACTIONS

Make a contraction of each of the following expressions. Be sure to place an apostrophe where letters are omitted, not in the space between the words.

1. he is _____

2. I am _____

3. could not _____

4. does not _____

5. she is _____

6. it is _____

7. they are _____

8. I will _____

9. that is _____

10. cannot _____

PRACTICE 2   USING APOSTROPHES IN CONTRACTIONS

In each sentence below, supply the missing apostrophe in the contraction and write the contraction in the blank provided.

_____ 1. Kwan says *shes* playing in the soccer tournament next Saturday.

_____ 2. Rodney *hasnt* heard from either of the firms where he applied.

_____ 3. This *isnt* the first time Jingles has deposited a dead mouse on the doormat.

_____ 4. *Its* a cool, cloudy day, perfect for travel.

_____ 5. "After *Ive* finished my degree," said Philip, "I hope to go on to veterinary school."

_____ 6. "Sorry," said the clerk, "but *were* out of the nine-grain bread."

_____ 7. "*Isnt* that the same outfit Professor Smith wore last Tuesday?" whispered the student.

_____ 8. When Karen *couldnt* find a parking place near her favorite store in the mall, she left.

_____ 9. I have been trying to figure out this math problem for half an hour, so please *dont* tell me the answer is obvious.

_____ 10. "Wait right here," said James. "*Ill* be back."

✍ Apostrophes to Show Possession

mywritinglab

Visit MyWriting Lab for additional practice with apostrophes.
If you could not use apostrophes to show **possession**, you would have to rely on long, tedious constructions such as "I drove the car of my father to the house of Ray to study for the test of tomorrow," instead of "I drove my father's car to Ray's house to study for tomorrow's test."

Making Nouns Possessive

There are two rules for making nouns possessive.

Rule 1: Add an apostrophe and *s* (*'s*) to form the possessive of singular nouns and of plurals that do not end in *s*.

Examples of Possessives of Singular Nouns and Plural Nouns Not Ending in *s*

✔ the bowl that belongs to the cat = the *cat's* bowl

✔ the ring of the telephone = the *telephone's* ring

✔ the cover of the book = the *book's* cover
✔ the work of a day = a *day's* work
✔ the vegetable garden belonging to Daphne = *Daphne's* vegetable garden
✔ the books that belong to the children = the *children's* books
✔ the office of my boss = my *boss's* office
✔ the boots of Jess = *Jess's* boots

PRACTICE 3   USING APOSTROPHES TO SHOW POSSESSION

Practice rule 1 by converting the five expressions in the exercise to possessives using *'s.*

1. the flame of the candle = _____

2. the red dress belonging to Cherie = _____

3. the lecture of Professor Ross = _____

4. the tools of the artist = _____

5. the meeting of next month = _____

Rule 2: Add an apostrophe (') to form the possessive of plural nouns that end in *s.*

Examples of Possessives of Plural Nouns Ending in *s*

✔ the cheers of the soccer fans = the *soccer fans'* cheers
✔ the lawn belonging to the Smiths = the *Smiths'* lawn
✔ the aroma of the flowers = the *flowers'* aroma

Grammar Alert!

When a singular word ends in *s*, it is also acceptable to use an apostrophe alone to make it possessive: *Mr. Jones'* job, *Dickens'* novel, the *boss'* office, the *crabgrass'* rapid growth.

PRACTICE 4   USING APOSTROPHES TO SHOW POSSESSION

Practice rule 2 by converting the ten expressions in the exercise to possessives using an apostrophe.

1. the names of my uncles =_____

2. the litter box of the cats = _____

3. the exhaustion of the workers = _____

4. the salaries of the athletes = _____

5. the taste of the cookies = _____

6. the demographic makeup of the classes = _____

7. the water levels of the lakes = _____

8. the disastrous vacation of the Robinsons = _____

9. the barking of the neighborhood dogs =_____

10. the voices of the speakers = _____

Distinguishing Possessives from Simple Plurals

To use apostrophes correctly, it is important to distinguish between possessives and simple plurals. A plural may be followed by a verb, by a prepositional phrase, or by nothing at all. Words that show possession will end in *s*, like plurals, but will be immediately followed by something that is being possessed, as in "*Mom's homemade chicken and dumplings*" or the "*horse's mane.*"

Possessive (Apostrophe Used)	Plural (No Apostrophe Used)
Amy's computer	computers in a lab
a day's work	days in a month
Mother's Day	Mothers Against Drunk Driving
a king's ransom	kings in the seventeenth century
the tornadoes' fury	several tornadoes
the washer's spin cycle	the broken washers

PRACTICE 5   DISTINGUISHING POSSESSIVES FROM PLURALS

In each sentence, underline the noun that ends in *s*. If the noun is possessive, write *possessive* in the blank provided. If the noun is simply a plural, remove the apostrophe and write the corrected plural form in the blank. The first one is done for you.

parents   1. Sometimes I think my <u>parents'</u> are hopelessly old fashioned.

_____   2. The dog's collar looked too tight.

_____   3. The speaker's viewpoint is controversial; therefore, a large turn-out is expected.

_____   4.   Our debate team and those of several other schools' will be participating.

_____   5.   Since no one used them anymore, the old, heavy computer monitors' were placed in storage.

_____   6.   Near the window, the sun had faded the carpet's color.

_____   7.   The Smith's have lived next door to me for nearly a year.

_____   8.   The oldest resident of the neighborhood has lived here for thirty year's.

_____   9.   The manatee's body looks heavy and awkward, but it swims easily.

_____   10. For older adults, the benefit's of weight training include improved coordination and stronger muscles and bones.

Possessive Forms of Pronouns

Personal pronouns (*I, we, you, he, she, it,* and *they*) have their own possessive forms that never require an apostrophe. These forms include *my, mine, our, ours, your, yours, his, hers, its, their,* and *theirs.*

Its and *It's*

The pronoun that is the focus of the most confusion is *its*. Since the possessive form of a pronoun never takes an apostrophe, *its* is the possessive form, meaning *belonging to it. It's,* the form with the apostrophe, always means *it is* or *it has.*

Examples Using *its* and *it's*

✔   The lawnmower seems to have lost *its* pep.

✔   *It's* too hot to mow, anyway.

PRACTICE 6   USING *ITS* AND *IT'S* CORRECTLY

Underline the correct form of *its* or *it's* in the following sentences.

1.   "(Its, It's) evident that you did not study," Professor Tate told the student.

2.   The car was new, and (its, it's) owner had parked it in the far end of the parking lot to prevent it from being scratched.

3.   That novel has been on the bestseller list for ten weeks, and (its, it's) still number five.

4. The mail truck slowly made (its, it's) way through the neighborhood.

5. Caroline has put off opening her mail, so (its, it's) piling up on her desk.

Proofreading for Apostrophe Errors

Apostrophes Incorrectly Omitted from Possessives

To find apostrophes incorrectly omitted from possessives, check each noun ending in *s* to see if it is followed by something it possesses.

✗ The corner delis roast chicken is the best in town.

Does *roast chicken* belong to *delis?* Yes. But does the apostrophe go before or after the *s?* Look for clues to whether the original word (before it was made possessive) was intended to be singular or plural. The main clue lies in the word *best*. Only one deli would have the *best* chicken. In addition, the deli is described as *the corner deli,* and there is unlikely to be more than one deli on the corner.

✔ The corner deli's roast chicken is the best in town.

✗ The girls bikes had been left lying in the carport.

Bikes belong to *girls,* but does the apostrophe go before or after the *s?* Since there is more than one bike, there is probably also more than one girl. The word *bikes* also ends in *s.* Does anything belong to *bikes?* No, the word is simply a plural and is correct without an apostrophe.

✔ The girls' bikes had been left lying in the carport.

PRACTICE 7   CORRECTING APOSTROPHE ERRORS

Supply the omitted apostrophes in the following sentences.

1. The cars windshield had been cracked by a grapefruit-sized hailstone.

   _____

2. The judge imposed the maximum sentence because of the thiefs lack of remorse.

   _____

3. The car lots no-haggle prices make it attractive to many potential buyers.

   _____

4. The restaurants atmosphere was pleasing; candles glowed on the tables and musicians played softly in the background.

_____

_____

5. The painters said it would take about three days work to finish the exterior of the house.

_____

_____

Review Exercises

Complete the Review Exercises to see how well you have learned the skills addressed in this chapter. As you work through the exercises, go back through the chapter to review any of the rules you do not understand completely.

REVIEW EXERCISE 1   FORMING POSSESSIVES OF NOUNS

Convert the ten expressions in the exercise to possessives using an apostrophe or 's.

1. the glow of the laptop = _____

2. the laughter of a young couple = _____

3. the address of the Wilsons = _____

4. the photos of the website = _____

5. the sweater belonging to Steph = _____

6. the orbit of Venus = _____

7. a vacation of two weeks = _____

8. the opinion of Prof. Simmons = _____

9. the daily rounds of the nurses = _____

10. the frames of the glasses = _____

REVIEW EXERCISE 2   SUPPLYING OMITTED APOSTROPHES

Each of the following sentences has an omitted apostrophe in a contraction or a possessive form. Cross through the error; then, in the blank, write the word with the apostrophe placed correctly.

_____ 1. Ron couldnt tell which of the twins was Daria.

_____ 2. The restaurants breakfast menu featured pancakes and waffles.

_____ 3. An ice pack helps reduce the swelling in Carolyns sprained ankle.

_____ 4. The sales of tabloids often depend on their headlines sensationalism.

_____ 5. Anita sat on a beach towel and stared out at the oceans broad expanse.

_____ 6. "Salary is important," said Amin. "But its job satisfaction that really matters."

_____ 7. Memos, notes, and photographs entirely covered the bulletin boards surface.

_____ 8. The buildings tumbledown appearance made it a neighborhood eyesore.

_____ 9. The vet said that the dogs operation should not be postponed.

_____ 10. Some scientists questioned the two researchers techniques.

REVIEW EXERCISE 3   SUPPLYING OMITTED APOSTROPHES

Each of the following sentences contains two omitted apostrophes. Cross through the error; then, in the blanks, write the words with the apostrophes placed correctly.

1. Though researchers are uncertain of the role of dreams, having dreams and getting a good nights sleep are important to a persons overall health.

_____   _____

2. The nursing homes smoke alarms were checked twice a month for the residents safety.

_____   _____

3. The clocks hands seemed to move at a turtles pace.

_____   _____

4. The childrens whispers made their parents wonder what mischief was brewing in the youngsters minds.

_____   _____

5. "Ive noticed youre not very talkative today," said Kim's mother.

_____   _____

REVIEW EXERCISE 4   EDITING A PARAGRAPH FOR APOSTROPHE ERRORS

Correct the ten apostrophe errors in the restaurant review below. Apostrophes may be misplaced, missing, or unnecessary.

[1]Restaurant Review: Leos Seafood House

[2]On Friday nights, theres always a line at Leo's Seafood House, and this past Friday was no exception. [3]The wait was short, however, and once we were seated, I ordered the Catch of the Day—grilled tuna—and my companion ordered the Fishermans Platter. [4]Service was slow, and our salads, a blend of greens topped with tomatoes and croutons, were just a memory by the time the entree's arrived at our table. [5]My companions' Fisherman's Platter was a sizzling delight with its crisply fried shrimp, tender flounder, and butter-drenched scallops. [6]The Catch of the Day, on the other hand, smelled as though it had been left to decay in the hold of a fishing boat while the fishers took two week's vacation. [7]The tuna was crisply grilled, but even a dousing of lemon could not disguise it's fishy flavor. [8]The server was apologetic and didnt mind substituting the more expensive Captain's Feast at no extra charge. [9]Dessert was a deliciously cold raspberry sorbet for me and Banana's Foster for my companion. [10]In spite of slow service and a Catch of the Day that should have been thrown back, its evident that there's a good reason for the lines outside Leo's on Friday nights.

1. _____

2. _____

3. _____

4. _____

5. _____

6. _____

7. _____

8. _____

9. _____

10. _____

mywritinglab

For support and practice meeting this chapter's goal, log in to www.mywritinglab.com and select Apostrophes.

CHAPTER 30

Quotation Marks, Italics, and Underlining

> ✍ **Chapter Goal:** Identify direct quotations, indirect quotations, and titles appropriately in your writing.

"Sorry, mister. They're all full of hot air."

Quotation marks, italics, and underlining are visual signals that give a reader information that would otherwise have to be conveyed in words. They say, "Someone is speaking or thinking"; "These words are a title of a long work"; or "These words are the title of a short work." Quotation marks, italics, and underlining are a kind of academic shorthand that enhances your ability to communicate within the academic world.

✎ Quotation Marks to Signal Quotations

Direct Quotations

mywritinglab

Visit MyWriting Lab for additional practice with quotation marks.

Quotation marks are used to signal a **direct quotation**; that is, they are placed around the exact words that someone speaks, writes, or thinks. As you look at the following examples, notice that when a comma or period comes at the end of a quotation, it is always placed inside the quotation mark. When a direct question is quoted, the question mark also goes inside the quotation marks.

Examples of Quotation Marks with Direct Quotations

"I'll wait for you in front of the fountain," said Paul.

Ann said, "I forgot to do my research for my paper on memory."

The clerk told the customer, "I can't help you now. It's time for my break."

The child asked, "Why don't people have fur?"

"Did you have a good time?" asked Harry.

PRACTICE 1   **USING QUOTATION MARKS WITH DIRECT QUOTATIONS**

Following the models above, place quotation marks around each of the direct "quotations" and add a comma or question mark where needed.

1. I wish it were Friday thought Sandra.

    _____

2. Did we do anything in class yesterday Tim asked the professor.

    _____

3. A sign on the hairstylist's mirror read I'm a beautician, not a magician.

    _____

4. I always read the comics first said Harold.

    _____

5. This milk is expired. I should throw it away said Tom.

    _____

Split Quotations

Some direct quotations are *split quotations*. Here are two rules for splitting quotations.

1. When you split a sentence, use commas to set off the tag (such as *she said*) that tells who said or thought the words you are quoting.
   - ✔ "If I've missed the bus," thought Alexandra, "I'll have to walk."

2. When there is a complete sentence before and a complete sentence after the tag, put a comma after the first sentence and a period after the tag.
   - ✔ "There's nothing good on TV," said Rick. "Let's go for a walk around the neighborhood."

PRACTICE 2   USING QUOTATION MARKS WITH SPLIT QUOTATIONS

Following the models above, place quotation marks around each of the direct quotations and add commas where they are needed.

1. Tonight will be clear with temperatures in the fifties said the meteorologist. Tomorrow, though, we can expect rain.

   _____

   _____

2. The elevator business is just like any other said the technician. It has its ups and downs.

   _____

   _____

3. Because Grandfather hated labels said Emil he always said 'human' when someone asked his race.

   _____

   _____

4. Go directly to jail the Monopoly card read. Do not pass go; do not collect $200.

   _____

5. For my birthday this year Carlton told his wife I'd like a gift certificate to the car wash.

   _____

   _____

Indirect Quotations

An **indirect quotation** is a paraphrase. It repeats the essence of what a person said, and it may repeat some or all of the words, but it is not a word-for-word quotation. The word *that* is stated or implied before an indirect quotation. Finally, an indirect quotation is not set off by quotation marks.

Examples

✔ Truman said that he had lost his best pen.

✔ Truman said he had lost his best pen.

The two examples above are indirect quotations. They do not repeat Truman's exact words (Truman did not use the words *he* and *his*). The word *that* is stated in the first example and implied in the second. Therefore, no quotation marks are used.

PRACTICE 3   **RECOGNIZING DIRECT AND INDIRECT QUOTATIONS**

On the line provided, label each quotation direct *(D)* or indirect *(I)*.

_____ 1. Earl said, "I might have gotten a better grade on the test if I had read the book."

_____ 2. Earl said that he might have gotten a better grade on the test if he had read the book.

_____ 3. The customer at table five said she needed extra salad dressing.

_____ 4. The bumper sticker said, "My other car is a piece of junk, too."

_____ 5. "If you are going to the post office," said Ann, "would you mind mailing my package?"

_____ 6. Brittany said, "Here, Mom. I drew this alligator for you at school."

_____ 7. James asked, "How much fertilizer should I feed the fern?"

_____ 8. James asked how much fertilizer he should feed the fern.

_____ 9. The mechanic told me I should have my car's oil changed every 3,000 miles.

_____ 10. Joy said that she could live without television but would be lost without her laptop.

Quotation Marks, Italics, or Underlining to Set Off Titles

mywritinglab

Visit MyWriting Lab for additional practice with quotation marks.

Quotation marks, italics, and underlining act as academic shorthand to signal a title.

> ### *Grammar Alert!*
>
> When you write *about* an essay, place the title of the essay within quotation marks. When you type the title of *your* essay on a cover sheet or at the head of the essay, do not use quotation marks.

Quotation Marks

Quotation marks set off titles of short works, including chapter titles, essays, episodes of a television series, newspaper and periodical articles, poems, and short stories.

1. Chapter titles: "Revising and Proofreading," "Introducing the Essay"
2. Essays: "Migraine Blues," "Should College Athletes Be Paid?"
3. Individual episodes of a TV series: "The Soup Nazi" (*Seinfeld*), "Hawaii: Crucible of Life" (*Nova*)
4. Newspaper articles: "Climbers feared dead on Everest," "Braves Beat up Pirates Again"
5. Poems: "To His Coy Mistress," "Harlem"
6. Short stories: "The Smallest Show on Earth," "A Good Man Is Hard to Find"

Italics and Underlining

Use of italics is the accepted way of setting off titles of longer works in published material; however, underlining has long been an acceptable substitute in handwritten, typed, and word-processed materials. The Modern Language Association used to recommend the use of underlining for clarity. However, the 2009 edition of the *MLA Handbook* recommends use of italic type rather than underlining. Therefore, if you are using a computer to write your document, use italics. If you are writing by hand, use underlining.

Instructions for the exercises in this text tell you to underline, since you will probably use pen and paper for the exercise. Keep in mind, though, that underlining and italics do the same job.

The titles of the following types of works are italicized or underlined.

1. Books: *A Tale of Two Cities, The Latin Deli*
2. Comic strips: *Jumpstart, Blondie*
3. Newspapers: *Miami Herald, Wall Street Journal*
4. Anthologies (collections) of poetry or short stories: *The Poem: An Anthology, The Best American Short Stories: 2010*
5. Music albums: *Loud, Mi Plan*
6. Television programs: *The CBS Evening News, Law and Order*
7. Movies: *True Grit, The Social Network*
8. Works of art: *Mona Lisa, Nude with a Hat*

PRACTICE 4   USING QUOTATION MARKS AND UNDERLINING WITH TITLES

In each of the following sentences, use quotation marks or underlining to set off titles.

1. Tonight's episode of Nature is titled Extraordinary Dogs.

   _____

2. For next week, the professor assigned a chapter called Memory in the book Psychology: An Introduction.

   _____

3. Jason's favorite cut on Best of the Blues is Stormy Monday.

   _____

4. The class read a poem by Gwendolyn Brooks called kitchenette building.

   _____

5. The newspaper headline read Dow up 50 points, but Ann did not feel any richer.

   _____

6. Many people know that Aretha Franklin recorded Respect, but few know that Otis Redding wrote it.

   _____

7. Carlos read Great Expectations for the third time.

   _____

8. Steve wondered why his wife was reading a magazine article called No More Chubby Hubby.

   _____

   _____

9. Before final exams, Pat tacked a poster of Edward Munch's painting The Scream above her desk.

   _____

   _____

10. Carol's favorite comic strip is Get Fuzzy.

   _____

Review Exercises

Complete the Review Exercises to see how well you have learned the skills addressed in this chapter. As you work through the exercises, go back through the chapter to review any of the rules you do not understand completely.

REVIEW EXERCISE 1   USING QUOTATION MARKS AND PUNCTUATING DIRECT QUOTATIONS

Place quotation marks around direct quotations in the following sentences and place commas and question marks where they are needed.

1. Something is going on. It's too quiet in here said Francine.

   _____

2. I don't care if the pet store is giving away free goldfish said Clark's mother. We already have enough pets.

   _____

   _____

3. Vernon said This looks like a catalog for people with more money than sense.

   _____

4. Do you know how far it is to the stadium the customer asked the clerk.

   _____

5. When we tried to see the movie said Curtis there was a line halfway around the theater.

   _____

   _____

REVIEW EXERCISE 2   **USING QUOTATION MARKS AND COMMAS WITH DIRECT QUOTATIONS**

Place quotation marks around direct quotations in the following sentences and add commas where needed. Two of the sentences are indirect quotations that do not require quotation marks.

1. The angry woman said My appointment was for two-thirty, and I have been waiting for an hour.

   _____

   _____

2. The veterinarian said Puddles was improving but should remain hospitalized for at least two more days.

   _____

3. Every work week should be a four-day week said Carla.

   _____

4. When her children cleaned the entire house and mowed the lawn, Paula said it was the best Mother's Day gift she had ever received.

   _____

5. Did you say this was thyme? said Paul. It looks like a weed to me.

   _____

REVIEW EXERCISE 3   **USING UNDERLINING OR QUOTATION MARKS WITH TITLES**

Use underlining or quotation marks to set off titles in each of the following sentences.

1. Chapter 14, Psychological Disorders, is the most interesting chapter in our psychology textbook.

   _____

   _____

2. John Williams has composed music for movies such as Jaws, E.T., Star Wars, and Jurassic Park.

   _____

   _____

3. Derek swears there is a country song called If My Nose Were Full of Nickels, I'd Blow It All on You.

   _____

   _____

4. David Hockney's painting, A Bigger Splash, contains no human figure, just a splash made by a diver entering a pool.

_____

_____

5. A small headline at the top of the page said Suspect arrested in Tuesday's robbery.

_____

mywritinglab   For support and practice in meeting this chapter's goal, log in to www.mywritinglab.com and select **Quotation Marks.**

Editing Exercises: Punctuation, Word Choice, and Mechanics

Punctuation, Word Choice, and Mechanics: Two Editing Exercises

EDITING EXERCISE 1   PUNCTUATION, WORD CHOICE, AND MECHANICS

Correct the following errors in punctuation, word choice, and mechanics:

1 quotation marks/underlining error
1 word choice error
2 apostrophe errors
1 capitalization error
2 punctuation errors
3 words commonly confused

[1]Susan Vreeland's novel, "Girl in Hyacinth Blue," traces a painting from its current owner's hands back to the moment of its origin. [2]The painting depicts a young chick sitting by the window, lost in thought, her sewing forgotten in her lap. [3]In a series of vignettes, Vreelands story traces the painting through its various owners. [4]A professor's love of the painting, which he believes to be a Vermeer, is overshadowed only buy his guilt. [5]He is consumed by the

knowledge that his father, a Nazi, took it from a jewish family as he sent them off to die in a prison camp. [6]In another vignette a married man keeps the painting because it reminds him of a lost love. [7]Another story tells of a father who sells the painting to feed his child after the child's mother is hanged! [8]As the story winds back threw the centuries through owner after owner, only the painting remains the same, luminous and beautiful, a scrap of ordinary life captured on canvas. [9]As the owner's admire the luminous beauty of the painting, so may readers appreciate the luminous quality of Vreeland's writing and the poignancy of the characters as scraps of their extraordinary lives are captured on paper. [10]*Girl in Hyacinth Blue* is a novel too be savored and enjoyed.

1. _____   6. _____

2. _____   7. _____

3. _____   8. _____

4. _____   9. _____

5. _____   10. _____

EDITING EXERCISE 2   PUNCTUATION, WORD CHOICE, AND MECHANICS

Correct the following errors in punctuation, word choice, and mechanics.

2 capital letter errors
3 apostrophe errors
2 italics/underlining errors
1 error in use of quotation marks

[1]Our local bookstore, Templeton's books, is a comfortable place to shop. [2]Opening the heavy wooden door that leads to the shop, a customer is greeted by a blast of air conditioning and the aroma of freshly brewed Coffee. [3]Inside the store, soft classical music plays in the background, and comfortable overstuffed chairs invite customer's to sit and read. [4]Templetons Books has paperback books, hardback books, and a small collection of books on tape. [5]Along the back wall, magazines such as *Psychology Today*, *Vogue*, and *Newsweek* are displayed in neat rows. [6]Templeton's also sells a wide variety of newspapers, from the *New York Times* to sleazy tabloids with headlines such as Mom Abducted by Two-Headed Alien. [7]At Templeton's customers are welcome to browse, so it is not unusual

to see people chatting in the coffee shop over cups of cappuccino or sitting in the comfortable chairs reading a copy of USA Today. [8]With such an inviting atmosphere, its no wonder Templeton's is the most popular bookstore in town.

1. _____   5. _____

2. _____   6. _____

3. _____   7. _____

4. _____   8. _____

Has the Internet Killed Privacy?

Richard Woods

Facebook's Mark Zuckerberg says that privacy is dead. Some people are worried; others say people can't expect privacy in the digital age.

Let's pick a person pretty much <u>at random</u>: Dan Braden of Austin, Texas. I do not know Braden at all, but I can tell you that in the past few days he has spent $373.46 on Louis Vuitton goods, $162.47 at a local grocery store, $20 at a fitness centre and $3.23 on iTunes. He is also a regular at Starbucks, went to a Maudie's Tex-Mex restaurant last week and spent $717.10 on new tires.   1

Is someone spying on Braden or hacking into his bank account? Nope. Instead, he has signed up to Blippy, a new website that puts online every purchase users make with a designated credit card. He is happy to publicize where he goes and what he buys. No privacy worries for him.   2

"If I buy some Britney Spears, I guess my friends would make fun of me," said Braden, who works for the computer company Dell. "But I'm not too concerned about privacy. I don't think I'm doing anything I would be embarrassed about."   3

Call it openness or <u>exhibitionism</u>, it is spreading everywhere. On Twitter you can post your thoughts minute by minute. On Facebook and Flickr personal photographs abound. One website will even broadcast your weight to the world every time you step on the bathroom scales.   4

Do we no longer care about privacy? Not much, claims Mark Zuckerberg, founder and chief executive of Facebook. Last week he declared: "People have gotten really comfortable not only sharing more information and different kinds, but more openly and with more people." He described such lack of privacy as a "<u>social norm</u>."   5

To those who grew up peeking at the neighbors from behind net curtains, it might seem crazy. To younger generations, born with the Internet in their DNA, Zuckerberg may have a point.   6

As Daniel Masoliver, a 24-year-old postgraduate student in London, put it: "The only reason privacy ever existed is because Facebook didn't. People have always liked talking about what they're into and the more people share information with one another, the more comfortable others are joining in."   7

Nevertheless, some online reaction to Zuckerberg's claims was hostile. "He's an idiot," wrote one social networker; "Poppycock," said another.   8

Experts in the social networking phenomenon are also concerned. The <u>erosion</u> of privacy, they say, brings dangers for both individuals and the wider body politic.   9

Sherry Turkle, professor of social studies of science at Massachusetts Institute of Technology, said insensitivity to privacy "shows a disregard of history and the importance of privacy to democracy and, I might add, intimacy. Young people are not unconcerned about this matter. But they feel <u>impotent</u>."   10

Even Zuckerberg, 25, is not truly comfortable letting it all hang out. When a change to Facebook's privacy settings happened recently, it revealed pictures on his profile page of him larking around with friends. In some he looked a bit of a dork. When news of the photographs spread, the images suddenly disappeared again.   11

Last week a Facebook spokeswoman was backpedalling vigorously, denying Zuckerberg had said privacy was dead. "His remarks were <u>mischaracterized,</u>" she said. "A core part of Facebook's mission has always been to deliver the tools that empower people with control over their information." She added: "If the assertion is that anything Mark chooses to make private is inconsistent with his remarks last week, here are a few other hypocritical elements of his life: he hides his credit card numbers in his wallet, he does not post the passwords to his online accounts, and he closes the door behind him when he goes to the toilet."   12

So is privacy no longer the social norm or not?   13

In a You.Gov poll for The Sunday Times this weekend, 30% of people said they agreed that privacy matters less than it did, and 63% disagreed. Just over 70% said they were worried about private information falling into the hands of others on the internet, while 28% said they were not worried. The differences of opinion may partly be down to age. The pace of technological change is so fast that researchers believe even small age gaps produce significantly different attitudes and behavior.   14

According to America's Pew Research Centre, 68% of teenagers send instant messages on the internet compared with 59% of twentysomethings, and a far lower proportion of older age groups. In the UK a study of social networking by Ofcom, the communications watchdog, found that 54% of internet users aged 16–24 had set up a profile on a social networking site, with the numbers falling steadily with age. The younger these "mini-generations" are, the more they appear to accept openness, if only through necessity. If everyone is revealing their lives online, they don't want to be left out.   15

"I remember thinking there was something distinctly creepy about Facebook when I went on it for the first time," said Jack Hancox, 24, of London. "Now it feels completely natural to put photos up and have various profiles on different sites. But still, I think people are quite <u>wary</u> about what they put online."   16

By contrast, Bryony, a 15-year-old Facebooker in Hampshire, said: "I don't   17
think people are worried about it. When you are writing on Facebook, you are
caught up in it and don't think about privacy."

One of her friends, Peter, said: "I'm not really concerned—except a little if my   18
future boss finds out what it [his Facebook profile] was like. But it would also be
cool looking back on it when I was 60."

Or maybe not. The follies of youth are a necessary <u>rite of passage,</u> says Turkle,   19
and used to be easily left to fade; now they may stick around forever.

"Adolescents need to fall in and out of love with people and ideas," said   20
Turkle, whose forthcoming book *Alone Together* examines friendships in the digital age. "The internet is a rich ground for working through identity. But that does
not easily mesh with a life that generates its own electronic shadow."

In other words, your youthful mistakes may remain forever on a computer   21
server and come back to haunt you.

Like many social network users, Sophie, another friend in the Hampshire   22
group, takes comfort from Facebook's privacy settings.

"I'm not really worried," she said. "I have it set up so only my friends can   23
see stuff."

Not everyone is convinced by such safeguards. For a start, Facebook has re-   24
duced the privacy level of its default setting. If you don't actively impose privacy,
lots of people will have access to your information. It can also become publicly
available if a friend's profile is not properly protected. Even if you do try to re-
strict your profile, the data that remains public can still give away a lot about you.
Facebook, for example, has no privacy restrictions on your name, photograph, list
of friends and certain other material. By analyzing such data, "spider" programs
can draw up social graphs that reveal your sexuality, political beliefs and other
characteristics. According to Ross Anderson, professor of security engineering at
Cambridge, it can be done even if you list as few as eight friends. That might not
matter so much in Britain, says Anderson, "but in a country like Iran, where they
punish gays, this is serious stuff."

Other concerns relate to how social networking sites use your data behind the   25
scenes. Facebook's privacy policy runs to more than eight pages and few users will
read it. If you do, you will learn that Facebook "may collect information about
you from other Facebook users"; keep details of any transactions you make; and
allow third parties access to information about you. It also admits it "cannot en-   26
sure that information you share on Facebook will not become publicly available."

Ever since George Orwell wrote *Nineteen Eighty-Four,* the Big Brother state has
been most people's first concern about diminishing privacy. Now private organizations and criminals are catching up fast.

The recent book *Delete: the Virtue of Forgetting in the Digital Age* cites the   27
case of Stacy Snyder, a student teacher in Pennsylvania. After she posted a picture
of herself apparently drunk on a social networking site she was denied a teaching
certificate.

Burglars are already thought to use Facebook to try to find out when proper- 28
ties may be left empty. And Anderson warns that "phishing" is a growing threat.
Using data gathered from social networking sites, criminals are sending people
emails that appear to come from their friends. Research shows that people are
far less wary of such emails than unsolicited spam, even though they can lead to
identity theft.

While the rest of us find our privacy is up for grabs, the rich and famous are 29
having theirs increasingly protected. Lawyers are using human rights legislation
to bring cases in British courts, which are favorable to protestations of privacy.
The latest action has been launched by Kate Middleton, the girlfriend of Prince
William, who claims her privacy was violated by a picture of her playing tennis
on Christmas Day.

A greater danger than there being one privacy law for the rich and another 30
for everyone else is that of a chronic <u>malaise,</u> at least in the view of Jaron Lanier,
author of a new book called *You Are Not A Gadget*. Lanier fears that the openness and "collectivity" of today's internet is leading us towards mediocrity. "We
shouldn't want the whole world to take on the quality of having been designed
by committee," he said. "When you have everyone collaborate on everything,
you generate a dull average outcome in all things." The best innovation relies on
privacy, he says.

The shift towards openness, however, has momentum and attitudes may well 31
be changing as Zuckerberg claimed. Young people are either unaware of the risks
or feel that less privacy is the price they have to pay to participate in social
networking.

Anderson is only half-joking when he says social networking has become a 32
"survival necessity" for the young. "At Cambridge all the party invitations go out
on Facebook," he said. "So if you don't have Facebook, you won't get invited to
any parties, so you won't have any sex, so you won't have any children, so your
genes die out. So it's an evolutionary necessity to be on Facebook."

Just remember, when you accept that Facebook invitation to a hot date, do 33
not use a Blippy card to buy contraceptives on the way there. Unless you want
the whole world to know what you are thinking.

Building Vocabulary

For each question, use your dictionary and context clues to choose the meaning that most nearly defines the underlined word or phrase as it is used in
the essay.

1. The phrase <u>at random</u> most nearly means
   a. without thought or planning.
   b. systematically.
   c. after establishing criteria.
   d. with a purpose in mind.

2. The word <u>exhibitionism</u> most nearly means
   a. modesty.
   b. fear of exposure.
   c. artistry.
   d. need to expose onself.

3. The phrase <u>social norm</u> most nearly means
   a. conformity.
   b. interacting socially before seeking privacy.
   c. expectation or behavior shared by a group.
   d. the idea that privacy is dead.

4. The word <u>erosion</u> most nearly means
   a. wearing away.
   b. soil condition.
   c. building up.
   d. disapproval.

5. The word <u>impotent</u> most nearly means
   a. important.
   b. powerless.
   c. unconcerned.
   d. intimate.

6. The word <u>mischaracterized</u> most nearly means
   a. misspelled.
   b. misquoted.
   c. detrimental to one's character.
   d. misrepresented.

7. The word <u>wary</u> most nearly means
   a. cautious.
   b. dishonest.
   c. accepting.
   d. weary.

8. The phrase <u>rite of passage</u> most nearly means
   a. anything posted on Facebook.
   b. something that is required.
   c. mysterious ritual to be inducted into a cult.
   d. step on the path to adulthood.

9. The word <u>malaise</u> most nearly means
   a. weakness.
   b. malice.

    c. any chronic disease.

    d. slow Internet connection.

10. The word <u>collaborate</u> most nearly means

    a. comment.

    b. work independently.

    c. work together.

    d. refuse to work.

Understanding the Essay

1. Which statement best expresses the main idea of the essay?

    a. The Internet is increasing the dangers of identity theft.

    b. Facebook enables thieves to target people who post their absences from home on Facebook.

    c. While many worry about the erosion of privacy on the Internet, others see it as a natural and inevitable effect of technology.

    d. The Internet has made privacy a thing of the past.

2. How did the author find out about Dan Braden's credit card activity?

    a. by hacking Braden's computer.

    b. by visiting Braden's Facebook page and putting in a friend request.

    c. through Blippy.com, where Braden allowed his transactions to be revealed.

    d. through data released by someone who hacked a credit card company's database.

3. The author implies that Mark Zuckerberg believes privacy is dead because

    a. technology is too intrusive.

    b. people want to reveal details about their lives.

    c. modern young people reveal too much information about themselves.

    d. Facebook encourages oversharing.

4. What can a "spider" program do, according to the article?

    a. connect people with friends through the Internet.

    b. find an individual's credit card and banking information.

    c. cure arachnophobia by exposing the phobic individual to detailed photographs of large hairy spiders.

    d. draw conclusions about one's sexuality and politics.

5. According to the article, which of the following might be interested in collecting data about individuals?

    a. the government.

    b. private organizations.

    c. criminals.

    d. all of the above.

6. According to the author, which group is increasingly having its privacy protected?

a. Facebook users

b. lawyers

c. the rich and famous

d. younger people

7. According to the student quoted at the end of the essay, people who do not have Facebook accounts also do not receive

a. party invitations.

b. "phishing" emails from criminals.

c. good grades.

d. job offers in technology.

Looking at Language

8. The essay contains many terms related to the Internet and its technologies. List five of these words.

_____

9. Some writers judiciously avoid using brand names in their writing so as not to promote any particular product. This writer uses many brand names. List five of them. Do you believe the use of brand names enhances or detracts from this essay? Why?

_____

_____

10. Choose three unfamiliar words from the essay that are not among the vocabulary questions. Define each.

_____

_____

_____

Discussing the Essay

Prepare to discuss the following questions in class by thinking about them or writing about them in your journal.

1. How much privacy should a person be able to expect on a social networking site?

2. Prospective employers have been known to search for job candidates on social networking sites to help finalize a decision about hiring. By the same

token, employees have been fired for inappropriate content or for posts disparaging an employer. Do you believe employers are within their rights to do these things?

Topics for Writing

Assignment 1: Your Social Network

Journal Entry or Small Scrawl

Do you have an account on a social networking site? What kinds of things do you post there? What information would you think twice about posting? Why?

Assignment 2: One Libation from Graduation

Essay

The article mentions Stacy Snyder, who was denied a teaching degree because of a photo posted on her MySpace page. The photo showed the then 25-year-old at a Halloween party wearing a pirate hat and drinking from a plastic cup. The cup's contents were not visible, but the photo was labeled "Drunken Pirate." Despite the student's good grades and performance reviews, the college denied her a teaching degree on the grounds that she lacked professionalism, and awarded her a degree in English instead. She sued the college for her teaching degree and lost. Do you think the college was justified in its decision not to award her an education degree? Write an essay explaining why or why not.

Assignment 3: Advantages or Disadvantages of a Social Network

Essay

What do you see as the advantages or disadvantages of social networking sites?

Assignment 4: Cyberbullying

Essay

As social networks have become more popular, cyberbullying has arisen as a threat among high school and sometimes college students. What are some ways that parents, teachers, and students can fight cyberbullying or prevent it in the first place?

Growing Up Bilingual

Sara Gonzalez

Does a parent have a duty to teach a child English and to speak English in the home, no matter what the parent's native language? Sara Gonzalez, who wanted her child to speak two languages, found herself at odds with a teacher and principal at her child's school.

About 30 years ago, I arrived in the United States as a refugee, accompanied by my two small children. I had been forced to abandon our beautiful island of Cuba. 1

A few months after getting settled (more or less) in Brunswick, N.J., I enrolled my son in kindergarten. Several weeks later, I received a letter from the principal asking me to come to school and meet with him and my son's teacher. I accepted the invitation and strolled into what was to become my first unpleasant experience in the United States: a lesson in <u>cultural prejudice</u> and exposure to a very <u>unsophisticated</u> American educational system. 2

All my life I had looked up to the education system, believing it to be filled with sophisticated, smart role models. I soon would learn differently. 3

As I entered the principal's office, greetings were exchanged. Then, without wasting any time, the principal and teacher confronted me with very blunt questions: "Is your son mentally retarded? Does he suffer from any kind of mental disability?" 4

My young heart grew 100 years old. The blood seemed to drain from my body and tears swelled in my eyes. Were they talking about my wonderful Luis? No, no, it can't be. What a helpless, lonely moment! I told them that Luis was not mentally disabled, that he was a quiet, sweet little boy. 5

To this they said, "Well, maybe he witnessed too many <u>atrocities</u> in your war-torn country and that has affected him?" No, I said again. We never witnessed any fighting or killings. I asked them why they were asking me all these questions. 6

My son was incapable of following the teacher's directions, they told me, and thus, he was <u>disrupting</u> the class. Lo and behold! Didn't they know my son did not speak English yet? 7

They were <u>outraged</u>: "Why hasn't your son been taught to speak English? Don't you speak English at home?" 8

No, I didn't speak English at home, I replied. I was sure my son would learn English in a couple of months, and I didn't want him to forget his native language. Well, wrong answer! What kind of person would not speak in English to 9 her son at home and at all times? "Are you one of those people who come to this country to save dollars and send them back to their country, never wanting to be a part of this society?"

Needless to say, I tried to tell them I was not one of "those people." Then 10 they told me the meeting was over, and I left.

As I had <u>anticipated</u>, my son learned to speak English <u>fluently</u> before the 11 school year was over. He went on to graduate from college and become <u>a part of corporate America</u>, earning close to six figures. He travels <u>extensively</u> and leads a well-adjusted, content life. And he has benefited from being <u>bilingual</u>.

Speaking more than one language allows people to communicate with 12 others; it teaches people about other cultures and other places—something very basic and obviously lacking in the two "educators" I encountered in New Jersey.

Building Vocabulary

For each question, use your dictionary and context clues to choose the meaning that most nearly defines the underlined word or phrase as it is used in the essay.

1. The phrase <u>cultural prejudice</u> most nearly means
   a. intolerance of the ways of other societies.
   b. fear and dislike of operas and art galleries.
   c. genocide.
   d. favoring other cultures over one's own.

2. The word <u>unsophisticated</u> most nearly means
   a. complex.
   b. elite.
   c. excellent.
   d. primitive.

3. The word <u>atrocities</u> most nearly means
   a. horrors.
   b. acrostics.
   c. soldiers.
   d. crimes.

4. The word <u>disrupting</u> most nearly means
   a. failing.
   b. not understanding.
   c. corrupting.
   d. disturbing.

5. The word <u>outraged</u> most nearly means
   a. understanding.
   b. angry.
   c. curious.
   d. sympathetic.

6. The word <u>anticipated</u> most nearly means
   a. precipitated.
   b. expected.
   c. taught.
   d. planned.

7. The word <u>fluently</u> most nearly means
   a. haltingly.
   b. smoothly.
   c. reluctantly.
   d. temporarily.

8. The phrase <u>a part of corporate America</u> most nearly means
   a. a salaried employee in a large corporation.
   b. a part-time worker.
   c. a union member.
   d. a company such as IBM.

9. The word <u>extensively</u> most nearly means
   a. at great cost.
   b. widely.
   c. briefly.
   d. luxuriously.

10. The word <u>bilingual</u> most nearly means
   a. biological.
   b. educated.
   c. able to speak fluently.
   d. able to speak two languages.

Understanding the Essay

1. Which statement most nearly expresses the main idea of the essay?
   a. Coming to a school in a country where one does not speak the language can be a frightening experience.
   b. The American education system is in need of reform and greater cultural awareness.

   c. The author encountered cultural prejudice when she enrolled her son in school.

   d. Living in a war-torn country can damage a child's ability to learn.

2. The author implies that on leaving her native land, she felt

   a. regretful.

   b. thankful to escape.

   c. glad for the opportunity to build a new life.

   d. frightened.

3. The author did not speak English to her child because

   a. she had not yet learned the English language.

   b. she thought it was the school's job to teach her son English.

   c. she wanted her child to have the benefit of two languages.

   d. she was afraid she would not teach her child properly.

4. When her son started school, the author was summoned by the principal

   a. immediately.

   b. after a few days.

   c. after a few weeks.

   d. after a few months.

5. Which of the following was *not* a stated result of the meeting between the author and school personnel?

   a. The author became disillusioned with the school system.

   b. School officials implied that the author did not want to contribute to American society.

   c. The author began speaking English at home.

   d. The author discovered that school officials were not aware her child did not speak English.

6. The essay is mainly developed by

   a. process.

   b. cause-effect.

   c. definition.

   d. narration.

7. With which statement would the author most likely agree?

   a. Parents owe it to their children to speak whatever language the child uses in school.

   b. Children of immigrants to the United States have a right to be educated in their native language.

   c. Culture and language taught in a child's home are not the business of school officials.

   d. School officials have a responsibility to call any problems to a parent's attention before the situation becomes serious.

Looking at Language

8. What specific words and phrases tell you how the author felt about the education system before and after the meeting with her son's teacher and principal?

_____

_____

_____

_____

9. What words show the emotional impact the school meeting had on the author?

_____

_____

10. Why do you think the author chooses to use dialogue in describing the incident in the principal's office? What effect does hearing the characters' exact words have on the reader?

_____

_____

Discussing the Essay

Prepare to discuss the following questions in class by thinking about them or writing about them in your journal.

1. In what ways did school officials handle their concerns about the author's son in an appropriate manner? In what ways did they handle the situation inappropriately? If you were a school principal, how would you handle a situation such as this?

2. Gonzales was confident that her son would learn English once he was enrolled in school. Some parts of the country have tried bilingual education programs in which teachers speak English along with the native language of the students they teach. Do you believe such programs are a good idea?

3. Gonzales says that speaking another language "teaches people about other cultures and other places." In many countries, children are routinely taught to speak a language other than their own. In the United States, learning a second language is the exception rather than the rule. Should children in the United States routinely be taught a second language?

Topics for Writing

Assignment 1: A Different Country

Journal Entry

Imagine that you are forced to leave your country and move to a country where a different language is spoken. You have a school-age child. Discuss in a journal entry whether you would speak the language of the new country at home or speak your first language. How important would it be to you to preserve your native language and culture? Why?

Assignment 2: Ancestral Journey

Essay

Because the United States is a fairly young country, most of its residents can look back just a few generations and find ancestors who began life in another country. In an essay, discuss the events that brought your family to this country, including some of the challenges they faced.

Assignment 3: Problems in Communication

Essay

Few people make it through twelve years of schooling without suffering setbacks and traumas. Have you (or your child, if you are a parent) ever had problems in school that stemmed from language or communication difficulties? How did you overcome these problems?

Assignment 4: Melting Pot or Patchwork Quilt?

Essay

The United States used to be termed a "melting pot" because it was a land in which many cultures blended into one and in which people celebrated their similarities. Recently, however, the idea of cultural diversity has challenged that of the melting pot. In this view, the United States is more like a patchwork quilt, with all the pieces joined yet with each possessing its own pattern. In a culturally diverse society, people celebrate their differences. Write an essay in which you discuss the advantages and/or disadvantages of one or both of these views.

The Game of My Life

Jeff Obafemi Carr

To succeed in unfamiliar arenas, it sometimes helps to have the support of a special person. Jeff Obafemi Carr, always more comfortable with books than with basketballs, searches the stands for one special face.

The atmosphere was tense. We were the top-rated team in the league, on a two-game losing streak. It was late in the season. Fatigue had settled in, and our top players were losing their touch. 1

I looked around in anticipation, scanning the <u>sparse</u> crowd for his face. No show. Maybe telling him about the game just three hours earlier had been too short a notice. Maybe he was busy at home. Maybe it just wasn't important enough to come to. 2

Of course it wasn't the intercity high-school marquee game or the NBA. It was only the Tuesday night winter league at the downtown YMCA. Yet for the past seven weeks, this aging gymnasium had been my field of dreams. 3

You see, I hadn't been an athlete while I was growing up. Sure, I ran in the neighborhood and climbed trees, threw rocks and shot bottle-cap guns. But except for a short <u>stint</u> on the seventh-grade track team and a <u>horrific</u> summer in Little League baseball, I stuck with the choir and the stage. I didn't know how to play basketball. My father hadn't taught me the game, probably because he had grown up in the hills of east Tennessee and had had me late in life, when he was in his mid-forties. Whatever the reason, I wasn't on the court Saturday mornings hooping. In childhood pickup games, I was a <u>liability</u> to the team. I didn't even look athletic—I wasn't very tall, I had no bulging biceps or explosive calves, and my round, slightly chubby face struck no fear in an opponent. After so many jokes about my <u>deficiencies</u>, I figured out the way to conquer them all: quit. But somehow quitting never stopped the desire within. It just made me dream harder and higher, all the while fearing the serious thought of picking up that ball or hitting that track. 4

So I grew up with my self-esteem coming from my intellect rather than my physical <u>prowess</u>. Then I went to college and met some brothers and sisters who put some funk into my soul. They helped me discover that my ancestors founded civilizations and were kings and queens and architects and doctors. After a few months of study, I began to believe I could do anything. Anything? 5

I hit the track one day, or should I say the track hit me? I <u>sputtered</u> along, covering a little more ground each day, until I was running a mile, then two, then three. (Now I run four miles without a problem and work out every day.)   6

For a year before the night of the big game, I had been playing basketball with a passion. My growth spurt at age 19 had helped me develop my slender six-foot two-inch frame, and I would work my legs extra hard. I had finally developed enough confidence to sign up for the league at the local YMCA.   7

It was also the place where I, at 29 years old, found a chance to live my dream. I might not ever be the lead scorer, but I figured that if I could just score a few points and snatch a few rebounds, I would be satisfied. I had already <u>surpassed</u> this goal, averaging ten points going into that night's game.   8

I was hanging around the perimeter practicing my now <u>potentially</u> deadly three-pointer. When I finally saw him come through the gym door, my heart leapt. There he was, just as he'd been there for me so many times before—at the choir concert, the play I was starring in or the speech I was giving. But this time my pops was coming to see his boy play ball. I ushered him to a seat in the bleachers as the ref blew the whistle for the opening tip.   9

I was in the starting lineup, and I found myself playing harder than I had ever played before. We lost the game by more than 30 points. But I had fun in a strange, boyish sort of way. I scored 13 points, a career high—9 of them from behind the arc. The last minute of the game I got a steal and passed it downcourt to our big man. He passed it back to me on the break. I went up hard and, you guessed it, made a slam dunk! My very first in a game, and my pops was a witness.   10

As I headed to the locker room in defeat, yet carrying an odd air of victory, I heard a voice in my ear. It was the voice that the <u>latent</u> athlete in me had longed to hear since I was young, uttering the words of empowerment, love and pride.   11

"You played a good game, son."   12

Better than you may ever know, Pops.   13

Building Vocabulary

For each question, use your dictionary and context clues to choose the meaning that most nearly defines the underlined word or phrase as it is used in the essay.

1. The word <u>sparse</u> most nearly means
   a. thin.
   b. cheering.
   c. unenthusiastic.
   d. large.

2. The word <u>stint</u> most nearly means
   a. limitation.
   b. coach.
   c. period of service.
   d. year.

3. The word <u>horrific</u> most nearly means
   a. dreadful.
   b. fun-filled.
   c. hot.
   d. playful.

4. The word <u>liability</u> most nearly means
   a. help.
   b. person of ability.
   c. key player.
   d. burden.

5. The word <u>deficiencies</u> most nearly means
   a. shortcomings.
   b. proficiencies.
   c. defeats.
   d. physical traits.

6. The word <u>prowess</u> most nearly means
   a. size.
   b. physique.
   c. body.
   d. skill.

7. The word <u>sputtered</u> most nearly means
   a. stammered.
   b. moved gracefully.
   c. sped.
   d. toiled.

8. The word <u>surpassed</u> most nearly means
   a. surprised.
   b. moved beyond.
   c. given up.
   d. set.

9. The word <u>potentially</u> most nearly means
   a. possibly.
   b. unquestionably.

    c. lethally.

    d. immediately.

10. The word <u>latent</u> most nearly means

    a. potent.

    b. talking.

    c. hidden.

    d. late.

Understanding the Essay

1. When he played the game he writes about, Carr was

    a. twelve.

    b. nineteen.

    c. twenty-nine.

    d. forty.

2. Which method of introduction does the author use?

    a. anecdote

    b. broad-to-narrow

    c. quotation

    d. contrast

3. Before he went to college, Carr's method of overcoming his problems with athletics was to

    a. believe in himself.

    b. practice occasionally, but not often enough.

    c. read books about sports.

    d. give up.

4. The author states that his father

    a. was an older parent and therefore too busy to give time to a young son.

    b. was always there to cheer his intellectual and artistic accomplishments.

    c. was habitually late.

    d. was disappointed that he had never made it as an athlete.

5. The author implies that he was spurred on to athletic achievement by

    a. the taunts of schoolmates who pointed out his deficiencies.

    b. his sense of athletic inadequacy.

    c. hearing about the accomplishments of his ancestors.

    d. his father's patient coaching.

6. The author implies that athletic prowess

    a. still eludes him.

    b. developed overnight.

c. came slowly but surely.

d. required too much work.

7. Which of the following is *not* a reason that the game was special to the author?

a. He played the best game ever.

b. It was an important intercity championship game.

c. His father was there to watch him.

d. He was competing in a field in which he had never excelled.

Looking at Language

8. Often, writers are advised to explain any technical or specialized language that they use in an essay, yet Carr uses basketball terminology without explaining it. Find four examples of basketball terminology and write them on the following lines. Do you believe that a person unfamiliar with basketball would have a hard time understanding the essay as a whole? Why or why not?

_____

_____

_____

_____

_____

_____

9. The author uses transitions of time to guide the reader through his essay. Find and list five.

_____

_____

_____

_____

_____

_____

10. Carr's father says, "You played a good game, son." But Carr hears much more than casual congratulations. What do the words mean to Carr?

_____

_____

_____

_____

_____

Discussing the Essay

Prepare to discuss the following questions in class by thinking about them or writing about them in your journal.

1. Though Carr was an adult when he played the basketball game he writes about, he describes himself anxiously scanning the crowd for his father. Do you think people outgrow the need for parental attention and approval?

2. Explain what Carr means when he says that he walked off the court "in defeat, yet carrying an odd air of victory."

Topics for Writing

Assignment 1: The Game of Your Life

Journal Entry or an Essay

Write a journal entry or a process essay describing your participation in a sport or athletic pastime that you enjoy. You might include such things as how you became interested in the game and how you improved your skills, or you might focus on your performance in a single game.

Assignment 2: Inspiration from the Past

Essay

Carr writes of drawing inspiration from studying the accomplishments of his ancestors. Are you inspired or otherwise affected by what your ancestors have done? Write a cause-effect essay showing how you are affected by those who have gone before. Alternatively, choose up to three of your older relatives or ancestors you have heard stories about and show how their example affects your life today.

Assignment 3: Struggle

Essay

Mastering skills we find difficult is sometimes more meaningful than doing well at skills that come easily to us. Discuss an accomplishment that you value because it was a struggle.

Assignment 4: Support

Essay

Carr writes of his father's support and how much it has meant to him. Write an essay about a person who has supported your efforts. In each body paragraph, give a different example showing how that person has supported you. Alternatively, write about three people who have supported you at various times in your life. Again, each paragraph should be supported by specific examples.

When Words Get in the Way

Athlone G. Clarke

Athlone G. Clarke finds that English is used differently in the United States than in his native Jamaica.

Coming from Jamaica, I have discovered that even among people who speak the same language, there can be artificial barriers. 1

In my island home, greetings are usually informal and taken at <u>face</u> value. I assumed it to be the same here, but I soon discovered there are deep historical wounds hidden behind everyday words. 2

One evening, as I passed my elderly neighbor Mr. Gabinsky on the stairs, he greeted me with his usual thick accent: "Hey there, young boy, how is the family doing today?" We exchanged a few <u>pleasantries</u> and went our separate ways. 3

That same evening, another neighbor who lived in the apartment upstairs dropped by. "You shouldn't let that man from across the hall get away with calling you 'boy,'" Al said. "He is disrespecting you in a big way." 4

This was news to me. Back home it was <u>commonplace</u> for elderly people to refer to younger adults as "boy" or "girl." Al, who is African American, explained that it was different here, that the "b" word has its roots in slavery and was to be <u>deemed</u> <u>derogatory</u> when used by my white neighbor. 5

So, the next time Mr. Gabinsky greeted me in such a manner, I quickly put a stop to it. He apologized profusely. As it turned out, he was from Hungary and, like myself, was not yet accustomed to choosing his words according to historical <u>context</u>. 6

And then there was the day I got lost trying to find a "shop" that sold milk. Many of us who grew up in the islands know what a vital link the "shop" is in the food chain. My journey would have been less complicated had I been looking for a "store" that sold milk. It is interesting to note that if my mission had been to buy clothes instead of milk, then that would mean I was out "shopping." 7

Here I am, an English-speaking man living in an English-speaking country, but with the feeling of looking in a mirror where everything appears the same, except it's reversed. 8

One of the most complex words I have had to work into my vocabulary is "minority." I had to learn what a "minority contract" was, and why someone like 9

Mr. Gabinsky, who is white, could not qualify. The word is almost always used in the context of racial classification. It hardly matters that there may be fewer Hungarian Americans living here than African Americans or Asian Americans or Hispanic Americans.

Sports is a subject dear to my heart, and my hopes were cruelly dashed when I dis-   10
covered there would be no African, European or Asian nations competing in the "World Series." One of my favorite athletes is now an <u>unrestricted</u> free agent. The words "unrestricted" and "free" at first seemed a little <u>superfluous</u>, until I learned there is no such thing as <u>excess</u> in American sports when it comes to words and salaries.

At least the language of business appears to be <u>universal</u>. The first time I   11
passed a certain Persian rug establishment in Atlanta, there was a big sign out front that said: "Going out of business sale. Fifty percent off." Ten years later, the sign is still there, touched up with a fresh coat of paint.

Building Vocabulary

For each question, use your dictionary and context clues to choose the meaning that most nearly defines the underlined word or phrase as it is used in the essay.

1. The word <u>face</u> most nearly means
   a. confrontational.
   b. surface.
   c. countenance.
   d. little.

2. The word <u>pleasantries</u> most nearly means
   a. serious insights.
   b. insults.
   c. Jamaican or Hungarian coins.
   d. friendly remarks.

3. The word <u>commonplace</u> most nearly means
   a. crude.
   b. communal.
   c. ordinary.
   d. unfair.

4. The word <u>deemed</u> most nearly means
   a. regarded.
   b. suppressed.
   c. dreamed.
   d. screened.

5. The word <u>derogatory</u> most nearly means
   a. forced.
   b. flattering.

    c. democratic.

    d. belittling.

6. The word <u>context</u> most nearly means

    a. custom.

    b. background.

    c. history book.

    d. fantasy.

7. The word <u>unrestricted</u> most nearly means

    a. casual.

    b. obsessive.

    c. free.

    d. signed.

8. The word <u>superfluous</u> most nearly means

    a. more than is necessary.

    b. perfect.

    c. less than is necessary.

    d. fluent.

9. The word <u>excess</u> most nearly means

    a. overabundance.

    b. success.

    c. lack.

    d. enough.

10. The word <u>universal</u> most nearly means

    a. changeable.

    b. widespread.

    c. subject to historical interpretations.

    d. on sale.

Understanding the Essay

1. A good alternative title for the essay would be

    a. "English and You."

    b. "Longing for Jamaica."

    c. "Language Barrier."

    d. "The Language of Business."

2. The thesis of the essay is

    a. implied.

    b. stated in the first paragraph.

   c. stated in the second paragraph.

   d. stated in the last paragraph.

3. The author implies that his neighbor, Mr. Gabinsky, is

   a. insensitive.

   b. malicious.

   c. well meaning.

   d. racist.

4. The method of development primarily used in the essay is

   a. description.

   b. definition.

   c. cause-effect.

   d. example.

5. The author's tone would best be described as

   a. objective.

   b. critical.

   c. humorous.

   d. bitter.

6. With which of the following statements would the author probably not agree?

   a. Whether a word causes offense may depend on who uses it.

   b. Storekeepers' use of language often is motivated by desire for profit.

   c. The government should make an effort to standardize English usage.

   d. Athletes in the United States are often overpaid.

7. Which statement best expresses the main idea of the essay?

   a. Only business English is consistent and predictable.

   b. A person from another country may not understand the historical context of American English usage.

   c. Even an English-speaking person can be tripped up by the idiosyncrasies of American English.

   d. Speaking a common language ensures that people will understand one another.

Looking at Language

8. Long before Clarke specifically tells us that his neighbor is Hungarian, he hints that his neighbor may not be a native of the United States. What specific phrase provides the clue?

_____

9. One of Clarke's points of confusion was the difference between the word *shop* and the word *store*. How would you explain the difference?

_____

_____

_____

_____

_____

10. Choose and define two unfamiliar words from the essay that are not in-cluded in "Understanding Vocabulary."

_____

Discussing the Essay

Prepare to discuss the following questions in class by thinking about them or writing about them in your journal.

1. The title of the essay suggests that words sometimes hinder communica-tion instead of enhancing it. Do you agree? Can you think of examples other than those given in the essay?

2. Clarke attributes his confusion over language to being from Jamaica. Do you think linguistic confusion also exists among people born in the United States? Can you think of examples?

Topics for Writing

Assignment 1: An Unintentional Offense

Journal Entry

Have you ever unintentionally offended someone through your use of language, or has someone offended you without meaning to? Discuss in a journal entry.

Assignment 2: Generation Gap

Essay

Write an essay contrasting the way members of two different generations use language. You may write about generations as a whole or choose a represent-ative of each generation (for example, your grandmother and your younger brother) to contrast. In either case, include specific illustrations of the types of language used.

Assignment 3: Pet Language Peeves

Essay

Write an essay discussing your pet peeves about the way people use language. Explain why you react as you do.

Assignment 4: The Language of Advertising

Essay

Write an essay analyzing how the language of three specific commercials or advertisements appeals to the particular needs and characteristics of its target audience. For example, an ad for a luxury car might use words associated with wealth, such as "rich leather," "a wise investment," or "platinum service guarantee," to appeal to a wealthy audience. If you use a radio or television commercial as one of your examples, record it or take notes so that you can discuss exact words used.

Letting in Light

Patricia Raybon

For author Patricia Raybon, washing windows is more than a chore; it is a link to the past and a bridge to the future.

The windows were a gift or maybe a bribe—or maybe a bonus—for falling in love   1
with such a <u>dotty</u> old house. The place was a wreck. A showoff, too. So it tried
real hard to be more. But it lacked so much—good heat, stable floors, solid walls,
enough space. A low interest rate.

But it had windows. More glass and bays and bows than people on a budget   2
had a right to expect. And in unlikely places—like the window inside a bedroom
closet, its only view a strawberry patch planted by the children next door.

None of it made sense. So we bought the place. We saved up and put some   3
money down, then toasted the original builder—no doubt some brave and gentle
carpenter, blessed with a flair for the grand gesture. A <u>romantic</u> with a T-square.

We were young then and struggling. Also, we are black. We looked with irony   4
and awe at the task now before us. But we did not faint.

The time had come to wash windows.   5

Yes, I do windows. Like an amateur and a dabbler, perhaps, but the old-   6
fashioned way—one pane at a time. It is the best way to pay back something so
plain for its clear and silent gifts—the light of day, the glow of moon, hard rain,
soft snow, dawn's early light.

The Romans called them *specularia*. They glazed their windows with <u>trans-   7
lucent</u> marble and shells. And thus the ancients let some light into their world.

In my own family, my maternal grandmother washed windows—and floors and   8
laundry and dishes and a lot of other things that needed cleaning—while doing
day work for a rich, stylish redhead in her Southern hometown.

To feed her five children and keep them clothed and happy, to help them walk   9
proudly and go to church and sing hymns and have some change in their pockets—and to warm and furnish the house her dead husband had built and added
onto with his own hands—my grandmother went to work.

She and her third daughter, my mother, put on maids' uniforms and cooked   10
and sewed and served a family that employed my grandmother until she was
nearly 80. She called them Mister and Missus—yes, ma'am and yes, sir—although
she was by many years their elder. They called her Laura. Her surname never
crossed their lips.

But her daughter, my mother, took her earnings from the cooking and serv- 11
ing and window washing and clothes ironing and went to college, <u>forging</u> a life
with a young husband—my father—that granted me, their daughter, a lifetime
of relative comfort.

I owe these women everything. 12

They taught me hope and kindness and how to say thank you. 13

They taught me how to brew tea and pour it. They taught me how to iron 14
creases and whiten linen and cut hair ribbon on the bias so it doesn't unravel.
They taught me to carve fowl, make butter molds and cook a good cream sauce.
They taught me "women's work"—secrets of home, they said, that now are looked
on mostly with <u>disdain</u>: how to sweep, dust, polish and wax. How to mow, prune,
scrub, scour and purify.

They taught me how to wash windows. 15

Not many women do anymore, of course. There's no time. Life has us all on 16
the run. It's easier to call a "window man," quicker to pay and, in the bargain,
forget about the secret that my mother and her mother learned many years before
they finally taught me.

Washing windows clears the cobwebs from the corners. It's plain people's 17
therapy, good for troubles and muddles and other consternations. It's real work,
I venture—honest work—and it's a <u>sound</u> thing to pass on. Mother to daughter.
Daughter to child. Woman to woman.

This is <u>heresy</u>, of course. Teaching a child to wash windows is now an act of 18
bravery—or else defiance. If she's black, it's an act of denial, a gesture that dares
history and heritage to make something of it.

But when my youngest was 5 or 6, I tempted fate and ancestry and I handed 19
her a wooden bucket. Together we would wash the outdoor panes. The moment
sits in my mind:

She works a low row. I work the top. Silently we toil, soaping and polishing, 20
each at her own pace—the only sounds the squeak of glass, some noisy birds, our
own breathing.

Then, quietly at first, this little girl begins to hum. It's a nonsense melody, 21
created for the moment. Soft at first, soon it gets louder. And louder. Then a rec-
ognizable tune emerges. Then she is really singing. With every swish of the towel,
she <u>croons</u> louder and higher in her little-girl voice with her little-girl song. "This
little light of mine—I'm gonna let it shine! Oh, this little light of mine—I'm
gonna let it shine!" So, of course, I join in. And the two of us serenade the glass
and the sparrows and mostly each other. And too soon our work is done.

"That was fun," she says. She is innocent, of course, and does this work by 22
choice, not by necessity. But she's not too young to look at truth and understand
it. And her heart, if not her arm, is <u>resolute</u> and strong.

Those years have passed. And other houses and newer windows—and other 23
"women's jobs"—have moved through my life. I have chopped and pureed and
polished and glazed. Bleached and folded and stirred. I have sung lullabies.

I have also marched and fought and prayed and taught and <u>testified</u>. Women's 24
work covers many bases.

But the tradition of one simple chore remains. I do it without apology. 25

Last week, I dipped the sponge into the pail and began the gentle bath— 26
easing off the trace of wintry snows, of dust storms and dead, brown leaves, of
too much sticky tape used to steady paper pumpkins and Christmas lights and
crepe-paper bows from holidays now past.

While I worked, the little girl—now 12—found her way to the bucket, proving 27
that her will and her voice are still up to the task, but mostly, I believe, to have
some fun.

We are out of step, the two of us. She may not even know it. But we can carry 28
a tune. The work is never done. The song is two-part harmony.

Building Vocabulary

For each question, use your dictionary and context clues to choose the meaning
that most nearly defines the underlined word or phrase as it is used in the essay.

1. The word <u>dotty</u> most nearly means
   a. eccentric.
   b. charming.
   c. beautiful.
   d. polka-dotted.

2. The word <u>romantic</u> most nearly means
   a. exhibitionist.
   b. lover of the opposite sex.
   c. lover of beauty.
   d. poet.

3. The word <u>translucent</u> most nearly means
   a. sheer.
   b. thick.
   c. transmitted.
   d. opaque.

4. The word <u>forging</u> most nearly means
   a. building through hard work.
   b. living.
   c. falsifying.
   d. working in metal.

5. The word <u>disdain</u> most nearly means
   a. approval.
   b. fear.

    c. cheer.

    d. contempt.

6. The word <u>sound</u> most nearly means

    a. noisy.

    b. worthy.

    c. secondhand.

    d. dangerous.

7. The word <u>heresy</u> most nearly means

    a. against religious beliefs.

    b. in tune with what everyone else thinks.

    c. against popular wisdom.

    d. against the writer's beliefs.

8. The word <u>croons</u> most nearly means

    a. cries.

    b. sings.

    c. talks.

    d. shouts.

9. The word <u>resolute</u> most nearly means

    a. timid and withdrawn.

    b. lively and active.

    c. determined and purposeful.

    d. expressive and emotional.

10. The word <u>testified</u> most nearly means

    a. made a will.

    b. spoken out.

    c. sworn in court.

    d. taken a test.

Understanding the Essay

1. The house that the author buys is

    a. small but new and filled with windows.

    b. odd and windowless.

    c. old, rundown, and small but with many windows.

    d. large, open, and filled with light.

2. Which of the following is *not* mentioned as one of the "clear and silent gifts" of a window?

    a. letting in sunlight

    b. affording a view of the snow

    c. keeping out rain

    d. letting in moonlight

3. The author's attitude toward window washing is

    a. mostly positive.

    b. mostly negative.

    c. neutral.

    d. inconsistent.

4. The author says that women today do not do windows because

    a. it is demeaning work.

    b. they are poor housekeepers.

    c. they are too busy.

    d. they consider it "men's work."

5. Along with narration, which pattern of development is used predominantly in the essay?

    a. comparison-contrast

    b. cause-effect

    c. argument

    d. process

6. According to the author, which of the following is "women's work"?

    a. fighting

    b. teaching

    c. cooking

    d. all of the above

7. In teaching her daughter to do windows, the author believes all of the following except one. Which one is it?

    a. She is passing on something important.

    b. She is doing something unconventional.

    c. She is out of step with the times.

    d. She is teaching her daughter that housework is strictly a woman's role.

Looking at Language

8. Look at the use of parallel structure in paragraph 9. Write the parallel phrases on the lines below.

_____

_____

_____

_____

_____

9. Look at the way Raybon describes the first time she and her daughter wash windows together. Which of the five senses does Raybon emphasize in her description? Write down four phrases from the description that convey a sense impression.

_____

_____

_____

10. Look at the following sentence from paragraph 27: "Last week, I dipped the sponge into the pail and began the gentle bath—easing off the trace of wintry snows, of dust storms and dead, brown leaves, of too much sticky tape used to steady paper pumpkins and Christmas lights and crepe-paper bows from holidays now past." How does Raybon feel about the task she is describing? Specifically, which words and phrases serve to tell you how she feels?

_____

_____

_____

Discussing the Essay

Prepare to discuss the following questions in class by thinking about them or writing about them in your journal.

1. How does Raybon feel about the work her mother and grandmother did?

2. Why does Raybon attach significance to the fact that her grandmother's employers called her "Laura" and never used her surname? Think about the relationships you have with others. Who addresses you by your first name? By your surname? How do you address them? Does it make a difference to you? Why or why not?

3. Look at the tasks mentioned by Raybon as "women's work." Are all of them "women's work" in the stereotypical sense? Are any of them normally stereotyped as "men's work"?

Topics for Writing

Assignment 1: "Wash Me"

Journal Entry

You are a window in a house or a car. You are so dirty that some prankster has written "Wash Me" in the grime that covers you. In a journal entry, convince the owner of the house or car to wash you. Include the advantages to the washer as well as the advantages to you.

Assignment 2: An Enjoyable Chore

Essay

Write a process essay telling your reader how you go about doing some chore that you enjoy. Perhaps you enjoy doing laundry, shopping for groceries, cleaning a closet, washing your car, or mowing the lawn. Make sure the essay conveys your enjoyment as well as the steps involved in the chore.

Assignment 3: Handed Down

Essay

In an essay, describe a special tradition, knowledge, or way of doing something that has been passed to you by older members of your family.

Assignment 4: What's in a Name?

Essay

Write an essay discussing the different messages people send through the way they use others' names. There are a couple of different approaches you might take. One is to write a process essay telling what rules should apply in using others' names. You might consider such matters as whether the other person is a stranger or an acquaintance, whether the person is older or younger, and whether the relationship is business or personal. Another is to write an example essay discussing the names various people call you and what those names convey to you.

Coping with Procrastination

Roberta Moore, Barbara Baker, and Arnold H. Packer

Procrastination—why do people put things off, and what should they do about the problem? The authors have some suggestions.

Any discussion of time management would not be complete without an exami- 1
nation of the most <u>well-intentioned</u> person's worst enemy—<u>procrastination</u>.
The dictionary *(Webster's New Collegiate)* defines procrastination as "the act
of putting off intentionally and habitually the doing of something that should
be done." Interestingly, most procrastinators do not feel that they are acting
<u>intentionally</u>. On the contrary, they feel that they fully *intend* to do whatever it
is, but they simply cannot, will not, or—bottom line—they *do not* do it. Procrastinators usually have good reasons for their procrastination (some would call
them excuses): "didn't have time," "didn't feel well," "couldn't figure out what
to do," "couldn't find what I needed," "the weather was too bad"—the list is
never-ending.

Even procrastinators themselves know that the surface reasons for their 2
procrastination are, for the most part, not <u>valid</u>. When procrastination becomes
extreme, it is a self-destructive course and yet, people feel that they are powerless to stop it. This <u>perception</u> can become reality if the underlying cause is
not uncovered. Experts have identified some of the serious <u>underlying</u> causes
of procrastination. Think about them the next time you find yourself struck by
this problem.

Often procrastination stems from a real or imagined fear or worry that is fo- 3
cused not so much on the thing you are avoiding but its <u>potential</u> consequences.
For instance, your procrastination over preparing for an oral presentation could
be based on your fear that no matter how well prepared you are, you will be
overcome by nerves and forget whatever you are prepared to say. Every time you
think about working on the speech, you become so worried about doing "a bad
job" that you have to put the whole thing out of your mind to calm down. You
decide that you will feel calmer about it tomorrow and will be in a much better
frame of mind to tackle it. Tomorrow the scenario gets repeated. The best way to
relieve your anxiety would be to dig in and prepare so well that you can't possibly
do poorly.

Being a perfectionist is one of the main traits that <u>spawns</u> fear and anxi- 4
ety. Whose expectations are we afraid of not meeting? Often it is our own harsh

judgment of ourselves that creates the problem. We set standards that are too high and then judge ourselves too critically. When you picture yourself speaking before a group, are you thinking about how nervous the other students will be as well, or are you comparing your speaking abilities to the anchorperson on the six o'clock news? A more calming thought is to recall how athletes measure improvements in their performances by tracking and trying to improve on their own "personal best." Champions have to work on beating themselves in order to become capable of competing against their opponents. Concentrating on improving your own past performance, and thinking of specific ways to do so, relieves performance anxiety.

On the surface this would seem to be the reason for all procrastination, and the obvious answer is for the procrastinator to find a way to "get motivated." There are situations where lack of motivation is an indicator that you have taken a wrong turn. When you seriously do not want to do the things you need to do, you may need to reevaluate your situation. Did you decide to get a degree in Information Systems because everyone says that's where the high-paying jobs are going to be, when you really want to be a social worker or a travel agent? If so, when you find yourself shooting hoops or watching television when you should be putting in time at the computer lab, it may be time to reexamine your decision. Setting out to accomplish something difficult when your heart isn't in it, is often the root cause of self-destructive behavior. 5

Often procrastination is due to an inability to concentrate or a feeling of being overwhelmed and indecisive. While everyone experiences these feelings during a particular stressful day or week, a continuation of these feelings could indicate that you are in a state of burnout. Burnout is a serious problem that occurs when you have overextended yourself for too long a period of time. It is especially likely to occur if you are pushing yourself both physically and mentally. By failing to pace yourself, you will "hit the wall," like the long distance runner who runs too fast at the beginning of the race. Overworking yourself for too long without mental and physical relaxation is a sure way to run out of steam. Learning to balance your time and set realistic expectations for yourself will prevent burnout. 6

Sometimes you put off doing something because you literally don't know how to do it. This may be hard to admit to yourself, so you may make other excuses. When you can't get started on something, consider the possibility that you need help. For example, if you get approval from your favorite instructor for a term paper topic that requires collecting data and creating graphics, you can be stymied if you don't have the necessary skills and tools to do the work and do it well. Does the collection and analysis of the data require the use of a software program that you don't have and cannot afford to buy? Sometimes it is difficult to ask for help and sometimes it is even hard to recognize that you need help. When you feel stymied, ask yourself, "Do I need help?" Do you need information but haven't a clue as to where to go to get it? Have you committed to doing something that 7 is really beyond your level of skills? Being able to own up to personal limitations and seek out support and resources where needed is a skill used every day by highly successful people.

Building Vocabulary

For each question, use your dictionary and context clues to choose the meaning that most nearly defines the underlined word or phrase as it is used in the essay.

1. The word <u>well-intentioned</u> most nearly means
   a. well-meaning.
   b. well-rounded.
   c. well-spoken.
   d. well-dressed.

2. The word <u>procrastination</u> most nearly means
   a. perfectionism.
   b. putting things off.
   c. predicting the future.
   d. time management.

3. The word <u>intentionally</u> most nearly means
   a. creatively.
   b. conventionally.
   c. carelessly.
   d. deliberately.

4. The word <u>valid</u> most nearly means
   a. false.
   b. valiant.
   c. genuine.
   d. reasons.

5. The word <u>perception</u> most nearly means
   a. reception.
   b. belief.
   c. condition.
   d. power.

6. The word <u>underlying</u> most nearly means
   a. false.
   b. surface.
   c. root.
   d. mild.

7. The word <u>potential</u> most nearly means
    a. potent.
    b. possible.
    c. confidential.
    d. favorable.

8. The word <u>spawns</u> most nearly means
    a. prevents.
    b. relieves.
    c. produces.
    d. spurns.

9. The word <u>burnout</u> most likely means
    a. fire.
    b. energy.
    c. productivity.
    d. exhaustion.

10. The word <u>stymied</u> most likely means
    a. helped.
    b. hindered.
    c. stylish.
    d. successful.

Understanding the Essay

1. Which of the following most closely expresses the main idea of the essay?
    a. People who procrastinate need to get motivated.
    b. Procrastination is unintentional.
    c. Procrastination can be understood and controlled.
    d. Some of the world's most famous people have been procrastinators.

2. Procrastinators tend to be
    a. lazy.
    b. male.
    c. perfectionists.
    d. low achievers.

3. Which of the following is not mentioned as a cause of procrastination?
    a. not being sure how to do something
    b. expecting too much of oneself
    c. not being sure when a project is due
    d. not being motivated

4. According to the authors, inability to concentrate or feeling overwhelmed and indecisive could be a sign of
   a. procrastination.
   b. physical illness.
   c. burnout.
   d. mental instability.

5. Which of the following methods of development is not used in the essay?
   a. narration
   b. example
   c. definition
   d. process

6. The authors imply that a tendency to procrastinate
   a. is always a problem for college students.
   b. can be controlled with several simple steps.
   c. is something the individual can at least partly control.
   d. is a sign of more serious problems.

7. To overcome procrastination, the authors suggest all but which of the following?
   a. Set realistic expectations.
   b. Do only the things you enjoy.
   c. Seek out support.
   d. Recognize your limitations.

Looking at Language

8. The authors' tone can best be described as
   a. helpful.
   b. stern.
   c. humorous.
   d. apologetic.

9. How do the authors define *burnout?* How can it be prevented?

   _____

   _____

   _____

10. The essay is written primarily from a second-person point of view, with the authors addressing the readers as "you." Why do you think the authors chose second-person point of view for this essay?

_____

_____

_____

Discussing the Essay

Prepare to discuss the following questions in class by thinking about them or writing about them in your journal.

1. Who is the intended audience for this essay? How do you know?

2. Does the essay change your views of procrastination? If so, how?

Topics for Writing

Assignment 1: Consequences of Procrastination

Journal Entry

Write a journal entry about a time when you procrastinated on something important. What were the consequences of your procrastination?

Assignment 2: Overcoming Procrastination

Essay

Write a process essay giving advice on how to overcome procrastination. Include specific examples as you write.

Assignment 3: Your Worst Habit

Essay

Procrastination is a real problem for some people. Others have different habits that they would like to break. Write an essay answering one or more of the following questions: What is your worst habit, and why do you want to break it? Alternatively, why don't you want to break it? What does it do for you that makes you want to keep it?

After 20 Years, I Want to See My Abusive Dad for His Money

Tony Kelso

His mother had to sue for access to his college account, and his abusive dad subsequently cut off all contact with him. Is it so wrong to think of getting some of Dad's money for the grandson's education? Tony Kelso ponders the issue.

Less than two months before my high-school graduation, my father told me he never wanted to see me again. He had received a summons that week and was furious that I had known but not warned him my mom was going to file a lawsuit against him.

The conflict involved a joint bank account my parents had set up for my future college education when I was a young child. For years, they mutually contributed to the modest savings plan. Yet after their divorce, a <u>protracted</u> and gut-wrenching break-up that gnawed away at my insides while I was on the verge of puberty in the sixth grade, only my mother continued to direct a slice of her earnings toward my schooling. Now that I was eighteen, the account had reached maturity. But my dad was refusing to sign the form that would allow my mom to apply the money to my tuition, books, and dorm expense. Consequently, she decided to press the issue through legal measures. From my perspective it was a messy affair the grown-ups should solve—not a situation that called for the engagement of a kid whose understanding of finances consisted of little more than knowing the price of a quarter pounder with cheese. My dad, however, felt differently. As a result, I would have to wave my diploma in front of only one proud parent clapping in the audience.

My father's rejection was definitely a blow. Still, I shouldn't have been surprised, given his track record. After all, this was a cruel man who had tormented me throughout my childhood, generating far too many <u>indelible</u>, piercing memories along the way. Like the time he went on a wild <u>tirade</u> through an entire wash cycle because I had splashed through a few puddles on my way home from school. Or the time he threw me into the bedroom after choking me in the hall, then a few minutes later called me out of the room to ask with a syrupy voice if he had hurt me, and finally screamed after I had nodded yes through my tears, "GOOD!" Or the time, as my mother came to a halt in the driveway to take me swimming after she had vanished for days to escape my father's unending wrath, he slugged her so hard that she bit her tongue, oozing her warm blood onto the front seat. Or the time he verbally assaulted me, then 11-years-old, for not fighting the divorce my mother had recently put in motion. Or the time, while my parents were separated before the divorce was final, my mom and I checked into a motel for the night because she had received a call from her best friend saying she had just heard from my father, who had revealed he was on his way to murder us. Or the time I came home after a pony-league baseball game to discover my battered mother shivering and huddled in a corner after my father had broken into the house through the milk chute to greet her with physical aggression. Or the Sundays he would pick me up after the divorce, speed 60-miles-an-hour down the residential street from my house with an expression straight out of a horror film, stop in a parking lot, then viciously explain to me that my mother was a pig and a whore who hung out with other pigs and whores. Needless to say, my dad was no Ward Cleaver.

Four years into my undergraduate studies, on the advice of the therapist 4 I had been seeing since the previous summer, I reached out to my father, hoping to reestablish a bond. Things were better for a while. As a perceptive young adult about to graduate from college, I knew how to appeal to his <u>narcissism</u> while avoiding anything that might set him off—although he no doubt unconsciously believed he was, as always, in charge of our <u>affiliation</u>, I was actually the one controlling the relationship. But about ten years after our reconciliation, it was my turn to bid adieu. Due to some twisted episode he had <u>fabricated</u> in his mind, he maniacally lashed out at me over the phone as though I were his mortal enemy. Soon afterward, I wrote him to announce I would no longer tolerate such abuse and, therefore, would not be in contact with him until he began to act like a father. Apparently that was a concession he has been unwilling—or unable—to make.

Two decades have passed since I dropped my poignant letter to my father in 5 the mailbox. Today, I am married and have a seven-year-old son. Lately I have been contemplating <u>extending an olive branch</u> to my dad once more. No, not because I want my boy to meet his grandpa. Nor do I myself miss the man who impregnated my mother. Instead, it boils down to only one thing: I just want his money.

A few years ago, I learned through my godfather who was still in touch 6 with my dad that he is worth over a million dollars. A high-school dropout, my father eventually went to trade school and became an electrician. Once he mastered the skill, he started his own business as an electrical commercial contractor. Throughout his career he not only performed all the duties associated with ownership—bidding jobs, purchasing materials, coordinating projects, and so on—he actually did the bulk of the day-to-day tasks as well. My father would often walk into a super-size building and singlehandedly lay the conduit, push through the wire, put in the light fixtures, assemble the giant fuse box that channeled all the power, and apply the finishing touches, such as plugs and covers, for the entire <u>edifice</u>. During his time as a blue-collar entrepreneur, he never hired more than one full-time employee, occasionally pulling temporary workers from the union hall (naturally, he hated unions) when he faced an especially daunting assignment. By owning and managing a large-scale operation while minimizing labor costs and running the company out of his house, he was able to accumulate significant wealth and retire young. If there is one trait I have always admired about my father, it is his amazing work ethic.

While my dad was forever motivated by the Almighty Dollar and what it could buy ("The only test of a man's IQ is how much money he makes" he repeatedly reminded me), I have always searched for employment that I felt could bring me a sense of meaning regardless of whether it commanded an impressive salary. (I certainly wouldn't have spent eight years pursuing a PhD and be currently serving as a college professor in the liberal arts at a small school if this weren't the case.) Likewise, I have never been the type of person who seeks handouts or devilishly schemes ways of bilking people for personal gain. Yet here I am, today, <u>devising</u> a plan to suck up to my father until he dies (now 72-years-old and a three- to four-pack a day smoker for much of his life, he could take his last breath any day), for no other reason than to be included in his will.   7

Does this make me a scoundrel? Am I guilty of a tiny (or even large) measure of hypocrisy? I admit, I feel considerably <u>sleazy</u> when I entertain the idea of following through with the manipulative act of embracing my father while slipping my hand into the wallet in his back pocket. But then I ask myself, Why shouldn't I? The least the guy could do, after a lifetime of meanness and neglect, is grant me an inheritance. Having alienated every family member except his also-aging, dysfunctionally timid second wife, who else would he leave money to but me?   8

The ultimate justification for my dubious undertaking, though, is that I don't want the money for me but for my seven-year-old son. Truth be told, I wouldn't even be thinking of contacting my father and re-establishing a relationship were it not for my boy. Should I be willed a tall stack of his bank notes, I would invest it and someday use the accumulated amount for my kid's college education. And this time, there would be no need for my dear ol' dad—busy nourishing maggots six feet below ground—to sign any paperwork.   9

Building Vocabulary

For each question, use your dictionary and context clues to choose the meaning that most nearly defines the underlined word or phrase as it is used in the essay.

1. The word <u>protracted</u> most nearly means
   a. proactive.
   b. intractable.
   c. lengthy.
   d. curtailed.

2. The word <u>indelible</u> most nearly means
   a. cannot be eaten.
   b. cannot be erased.
   c. cannot be believed.
   d. cannot be remembered.

3. The word <u>tirade</u> most nearly means
   a. exhaustion.
   b. ebb and flow.
   c. drinking binge.
   d. rant.

4. The word <u>narcissism</u> most nearly means
   a. concern with self.
   b. enjoyment of flowers.
   c. addiction to narcotics.
   d. concern with the needs of others.

5. The word <u>affiliation</u> most nearly means
   a. relationship.
   b. enrollment in a college.
   c. bank account.
   d. choices.

6. The word <u>fabricated</u> most nearly means
   a. remembered.
   b. created.
   c. refreshed.
   d. enjoyed.

7. The phrase <u>extending an olive branch</u> refers to
   a. researching one's family tree.
   b. working in an olive grove.
   c. an act of hostility.
   d. an act of peace.

8. The word <u>edifice</u> most nearly means
   a. building.
   b. wiring.
   c. principle.
   d. blueprint.

9. The word <u>devising</u> most nearly means
   a. rejecting.
   b. avoiding.

    c. making.

    d. deriding.

10. The word <u>sleazy</u> most nearly means

    a. clever.

    b. triumphant.

    c. ambivalent.

    d. trashy.

Understanding the Essay

1. Which statement most nearly expresses the main idea of the essay?

    a. After a long period of estrangement, the author is thinking of contacting his abusive father in hopes of being named in his will.

    b. We should all treasure our parents while we have them with us because we cannot predict when death will take them away from us.

    c. Parents who abuse their children should not expect to be loved or respected.

    d. The author's father abused both the author's mother and the author himself.

2. Which method of introduction does the author use?

    a. quotation

    b. broad to narrow

    c. historical

    d. contrast

3. The first estrangement between the author and his father was caused by

    a. the father's habit of calling the author's mother a pig and a whore.

    b. a suggestion from the author's therapist.

    c. the father's focus on the almighty dollar.

    d. the father's anger at not being tipped off to a lawsuit that the author's mother was filing.

4. How would you characterize the author's childhoood?

    a. He had a normal, average childhood.

    b. He was treated harshly yet fairly by his father, who had a strong work ethic and expected much from his son.

    c. He suffered abuse and watched his mother suffer abuse.

    d. His happy childhood was marred only by his parents' arguments.

5. Which pattern of development is used predominantly in Paragraph 3 of the essay?

    a. comparison-contrast

    b. example

    c. argument

    d. process

6. The author's father said, "The only test of a man's IQ is how much money he makes." Which of the following does the essay imply about the author's own feelings?

    a. He agrees with his father on that point, if no other.

    b. He dismisses money as being of no importance.

    c. He values job satisfaction and sense of purpose above salary.

    d. He consistently finds himself seeking higher-paying jobs in an effort to make his father proud.

7. What does the author say is the *main* reason he wants his father's money?

    a. It's the least his father can do to make up for the abuses in his childhood.

    b. He wants to use the money for his own son's education.

    c. There is no one else his father might leave it to, except a dysfunctionally timid second wife.

    d. He wants to fund an abused children's foundation.

Looking at Language

8. Death is often referred to with *euphemisms* (Greek for "good speech"), or words that will not offend or shock. Expressions such as "passed away," "entered into rest," or "is no longer with us" seem less harsh than the word "died," and are used to approach the subject delicately. Why, then, does the author choose to say that his father will be "busy nourishing maggots six feet below ground"? Does the expression achieve the effect intended?

_____

_____

_____

_____

_____

9. To "mince words" means to be polite and tactful so as not to offend anyone. Does Kelso mince words in his discussion of his father? Give three examples to support your answer.

_____

_____

_____

_____

_____

_____

_____

_____

_____

_____

_____

Discussing the Essay

Prepare to discuss the following questions in class by thinking about them or writing about them in your journal.

1. What is the author's attitude toward his father? What three words would you use to describe it? Why does the author feel as he does?

2. How does the author feel about his plan to reconcile with his father for the purpose of being included in his father's will? Do you think the author is justified in his plan?

Topics for Writing

Assignment 1: A Letter to Someone in Your Life

Letter

Tony Kelso wrote a letter to his father saying that he could not continue the relationship unless his father began to act like a father. Write a letter to someone you are having a problem with. Express your feelings and tell that person what it would take to make you happy.

Assignment 2: Good Parenting

Essay

What qualities does it take to be a good parent? Discuss those qualities as they relate to a person, perhaps one of your parents, or discuss the qualities as they relate to you—do you have the qualities it takes to be a good parent?

Assignment 3: Preventing Child Abuse and Spousal Abuse

Essay

What steps can be taken to prevent child and/or spousal abuse in our society?

Assignment 4: Money, Money, Money

Essay

Would you rather inherit, win, or marry into money, or would you prefer to earn it yourself? Discuss.

Why Chinese Parents Are Different

Amy Chua

Chinese parents are known for raising high-achieving children. How do they do it . . . and why?

Chinese parents can get away with things that Western parents can't. Once when I was young—maybe more than once—when I was extremely disrespectful to my mother, my father angrily called me "garbage" in our native Hokkien dialect. It worked really well. I felt terrible and deeply ashamed of what I had done. But it didn't damage my self-esteem or anything like that. I knew exactly how highly he thought of me. I didn't actually think I was worthless or feel like a piece of garbage.   1

As an adult, I once did the same thing to Sophia, calling her garbage in English when she acted extremely disrespectfully toward me. When I mentioned that I had done this at a dinner party, I was immediately <u>ostracized</u>. One guest named Marcy got so upset she broke down in tears and had to leave early. My friend Susan, the host, tried to <u>rehabilitate</u> me with the remaining guests.   2

"Oh, dear, it's just a misunderstanding, right, Amy? You didn't actually call Sophia 'garbage.'"   3

"Um, yes, I did, But it's all in the context," I tried to explain. "It's a Chinese immigrant thing."   4

"But you're not a Chinese immigrant," somebody pointed out.   5

"Good point," I conceded. "No wonder it didn't work."   6

I was just trying to be <u>conciliatory</u>. In fact, it had worked great with Sophia.   7

The fact is that Chinese parents can do things that would seem unimaginable—even legally actionable—to Westerners. Chinese mothers can say to their daughters, "Hey fatty—lose some weight." By contrast, Western parents have to tiptoe around the issue, talking in terms of "health" and never ever mentioning the f-word, and their kids still end up in therapy for eating disorders and negative self-image. (I also once heard a Western father toast his adult daughter by calling her "beautiful and incredibly <u>competent</u>." She later told me that made her feel like garbage.) Chinese parents can order their kids to get straight As. Western parents can only ask their kids to try their best. Chinese parents can say, "You're lazy.   8

All your classmates are getting ahead of you." By contrast, Western parents have   9
to struggle with their own conflicted feelings about achievement, and try to persuade themselves that they're not disappointed about how their kids turned out.

I've thought long and hard about how Chinese parents can get away with   10
what they do. I think there are three big differences between the Chinese and
Western parental mind-sets.

First, I've noticed that Western parents are extremely anxious about their   11
children's self-esteem. They worry about how their children will feel if they fail
at something, and they constantly try to reassure their children about how good
they are, notwithstanding a <u>mediocre</u> performance on a test or at a recital. In
other words, Western parents are concerned about their children's psyches. Chinese
parents aren't. They assume strength, not fragility, and as a result they behave very
differently.

For example, if a child comes home with an A-minus on a test, a Western   12
parent will most likely praise the child. The Chinese mother will gasp in horror
and ask what went wrong. If the child comes home with a B on the test, some
Western parents will still praise the child. Other Western parents will sit their
child down and express disapproval, but they will be careful not to make their
child feel inadequate or insecure, and they will not call their child "stupid,"
"worthless" or "a disgrace." Privately, the Western parents may worry that their
child does not test well or have aptitude in the subject or that there is something wrong with the curriculum and possibly the whole school. If the child's
grades do not improve, they may eventually schedule a meeting with the school
principal to challenge the way the subject is being taught or to call into question the teacher's <u>credentials</u>.

If a Chinese child gets a B—which would never happen—there would first be   13
a screaming, hair-tearing explosion. The devastated Chinese mother would then
get dozens, maybe hundreds of practice tests and work through them with her
child for as long as it takes to get the grade up to an A. Chinese parents demand
perfect grades because they believe that their child can get them. If their child
doesn't get them, the Chinese parent assumes it's because the child didn't work
hard enough. That's why the solution to substandard performance is always to <u>ex-
coriate</u>, punish and shame the child. The Chinese parent believes that their child
will be strong enough to take the shaming and to improve from it. (And when
Chinese kids do excel, there is plenty of ego-inflating parental praise lavished in
the privacy of the home.)

Second, Chinese parents believe that their kids owe them everything. The   14
reason for this is a little unclear, but it's probably a combination of Confucian
filial piety and the fact that the parents have sacrificed and done so much for
their children. (And it's true that Chinese mothers get in the trenches, putting
in long grueling hours personally tutoring, training, interrogating and spying
on their kids.) Anyway, the understanding is that Chinese children must spend
their lives repaying their parents by obeying them and making them proud.

By contrast, I don't think most Westerners have the same view of children   15
being permanently indebted to their parents. My husband, Jed, actually has the
opposite view. "Children don't choose their parents," he once said to me. "They
don't even choose to be born. It's parents who foist life on their kids, so it's the
parents' responsibility to provide for them. Kids don't owe their parents anything.
Their duty will be to their own kids." This strikes me as a terrible deal for the
Western parent.

Third, Chinese parents believe that they know what is best for their chil-   16
dren and therefore override all of their children's own desires and preferences.
That's why Chinese daughters can't have boyfriends in high school and why
Chinese kids can't go to sleepaway camp. It's also why no Chinese kid would
ever dare say to their mother, "I got a part in the school play! I'm Villager
Number Six. I'll have to stay after school for rehearsal every day from 3:00 to
7:00, and I'll also need a ride on weekends." God help any Chinese kid who
tried that one.

Don't get me wrong: It's not that Chinese parents don't care about their chil-   17
dren. Just the opposite. They would give up anything for their children. It's just
an entirely different parenting model. I think of it as Chinese, but I know a lot
of non-Chinese parents—usually from Korea, India, or Pakistan—who have a very
similar mind-set, so it may be an immigrant thing. Or maybe it's the combination
of being an immigrant and being from certain cultures.

Building Vocabulary

For each question, use your dictionary and context clues to choose the meaning that most nearly defines the underlined word or phrase as it is used in
the essay.

1. The word <u>ostracized</u> most nearly means
   a. rejected.
   b. optimized.
   c. minimized.
   d. made popular.

2. The word <u>rehabilitate</u> most nearly means
   a. ignore.
   b. chide.
   c. alienate.
   d. redeem.

3. The word <u>conciliatory</u> most nearly means
   a. authoritative and overbearing.
   b. concerned and kind.

     c. polite and accommodating.

     d. insistent and assertive.

4. The word <u>competent</u> most nearly means

     a. skilled.

     b. competitive.

     c. incapable.

     d. complaining.

5. The word <u>mediocre</u> most nearly means

     a. fearless.

     b. perfect.

     c. average.

     d. outstanding.

6. The word <u>credentials</u> most nearly means

     a. experience.

     b. caring.

     c. accreditation.

     d. honesty.

7. The word <u>excoriate</u> most nearly means

     a. praise.

     b. excuse.

     c. accept.

     d. chastise.

8. The phrase <u>coercion</u> most nearly means

     a. forcing someone to do something.

     b. persuading someone to do something.

     c. letting people do as they please.

     d. sticking together as a family.

9. The word <u>imperturbable</u> most nearly means

     a. gawky and ungraceful.

     b. loud and raucous.

     c. uncertain and shaky.

     d. cool and confident.

10. The word <u>callous</u> most nearly means

     a. kind.

     b. hardened.

     c. inspirational.

     d. lazy.

Understanding the Essay

1. Some examples of things that Chinese parents "get away with" that are mentioned in the essay include
   a. calling a child "garbage."
   b. calling a child "fatty."
   c. telling a child she is lazy.
   d. all of the above.

2. According to the author, three major differences between Chinese parents and Western parents include the degree to which they focus on
   a. self-esteem, indebtedness to parents, and knowing what is best for the child.
   b. grades, athletics, and extracurricular activities.
   c. self-esteem, grades, and hard work.
   d. getting straight A's, respecting parents, and working hard.

3. The author implies that Chinese parents demand perfection because they
   a. would be shamed by less.
   b. are less reasonable than Western parents.
   c. believe in their children.
   d. have no sympathy for their children.

4. According to the essay, the author and her husband disagree over which of the following parenting concepts
   a. The idea that children should make sraight A's.
   b. The idea that children owe parents everything.
   c. The idea that children's self-esteem is not a fragile flower to be protected.
   d. The idea that parents know what is best for their children.

5. Which of the following statements from the essay is probably not an exaggeration?
   a. If a Chinese child gets a B—which would never happen—there would first be a screaming, hair-tearing explosion.
   b. Anyway, the understanding is that Chinese children must spend their lives repaying their parents by obeying them and making them proud.
   c. Chinese parents believe that they know what is best for their children and therefore override all of their children's own desires and preferences.
   d. Chinese parents can say, "You're lazy. All your classmates are getting ahead of you."

6. The author concludes that Chinese parents
   a. have a different parenting model.
   b. would give up anything for their children.
   c. may share their parenting approach with some other cultures.
   d. All of the above.

7. Through which of the following techniques is the essay mainly developed?
   a. comparison–contrast.
   b. cause–effect.
   c. process analysis.
   d. narration.

Looking at Language

8. The author speaks of being called "garbage" by her father, and feeling ashamed of her action while still knowing he valued her. She also speaks of a Western father who calls his daughter "beautiful and incredibly competent." The daughter later tells the author that the compliment "made her feel like garbage." Can you explain how a compliment can make a person feel inferior while an insult might not? Can you think of other examples?

_____

_____

_____

_____

_____

_____

9. The author says that when it comes to the issue of overweight children, Western parents "tiptoe around the issue, talking in terms of "health" and never ever mentioning the f-word." From your own observation, is that true? If so, does the "tiptoe" approach apply to other issues?

_____

_____

_____

10. Choose three unfamiliar words from the essay that are not among the vocabulary questions. Define each.

_____

_____

_____

_____

_____

Discussing the Essay

Prepare to discuss the following questions in class by thinking about them or writing about them in your journal.

1. The author contrasts the Chinese idea that children owe their parents everything with the Western idea that children don't choose to be born (and therefore presumably owe the parents nothing). Discuss the merits and drawbacks of both ideas.

2. When Amy Chua's book, *Battle Hymn of the Tiger Mother*, was released, it provoked a firestorm of controversy. Chua said in an interview that much of the book was deadpan humor and exaggeration. Look at paragraphs 3–7 and 12, 13, and 17. Do you see some of this as humor or exaggeration, or do you believe she is entirely serious?

Topics for Writing

Assignment 1: Played Out

Journal Entry or Small Scrawl

You are in charge of seeing that a child completes an hour of math homework. The child would rather play, eat, go outside, or do almost anything except do the assignment. In one page, describe how you would convince the child to memorize multiplication tables and solve math problems for an hour.

Assignment 2: Contrasted Upbringing

Essay

The essay contrasts two styles of parenting. Do you have a friend or relative who was brought up quite differently from you? Alternatively, is your child-rearing philosophy quite different from that of a relative or close friend? Contrast two styles of parenting, making sure to use examples effectively.

Assignment 3: Qualities of a Good Parent

Essay

What are the qualities of a good parent? Do you believe you would make (or are) a good parent?

Assignment 4: This or That?

Essay

Think carefully about Chinese and Western parenting as defined in the essay. Which do you believe is preferable? Why? Write an essay defending your choice.

Date Rape: Exposing Dangerous Myths

John J. Macionis

Rape is almost always committed by a stranger . . . isn't it? Sociologist John J. Macionis sheds light on the dark subject of date rape and exposes the myths that surround it.

Completing a day of work during a business trip to the courthouse in Tampa, Florida, thirty-two-year-old Sandra Abbott <u>pondered</u> how she would return to her hotel. An attorney with whom she had been working—a pleasant enough man—made the kind offer of a lift. As his car threaded its way through the late afternoon traffic, their conversation was <u>animated</u>. "He was saying all the right things," Abbott recalled, "so I started to trust him."

He asked if she would join him for dinner; she happily accepted. After <u>lingering</u> over an enjoyable meal, they walked together to the door of her hotel room. The new acquaintance <u>angled</u> for an invitation to come in and talk, but Abbott hesitated, sensing that he might have something more on his mind. She explained that she was old-fashioned about relationships but would allow him to come in for a little while with the understanding that talk was all they would do.

Sitting on the couch in the room, soon Abbott was overcome with drowsiness. Feeling comfortable in the presence of her new friend, she let her head fall gently onto his shoulder, and, before she knew it, she fell asleep. That's when the attack began. Abbott was startled back to consciousness as the man thrust himself upon her sexually. She shouted: "No!" but he paid no heed. Abbott describes what happened next:

> I didn't scream or run. All I could think of was my business <u>contacts</u> and what if they saw me run out of my room screaming rape. I thought it was my fault. I felt so filthy, I washed myself over and over in hot water. Did he rape me? I kept asking myself. I didn't consent. But who's gonna believe me? I had a man in my hotel room after midnight.

Abbott knew that she had said "No!" and thus had been raped. She notified the police, who conducted an investigation and turned their findings over to the state attorney's office. But the authorities backed away. In the absence of evidence like bruises, a medical examination, and torn clothes, they noted, there was little point in prosecuting.

The case of Sandra Abbott is all too typical. Even today, in most instances of sexual attack, a victim makes no report to police, and no offender is arrested. The reason for such inaction is that many people have a misguided understanding of rape. Three false notions about rape are so common in the United States that they might be called "rape myths." **5**

A first rape <u>myth</u> is that rape involves strangers. A sexual attack brings to mind young men lurking in the shadows who suddenly spring on their unsuspecting victims. But this pattern is the exception rather than the rule: Four out of five rapes are committed by offenders known to their victims. For this reason, people have begun to speak more realistically about *acquaintance rape* or, more simply, *date rape*. **6**

A second myth about rape holds that women provoke their attackers. Surely, many people think, a woman claiming to have been raped must have done *something* to encourage the man, to lead him on, to make him think that she really wanted to have sex. **7**

In the case described above, didn't Sandra Abbott agree to have dinner with the man? Didn't she invite him into her room? Such self-doubt often paralyzes victims. But having dinner with a man—or even inviting him into her hotel room—is hardly a woman's statement of consent to have sex with him any more than she has agreed to have him beat her with a club. **8**

A third myth is the notion that rape is simply sex. If there is no knife held to a woman's throat, or if she is not bound and gagged, then how can sex be a crime? The answer is simply that *forcing a woman to have sex without her consent is a violent crime*. To accept the idea that rape is sex one would also have to see no difference between brutal combat and playful wrestling. "Having sex" implies intimacy, caring, communication, and, most important of all, consent—none of which is present in cases of rape. Beyond the brutality of being physically <u>violated</u>, date rape also <u>undermines</u> the victim's sense of trust. This psychological burden is especially serious among rape victims under eighteen—half of the total—about one-fourth of whom are attacked by their own fathers. **9**

The more people believe these myths about rape, the more women will fall victim to sexual violence. The ancient Babylonians stoned married women who became victims of rape, convinced that the women had committed adultery. Ideas about rape have changed little over thousands of years, which helps to explain why, even today, only about one in twenty rapes results in an offender being sent to jail. **10**

Nowhere has the issue of date rape been more widely discussed than on the college campus. The collegiate environment promotes easy friendships and a sense of trust. At the same time, many students have a great deal to learn about relationships and about themselves. So while college life encourages communication, it also invites sexual violence. **11**

To counter this problem, colleges have been facing—and <u>debunking</u>—myths about rape. In addition, attention has centered on the <u>prevalence</u> of alcohol **12** in campus life and the effect of cultural patterns that define sex as a sport. To address the crisis of date rape, everyone needs to understand two simple truths: Forcing sex without a woman's consent is rape, and when a woman says "no," she means just that.

Building Vocabulary

For each question, use your dictionary and context clues to choose the meaning that most nearly defines the underlined word or phrase as it is used in the essay.

1. The word <u>pondered</u> most nearly means
   a. perused.
   b. reserved.
   c. wondered.
   d. plotted.

2. The word <u>animated</u> most nearly means
   a. meaningless.
   b. animalistic.
   c. dull.
   d. lively.

3. The word <u>lingering</u> most nearly means
   a. spending time.
   b. salivating.
   c. spending money.
   d. kissing.

4. The word <u>angled</u> most nearly means
   a. turned.
   b. longed.
   c. became eligible.
   d. hinted.

5. The word <u>contacts</u> most nearly means
   a. contracts.
   b. associates.
   c. conduct.
   d. corrective lenses.

6. The word <u>myth</u> most nearly means
   a. legend.
   b. lie.
   c. false belief.
   d. theory.

7. The word <u>violated</u> most nearly means
   a. threatened.
   b. sexually active.
   c. touched.
   d. assaulted.

8. The word <u>undermines</u> most nearly means
   a. weakens.
   b. reinforces.
   c. precludes.
   d. determines.

9. The word <u>debunking</u> most nearly means
   a. discrediting.
   b. hiding.
   c. proving.
   d. debasing.

10. The word <u>prevalence</u> most nearly means
    a. enjoyment.
    b. widespread existence.
    c. condemnation.
    d. sale.

Understanding the Essay

1. Which statement most nearly expresses the main idea of the essay?
   a. Date rape is a common occurrence on college campuses.
   b. False ideas about rape can encourage sexual crime against women.
   c. To prevent rape, women should "just say no."
   d. Increasing penalties for rape and decreasing campus alcohol use are the solutions to the problem of date rape.

2. Which method of introduction does the author use?
   a. anecdote
   b. broad-to-narrow
   c. quotation
   d. contrast

3. The author implies that Sandra Abbott did not run or physically resist the man who raped her because
   a. she was afraid her attacker would kill her if she resisted.
   b. she felt inviting him in was the same thing as inviting him to have sex.
   c. she was afraid of looking foolish in front of her colleagues.
   d. she was asleep at the time of the attack.

4. According to the author, which of the following is *not* a myth about rape?
    a. Most rapes do not result in the rapist being sent to jail.
    b. Victims are often guilty of behavior that implies an invitation to sex.
    c. Most rape victims do not know their attackers.
    d. If no weapon is used, then what some call rape is simply sex.

5. Which pattern(s) of development does the author use most predominantly?
    a. comparison-contrast
    b. definition and classification
    c. cause-effect
    d. narration and description

6. Which is *not* mentioned as a reason date rape is prevalent on college campuses?
    a. Alcohol use is relatively common.
    b. Students are naive and too trusting.
    c. Morals are more lax than in the past.
    d. Some students have much to learn about relationships.

7. With which statement would the author most likely agree?
    a. Blaming women for rape began with the rise of feminism when women were no longer seen as under the protection of husbands and fathers.
    b. All instances of rape involve alcohol use.
    c. When a woman says "no," sometimes she means "yes" or "maybe."
    d. Not much progress has been made in the way people think about rape.

Looking at Language

8. Look at the language that Macionis uses to describe date rape, rapists, and rape victims. What specific word choices emphasize the seriousness of this crime?

   _____

   _____

9. Reread Sandra Abbott's statement in paragraph 3. The answer to her question, "Did he rape me?" ultimately requires Abbott to define the word *rape*. How do you define rape? Based on your definition, how would Abbott's question be answered?

   _____

   _____

10. The author writes, "'Having sex' implies intimacy, caring, communication, and, most important of all, consent." In your opinion, which of the four

listed items is implied most strongly by the words *having sex?* Why? Which is implied least strongly? Why?

_____

_____

_____

Discussing the Essay

Prepare to discuss the following questions in class by thinking about them or writing about them in your journal.

1. According to the author, how did the ancient Babylonians define rape? How did this definition affect women? What does your answer suggest about the power of language? About the power of those who define?

2. Is date rape a problem on your campus? What can be done to eliminate it on your campus or at other colleges?

Topics for Writing

Assignment 1: A Definition

Journal Entry

Write a journal entry giving your definition of rape.

Assignment 2: Police Business

Journal Entry

You are a police officer taking the statement of John L., a suspect arrested in a crime against his neighbor Kristen G. The suspect, John, uses the following excuses: "She invited me in." "She was always flaunting it." "What else was I supposed to do, with temptation right there in front of me?" John's crime, however, is not rape. Instead, he locked Kristen in a closet and stole her new Sony high-definition television. Use your imagination and write up John's statement in a journal entry.

Putting the traditional excuses for rape in the mouth of a television thief presents them in a new light and exposes their absurdity. This form of writing, called satire, uses humor to expose the faults of humanity or society.

Assignment 3: Causes of Date Rape

Essay

What factors do you believe account for the prevalence of date rape? Write an essay discussing them.

Assignment 4: Reluctance to Report

Essay

Write an essay discussing some reasons women might be reluctant to report date rape.

Assignment 5: Solving the Problem of Date Rape

Essay

What can be done to solve the problem of date rape on college campuses? Write an essay proposing your solutions to the problem, including why you think your solutions would work.

Assignment 6: Advice for a College Student

Essay

Macionis suggests that while a college atmosphere promotes trust, many students may be vulnerable because they "have a great deal to learn about relationships and about themselves."

Imagine that you have been asked to give advice to a student just beginning college. What are the three most valuable things that student needs to know before entering college? Your essay may be addressed to male students, female students, or both. It may touch on the subject of date rape or it may deal with other things entirely. It is simply your best advice to a beginning college student.

Is National Service a Cure for America's Woes?

Larry Fennelly

Not everyone can serve in the military, but national service does not have to mean military service. Will "asking what we can do for our country" strengthen the American backbone?

It's hard to pick up a newspaper, newsmagazine or other serious publication in recent days without some observer of the American scene speculating that our systems of education, industry or commerce are in serious decline, that the national backbone is weakening and that we are losing our collective will to win. <u>Lassitude</u> and complacency, we are told, are taking over our classrooms, workplaces and even our research facilities.   1

Older Americans point with pride to achievements of the men and women of "the Greatest Generation." They <u>scoff at</u> today's crop of young adults, most of who have never lived in a house without central heat and air conditioning, never mind experienced the <u>rigors</u> of military service. Are these concerns just another example of the older generation whining about the young? Or is there reason for genuine concern?   2

Certainly the world is changing: In 1950, when baby boomers were starting out, the New York/Newark area was the largest metropolitan area in the world. By last year, New York had been surpassed by cities in Japan, India (two) and Mexico. China is said to be ahead of America in patent creation.   3

Every educational organization worth its salt has published statistics <u>lamenting</u> an American decline in academic achievement. While our country remains atop the world, many educators worry that today's students are not going to be able to <u>pick up the baton</u>.   4

A World War II vet friend of mine died recently, and as I attended his funeral and thought about his decision to be buried with full military honors, I realized that for most people who served their country, even many years later, that period remains the defining experience of their lives. I also recalled that retired Gen. Stanley McChrystal had recently penned a piece for *Newsweek* magazine proposing a period of national service. Although McChrystal's proposal is not new, it does make the important point that with "<u>inalienable</u> rights" come "inalienable responsibilities."   5

Those who have worn a uniform know that military service is known for imbuing slackers with a whole host of practical virtues, such as self-discipline, reliability, leadership and a commitment to democracy. It is also known that the <u>acquisition</u> of such virtues through military means sometimes comes at a dreadful price.   6

McChrystal's proposal, then, to include other service options—Americorps, Peace Corps, Teach for America and others—would make his suggestion more <u>palatable</u> to those opposed to military service for various reasons. And there are many. Yet, we also know of many former servicemen and women who credit their military training with "making something" out of them. They thank their Uncle Sam for teaching them the virtues which subsequently enabled them to become successful citizens. I know that in my own case, several of my experiences in the U.S. Army—particularly my time as the only ROTC product in an Armored Cavalry Squadron otherwise staffed by West Point graduates—helped me to overcome a paralytic shyness and acquire <u>sufficient</u> social poise to lead a reasonably normal life.   7

Certainly, a key ingredient, whatever form the service takes, must be rigor. If the experience is to benefit both the participants and the nation, it must entail a certain amount of hardship or sacrifice—call it character-building, if you will. It is the concept of a burden shared for the common good that will generate the true rewards of such service. Ask anyone who has served.   8

President Kennedy once upon a time urged us to ask not what our country could do for us, but rather what we could do for our country, knowing all the while that we would be benefitting ourselves immeasurably—not merely because we <u>constitute</u> the country but because of the ineffable change that occurs within the human heart when, not for gain but for love, it gives of itself.   9

Building Vocabulary

For each question, use your dictionary and context clues to choose the meaning that most nearly defines the underlined word or phrase as it is used in the essay.

1. The word <u>lassitude</u> most nearly means
   a. attitude.
   b. certitude.
   c. apathy.
   d. smugness.
2. The phrase <u>scoff at</u> most nearly means
   a. belittle.
   b. admire.

    c. look up to.

    d. worry about

3. The word <u>rigors</u> most nearly means

    a. privileges.

    b. joys.

    c. boredom.

    d. difficulties.

4. The word <u>lamenting</u> most nearly means

    a. bemoaning.

    b. laminating.

    c. declining.

    d. embracing.

5. The phrase <u>pick up the baton</u> most nearly means

    a. conduct an orchestra.

    b. continue a tradition of leadership.

    c. pick up the pieces.

    d. choose the correct instruments.

6. The word <u>inalienable</u> most nearly means

    a. very fragile.

    b. not understandable.

    c. not given to everyone.

    d. can't be taken away or transferred.

7. The word <u>acquisition</u> most nearly means

    a. agreement.

    b. attainment.

    c. loss.

    d. overcoming.

8. The word <u>palatable</u> most nearly means

    a. delicious.

    b. reprehensible.

    c. disagreeable.

    d. acceptable.

9. The word <u>sufficient</u> most nearly means

    a. inadequate.

    b. not preferred.

    c. enough.

    d. arrogant.

10. The word <u>constitute</u> most nearly means

   a. make up.

   b. make up for.

   c. make out.

   d. make sure of.

Understanding the Essay

1. According to the author, people are concerned that America is falling behind in all but one of the following. Which one is it?

   a. education.

   b. military might.

   c. patent creation

   d. industry.

2. Based on the essay, among which group would you *not* expect to find lassitude and complacency?

   a. Students in a tenth-grade classroom.

   b. Office workers in an insurance company.

   c. Players at a pickup game of basketball.

   d. Scientists reserching a cure for cancer at a prestigious university.

3. What is retired general Stanley McChrystal's proposal?

   a. A period of national military service.

   b. A period of service which might or might not include military service.

   c. A return to the values of the "Greatest Generation."

   d. Rigorous boot-camp-style training to build character.

4. How did the author say he benefited from military service?

   a. He earned the right to be buried with full military honors.

   b. His Uncle Sam taught him virtue.

   c. He overcame shyness and gained poise.

   d. He served in an armored cavalry squadron.

5. The author believes that enduring hadship and sacrifice for one's country

   a. builds character.

   b. was only done by the Greatest Generation.

   c. is too difficult for today's young people.

   d. should not be necessary.

6. Which of the following bumper stickers would you be most likely to find on the author's car?

   a. Make love, not war.

   b. My country, right or wrong.

    c. Keep honking . . . I'm reloading.

    d. Freedom is not free.

7. Which statement most nearly expresses the main idea of the essay?

    a. The United States is a declining country.

    b. A rigorous national service program would benefit the country and the people who served.

    c. The Greatest Generation was the one that came of age during World War II.

    d. President Kennedy would be horrified by the state of the United States today.

Looking at Language

8. What is the level of vocabulary in the essay? What assumption do you think the author makes about his audience?

    _____

    _____

9. In paragraph 4, the author uses the expression "worth its salt." What does this expression mean? Use a dictionary or the Internet to find the answer.

    _____

    _____

    _____

    _____

    _____

10. In paragraph 5, the author writes that Gen. McChrystal made the point that with inalienable rights come inalienable responsibilites. What do you think McChyrstal meant?

    _____

    _____

    _____

    _____

    _____

    _____

_____

_____

_____

_____

_____

Discussing the Essay

Prepare to discuss the following questions in class by thinking about them or writing about them in your journal.

1. What would be the advantages of a national service program to the country? To those who served?

2. What does Fennelly mean when he says that for the World War II generation, military service often "remains the defining experience of their lives"?

Topics for Writing

Assignment 1: Greatest Generation?

Journal Entry

The term "the Greatest Generation" is often used to describe the generation that came of age during World War II. This generation, which supported World War II and generally "played by the rules," is considered patriotic and hardworking. What term would you give your own generation? Why?

Assignment 2: Benefits of National Service

Essay

Discuss the possible benefits of a national service project which required young people to spend the first year out of high school in the service of their country if they did not choose to join the military. The service could be at home or abroad and would require serving an organization such as the Peace Corps or Americorps, as mentioned in the essay, or perhaps organizations such as Habitat for Humanity or the Red Cross. Consider the benefits to the country and to the individuals who serve.

Assignment 3: Strength from Adversity

Essay

The essay suggests that facing difficulties and working in the service of others builds character and changes lives. Describe a period in your life that may have been difficult but that made you a stronger person.

Alternatively, interview an older peson such as a parent or grandparent, ask about the experiences that changed their lives, and write about those experiences in an essay.

Assignment 4: Challenges to a New Generation

Essay

Fennelly writes about older Americans scoffing at young people, most of whom have never lived without air conditioning and other modern comforts and have never served in the military. Yet every generation faces its own set of challenges, and every generation fights in some way to make the world a better place to live. What challenges does your generation face?

Credits

Maya Angelou, "Complaining" from *Wouldn't Take Nothing for My Journey Now* by Maya Angelou, copyright © 1993 by Maya Angelou. Used by permission of Random House, Inc.

Jeff Obafemi Carr, "The Game of My Life" from *Essence* (March 1997). Copyright © 1997 by Jeff Obafemi Carr. Reprinted by permission.

Amy Chua, "Why Chinese Mothers are Different." From "Battle Hymn of the Tiger Mother" by Amy Chua, copyright © 2011 by Amy Chua. Used by permission of The Penguin Press, a division of Penguin Group (USA) Inc., and Bloomsbury Publishing Plc.

Amy Chua, "Why Chinese Mothers are Different." (Rights for United Kingdom—other rights by Penguin Group.) From "Battle Hymn of the Tiger Mother" by Amy Chua, copyright © 2011 by Amy Chua. Used by permission of The Penguin Press, a division of Penguin Group (USA) Inc., and Bloomsbury Publishing Plc.

Athlone G. Clarke, "When Words Get in the Way" from *The Atlanta Journal Constitution*, January 30, 1995, © 1995 The Atlanta Journal-Constitution. All rights reserved. Used by permission and protected by the Copyright Laws of the United States. The printing, copying, redistribution, or retransmission of this Content without express written permission is prohibited.

Definition of "burden." From *The New American Webster Handy College Dictionary*, 3/E. Published by Penguin Group (USA).

Fennelly, Larry, "Is National Service a Cure for America's Woes?" (editor's title, originally titled "Old-School Style Character" from *The Telegraph* (February 10, 2011). Reprinted with permission of the author.

Sara J. Gonzalez, "Growing Up Bilingual" from *The Atlantic Journal Consitution* (September 18, 1995). Copyright © 1995 by Sara J. Gonzalez. Reprinted by permission.

Franz Kafka, from *The Metamorphosis*. 20 words from Franz Kafka's *The Metamorphosis*.

Tony Kelso, "After 20 Years, I Want to See My Abusive Dad for His Money." First appeared in Open Salon (www.salon.com), June 15, 2011. Copyright © 2011 by Tony Kelso. Tony Kelso is an Associate Professor of Media Studies at Iona College in New Rochelle, New York. Reprinted by permission of the author.

Steve Kotler, "The Perils of Higher Education" from *Psychology Today*, Mar/Apr 2005.

John J. Macionis, "Date Rape: Exposing Dangerous Myths" from *Sociology*, 6th Edition, copyright © 1997, pp. 218-219. Reprinted by permission of Pearson Education, Inc., Upper Saddle River, NJ.

Roberta Moore, Barbara Baker, and Arnold Packer, "Coping With Procrastination" from *College Success*. Copyright © 1997 Prentice Hall. Reprinted with permission of the author.

Reuse of "Percent of Adults Polled Who Rate the Following Items as Necessary (Save Big with the Flashback Budget)," December 2006 © 2006 Pew Research Center, Social and Demographic Trends Project. Things We Can't Live Without: The List Has Grown in the Past Decade. http://pewsocialtrends.org/2006/12/14/luxury-or-necessity/. Reprinted with permission.

Letty Cottin Pogrebin, "Superstitious Minds" from *Ms. Magazine*, February 1988. Reprinted by permission of *Ms. Magazine*. Copyright © 1988.

Patricia Raybon, "Letting in Light" Copyright © 1993 by Patricia Raybon. Reprinted by permission of the author.

J. K. Rowling, from *Harry Potter and The Sorcerer's Stone*. 22 words from J. K. Rowling, *Harry Potter and The Sorcerer's Stone*.

Ann Tyler, from *Back When We Were Grownups*. 17 words from Ann Tyler's *Back When We Were Grownups*.

Liz Pulliam Weston, "Save Big With the Flashback Budget" *MSN Money* (April 26, 2007). Copyright © 2007. Reprinted with permission of the author.

Richard Woods, "Facebook's Mark Zuckerberg Says Privacy Is Dead. So Why Does He Want to Keep This Picture Hidden?" Renamed "Has the Internet Killed Privacy?" From *The Sunday Times*, January 17, 2010. The Times/NI Syndication. Reprinted with permission.

Photo Credits

P. 1: Dave Cutler/Stock Illustration Source, Inc.-Images.com; p. 2: Spencer Grant/PhotoEdit; p. 20: Images.com/Corbis; p. 21: AP Photo/Danny Moloshok; p. 33: Stockbyte/Getty Images; p. 34: Computer Earth/Shutterstock.com; 55: Nancy R. Cohen/Photodisc/Getty Images; p. 67: AptTone/Shutterstock.com; p. 68: David Young-Wolff/PhotoEdit; p. 91: Pearson; p. 92: Archives du 7eme Art/Photos 12/Alamy; p. 101: Dorling Kindersley; p. 102: North Wind Picture Archives; p. 117: Barry Robson/Dorling Kindersley; p. 118: Mtkang/Shutterstock.com; p. 121: Kent Knudson/PhotoLink/Getty Images; p. 134: Denise Hager/Catchlight Visual Services/Alamy; p. 142: fokusgood/Shutterstock.com; p. 143 (top): Francis G. Mayer/CORBIS; p. 143 (bottom): The Art Gallery Collection/Alamy; p. 146: VisionsofAmerica/Joe Sohm/Getty Images; p. 153: Pamela Arlov; p. 157: Lee O'Dell/Shutterstock.com; p. 158: Bettmann/Corbis; p. 162: Steve Cole/Photodisc/Getty Images; p. 172: Jayme Thornton/Photodisc/Getty Images; p. 184: Monkey Business Images/Shutterstock.com; p. 191 (left): olly/Shutterstock.com; p. 191 (right): Erik Reis/Alamy; p. 195: Dave King/Dorling Kindersley; p. 196: Marty Loken/Riser/Getty Images; p. 201: Steve Cole/Photodisc/Getty Images; p. 209: Michael Pettigrew/Shutterstock.com; p. 210 (left): lyf1/Shutterstock.Com; p. 210 (right): Comstock/Thinkstock.com; p. 212: Pearson; p. 218 (top): Valentyn Volkov/Shutterstock.com; p. 218 (left): BananaStock/Thinkstock.com; p. 218 (right): Pamela Arlov; p. 219 (top): Bob Pardue—Lifestyle/Alamy; p. 219 (bottom): jon le-bon/Shutterstock.com; p. 226: Pamela Arlov; p. 237: Dieter Wanke/Alamy; p. 240: Photodisc/Getty Images; p. 241: 20th Century Fox. All rights reserved/Courtesy Everett Collection; p. 260: Pearson; p. 261: Benita Epstein, Cartoon; p. 289: Paul Gilligan/Photodisc/Getty Images; p. 307: ImageZoo/Alamy; p. 321: Hans Neleman/Stone+/Getty Images; p. 334: Evgeny Murtola/Shutterstock.com; p. 350: David Young-Wolff/Stone/Getty Images; p. 366: Pearson; p. 380: Hulton Archive/Archive Photos/Getty Images; p. 402: Franco Volpato/Shutterstock.com; p. 415: Andy Crawford/Dorling Kindersley; p. 422: Nick Koudis/Photodisc/Getty Images; p. 443: Goga S/Shutterstock.com; p. 452: Pearson; p. 464: Illustration Works/Corbis; p. 476: Photos.com/Getty Images/Thinkstock.com; p. 491: Dorling Kindersley; 501: Photodisc/Getty Images; p. 513: Pearson; p. 524: Stockbyte/Getty Images; p. 535: Cre8tive Images/Shutterstock.

Index